D0916120

Missing

Missing

YOUTH, CITIZENSHIP, AND EMPIRE AFTER 9/11

Sunaina Marr Maira

Duke
University
Press

Durham & London 2009

© 2009 Duke University Press
All rights reserved

Printed in the United States of America on acid-free paper ∞
Designed by Jennifer Hill
Typeset in Adobe Jenson by Achorn International

Library of Congress Cataloging-in-Publication Data
appear on the last printed page of this book.

For the young people in this book

and for Majeed

Contents

Acknowledgments   ix

Introduction   South Asian Muslim Youth
in the United States after 9/11   1

One   Imperial Feelings: U.S. Empire
and the War on Terror   37

Two   Cultural Citizenship   76

Three   Transnational Citizenship:
Flexibility and Control   95

Four   Economies of Citizenship:
Work, Play, and Polyculturalism   128

Five   Dissenting Citizenship:
Orientalisms, Feminisms,
and Dissenting Feelings   190

Six   Missing: Fear, Complicity,
and Solidarity   258

Appendix   A Note on Methods   291

Notes   293

Bibliography   305

Index   329

Acknowledgments

The acknowledgments are usually the place where the author names the individuals or groups that have enabled the production of what is inevitably a collectively shaped artifact, despite the often solitary process of writing. In my case, I am unable to name those I would really like to thank for making this book possible—the young people whose stories I include in this book, as well as their families and friends, whose names I cannot reveal for reasons of confidentiality and safety but who allowed me to narrate their experiences and share their critique. I am indebted to them for being willing to be so candid with me at a time when not just immigrants, but also citizens, were hesitant to share their views for fear of backlash. This was a moment that was variously frustrating, scary, painful, infuriating, and depressing for many—including myself—and I want to thank these students for their courage and candor that kept me sane and helped me keep my eyes on the prize.

I am very grateful to the public high school for letting me do this research and for giving me such open access to the teachers and staff, who were incredibly generous with their time and let me intrude into their classrooms. In particular, the director of the International Student Center was extremely thoughtful and willing to share his experiences and insights with me. It is largely due to his support of the Muslim immigrant students that many of them found spaces where they could publicly express their political views and challenge everyday racism. The staff at the center were a great help and also made me feel welcome as I hung around on a regular basis.

Thank you to my colleagues in the South Asian Mentoring and Tutoring (SAMTA) program who gave me the opportunity to work in the high school and get to know the students better. Among the several volunteers in SAMTA I would like to especially thank Asha Balakrishnan for her commitment and creativity and Anjali Adukia for her constant support. My research assistants—Palav Babaria, Sarah Khan, and Aaron Spevack—helped to make the interviews and fieldwork possible and deepened my understanding of these issues. The ethnographic research was funded by the Russell Sage Foundation, which also gave me opportunities to share my work with other scholars and collaborate with researchers who have long been working on similar issues, such as Louise Cainkar. I also received a Research Fellows grant in 2002 from the Institute for Asian American Studies at the University of Massachusetts, Boston.

There were many individuals in the community who were doing exemplary work at the time on civil and immigrant rights, against the war, and for justice in the Middle East. My deepest admiration and respect goes to Rakhshanda Saleem for her principled stance and extraordinary humility, and to comrades in the South Asian Committee for Human Rights—"Bunty," Praveen, Raju, Aparna, Anjali, Rajini, Gautam, Molly, and others. I was also given many opportunities for organizing, from which I learned a great deal, by Bobbie Louton of the New England Immigrant and Detainees Response Network, Abira Ashfaq and members of the Alliance for a Secular and Democratic South Asia, Nancy Murray at the ACLU, Merrie Najimy of the American Arab Anti-Discrimination Committee, Jaspal and Hardeep of the South Asia Center, as well as countless others from various immigrant communities who worked consistently and quietly on the ground. In the Bay Area, I was welcomed into a political community including the Justice in Palestine Coalition, Direct Action to Stop the War, and the Association of South Asians Taking Action (ASATA). The memory of Birjinder Anant, who was an inspiration to many of us but who left us early in his life, still lives on.

While working on the book, I was lucky to have the support and feedback of friends and colleagues such as Rajini Srikanth, Veena Dubal, Kasturi Ray, Gautam Premnath, Susette Min, Purnima Mankekar, Piya Chatterjee, Kent Ono, and Evelyn Al Sultany, and mentors such as Gary

Okihiro, George Lipsitz, and Marcelo Suárez-Orozco. Christine Cooper and Vijay Prashad took the time to read parts of the manuscript and give me their always lucid and detailed feedback. Thanks to the indefatigable chair of my program, Wendy Ho, for consistently supporting me politically and intellectually and for her principled commitment to academic freedom, social justice, and feminist praxis. She and others in the Asian American Studies program at the University of California, Davis, work hard to maintain the best ideals of ethnic studies.

I am grateful to my editor, Courtney Berger, for her patient support and constant encouragement and to the anonymous reviewers at Duke University Press for their astute feedback. This book is clearly better for it. Thanks to Mark Mastromarino at Duke Press for guiding the manuscript through the production process, and to Dawn Lee Tu for preparing the index. And special thanks to Chitra Ganesh for the brilliant art on the book's cover and Irum Sheikh for letting me use so many of her wonderful photos.

I want to thank my parents and my brother, Sandeep, for their love and support even when they had no idea what the hell I was up to or when they did and loved me anyway. Finally, I thank Majeed for his engaged reading of my work, inspiring insights, thoughtful suggestions, and caring partnership in our shared struggle for the freedom that many are missing.

Introduction

South Asian Muslim Youth in the United States after 9/11

Amin

"The first week when I came to the Wellford High School, we talked about religion and Muslims in class, which was a bit strange for me. It was in my ESL class, and my teacher, Miss Daniels, put up some pictures of people praying from different religions. She asked us if we knew what religions they were from. I noticed that one of the pictures was of Mecca, so I said that they were following Islam. She asked me to tell the class what Islam was about. I tried to tell them, but my English was not very good at that time because I had just come from India. I said that there were five pillars of Islam. I was thinking that I was the only Muslim student in the class, so I have to explain it to them. Miss Daniels also tried to talk a little about Islam, and about the other religions. Then this girl put up her hand, an American girl, and she asked Miss Daniels why one of the rules of Islam is that women have to cover their head. I don't know why she was asking that, because I don't think that's true, but Miss Daniels said, 'Is there any one in the class who knows why?' I didn't really feel like talking about that, because I was new to the country, and I didn't understand why that girl thought all Muslim women should cover themselves.

"Then I saw that there was an Indian girl sitting in the corner, in a pink salwar kameez [long shirt and pants]. She had brown hair and light eyes; she looked like maybe she was also from Gujarat. She was putting her hand up, and Miss Daniels looked at her. The girl said, 'But it's not true. I know all Muslim women don't have to wear headscarves, they don't have to wear burka.'

"Miss Daniels was looking at her, and looking at the American girl. The American girl said, 'But then why do they talk about that on television? I saw this program on Islam on CNN, and they showed how they have to cover their head, and they are afraid to walk around without wearing big sheets and the girls can't go to school. That's what they're making them do in Afghanistan, and that's why we went to war there, so we can free the women, from the Taliban.'

"The students all started talking and looking at me and the girl, and I was feeling very bad. Not because of what the American girl was saying—she didn't sound right to me—but because of the Indian girl in the salwar kameez. I saw her face was becoming red, and she put up her hand again. 'It's not true. I am Muslim, and I don't have to wear it, and none of us do in my family. Many women in Gujarat don't.'

"I think Miss Daniels didn't know about Gujarat, so she was confused. I tried to tell her, 'Miss, Gujarat is in India.'

"Then another boy—I think he was Spanish—he said to me, 'Do you speak Arabic then? I thought all Arabs speak Arabic.' I was thinking I do know a little Arabic because I read the Koran, but I didn't know how to tell him we are not Arab.

"I remember Miss Daniels ended the lesson right then, and she made us do an English quiz. I wanted to talk to the Indian girl but she had left. I was thinking, She is so pretty and nice. Will she talk to me? So I asked Ismail about her, and he told me that she lived in the third building in our compound. He said many of the boys also thought she was pretty. But she never really came downstairs with the other girls so they did not know much about her."

Sara

"I like the school here much better now. In the beginning, I used to go to class, and I kept waiting for school to end so I could go home. The teachers are good, but the classes are very different from India. People ask a lot of questions and sometimes I want to say something, but I don't know if they understand me. I remember this one time when I was in the class with Miss Daniels, and she kept asking about being Muslim. I didn't know why she is asking about that, because it is an English class. And then there was only this one other Muslim boy in the class, and he just came from Gujarat so his English was not very good. So I felt like I need to tell them something, but this one girl kept talking about burka and everyone was looking at me. But we don't wear burka. Why do Americans want to know about burka? I don't know why. This girl said something about the war and about those people in Afghanistan. And I was thinking about what this has to do with the war. I wish that thing did not happen on September 11, and I wish they did not kill those people in the buildings. But I wish America did not send the bombs over there, to Afghanistan. My father told me that I should not say these things outside, because people think that the Muslims had something to do with that thing on September 11. What did we do? I don't understand. My history teacher told me it was some men, from Saudi [Arabia], I think. Is that in Afghanistan?

"Anyway, my father is afraid that he will get sent back to India if he talks about these things. My mother says not to worry, if we get sent back, we will just go back to our village. My mother misses her family there a lot! I do too, but now I'm here and I don't want to move again. My uncle in Hartford knows someone who got sent to prison in New Jersey. He works in a restaurant with this man and someone saw them coming in a van at night with the food, and they told the police. I don't know, I think they thought they have some bombs or something. So they took him to prison, and now they don't know when he will get out of the jail. I think he's from Pakistan.

"There are some Pakistanis in our building, but mainly, there are Indians and other people, like Spanish, African.[1] I like it because I have friends there—I used to go down and take walks with the other Indian girls. But now my father is scared about who we will talk to outside, so I don't go out that much. I watch videos of the Hindi TV shows at home with my sisters. We get the tapes from the store where I work, so we watch them nearly every night. One time when I was going to work on the bus, I saw that Gujarati boy from my class waiting for the other bus. He said that he also lived in the building, but I never saw him before. He just came to the school so he was still new. He said he was from Billimoria, his name is Amin. I remember it because there is one guy called Amin in the Hindi serial I watch on video, and who likes the girl called Asha. You know that show?"

Coming of Age in a Moment of Empire

What does it mean to be a young person living in the heart of the empire? How do you grow up, work, study, play, and fall in love when you know you are, at a particular moment, considered the enemy population of the nation-state in which you live? What do you do if you know that your father or brother could one day disappear and be taken from your home, detained in prison, and then sent away on a plane? What is the texture of your fear when the state turns its intelligence apparatus on surveilling and documenting your community from Islamabad, Pakistan, to Albany, New York? Where do you feel you belong if your parents left your home country to make a better living in the United States? How do you speak of war and terror if political speech is potentially dangerous? Who are your friends and whom do you to turn to for an understanding of what it means to be American?

This book looks at the ways in which young South Asian Muslim immigrants in the United States express ideas of national belonging and citizenship during the War on Terror. It focuses on the experiences of a group of Muslim youth from India, Pakistan, and Bangladesh, such as Amin and Sara, who were living in a New England town I call Wellford and grappling with issues that extended well before and after the events of September 11, 2001. However, in the wake of the 9/11 attacks, questions of citizenship, racialization, religion, and national identification took on new, urgent meanings for South Asian Muslims living in the United States and Muslims and Arab Americans more generally, as well as for South Asians mistakenly profiled in the post-9/11 backlash, particularly (turbaned, male) Sikh Americans. Muslim immigrant youth, in particular, are coming of age in U.S. society at a moment when their religious and national affiliations are politically charged issues tied to the state's War on Terror, both within and beyond U.S. borders. The national allegiances of Muslim, Arab, and South Asian Americans have come under intense scrutiny for signs of betrayal to the nation, and for any wavering in allegiance to the project of freedom and democracy as defined in the neoconservative vision for the "New American Century."

I connect the experiences of young immigrants to issues of state policy, domestic and foreign, to show how their lives are shaped by historical and political forces they are forced to grapple with in their everyday lives. How do South Asian Muslim youth make sense of the imperial state and its powers as it shapes their experiences of family, migration, work, and education? How do they think of "the nation" and national belonging in relation to the United States as well as to India, Pakistan, or Bangladesh, and to other countries in which their families have lived? How do they imagine their relationships with young people from other ethnic and national groups and other histories of belonging, exclusion, and dissent?

As Amin's and Sara's reflections suggest, ideas of religion, nationalism, war, terrorism, retribution, justice, and human rights collide with one another in ways that entangle young immigrants, especially South Asian Muslim immigrant youth, in the taken-for-granted premises as well as distortions underlying the War on Terror. Sara and Amin had to confront these ideological notions, and confusion about language and geography pertaining to the "Muslim" or "Arab world," soon after they arrived in the United States in 2001 and experienced their own displacements of culture, sociality, language, and geography. This book uses an ethnographic approach to analyze young people's own understandings of war, global politics, and the state in the everyday social contexts they inhabit, such as school, work, home, and youth culture. This book is based on an ethnographic study that involved interviews and fieldwork in the school and city in 2001–3.[2] I interviewed South Asian Muslim immigrant students, second-generation South Asian youth and Muslim immigrant students from other regions, parents of both immigrant and nonimmigrant students, teachers, staff, youth program organizers, community and religious leaders, and activists working on immigrant and civil rights. I also did fieldwork in the school and at a range of sites in Wellford, including homes, workplaces, social gatherings, and cultural and political events. The research demonstrates how the micropolitics of citizenship practices and performances of immigrant youth in these everyday contexts are linked to the macropolitical processes of the imperial state and global capital.

My conversations with these young immigrants and their families inevitably turned to the issue of citizenship, for like other immigrants they were concerned with the ever pressing issue of legal citizenship—and the possibilities of residence, work, education, financial aid, and health care—as well as the increasingly fraught question of cultural belonging and alienation. Citizenship is a fundamental notion underlying relationships among individuals, communities, and the nation-state as these are inflected by issues of ethnic and racial identity, class, gender, religion, and transnational identification (I. Young 1990). Citizenship has become an increasingly prominent theoretical lens, as well as organizing principle for movements, that represents the nexus of pressing issues of nationalism, globalization, immigration, cultural pluralism, democracy, empire, and human rights. An analysis of citizenship is crucial to understanding the ways the imperial state manages and controls its subjects; the possibilities and limitations of citizen rights have been shaped by the evolving form of the nation-state, the administrative practices of colonial (and postcolonial) regimes, the demands of the market, and emerging supranational governmental institutions (Hindess 2005). The research explores the cultural values and national ideologies that infuse ideas of citizenship for immigrant youth after 9/11, such as achievement, productivity, autonomy, self-reliance, freedom, mobility, loyalty, and security.

The book has three major focal points—youth, citizenship, empire—and it questions the relationship among and between these three pivotal concepts in order to provide a deeper, more critical understanding of the moment in which we live, one that has been glossed as the "post-9/11 moment." I connect different bodies of literature and theoretical debates that address these concepts, and that are not always in conversation with one another, to show the analytic importance, and political urgency, of tying together these issues. While the term "empire" has recently become attached (or reattached) to the United States in ways that are normalized, and even au courant after 9/11, the meaning of this word in association with the United States is not always clear. In this book, I offer an analysis of empire that shows how the post-9/11 moment is not exceptional, but part of a longer history of U.S. imperialism and political repression that has generally been evaded or erased. The book shows how citizenship is not just embedded in, but actually constitutive of, the workings of empire and the management, and resistance, of its subjects. It situates the meanings of national belonging for South Asian Muslim immigrant youth in relation to a particular moment of U.S. empire and connects questions of empire to everyday notions of national belonging, or cultural citizenship, and constructions of "youth" and cultural "difference."

South Asian Immigrant Youth in Wellford

Understanding the experiences of South Asian Muslim youth in the United States after 9/11 requires situating the narratives of Sara, Amin, and the other immigrant students in the larger history of South Asian immi-

gration and its links to global capitalism and U.S. ra
needs, and foreign policies. Transnational migration
historically been shaped by U.S. foreign policy and
derscoring the link between migration and empire. 1
South Asian immigrants came after 1965 when U.S
century-old policy of restrictions on Asian immigr:
of new immigrants from India and Pakistan incr
is important to note that the changes in immigra.....
part due to the politics of the Cold War. The United States was forced
to acknowledge the hypocrisy of enforcing racially biased immigration
restrictions while championing itself as the defender of the "free world";
it also needed to import skilled scientific and technical labor to compete
with the Soviet Union in the arms and technology race (Chan 1991;
Prashad 2000). The new immigration laws gave preferential treatment to
professionals, hence the early wave of post-1965 South Asian immigrants
consisted of highly educated, skilled professionals most of whom, but not
all, acquired middle- to upper-middle-class status and moved into suburban communities (Agarwal 1991; Helweg and Helweg 1990). For example,
Bangladeshis who came to the United States as needed pharmacists in
the early 1970s were sometimes unable to find jobs in their profession and
moved into service-sector jobs (Ahmed, Kaufman, and Naim 1996, 161).

The South Asian immigrant youth in Wellford I focus on in this book
are part of the most recent wave of immigration from South Asia to the
United States and are predominantly working class to lower middle
class. Since the 1980s, there has been a second wave of South Asian immigrants, which includes a substantial working- and lower-middle-class
population, as well as relatives of earlier immigrants who enter with
family reunification visas, changing the presumed "model minority" profile of the South Asian immigrant community.[4] In addition, in the early
1990s, many Bangladeshi and Pakistani immigrants entered through the
"visa lottery" program, for which Indian citizens were not eligible; many
of these immigrants worked in gas stations, restaurants, construction,
and sales (Ahmed, Kaufman, and Naim 1996, 160). Chain migration, or
sponsorship for immigration visas for family members who then sponsor other relatives, has helped create growing urban enclaves of working-
to middle-class Indian immigrants from particular regions or towns
(Rudrappa 2004; Shukla 2003). For example, immigrants from Gujarat in
western India (who are Hindu and Jain, as well as Muslim) have clustered

ular towns in the Boston area, as I found in an earlier study of
rati Indian immigrants in Lowell, Massachusetts (Maira and Levitt
97).

When I began this research, I discovered that the majority of the Indian
immigrant youth in the public high school in Wellford were from Muslim families, from small towns or villages in Gujarat. Most of the South
Asian immigrant students had migrated within the last five to seven
years, though some had fathers or relatives who had come to the United
States much earlier. Several of the South Asian Muslim youth were related to one another, as their families had sponsored relatives as part of
an ongoing chain migration. Whole families had migrated from the same
village in Gujarat, for example, re-creating extended family networks in
the same apartment building in Wellford. The parents of these South
Asian youth generally worked in low-income jobs in the service sector,
their employment prospects limited by their minimal fluency in English,
and the students themselves worked in part-time jobs, up to thirty hours
a week, in fast food restaurants, in gas stations, in retail stores, and as
security guards.

At least half of the South Asian immigrant youth in the school lived in
high-rise apartment complexes in North Wellford. The remainder lived
in the Prospect Square area, an ethnically and racially diverse neighborhood that is undergoing gentrification. The families of these South Asian
(Sunni) Muslim youth were not very involved in local Muslim organizations or mosques—that draw a diverse Arab, North African, Asian, and
African American population—largely because they were so busy struggling with work and survival. They tended to socialize mainly with people
from their own ethnic community, but they did not seem to affiliate with
the Indian American or Pakistani American community organizations
in the area either, which involve mainly middle- to upper-middle-class,
suburban families. The experiences of these immigrant youth are rooted
in the specificities of their urban, working-class experience, one that is often completely unknown to their more privileged South Asian American
counterparts in the area.

Wellford is a small, predominantly white city that was transformed in
the 1990s by the abolition of rent control and accelerated gentrification,
and by increasing immigration which expanded the population of immigrant workers from different parts of the world.[5] The 2000 Census
for Wellford reported that 2,720 Indian immigrants (2.7 percent of the

population), 125 Pakistanis, and 120 Bangladeshis lived in the city, which is very likely an underestimate of the South Asian population given the underreported presence of undocumented immigrants (U.S. Census Bureau, 2000). Wellford is an interesting site for this research, for while media attention and community discussions of racial profiling after 9/11 have primarily focused on South Asians in the New York / New Jersey area, there were hundreds of incidents around the country in places where South Asians have not been as visible in the public sphere or as organized, such as in New England. It is interesting to focus on a community such as Wellford that is known to be politically liberal; it sheds light on the kinds of political expressions such a setting enables, encourages, or fails to safeguard in a climate of repression, particularly for Muslim immigrant youth.

The Wellford public high school has an extremely diverse student body reflecting the city's changing population, with students from Latin America, the Caribbean, Africa, and Asia.[6] The high school has approximately 2,000 students, of which about 40 percent are white and the remaining 60 percent are students of color. African Americans are the largest group of students of color (about 25 percent), followed by Latinas and Latinos (15 percent), and Asian Americans (about 7 percent). Fred Ellery, who was at the time director of the Bilingual Program and International Student Center, noted that in the 2002–3 academic year there were about 400 foreign-born students in the high school, of which the largest group were Haitians, followed by Latinos, Portuguese-speaking students from Brazil and Cape Verdes, and South Asians, who were the fourth-largest group. Yet the international student population has reportedly declined in the years since, for accelerated gentrification and soaring housing costs have squeezed most working- and lower-middle-class families out of the city. The period during which I was doing the research was thus a moment when the immigrant student presence was very visible in the school and a source of pride in its claims to multicultural diversity.

Students from India, Pakistan, Bangladesh, and Afghanistan constituted the largest Muslim population in the school, followed by youth from Ethiopia, Somalia, and Morocco. In the year I was doing my fieldwork, there were about sixty students of South Asian origin in the high school, who were almost evenly split between immigrant students and second-generation youth. Reflecting more or less the national immigration trends for South Asians in the United States, the largest group of South Asian students was from India, followed by youth from Pakistan, Bangladesh, Nepal, Tibet, and Afghanistan. South Asian students have been coming to the high school since they started migrating to Wellford about fifteen years ago, with some Afghan students coming in the late 1970s and 1980s, but the South Asian presence increased visibly in the mid- to late 1990s.

Cultural Citizenship

My research explores the ways in which young South Asian immigrants make sense of citizenship, particularly cultural citizenship or everyday understandings of belonging and exclusion, a charged trope in the War on Terror. After 9/11, but also at earlier moments in U.S. history, cultural definitions of citizenship and dominant understandings of who is truly American mediate the rights afforded to citizens and immigrants and cultural constructs of "terrorists" (now "jihadists"), "borders," and "security." Young Muslim men, such as Amin, became inextricably associated with the specter of radical Islam and with an explicit, or sometimes implicit, suspicion exacerbated by anti-Arab racism and conflations of "Muslims" and "Arabs." As I will discuss at greater length in chapter 2, cultural citizenship is a critical issue for immigrants and nonwhite Americans because it highlights the ways in which the trope of national belonging, so powerful in modernity, is not just based on political, social, and economic dimensions of citizenship but is also defined in the social realm of belonging.[7] These questions are especially pertinent to youth, who are viewed as the next generation of citizens and whose future cultural and political role in the nation is a concern for both the Right and the Left (France 1998). The issue of cultural citizenship is a critical one, as it goes to the heart of issues of equality and exclusion, rights and justice, and extends beyond official definitions of citizenship.

At the same time, cultural belonging is still intertwined with legal distinctions between citizens and noncitizens and issues of immigrant rights and worker rights in the neoliberal economy. My research demonstrates how issues of exclusion and inclusion play out in the sphere of labor for young immigrant workers, linking economic citizenship to consumption, subcultural affiliation, and (trans)national belonging for South Asian Muslim youth, questions that have been underexplored in existing work on Muslim American youth, in particular. Sara was one of several youth in this book who engaged with national (Indian) identity by consuming South Asian films and television shows, in the little time she had between school and her part-time job. Like other South Asian immigrant students, she also expressed a dissenting critique of the U.S. war in Afghanistan, challenging the use of the veil as an alibi for the War on Terror.

South Asian immigrant youth spoke of their relationship to the nation-state in various ways, as I will discuss in the chapters that follow: through transnational ties embedded in global labor and family networks (flexible citizenship), multicultural and political affiliations, popular culture, local and urban cultures (multicultural and polycultural citizenship), and dissent or critique of state policies (dissenting citizenship). These forms of cultural citizenship are overlapping and simultaneously expressed, and they highlight the interconnections between transnational migration, the neoliberal economy, multicultural management of "difference," and political subversion and complicity.

The book explores how the War on Terror operates on the terrain of cultural citizenship, and is infused with cultural constructions of "terrorist threats" and "alien civilizations" that justify so-called racial profiling polices that targeted populations based on U.S. foreign policy concerns, as I will explain in chapter 5. The cultural reimagining and political persecution of Muslims and Arabs as suspect citizens in the War on Terror have roots in Orientalist views of Islam and the Middle East that have long been tied to imperial engagements with the region (Said 1981 [1978]). However, this suspicion emerged in intensified form after 9/11 through hyper-Orientalized media representations, state surveillance and profiling, and hostility and harassment of Arab and Muslim Americans in the public sphere.

After 9/11, there was a violent backlash in the United States against Muslims, or those thought to be Muslims, with 700 hate crimes against South Asian Americans, Arab Americans, and Muslim Americans in the three weeks following the Twin Towers attacks. There were four homicides (two involving South Asian American victims, one Sikh and the other Muslim, and others targeting Arabs and even one Native American woman), reported as hate crimes in this period.[8] At least 200 hate crimes were reported against Sikh Americans alone; Balbir Singh Sodhi, a Sikh gas station owner, was the first to be murdered in connection to the events of 9/11.[9] The Council on American-Islamic Relations (CAIR) documented 960 incidents of racial profiling just in the five weeks after

Flier for art exhibit at Asian
Resource Gallery,
Oakland, California, 2006.
Graphic by Kasi Chakravartula;
design by Joy Gloria Liu.

September 11, 2001; reported hate crimes against those believed be Muslim in 2001 increased by 1,600 percent from the previous year, in the FBI's estimate.[10] In addition to the official statistics for reported incidents of profiling, harassment, or assault—which are a conservative estimate since many more instances went unreported—there was also a much broader range of formal and informal practices of ongoing exclusion, profiling, and surveillance of South Asian, Arab, and Muslim Americans in the mainstream media and public sphere, as I will discuss later.

Under the guise of the War on Terror, there were mass detentions and deportations of Muslim and Arab Americans, mainly immigrant men rounded up on public suspicion or for immigration violations. They had a chilling effect on Muslim and Arab American communities, as did the "Special Registration" program requiring Muslim immigrant men to register with the government and submit to questioning. The state's program of surveillance, detentions, and deportations of South Asian, Arab, and Muslim Americans has largely receded from the mainstream media's attention (except in a few sensationalized cases), but it continues to target these communities, particularly through ongoing FBI monitoring and surveillance, the use of Muslim and Arab informants, and interviews targeting Muslim males and mosqued communities (e.g., Maira 2007).[11] The War on Terror is also, in part, a battle about the meaning of cultural citizenship: it uses a cultural discourse to emphasize values about clashing civilizations that presumably explain the "radicalization" of Muslim youth alienated from "Western" values and notions of liberal (and supposedly secular) democracy. The imperial state is constituted in these political as well as cultural processes of contestation, representation, classification, surveillance, and everyday disciplinary practices that shape cultural citizenship.

Exploring expressions of cultural citizenship by youth who are from communities targeted with suspicion after 9/11 allows us to understand some of the paradoxes of national belonging, exclusion, alienation, and political expression for a generation of immigrants that is coming of age at this particular moment, and it also sheds light on larger cultural and political debates about citizenship and dissent in the United States. These discussions of the political views of Muslim youth are shaped by deeper national anxieties, not just about "radical Islam" but also about the national consensus, the positioning of white middle-class America, and the role of U.S. empire. This anxiety is most evident in the fear and loathing evoked by reports of alleged terrorist plots by young Muslim Americans, such as the sensationalized case of Hamid Hayat, a Pakistani American from Lodi, California (Dubal and Maira 2005; Maira 2007), which generate panic about a "fifth column." But it also surfaces in the horror, confusion, and moral reprobation provoked by stories of young, white, middle-class and upper-middle-class Americans who convert to Islam and join the "other side" in the War on Terror. The so-called American Taliban, John Walker Lindh (Best 2003), and the al-Qaeda spokesperson, Adam Gadan, are viewed as betraying the nation not just because of their treacherous assistance to "the enemy" but also due to their apparent rejection of the cultural values underlying "Western" liberal democratic citizenship.

Youth, Citizenship, and Politics

Debates about citizenship and national belonging in relation to Muslim American youth are infused with layered assumptions about the meaning of "youth," the definition of "citizenship," and the possibilities of "politics" for young people. The category of youth is itself socially and politically constructed and, in traditional Western perceptions of adolescence, is viewed as a liminal stage when social identities and political commitments are being formed (Erikson 1994 [1968]).[12] The construction of youth as a transitional category of citizenship underlies the preoccupation with youth in relation to the social order and civic personhood. Young people symbolize the unknown future or possible direction of the nation and become the site of projection of adult hopes and fears about their own society (Maira and Soep 2005). Much of the discussion of Muslim American youth after 9/11 is tinged with these deeper social and national anxieties about how Muslim, South Asian, and Arab Americans will position themselves in relation to the nation-state and what kinds of citizens they will become.

In the United States, there is a tendency to define generational cohorts as representing certain cultural values—the '60s generation, the Baby Boomers, Generation X, and now what some now call Generation 9-11 (Fields n.d.). These labels encapsulate what U.S. national identity means in different historical periods by linking it to the political culture of that generation of youth, generally reducing a complex range of experiences to a single catchy term. The interest in classifying and surveying young people in order to create a distinct cultural and political profile is partly a result of adult concerns, hopes, and worries about the shape of the social landscape and how youth conform to, challenge, or reshape the status quo; it is also a marketing strategy for predicting and generating consumption patterns based on lifestyle and generational categories (Hall and Jefferson 1976; Lopiano-Misdom and De Luca 1997).

The presumed liminality of adolescence cannot be taken for granted nor the very notion of age or the process of "coming of age" in modernity. Youth are supposedly between "childhood" and "adulthood" but can be defined as either—or neither—depending on the minimum age designated for certain citizen rights. For example, the right to vote at the age of eighteen was bestowed on youth in the United States only in 1972 after those who came of age during the Vietnam War decided that if they were old enough to be in the military, they were old enough to vote (Fields n.d.; Sigel and Hoskin 1981). Focusing on how citizenship rights are linked to age reveals the role of the state in defining youth and points to what Philip Mizen calls "the importance of age to the political management of social relations" by the state (2002, 6). Age-based concepts of youth or generation are often tied to the naturalization of the social order for social reproduction, which is key to the cultural, political, and economic processes—and hierarchies—that shape biopolitics, or the management of populations (Cole and Durham 2007, 2, 7). The category of youth is part of the broader age-graded relations that underpin systems of labor, education, criminal justice, taxation, property, marriage, and family (Mizen 2002). The notion of youth-as-transition is necessary to the division of labor and the hierarchy of material relations specific to various formations of the capitalist state. Youth are implicated in notions of citizenship emerging in the shift from the welfare state to the neoliberal privatization of state services in Britain and in the United States (Harvey 2005; Mizen 2002), as will be discussed in chapter 4. Age is a category that is deployed by the state, and that is used to understand what constitutes "good" citizenship or mature selfhood. Mizen, along with other scholars who deconstruct the notion of youth, shows how "age provides a precise method of calibration for state administrative practices as the means to define subordinate populations in order to effect their control" (2002, 12).

For many of the Muslim immigrant youth in this book, there is a clear awareness that the state is not a protector of their civil rights, even as it purportedly offers them other rights: to work, residence, or voting. The discourse of rights, including human rights, has also been critiqued as concealing systems of domination and repression (Hansen and Steputat 2005, 10). These young immigrants are aware that citizenship is a compromise, a transaction in which they trade some rights for others—if only hoped-for opportunities—and that they have emigrated knowing that their home states, too, are limited in what they can offer them. In focusing on young people's understanding of citizenship as embedded in daily experiences, this research also examines their relationship to the state in their everyday lives and the ways in which the imperial state is constructed in this encounter.

It is important to examine what "citizenship" and "dissent" mean when juxtaposed with "youth," particularly immigrant youth who are the object of national anxieties about assimilation and the economy that are culturally and racially coded. Immigrant youth are often viewed as not being American enough, or desiring to "become American" but being "caught between two worlds" and thus culturally and even politically suspect. If the category of youth has been viewed as a liminal stage in the development of political and national identity (France 1998), then immigrant youth are perceived as doubly liminal, because of their age and also their national affiliations. For Muslim immigrant youth this perception is even more acute, especially after 9/11; they are constructed in mainstream discourse as culturally or religiously alien and also as potential threats to the nation. The images of Muslim and Arab American youth in the mainstream media are linked to religious fundamentalist movements or anti-American ideologies, or at best, they are seen as having divided loyalties at a time when national unity is seen as critical. This book reveals the ways that young South Asian Muslims engaged with questions of national belonging and notions of terrorist or enemy threats by focusing on their own narratives and performances of national belonging or cultural citizenship in a range of sites.

Youth are the targets of nationalizing discourse by the state and civil society, for example, in institutions such as public high schools where ideas of national identity and history are inculcated for the purposes of producing good citizens (Cole and Durham 2007, 10), as the experiences of Amin, Sara, and other youth in this book will demonstrate. Young people express notions of national belonging and imagine the state in various ways, in the contexts of their experiences of youth culture, schooling, work, immigration, policing, social services, the military, or the prison system—what Timothy Mitchell describes as "small-scale polymorphous methods of order," drawing on Michel Foucault's seminal analysis of sites where populations are regulated and disciplined by regimes of "governmentality" (Mitchell 2006, 177). Yet until recently the issue of "youth citizenship" has not received enough attention: it falls between the cracks of literature on children's rights and adult citizenship but draws on issues from both these areas (e.g., on children's rights see Roche 1997; Stephens 2005). Research on youth and citizenship has traditionally drawn on developmental psychology or functionalist socialization theory, reinforcing approaches to youth as a transitional stage on the path to adulthood. In both scholarship and public discourse, young people's ideas of citizenship are viewed as not fully formed, and so unresolved and more susceptible to shaping by external forces than for adults. It is certainly true that youth are engaged in an ongoing process of social and cognitive development and do acquire more legal rights and responsibilities as they move into adulthood. Young people undeniably have to negotiate particular concerns due to their positioning in the family, social structure, and educational system. But at the core of this perspective about youth as protocitizens are taken-for-granted assumptions about citizenship that reify, and consolidate, state power and neoliberal capitalism.

The traditional literature on the political socialization of youth often suggests that they need to be drawn into "consensual citizenship," inherently maintaining the status quo and leaving the definition of citizenship or national belonging largely unchallenged (France 1998, 105). Such approaches imply that young citizens must be socialized into adult norms of political involvement, rather than considered as thinking agents who may express important critiques of citizenship and nationhood, even if their rights are limited (Buckingham 2000, 13). Researchers interested in citizenship suggest various ways young people should learn about citizenship, for example, through "apprenticeship in democratic citizenship" (Storrie 1997). However, these approaches are generally based on a normative view of citizenship in which "terms such as good citizenship, democratic citizen, and involved citizen are used almost interchangeably," without much questioning of what "democracy" really means (Sigel and Hoskin 1981, 39). There is also an assumption that citizens should feel "loyalty or affection" for the nation and express patriotic citizenship (Sigel and Hoskin 1981, 39), as particularly evident in post-9/11 America.

The experiences of these working-class youth demonstrate the interconnections between the cultural and economic forms of citizenship and notions of the ideal citizen. The research shows how the experiences of young immigrants who are also workers and students shape ideas of national belonging in relation to education and the labor market under neoliberal economic regimes. Citizenship in the neoliberal capitalist state means being a productive worker who is not automatically entitled to social services as a citizen but must try to gain access to them as an individual consumer. Many U.S. youth come to understand social problems and citizenship through the particular political lens of economic individualism within neoliberal capitalism, as youth increasingly do in Britain and Europe (France 1998). The notion of youth as active citizens is often translated into youth as active consumers whose presumed "right to choose between services," rather than rights to basic needs, is emphasized by the neoliberal state (Jones and Wallace 1992, 140), as elaborated in chapter 4. Discourses of active citizenship that emerged in the 1980s in the United States as well as in Europe, in response to economic restructuring and the erosion of the welfare state, have promoted volunteering as one of the modes in which citizens, including youth, construct their civic identity (France 1998; Storrie 1997). Community service programs targeting youth are often linked to neoliberal economic policies that rest on "tutoring people to build their own capacities and become self-dependent, responsible citizens who can take care of their own welfare," allowing the state to privatize public services and making citizens "complicit in the contemporary workings of power and governance" (Sharma and Gupta 2006, 21).

Immigrant youth engage with notions of citizenship in the context of national and global economic restructuring and shifts in ideas of productivity and virtue in neoliberal capitalism. Theorists of youth citizenship argue, rightly, that young people have different expectations of work and future careers than those of earlier generations, due to changes in the economy and labor market, and that working-class youth experience heightened uncertainty about their economic futures in the nation (e.g., Bhavnani 1991; France 1998; Rogers et al. 1997; Sigel and Hoskin 1981). These South Asian immigrant youth understand national belonging as an aspiration for class mobility, but in their daily struggles with education and work they confront the many obstacles that make the American Dream a distant mirage for working-class immigrants, as the unfolding stories of Amin, Sara, and other youth will underscore.

However, research on youth and citizenship has traditionally underemphasized the ways young people who have grown up with globalized media and immigration imagine their futures *beyond* the border of the nation-state or in relation to multiple nation-states, and has generally persisted in viewing citizenship for youth as largely confined within national borders. As other political theorists have pointed out, there has been a "globalization" and "flexibilization" of citizenship with the increasing flows of people and capital across national borders, but this has not led to greater flexibility of rights for all (Hansen and Steputat 2005, 10; Hindess 2005, 255–56). Sara made the poignant observation that her mother was not afraid of being deported, because she missed her village in Gujarat, unlike her father who was worried that they might have to return after uprooting themselves to pursue a "better life" in the United States. For these immigrant youth, the ties of love and family crisscross national borders, as families are reunited and divided through the workings of immigration and foreign policies of the U.S. state, as well as the policies of the nation-states from which they emigrate. Building on more recent work that has a transnational perspective, the book demonstrates that young immigrants think of citizenship in ways that span national borders, and that these views of transnational citizenship are linked to notions of economic citizenship shaped by global capitalism and to political understandings of nationalism and dissent.[13]

However, the traditional approach to youth and citizenship also assumes a limited definition of what it means for young people to be political. A prominent and problematic refrain in the research on youth and citizenship as well as in public discussions of youth politics, in the United States and elsewhere, is the pervasive concern that youth are apparently not sufficiently politically engaged. It is certainly true that youth movements in the United States are not as visible, cohesive, or militant as they were in earlier moments. Neoliberalism has been accompanied by an assault on political movements demanding structural changes of the state and by a growing retreat to the private sphere, or a privatization and individualization of politics itself, that is reflected across generations. Some researchers also point out that assessment of young people's politicization also leads to a temporal conundrum, for it is not always possible to predict young people's political attitudes based on the experiences of a different generation, but they still conclude that young people today do not express the "overtly political values" identified among young people in the 1960s, the benchmark of youth politicization in the United States (e.g., Rogers et al. 1997, 27–28).

The 1960s and 1970s were certainly a time of worldwide involvement of youth in struggles against the depredations of capitalism, militarism, imperialism, and repression; the discussion of youth politics today is, implicitly or explicitly, imbued with both fear and hope about whether youth and students will emerge as a radical or militant force. But it is important to note that there are many groups of youth today who are involved in responding to the political crises of globalization, late capitalism, and U.S. militarism as they affect their generation, and that politics today generally looks different than it did in earlier moments, for better or worse. It is clear that on the ground, even in the United States, young people are engaged in a variety of political realms (Bhavnani 1991; Fields n.d.; Storrie 1997) and that these mobilizations are often led by youth from disenfranchised communities, immigrant or minoritized, whose collective organizing continues to be met with state repression and media demonization. Young people are involved in campaigns ranging from anti-sweatshops organizing and feminist coalitions to prison abolition

Active Arts Youth Conference, Boston, Massachusetts, 2002.

movements and counter-recruitment programs to resist military induction (Allison and Solnit 2007; Faith 2000; Fields n.d.; Mariscal 2005; Poitevin 2000; Shepard and Hayduk 2002). Since 9/11 and the war in Afghanistan, young people have been engaged in antiwar politics in various ways, from engaging in civil disobedience actions and organizing rallies to producing and participating in alternative media. There is a growing genre of political music that is critical of the United States and of empire and militarism, including hip-hop by artists such as Paris, Dead Prez, and the Coup, among others.[14] The book explores the ways in which South Asian immigrant youth are engaged with, or disengaged from, these American youth subcultures and the implications of their affiliations with other youth of color for notions of liberal multiculturalism and interethnic alliances after 9/11.

Popular culture is also a site where youth articulate the convergences between these various political movements. For instance, in September 2002 I attended the Active Arts Youth Conference in Boston, designed to mobilize the "hip hop generation" by featuring spoken word by artists such as Palestinian American poet Suheir Hammad and offering workshops by antiwar groups, alternative media projects, the Prison Moratorium Project, and Military Out of Our Schools, among other youth organizations challenging state policies. At the same time, there are also youth, including immigrant youth, who support the U.S. wars and enlist in or want to join the military for various reasons, so dissent is uneven and not guaranteed by identities—racial, ethnic, gender, or sexual—as I will discuss in chapter 5. Many young Americans identify with the model of "patriotic citizen" that coalesced strongly in the United States after 9/11 and believe the nation is justified in waging its War on Terror. Being a patriotic citizen has increasingly replaced "democratic citizen" and "involved citizen" as the primary definition of "good" citizenship, and it one that some Muslim and Arab Americans have tried to perform to assert their national loyalty, as I will explore later.

However, some complaints about the lack of politicization of youth are based on a perspective that defines the political as formal or electoral politics, and that assumes that this is the litmus test of "participatory" citizenship (Fields n.d.). The political subjectivity of youth is often expressed not just in different arenas than for adults but through an informal logic of politics and citizenship (Storrie 1997, 60; see also Bhavnani 1991). The fundamental assumption about the meaning of politics for young people is questioned in this book, which focuses on the micropolitics of youth in their daily lives beyond the realm of official, electoral politics. It builds on recent work that pays attention to young people's own understandings of politics and the ways they negotiate relationships of power in different realms in their everyday life (Bhavnani 1991; Buckingham 2000; France 1998). Young people express a political awareness of the ways their lives and social relations are shaped by the "government" and offer an analysis of the public sphere and the state without necessarily using the official language of citizenship, rights, or formal politics. Kum-Kum Bhavnani (1991, 53, 9) points out that studies of youth political development are often limited by research methodology, for young people's subjective awareness is difficult to assess through the traditional survey methods of political science or social psychology. Thus an ethnographic perspective pays attention not just to verbalized discourse by youth about politics but to nonverbal, daily experiences of young people, which is particularly important for immigrants, young people, and any group whose political speech is targeted in a climate of repression.

My approach draws on the insights of Paul Willis (1990, 145), who suggests that the work of citizenship for youth is grounded in popular

culture, social affiliations, and everyday discourse. His analysis focuses on
the creativity of political and social meanings that is expressed by youth
through "common culture," rather than in the increasingly constrained institutional spheres of work, formal politics, and education. A focus on
the everyday experiences of young people reveals how they grapple with
the meaning of the state's role in their lives and with the implications of
war, violence, and racism for an ethics of belonging. This analysis helps
us understand how South Asian immigrant youth use an "informal" logic
to understand the work of empire and the state in their everyday lives. It
is this informal politics of immigrant youth that I focus on in this book
and from which I draw insights to complicate a theoretical and "formal"
political logic of citizenship and empire. Looking at the varying meanings
of citizenship and belonging for youth after 9/11 in relation to the cultures of U.S. imperialism helps to understand the source of these deeper
anxieties about citizenship and youth and how to imagine our own relationship to empire.

Empire, Imperialism, and Imperial Feelings

The existence, or nature, of a U.S. "empire" is the focus of a global debate
that has slowly reemerged since the fall of the Berlin Wall and the breakup
of the USSR, the only other superpower. Some proponents of empire
view the current role of the United States as democratizing, benevolent,
or simply necessary, if accompanied by certain problems and burdens for
the sole superpower today. On the other end of the spectrum in this debate are those who view U.S. imperial power as coercive, violent, and repressive, and opposed to the very "democracy" and "freedom" it purports
to bring to the rest of the world. This debate needs to be historicized because the War on Terror and the assault on civil liberties unleashed by the
PATRIOT Act were not immaculately conceived on September 11, 2001.
They have a long gestation in the plans for aggressive military expansion
and global political and economic domination, developed by the group of
neoconservatives aligned with George W. Bush well before 2001, and also
in the military interventions and anti-immigrant policies of previous regimes that laid the groundwork for this intensified, unilateralist assertion
of American power after 9/11, as I will explain in the following chapter.
These policies of U.S. military, political, and economic domination are
rooted in a long history of imperial power and designs that is tied to the

formation of the nation as a settler-colonial state, built on the conquest and cleansing of new frontiers and the control of territories through direct and indirect methods. Yet collective amnesia and suppression of this history have obscured the realities of U.S. empire for those who benefit from its spoils.

The rehabilitation of the term "empire" has in many ways led to an obfuscation, rather than clarification, of how empire really works, as will be explored in chapter 1. I argue that returning to the less sexy, but more analytically precise, notion of imperialism is important to understand the nature of U.S. imperialist power at the current moment. The shape of U.S. imperialism has morphed and evolved over time, from the genocide of Native Americans to the colonization of the Philippines and Puerto Rico; the annexation of parts of Mexico as well as Hawaii, Guam, and other Pacific territories; the proxy wars in Latin America and Africa; the weapons of mass destruction used against Japan; the devastation of Southeast Asia; and the contemporary mix of covert and overt strategies of domination, including the bombing of Afghanistan, the occupation of Iraq, and the client regimes installed in both countries. This imperialism is marked by invisibility, secrecy, and flexibility in its operation of power, and by nebulous, nonterritorial forms of domination that do not resemble traditional forms of territorial "colonialism."[15] The beast whose belly we live in is the proverbial elephant in the room that no one can accurately name, but its form can be grasped if we reach for more than its discrete parts.

A crucial point is that the "post-9/11" moment is not a radical historical or political rupture, but rather a moment of renewed contestation over the state's imperial power and ongoing issues of war and repression, citizenship and nationalism, civil rights and immigrant rights. The "state of emergency" in empire—this crisis of civil rights and the forms of dissent it provokes—is not exceptional in the United States even if it becomes more apparent at certain historical moments (Ganguly 2001). The broader theory of the "state of exception," drawn variously from the work of Carl Schmitt and Walter Benjamin, suggests that the expansion of executive power and suspension of democratic rights is, in fact, not the exception but the rule—the constitutive paradigm of Western government and law since World War I—blurring the distinction between peace and war (Agamben 2005, 22). As Michael Hardt and Antonio Negri (2000, 17) argue, the state of exception is permanent for empire which, as a rule, exercises repressive, preventive, and military force. The post-9/11 moment builds on measures and forms of power already in place—this is a state of everyday life in empire. While there has been growing discussion of these issues, the questions this book raises are: What does it mean to express dissent against empire during this particular state of exception? What forms does dissent take for young people, immigrants, and those who are targeted by the state? How is citizenship, including cultural citizenship, a crucible for imperial state policies of subordination, repression, and division? My research addresses these complex questions in ways that challenge the current discourse of empire and our conventional understandings of political dissent or activism.

The book reflects on how we can think about young people's politics after the events of 9/11, and how we can connect their political responses to a global analysis of imperial power. It does this by tracing the forms of national belonging expressed by South Asian Muslim youth in their everyday lives at a time when they were considered potential threats to the state, or at least alien to the "American way of life." Amin's and Sara's narratives highlight the ways in which their own lives were transformed by the discourse about Islam used in the War on Terror and the fear of being detained or "disappeared." The state's policies of surveillance, detentions, and deportations targeting Muslim and Arab Americans after 9/11 have altered Muslim American publics and also counterpublics, as I discuss in chapter 5. Sara no longer hung out with her friends outside her building, and Amin found himself having to represent, and speak for, Islam in the classroom. Stories of Muslim immigrant men who disappeared mysteriously, never to return or to be deported weeks or months later to Pakistan or Bangladesh, seeped into the community and tightened the noose around expressions of public dissent or even private political discussion. Yet Amin and Sara were also young people: teenagers who were trying to figure out a new educational system, new forms of popular culture, and new social relations and languages of difference, while grappling with feelings of confusion, fear, frustration, alienation, anger, attraction, sorrow, and hopefulness.

The book links the experiences of these youth to what I call the "imperial feeling" of post-9/11 America, a concept I elaborate on in chapter 1. Imperial feelings are the everyday "structures of feeling" that undergird what William Appleman Williams (1980) called "empire as a way of life," or the "habits of heart and mind" that infuse and accompany structures of difference and domination (Stoler 2006a, 2). The affective and cultural dimensions of imperial nationalism are inextricably intertwined with issues of war and terrorism, and also education and work, popular culture and global media, family and belonging, as the narratives of Sara and Amin suggest. The notion of an imperial feeling unifies the emotional and structural dimensions of citizenship, and the public and private domains of politics, for it acknowledges that like nationalism, political identification is based on subjective feelings as well as "rational" discourse (Young 1990, 117). Citizenship—identification with or dissent from the nation-state—is built on an affective as well as political logic of national belonging that has different meanings for various groups within the nation and is a crucial site for the constitution of imperial power.

Doing an Ethnography of Empire

This book uses an ethnographic approach to explore the everyday understandings of citizenship of South Asian Muslim youth at this particular historical moment—the many ways in which these young people construct their relationship to the nation-state in the contexts of school, work, family, and popular culture. In doing so, I am developing an ethnographic method for studying empire through the lens of young immigrants' experiences. The methodology I develop here draws on the work of scholars such as Thomas Hansen and Finn Steputat (2001, 5), who propose that an ethnography of the state focus on everyday, local practices that engage with the "languages of stateness" evident in "mythologies of power": the "practical, often nonpolitical routines" or "violent impositions" of the state. My research offers an ethnography of life in an imperial nation-state, exploring how the "effect of the state" is created through structural and everyday processes that produce the state and manifest its disciplinary power for immigrant youth, through their encounters with institutions such as the school, workplace, media, and immigration bureaucracy.

Traditional conceptions of the state in the social sciences took for granted its abstract, dominant, and autonomous nature, thus reifying the power of the state and its presumed separation from society. More recent work on the state shows that it is not constituted by an abstract or static disciplinary power but comes into being and asserts its power through cultural practices and everyday social relations (Sharma and Gupta 2006).

The state is described by Aradhana Sharma and Akhil Gupta (2006, 6) as "a multilayered, contradictory, translocal ensemble of institutions, practices, and people in a globalized context" that is variously imagined as unitary, outside of the private sphere, and all-powerful in governance. Timothy Mitchell (2006, 176) points out that the power of the state is consolidated by structural processes that make it possible to view it as unitary, discrete, and distinct from civil society so that the state is actually a structural effect of this abstraction; the state is conceived as based on a system of law, linked to the "economy," and conflated with the "nation" as the "fundamental political community" in modernity.

Anthropological work has explored cultural struggles and disciplinary practices associated with state power and focused on people's imaginings of the state as being powerful, necessary, limited, irrelevant, or disruptive. Muslim American youth, too, may understand the state in diverse and shifting ways, but they also confront the power and coercion of the U.S. state, however dispersed or refashioned in the era of globalization, and view it with a mixture of fear, hope, uncertainty, and disillusionment. As a group of young people from a community whose civil, immigrant, and human rights have been under intensified assault since 2001, the experiences of these South Asian immigrant youth help us understand the possibilities, and limitations, of agency and resistance in these everyday encounters with the state. The research shows how young people narrate their encounters with the imperial state—its officials and institutions—in a variety of arenas and grapple with issues of state power in their daily lives.

This is also an ethnography of imperial feelings, for it reveals the *intimacy of empire* by exploring the everyday encounters with the state that have increasingly dissolved the boundaries between "private" and "public" spheres for communities surveilled by the state, and the feelings of fear, dissent, complicity, and solidarity that emerge from the imperial. Scholars in postcolonial studies, such as Ann Stoler (2006a, 4), have drawn attention to "the distribution of sentiments within and between empire's subjects and citizens as part of an imperial statecraft" that works through "close encounters, unspoken knowledge" and intimate "proximities of power." This book is unique because it focuses on the intimacy of power in an existing imperial regime, not a former European colonial power or postcolonial state; furthermore, it conceives of intimacy not just in relation to actual intimate, domestic, or social relations as a site of colonial control, but also in terms of Martin Heidegger's concept of nearness—a broader notion of the "degree of involvement, engagement, concern" with imperial power (cited in Stoler 2006, 15).

How far, or how close, are we willing to go with an ethnography of empire? The particular approach I have taken to writing about the experiences of South Asian Muslim youth in this book highlights that what is *in* the story of Muslim immigrant youth after 9/11 is itself politically constituted. If Muslim youth are understood as potential terrorists, religious fundamentalists, or "anti-American" subjects, it is because of the story the U.S. state tells about them through its policies and discourse, and the ways this is filtered through mass media and public culture through the lens of Islam (and what is now branded by the antiterrorism industry and lecture circuit as "jihadism"). Framed almost exclusively in relation to religion, and the trope of a "clash of civilizations," the fuller stories of Muslim American youth—as students, workers, cultural consumers, or critical political subjects—are never known (Moallem 2005, 53). This simultaneous use of reductionism and voyeurism is, of course, an old strategy in constructing the enemy "other" or scapegoating those perceived as non-American for being un-American (Saito 2005, 61).

In this book, I wanted to challenge the dominant fictions about Muslim immigrant youth and the desire to "know" them as a distinct, and potentially suspect, other. Yet at the same time, I also wanted to articulate the experiences, observations, and critiques of these young people that I believe to be important and illuminating. So rather than accept at face value the categories—particularly that of "the Muslim"—that are assumed to be the most obvious frames in which to place the stories of the South Asian youth in this study, I have purposefully tried to complicate how the identities and experiences of Muslim immigrant youth are imagined in the mass media and public discourse after 9/11. This book considers its subjects to be much more than just Muslim youth, portraying them also as immigrants, students, workers, family members, and cultural consumers, as the stories of Sara and Amin suggest. I explore these young people's views of politics, national belonging, and the imperial state by drawing on their own narratives, which are often critical of their profiling as Muslims but at the same time position themselves within the nation in ways that extend beyond simply being "Muslim."

The research literature, too, has largely framed Muslim American youth in relation to religious identity or practice and cultural values and conflicts. In putting U.S. imperialism at the center of the story, I have

shifted the frame from worn dichotomies of assimilation versus ethnicization—or coded anxieties about "Islamicization" (do they hate us?)—
and a narrowly nation-based focus on immigration to an analysis linking the domestic and global faces of imperial state policies. In doing so,
the book demonstrates that the stories of these youth speak to broader
questions of war, foreign policy, globalization, labor, gender, racialization,
Orientalism, multiculturalism, nationalism, solidarity, and dissent that
course through U.S. society and that shed light on larger social and political processes at work at this historical moment.

For this study, I chose to focus on a group of young people who would
not conventionally be defined as political activists and who did not belong to any organized political groups. I was interested in learning how
the events of 9/11 and their aftermath would shape the everyday, political
understandings of Muslim youth who had just come to the United States
and whose own perspectives have not always been included in discussions
of these events, except as victims of racial profiling and as token representatives of Islam within liberal multiculturalism. The analysis of these
young people's notions of national belonging and evolving political understandings goes beyond the question of political rights and organized
activism to the many contexts in which citizenship and political subjectivity are produced. One of the aims of this book is to reflect on what it
means to express political views or opinions dissenting from the majority
when the freedom to critique the state is particularly tenuous for certain
groups, based on national origin and religion, and to some extent also
for the public at large in the aftermath of 9/11. The state evokes fear as a
tactic of intimidation and repression, but fear coexists with other kinds
of responses in targeted communities: with feelings of affiliation or solidarity, and also with intimations of betrayal or complicity, as discussed in
chapters 5 and 6.

Talking to these young people demonstrates that although they did not
explicitly use the vocabulary of "empire" or "dissent"—which is also true
of many others in the United States—they did articulate strong feelings
about the actions of the United States, and of other nation-states, and
expressed a range of critical reflections on political events through their
vernacular dissent. Focusing on the everyday lives of these youth helps
shed light on the connections between state power and experiences related to school, work, family, social relationships, and popular culture and
to provide a broader analysis of citizenship and empire grounded in daily

experience. Issues of national belonging in relation to the imperial state are evident in each of these everyday contexts, directly and indirectly, so this book provides the connection between social life and empire that is missing in most theoretical discussions of empire. Clearly, this is a story about citizenship and empire, but it is necessarily intertwined with issues of labor, leisure, dissent, betrayal, and loss that these young immigrants faced.

Post-9/11 Area Studies

Doing an ethnography of empire, and particularly of immigrant youth after 9/11, raises several tangled questions about what I call "post-9/11 area studies" and its complex ethics of research. Since 2001, there has emerged a new kind of area studies of the United States, a post-9/11 area studies evident in the profusion of books in the aftermath of the events of September 11, 2001. The term "post-9/11" has become a shorthand to signify a range of issues: the War on Terror and national security regimes; the relation between the U.S. state and Muslim, Arab, and South Asian Americans; Islam and fundamentalism; and almost anything to do with Muslims and Arabs in the current moment. After 9/11 there was a flurry of interest in the media—and also in schools, colleges, churches, and community groups—in learning about "the Muslim world" and the Middle East as an explanatory rubric for 9/11, but with a particular focus on culture and religion, rather than on politics. A burgeoning body of work by various scholars and commentators has focused on Islam, fundamentalism, terrorism (some contributing to the growing "jihad" industry), and also the Bush regime, the civil liberties crisis, and war, but with uneven analyses of the role of the U.S. state.[16]

Islam has become packaged for U.S. and Western consumers in ways that obscures historical and political conflicts and movements tied to U.S. empire, as I will discuss in chapter 5, and constitutes "Muslim" subjects in narrow and often Orientalist ways. In post-9/11 studies, there are various ways of positioning Muslim Americans: as adherents of Islam (often viewed as a distinctly un-Western religion and conflated with Arab culture); as immigrants (to be placed within the framework of assimilation or multiculturalism); as transnational subjects (with the complex and potentially charged implications of dual allegiances that that implies); as victims of the state's War on Terror (the latest group to be "racially profiled"); or as a potentially suspect population to be documented and identified by the state.

Some of this writing that emerged in the United States after 9/11 is motivated by benign interest to compensate for previous ignorance, even if in the context of fear or a sense of cultural and religious distance from Muslims and Arabs. At the same time, the hypervisibility of Muslim Americans after 9/11 is tied to the state's desire to map Muslims, and especially Middle Eastern and Pakistani communities, within the U.S. in order to monitor them and convince the American public that it is guarding against the threat of terrorism. Post-9/11 studies thus raises troubling questions, given the various state projects of surveillance and documentation of Muslims in the United States; for example, the now revised Special Registration program targeting Muslim immigrant men and the interviewing of Muslim Americans by the FBI. Research that focuses only on the dimensions that the state has chosen to highlight with regard to this population—their religion and political views—is potentially of use to the state to map the "enemy within." At the very least, it perpetuates the underlying premise of the War on Terror by continuing to position these youth only in relation to Islam, thus perpetuating the Orientalist framework of the "clash of civilizations," supposedly between Islam and the West (Huntington 1996). In doing this ethnographic study, I grappled with the question: How can we produce an ethnography of everyday life in empire that is not completely complicit with intelligence gathering and surveillance of the target population after 9/11? Are there methods, modes of interpretation, and means of dissemination that can allow our research to safeguard vulnerable individuals—and the possibilities of dissent and resistance—while still offering a complex and critical analysis?

Social scientists and area studies scholars, in different fields and of various backgrounds, have always had to struggle with questions of "intelligence gathering" in relation to state policies of profiling, interrogation, detention or internment at home, and military intervention overseas. State interest in post-9/11 area studies is not a figment of paranoid imagination, but is clearly illustrated by H.R. 3077, the legislation proposed by the U.S. Congress to regulate TITLE VI funding for area studies through an International Education Advisory Board constituted by no less than members of the Department of Defense, the National Security Agency, and the infamous Department of Homeland Security. The area of knowledge explicitly targeted by hearings on this bill was postcolonial theory, Middle Eastern studies, and the work of Palestinian American scholar Edward Said, in particular, which was accused of being anti-American by the bill's proponents (Beinin 2006; Doumani 2006). Although the bill was not approved, the push for passing H.R. 3077 made it clear that in the present moment, the stakes in doing academic work related to the Middle East or the "Muslim world" are high enough to warrant overt government regulation. In September 2005, the FBI announced the creation of the National Security Higher Education Advisory Board to foster links between higher education and the FBI's interests in intelligence recruitment and to shape research agendas in accordance with national security issues. There has also been a broader, private monitoring of academic research and blacklisting of scholars perceived to be "anti-American," such as by Lynne Cheney and Senator Joseph Lieberman's American Council of Trustees and Alumni (ACTA) which documents "unpatriotic acts" by academics (Hammer 2003, 300; Schrecker 2005, 165).

While repression by the state and by civil society groups, such as Cheney's ACTA or Daniel Pipes's Campus Watch, stifles open expression by academics and writers, it is even more chilling for those who are presumed to fit "the profile" of "terrorists" or supporters of "enemy" groups ("jihadists"). I was constantly aware in this study that questioning South Asian Muslim immigrants about issues of immigration and national belonging after 9/11 could cause anxiety and fear for many, given the state's scrutiny of their lives, relatives, associations, and religious and political views, and the detention and deportation of many South Asian and Arab immigrants based on suspicion of their political views. The fact that my research focused on the impact of the post-9/11 political climate only made more acute the reflexivity of my position as a researcher and also as a member of the target communities, without making my own anxieties about doing this research more resolved. However, I think this reflexive awareness is a necessary component of any ethnographic project which deals with issues that are politically and ethically charged. A politically reflexive approach is important in order to acknowledge the role of academic knowledge vis-à-vis the state's domestic and foreign policy agendas. The story of my own involvement in the space of the community and the city—as it was constituted and reconstituted by the politics of affiliation, fear, and dissent—is very much a part of this story.

What can be revealed, or how one is identified, are questions intimately bound up with a moment of empire in which the secrecy and surveillance of the state's "homeland security" policies and the interrogation and detention of selectively targeted immigrant subjects make knowledge feel like a slowly burning fuse. Methodologically, such a moment demands that researchers explicitly situate themselves within the context of their research. This moment is not exceptional in U.S. history, as I pointed out, but it does highlight ongoing tensions for researchers over modes of identification and revelation, collusion and betrayal, intimacy and evasion that I will touch on throughout the book. It is the reflexive relationship of the researcher to the "research subject" in such a project that illuminates the ways in which empire acts as the hinge between the institutional matrix of knowledge production and the everyday expressions of citizenship and political understandings of immigrant youth. The academy is part of the context created by empire, and so is not outside of the larger culture of imperialism and imperial feelings, as I will discuss in the following chapter.

Writing of Youth and Empire

This book tells the stories of these youth as they speak of empire and the War on Terror, cultural citizenship, transnational ties, work and leisure, and dissent. These are the major organizing themes for chapters 1 through 5 and each telescopes into the other, leading to the final discussion in chapter 6 of what and who are missing in this moment of empire, and to responses of fear, courage, complicity, and solidarity. These themes all emerged from conversations with and observations of the youth in this study, and my analysis of empire was produced and complicated by *their* ideas and experiences. These young immigrants (obviously) did not use the abstract terms of academic discourse, but they nonetheless spoke to issues embedded in the historical and political context of U.S. empire. I have purposefully outlined my conceptual framework and political investments at the outset, and at the same time I have tried to expose the tensions and contradictions that emerge from the views of the young people by presenting their narratives as complete, first-person accounts, as told to me. I have deleted the questions I asked so as to allow the first-person narratives to flow more coherently, but I have indicated in the text where there is a response to my questions or comments so as not to completely erase my presence nor deny its influence. While I have lightly edited the narratives to make them legible, given that English was not these young immigrants' first language, I have tried to keep intact their expressive style.

I intentionally present the interview narratives as discrete accounts, rather than only as interspersed fragments seamlessly woven into the critical analysis, so that they speak in multiple voices and through subtle inflections to the issues raised in the chapter and throughout the book. It is the tensions, contradictions, and gaps between their narratives (as translated by me) and my own telling of empire, citizenship, and youth that I wish to offer in this multilayered account. The stories the youth tell can thus be juxtaposed with the stories I tell about them, but this is not in order to somehow recuperate their "authentic" voices. Their stories were filtered through the lens of my questions and interests, as well as my evolving connections with different students. The presentation of these narratives and the ethnographic vignettes also does not rest on an assumption that there is an opaque partition between "theory" and "ethnography," for my theoretical questions and analyses undeniably shaped the research.

I document in the book the many instances in which I was involved not just in various activities with these young people, but also in creating the very contexts in which discussions about national belonging, culture and rights, and domestic and international politics took place. While doing research in the school, I was working as a volunteer with the South Asian Mentoring and Tutoring Association (SAMTA), a program for South Asian immigrant students in the high school's bilingual program. In coordination with the International Student Center at the school, I helped organize biweekly workshops for South Asian students on academic, cultural, and political issues, some of which I will discuss in this book, and SAMTA also organized after-school activities for the students, such as taking them to see a film about South Asian immigrants or to cultural performances at local college campuses, events at which I often acted as unofficial chaperone. I also became involved in some of the bilingual program's activities, which gave me an opportunity to interact with students from other immigrant communities and with teachers.

Many of the South Asian immigrant students came to perceive me as someone associated with the school, however semiofficially, a role more comprehensible to them than that of the ambiguous identity of "researcher." The fact that I had grown up in India myself and could speak

Hindi allowed many of them to feel quickly at ease with me; a few of them began calling me to ask for academic as well as personal advice, turning to me if not quite as an older sister, then at least as someone who was from their country but who also knew the ropes of living in Wellford and the United States. Yet there were also gaps in our histories and experiences that could not be translated, such as differences in class, among other issues. Many of these youth and their parents would ask me if I was Muslim, and I would reply that I was not but that I had a Christian mother, a nominally Hindu father, Christian and Hindu grandparents (including a grandmother who followed Tibetan Buddhism), and Sikh and Muslim great-grandparents, so my family clearly represented the religious pluralism of India. They generally seemed either slightly confused or slightly pleased by this mixed identity, a response no different from that of most other Indians or South Asians I have encountered. This book is informed by a range of experiences and connections with these young people in the time I spent with them, and shaped by the familiarity and gaps in my own history—having lived in New England since I came to the United States as a student at the age of seventeen, and never having attended an American high school, that unique rite of passage in American culture.

There has been a growing inclination in ethnographic writing to expose the ways in which ethnographers coproduce the research context and in which the accounts of "informants" challenge researchers' interpretations, in order to lay bare the reflexivity of the research process—the relationship between the researcher and researched (see Caplan 2003, for example). This has been driven by an impulse in critical ethnography to make more explicit the politics and scaffolding of doing ethnographic research and also to show the limitations or partiality of theoretical analysis (Clifford and Marcus 1986). The forms of writing and structure I have chosen in this book, including the sometimes self-reflexive ethnographic vignettes, reflect this impetus to challenge the notion of transparently objective knowledge and "pure" lived experience as somehow completely outside of the contamination of "theoretical ideas."

This critique of the work of interpretation and translation in ethnography also emerged from my concerns about documenting the experiences and political views of Muslim immigrant youth at a time of heightened state surveillance and public scrutiny of their communities. There have been many cases of detention and deportation of Muslim Americans linked to political speech and statements about U.S. foreign policy involving Muslim American youth, such as a teenage Bangladeshi girl from New York who was deported after she wrote an essay about suicide bombing and Islam and visited radical Islamic chat rooms on the Internet (Bernstein 2005). In order to protect the identity of these young immigrants, as much as is really possible, I changed the name of the town in New England where I did the research while still trying to provide a description of the local context. I have used pseudonyms for all the students I interviewed and have also created composite portraits in certain cases to make it difficult to identify these youth. All the experiences and incidents here are true, but minor details are mixed in some instances so that they cannot be as easily traced to identifiable individuals. While I am aware that these devices are perhaps largely symbolic rather than practical shields of protection, this attempt, however limited, is probably the minimum responsibility of an ethnographer during a time of war and surveillance. An equally important motivation for these exercises is that they will hopefully force some reflection on the thirst for knowledge of targeted communities and the ways these groups are framed by the state, academy, media, and public discourse as part of a culture of surveillance.

The narratives of youth—as all interview narratives or oral histories—and my own reflections, as well as the critical analysis, are infused with and driven by feelings of fear, frustration, alienation, closeness, longing, despair, outrage, remorse, desire, confusion, and pain. This is the affective side of issues of belonging and exclusion that underlie the politics of this period. I sat down to write this book after I had moved to California after living in New England for fourteen years. At the time, I had one overwhelming feeling, that of missing: missing these youth, missing the city, missing my work and friends, missing the missing. The feeling of missing is a testament to the presence of someone or something not completely there, but it is not completely born of imagination. This book does not pretend to offer "absolute facts," but it also does not pretend that there is no truth.

Some months after I began working on the book, however, I realized that the book really was a testament to the presence of something so powerful that it needs to be perceived as absent: the idea of "missing" is both illusion and fact. What has been missing from mainstream debates about U.S. policy both before and after 9/11 is an analysis of U.S. empire; restoring this notion to the center of discussion is one of the aims of this book. We need to insert the category of empire, in a critically defined way, into debates about youth, citizenship, and South Asian, Muslim, and Arab American experiences after 9/11 and, more generally, into discussions of the War on Terror at home and abroad. The title for this book is, in part, inspired by the film *Missing* (1982), by the extraordinary Greek filmmaker, Constantin Costa-Gravas, about the disappearances in Chile under the right-wing military dictatorship and the U.S.-backed coup against President Salvador Allende which took place, coincidentally, on September 11, 1973. So the title gestures, on many levels, to empire and (willed) forgetting: the global reach of U.S. empire, the historical amnesia about U.S. military interventions, and the courage of those who expose and challenge the violent assaults on true "democracy" and "freedom" around the world. The book begins by defining empire so as to foreground this framework, for although the word may have now become incorporated into American public discourse, using the word "empire" alone is not sufficient.

The book has three strands or modes of writing: first, narratives about and by the youth; second, analysis based on my fieldwork and engagement with theoretical and political ideas; and third, an account of my own involvement in community and political issues in relation to the questions of the book. This introduction began by introducing Sara and Amin, two of the South Asian immigrant youth whose stories bind the book together as I trace their lives over a period of time, and at the same time, showed the range of emotions and ideas that spill over in a moment of empire. Sara and Amin are not "representative" of Muslim American youth in general, nor even necessarily of the youth in this book, but they were the most candid and generous in sharing their views with me, forcing me to think more deeply about the ways everyday life was knotted with the everyday-ness of U.S. empire after 9/11.

Chapter 1 offers an analysis of U.S. empire and the historical events of the War on Terror in which the subsequent discussions of citizenship and youth are embedded. The concept of empire is vital for understanding the experiences and expressions of South Asian Muslim immigrant youth and issues of citizenship the book explores, yet it is one that has rarely been foregrounded in work on immigrant youth, or even on Arab or Muslim American youth. The book begins with a discussion of U.S. empire in order to highlight the importance of this framework for research on a range of issues related to citizenship, culture, and politics in this historical moment, and to reinsert an approach into the study of youth and immigration that has long gone missing.

One

Imperial Feelings:
U.S. Empire and the
War on Terror

The country was up in arms,
the war was on, / in every breast / burned the holy fire of
  patriotism;
. . . a fluttering wilderness of flags / flashed in the sun; daily
  the young volunteers marched / down the wide avenue /
. . . and the half-dozen rash spirits / that ventured to
  disapprove of the war /
and cast a doubt upon its righteousness
straightway got such a stern / and angry warning
that for their personal safety's sake / they quickly shrank
  out of sight
And offended no more in that way.
· ·
When you have prayed for victory / you have prayed for many
  unmentioned results / which follow victory—must follow it.

MARK TWAIN, *The War Prayer* (2000 [1923])

Osman

*"I came to Wellford when I was thirteen years old; it's
been four years now. I used to live in Pakistan before.
My family comes from Karachi in Pakistani. Yes,
we're Sindhi. My father was living in America for fifteen years before we could come over. He was in Malden, and he also moved around and lived in different
places. When I first came here, I lived in Malden for,
like, two or three months. Then we moved to Wellford
when we got an apartment there. Why did we move
here? Because there are a lot of people from Pakistan.*

There are people from Karachi living here too—in Wellford, Revere, Brighton. There are many Pakistanis in Prospect Square, where I live. There's a mosque there; the people are mostly Middle Eastern. I go there sometimes, and for Eid [Muslim festival] we go to Sharon or Wayland Mosque. I think that Wellford is better than other cities, but I've only seen Malden and New York, when we first came to America.

"I was very excited when I first came here. I knew about America from my relatives who went abroad. I have an uncle in Sweden and another uncle in Canada. But my uncle from Sweden came here because he found the language difficult; now he lives in Prospect Square too. After I got here, I started to miss Pakistan. I missed seeing my relatives and friends everyday. I went back two years ago and when we had to come back, I didn't feel like coming home. I still talk to my friends in Karachi. I call them and sometimes I e-mail them, but mainly I just chat with them on the phone. With the time difference, it's hard, though; they're very far away. I don't know when I'll see them again. I'm waiting to get an American passport; then I can go back when I want.

"I went to an English-medium school in Karachi. It was also boys-and-girls, but it's pretty different from the school here. I like the school, but I think it's a lot easier here than in Pakistan. The work was much more in my school in Karachi; the subjects were much tougher. The only thing here is the MCAS [state high school graduation test]. It's hard! You have to take English and math, and if you fail, you can take it four or five times, I think. But if you don't pass it in the eleventh grade, you cannot go to the twelfth. I hope I pass it next time. I did okay on math, but I failed in English the first time. The teachers are good, though; they think I'll pass when my English gets better. They say that I might even be put in "standard" [curriculum] next year and I won't have to be in the bilingual program. Let's see.

"There are no Indians or Pakistanis in my class. There's just one kid—he's from Afghanistan. I'm friends with him, and I also know a lot of people in the school now. So after the first year it was much better. Kids in the school mostly hang out with people from their own country. Yes, it's true that all the Indian and Pakistani kids sit on one table in the cafeteria. They don't speak English so well, so they like to talk to each other in Urdu, or Gujarati or whatever.

"After September 11, no one said anything to me in the school. No, not even in Wellford. The teachers were telling us we should be careful, because of what was happening to Muslims, but I didn't really follow that. What will happen will happen; I'm not afraid of that. My mother and sisters didn't go out for a few days, but that was it. What do I think about what happened on September

11? I think it was crazy. I was very shocked when I heard about it. What do I think about the U.S. attacking Afghanistan? I can't talk about that. But I think that's what the people wanted the government to do, 'cos they were scared that there might be another attack. I don't know how I feel about that. It's kinda hard . . . I think they're both right: the people of Afghanistan who don't want to be attacked, and the people here that's scared. One of my friends was against the war, he's American—yes, white. I think plenty of people just don't care about the war. But I don't really talk to other people about this. It's just something you don't want to talk about it. That's what my father says too.

"My father drives a cab in Wellford, for City Cab. He doesn't have his own hack license; he gets it from the garage in Wellford. I don't see him much in the evenings, because he's working. I don't know if anything happened to him after September 11. He didn't say anything to us, but I know he stuck a big American flag on the cab. His friend, who's Sikh, took off his turban and shaved his beard. My father told him not to do it, but some men who took his cab shouted at him about trying to kill Osama's brother, so he was scared. We felt bad for him about that. There are many Punjabi cab drivers, also African, Haitian.

"I had a job last year at the mayor's office. After school, I used to work two hours every day, ten to twenty hours a week. I was dealing with papers, typing, that kind of thing. Before that, I was working in the police station in Prospect Square. I got the job because of Maria, in the internship office; you know her, right? It wasn't anything exciting, just doing paperwork. Yes, maybe I was working there if you came to the police station in the summer, but I was in the back. You can apply to the internship if you are a bilingual student; you just have to speak two languages. There's a lot of people who speak Spanish—Spanish people, Portuguese, Indians, in the program. I am trying to get another job right now—I would like a computer job. I was not interested in computers in Karachi, but I got into it here and I like it a lot. I am going to take a web design class this year, so let's see. I would like to do computer programming after I finish high school. My parents want me to do that too. I may go to a community college first, then try to get into another college for four years. My big sister got into the University of Massachusetts. She is studying biology, I think. She got in right away—she's very smart!

"I go out sometimes with my friends, now that I'm not working. We go to the mall, sometimes we watch movies at my house. I like action movies, Hindi movies; I like the Hindi film music too. I get the music from the web. You don't know how to download music? I'll show you; it's easy! I used to play basketball, but I haven't played for, like, three or four months. I just don't *like it anymore, and now I'm playing cricket. I go to Revere with the other Pakistani boys; we've been playing for three or four months. Yes, I saw the movie* Lagaan. *It's good how they showed the Indians playing cricket against the English. I don't know why it didn't get the prize for foreign movies; I think that they probably didn't want that here. There's a lot of good movies out now; I like* Devdas. *It has good music. My parents like the old movies because they like the older singers. Sometimes I watch those with them too, when my father has a few hours off."*

Nasreen

"I came to the U.S. on January 17, 1999. I remember the date, because it was the first time I saw snow. It was very cold when we first came to Wellford. My father had been here for twelve or thirteen years; he was in New York for a few months, then he came to Wellford. He liked it here because it is not so crowded, and he thought the schools are better for us. My uncle has been here in Wellford since I was a little girl. He went to New York first too. He drove a taxi there for a few years, then he moved here. He works at the Taj Mahal restaurant. My father works at the Passage to India restaurant. He's been there a while, so now he's the manager. I hope you can visit the restaurant sometime and he can give you a taste of the food—will you come? My mother works in a Store 24 close to Prospect Square.

"We're from Bangladesh—from Sylhet, a city there. My grandparents' house is in a village nearby. There are many people from Sylhet in America, in New York and also here. Shamita, the girl who just joined the school, her family is also from Sylhet [which became part of Bangladesh after the war with (West) Pakistan in 1971] but she lived in India. She's Hindu; her family is in India and also in Bangladesh. [Bengal was partitioned between predominantly Hindu India and predominantly Muslim East Pakistan in 1947.] I can speak Bengali to her, which is really nice. When I came here, it was the first time that I met people from India and Pakistan. I had never met them before. My best friend is from India: Samira. She speaks Gujarati, but her culture is not that different from mine. She comes to my house sometime. She likes the food my mother makes!

"I have four sisters and three brothers. My brothers are all older than me, and I have one older sister, so I am kind of in the middle. I came here with all of them, except my oldest sister who was over twenty-one. She couldn't get

the papers to come with us, so I don't know if she'll be able to come here. Yes, America is pretty much what I expected it to be like. We saw it on the news, and read about it in the newspapers when we were in Bangladesh. My father also told me what New York and Wellford are like, and he said it's good to study here. One thing is that in my country, I didn't have to work, but here I do. It's not really hard, and my family doesn't really care if I work or not. But I always give my check to my parents. I think work gives me some experience, and I meet different people. If I go to college, my brother is going to help me pay for it. He works in a hotel in the city, and the older one used to work there too but he kinda got laid off after September 11.

"I used to work in a dental clinic last summer; I was there thirty-five hours a week. They knew my father at the clinic, and I liked the job—I got to do different things. I had to help the doctor do the suction thing, clean up after the patient leaves, answer the phone, and play with the dog. Yes, if you want to work there, you have to love the dog! Now that I'm in my senior year, I have a lot of work so I may try to get a job in the school office, like my younger sister who works in the library. After I graduate from high school, I'm not sure what I want to do. I used to say that I want to work in a bank, but when I started working in the school bank downstairs, I read the rules and became afraid of all the risk. But I think I still want to work in a bank, maybe. I'm not sure what kind of job my parents want me to have; they wouldn't force me to do anything. My father went to college, and when he was in Sylhet he used to teach my aunties at home because he really wanted women to have an education. My mother told me that my father also taught her. She finished tenth standard, but my father wanted her to go to college. She never went, even though my mother's mother was a teacher. So women in Bangladesh are not like what people here think.

"After 9/11, I felt very, very sad about what happened. The last time I went to New York was just two months before it happened, and I went to the World Trade Center with my family. I was also sad about the war in Afghanistan because they were killing poor people who did not have anything to do with 9/11. My friends in school also felt the same thing about 9/11. I was scared for the first week after 9/11, because I was wearing my salwar kameez and people always looked at me funny, even before 9/11 happened. Then one day, some students were talking in class about why Muslims hate the U.S. and Ms. Scott said that just because a few Muslims did the attacks, it doesn't mean all of them think that way. If some African Americans did something, you wouldn't bomb all African Americans, would you? We talked about it a lot in Mrs. Scott's class and I told them that not all Muslims are fundamentalist or hate women or whatever.

"I think of myself as Bangladeshi. After 9/11, I don't really go around telling people I am Muslim, but if people ask me what religion I am, I say I'm Muslim. Because I really want to see what their reaction will be. Most of the people just say, 'Okay, okay'; they don't say anything about it. Some people are ignorant: they don't know a lot about Muslims or about Afghanistan or Iraq. I didn't know much about it myself but ever since 9/11, I started watching the news and now I have so much stuff in my head, I don't know. . . . . I mean, America thought that bin Laden was hiding in Afghanistan, so they attacked them but I don't understand why they were sending him arms and food before. And now what's happening with Saddam—it's just hitting my head. Basically, the first question I have is that a group of people did a wrong thing on September 11, and they are terrorists because they attacked the country. So how does America go after a country? How does a group of people destroying something in America lead America to have a war with a whole country? Because the terrorists who killed all those people on 9/11, they were from Saudi Arabia, but I heard in the news that Saudi Arabia has the most oil. So Americans may hate Saudi Arabians, but they still have to keep in touch with them because of oil. And so one guy on the news said that Iraq has the second-most oil so if America takes over, they don't have to worry.

"But my friend also said that Saddam tried to kill Bush's father, and I was just like, if somebody tried to kill my father, personally I would try to kill them too! But then my friend said, Bush is the president and he is putting his own personal problems before that of the whole country; the whole country depends on him and he is putting them in danger. So I think Bush got a little carried away and brought other excuses about going to war with Iraq. I don't know why Saddam tried to kill Bush's father, but I was watching MSNBC and Hardball and what's his name, Donohue? And they were saying that Saddam was friends with America before and they used him to fight Iran, and Iran hates America. But after that, Saddam wanted to lead his own country because he loved it, but I guess somehow Bush wanted a part of it too. Well, this is what I'm guessing. I heard that Saddam let America search his house, search through his stuff, but America still started the war. I don't talk about politics with many people, but if the subject comes up, I can't stop talking. I was never interested in politics before, but my history teacher is really good and he can teach very well. It's fun, because he gets me into it. Like, why does America *have soldiers all over the world? And why don't wars happen in America, but they happen all over the world? Because nobody wants to fight America; that's what I think.*

"I'm already a U.S. citizen and so is my father, so I'm not so worried about him. I became a citizen when I was sixteen years old, and my sisters are all citizens too but not my brothers, because they are over eighteen so they have to wait. My mother was also sponsored by my father, but she failed her English test the first time. For me, citizenship is not that different from having a green card, but I heard it's better if you want to go to college, because you get financial aid. But the laws keep changing so I hope I can stay here. The reason people came here is because of the laws and the rights they get, and they like the way they live. But things are changing, and the laws are changing. If the rights are gone, then what's the point of living here?"

Empire and Imperialism

This book is about a historical moment, after the events of 9/11, when the "feeling" of U.S. empire became particularly visible in the national and global political imagination, as Osman and Nasreen suggest in their allusions to U.S. power on the global stage and regimes of surveillance and profiling of citizens and noncitizens. Neither Osman and Nasreen used the word "empire," not surprisingly, since they were immigrant youth talking about everyday experiences, but they were clearly concerned with issues of citizenship, racism, labor, civil and immigrant rights, and political dissent in a time of war and racial profiling. Nasreen, in particular, voiced an analysis countering dominant rationalizations for the War on Terror and the invasion of Iraq to preempt an attack by Saddam Hussein's weapons of mass destruction. These observations were filtered through her own teenage lens of family loyalty and feelings about home, sentiments that also alluded to deeper allegories of nation as home or family. Nasreen astutely exposed U.S. support for the same mujahideen in Afghanistan who helped fight their war with the Soviets and were now their enemies, implicitly questioning the instrumentalist alliances, proxy wars, and government deception that underlie U.S. imperial policies.

The discourse of empire has long been absent from mainstream discourse about U.S. global power, though it crystallized briefly at certain historical moments such as the 1898 war on the Philippines—that prompted Mark Twain and others to join the Anti-Imperialist League—and the Vietnam

War—that provoked a critique of U.S. imperialism in the global context of Third World decolonization movements—only to disappear from all but the most radical corners of intellectual and political critique (Zwick 2002). After 9/11, the word "empire" proliferated in the pages of magazines, on the lips of U.S. politicians and even administration officials, and on the covers of a slew of books on empire. Now that this term has come out of the closet, so to speak, what is needed is a grounded analysis that focuses on the impact of imperial power on everyday life for different groups of people, so that we can understand the connections between the many understandings of the word "empire" in relation to questions of belonging, justice, and dissent.

Empire is not simply an abstract idea carried on the currents of political thinking about the role of the United States on the global stage since the events of September 11, 2001, but a specific lens for understanding the history of U.S. imperial power that took form long before 2001. It is a term that has various theoretical and historical genealogies, which I will not elaborate on here (see Kaplan 1993; Rosenberg 2006; Stoler 2006a, 2006b), but I will provide an analysis of empire as the key framework for understanding the political and cultural shifts after 9/11 and situating the experiences of the youth in this book. How do the notion of empire and the concept of imperialism help explain the moment in which we live and the role of U.S. global power today? For many decades, and especially with the conservative shift in U.S. politics after the 1960s and 1970s, those who spoke of U.S. imperialism were dismissed simply as crazy, old-fashioned leftists using a terminology that was out of touch with the times and inaccurate in its conception of U.S. power.[1] The analysis of U.S. imperialism was suppressed and marginalized, even in the academy, and "empire" was not a term to be used in association with the United States. Ann Stoler (2006a, 10), a scholar of European colonialism, questions "why the imperial frame seems 'forced' to some and the rubrics and vocabulary of postcolonial scholarship 'contrived' in U.S. contexts." "Do these terms seem forced," she asks, "because they have been made not to fit, because historical actors refused the term empire while practicing its tactics?" Stoler answers her own question, by pointing out that the denial of U.S. empire was part of national mythologies and cultures of U.S. imperialism that allowed imperial policies to persist without being acknowledged as such.

Today, the idea of empire has been reattached to the United States with a profusion of books and also articles in the mass media in the aftermath of 9/11 about what some call "the new empire," discussing not just whether the United States is an empire, but what form of empire it could, and should, take. For example, Michael Ignatieff (2003) gained wide attention in a cover story focusing on U.S. empire for the *New York Times Magazine*, where he argued that although President George W. Bush had proclaimed, "America has no empire to extend or utopia to establish," it was necessary for the United States to find, even if reluctantly, the will to sustain empire as the "last hope for democracy and stability," particularly in the Middle East. In the same proclamation made by Bush at West Point in June 2003, the president announced the doctrine of preemptive war, a new logic justifying U.S. military interventions against the "Axis of Evil," and later in Iraq: "We must take the battle to the enemy, disrupt his plans and confront the worst threats before they emerge." The War on Terror was framed as part of a moral vision for America linked to an imperial crusade against "evil": "Because the war on terror will require resolve and patience it will also require firm moral purpose" (cited in Koshy 2003, 8). Niall Ferguson (2003, 54), a historian of British empire, urged Americans in the pages of the same magazine and in his much-publicized book, *Empire* (2002), to stop being wimpy about assuming the mantle of the new imperialism and to learn from the British both the "stamina" and art of professionally managing the empire. The discourse of empire has shifted and the meanings of empire are rewritten and revised by political conservatives as well as liberals, not just reintroducing and normalizing the term, but rehabilitating the concept of empire as a just, necessary, and benevolent force. "Imperialism," however, has been resistant to this makeover and has retained the taint of an undesirable form of power. What has made "empire" so acceptable in academic as well as public discourse, and why does "imperialism" seem so inappropriate in relation to the United States?

It is important to clarify that the words "empire" and "imperialism" are not synonymous; they have different meanings, carry particular genealogies of thinking, and are put to varying political use. "Empire" sounds abstract and grand, perhaps glamorous in its evocation of planetary rule and older moments of historical certainty and European colonial domination, but is ambiguous in its meaning. It hints at corporate empire and economic monopoly, a palatable if not comforting notion for those who support the notion that "the hidden hand of the market will never work without a hidden fist" (Koshy 2003, 169). "Imperialism," on the other hand, has been for many a dirty word reeking of leftist, Marxist, and nationalist critique, and for others, simply passé. In this book, I want to reclaim parts of the analysis that make the concept of *imperialism* a revealing model of global power, showing how it is has been manifested and modified in the case of the United States, and to reveal the pain, terror, and fear that are intrinsically part of imperial power and that affect young people, like Osman, Nasreen, and many others. I am not providing here a review of various approaches for studying imperialism that have developed over time in different fields (see R. Young 2001). Rather, I am interested in offering a brief analysis of the form of imperialism that the United States represents at the current moment to illuminate the relationship of South Asian Muslim immigrants to the imperial state and to guide us in our research and thinking on the cultural and political questions of our times, such as the questions of war, nationalism, sovereignty, justice, and dissent that both Nasreen and Osman raised in their reflections.

Empire, or Imperialism without Colonies?

Since September 11, 2001, there has been a proliferation of approaches to thinking and rethinking empire; a new book with the word "empire" in the title seems to appear in stores with increasing regularity, some for academic audiences but many for general readers.[2] There is one book that took special hold in the American intellectual imagination after the events of 9/11 and that I want to use an entry point for engaging with larger debates about empire and imperialism: Michael Hardt's and Antonio Negri's *Empire* (2000). I think the flurry of interest in Hardt's and Negri's model of empire is actually very revealing, and sheds light on the question about the nature of U.S. power and the possibilities for critical response or dissent at this historical moment. *Empire* was very timely in its moment of publication and has been credited with "[rehabilitating] the concept of empire as a tool for analysis of world politics," according to Mark Laffey and Jutta Weldes (2004, 128). Hardt's and Negri's theory is that, in contrast to earlier forms of the imperialist state, "empire" today is constituted by decentered networks of *imperial* power and of global sovereignty based not in any one nation-state, but rather in the current mode of global capitalism. I focus on their theory of empire, in particular, not as a convenient straw model that overshadows other, more comprehensive analyses but because the notion of network power tied to global capitalism shapes much current thinking and rationalization for "empire," and is important to consider but, in my view, incomplete and even potentially obfuscating.

In Hardt's and Negri's framework, the United States is not "imperialist," because it does not always exercise direct governance of other nation-states, but is part of a new, all-enveloping "imperial sovereignty," based in deterritorialized networks. They acknowledge that there have been historical "aberrations" and temptations to engage in imperialist-style ventures in U.S. history, such as the Spanish-American War under Theodore Roosevelt, not to mention the genocide inflicted on Native Americans and the treatment of black slaves (Hardt and Negri 2000, 168–72), but these contradictions are never reconciled in their model.[3] This is a largely abstract analysis of empire as a form of late capitalist globalization, and it underestimates the continuing power of nation-states, even if transformed by shifts in capitalism; it ignores what Richard Falk calls "statist American patriotism" associated with American military assaults on sovereign states (Falk 2004, 181). *Empire* neglects the role of the United States in institutions such as the World Bank, World Trade Organization, and the International Monetary Fund, as many critics have pointed out by now (Aronowitz 2003; Arrighi 2003; Tilly 2003). Little to no attention is paid to the role of U.S. militarism and to the global policing of borders and exporting of U.S. security regimes to other parts of the world (Laffey and Weldes 2004), including "antiterrorist" repression in Pakistan and India (Chari 2006, 43; Koshy 2003, 93–95). *Empire's* vision of the global "multitude," particularly immigrants who cross national borders, is also amorphous and romanticized, and the final recommendation for creating "global citizenship" is a rather utopian notion of resistance (Aronowitz 2003, 24; F. Cooper 2004; Harvey 2003, 169). *Empire* reads like a celebration of the potential of globalization, but it is a party where the enormous elephant standing in the room has been stomping on the furniture.

In my view, Hardt's and Negri's *Empire* offered an appealing model to many, both inside and outside the academy, for it denied the centrality and tangibility of U.S. imperialist power while offering a grand theory centered largely on economic globalization. This was especially enticing for American intellectuals and liberals who could be absolved of feelings of imperial guilt, especially after 9/11, an issue I will return in chapter 6. Some claim that *Empire*'s contribution was that it brought to the fore the notion of resistance to global capitalism (Balakrishnan 2003, xviii; Passavant 2004, 4), but this was after all an issue that had been discussed for years by those writing about globalization and social movements in more grounded analyses. My book intervenes in the debate about empire and imperialism by building on the critical tradition of discussing globalization and imperialism in relation to the tangible manifestations of U.S. power. It provides an ethnographic analysis of both imperial power and the role of specific groups of immigrants and young people in shaping expressions of dissent, discussing concrete instances of the ways in which ideas and practices of citizenship spill over the territorial borders of nation-states in response to the global flows of labor, capital, technology, and media (Appadurai 1996).

Hardt and Negri did highlight important issues that need to be considered in any model of U.S. empire and were right to point to the distinct form of empire evident in the moment in which we live: capital, as well as labor, are globalized and the power of nation-states has, if not declined, at least been rescaled (Laffey and Weldes 2004, 124; Passavant 2004). In their sequel, *Multitude*, Hardt and Negri (2004, 9, 59) respond to their critics and concede that the United States plays an "exceptional role" in its dominance of the global order and that its military is "midstream between imperialism and Empire," in their view, between national and universalizing logics of war and intervention. Earlier work on U.S. empire has already shown that the United States has a long history, since its wars in Cuba, Puerto Rico, and the Philippines in 1898, of "imperialism without colonies" or of "informal empire" (Kaplan 2005; Magdoff 2003; Panitch and Gindin, 2003; Román 2002). This neocolonialist model is rooted in what some call the strategy of "New Empire," promulgated by Theodore Roosevelt and other early twentieth-century figures who wanted to expand U.S. economic and military power without the burden—and stigma—of administering overseas colonies (Kaplan 2005, 837).

The revisionist historian William Appleman Williams described this seemingly "non-colonial imperial expansion" as a policy of "open door" imperialism developed by the United States to aid its conquest of economic frontiers without the material, military, or political costs of administering overseas territories, in the wake of the Spanish-American War of 1898 and annexation of the Philippines and Puerto Rico (cited in Bacevich 2002, 26). The United States strategically chose to avoid the direct territorial control generally practiced by formal European-style empires, for Woodrow Wilson and other architects of American expansionism realized that it could be achieved through the market, thus upholding the "liberal rhetoric of democracy and self-determination" professed by the United States (Smith 2005, 49). However, Neil Smith (2005, 47) argues that 1898 was not a sharp break between "formal" and "informal" modes of empire, but rather a transition in evolving forms of U.S. expansionism that continued to use territorialized forms of domination, globally and also domestically (confining Native Americans, enslaving African Americans, and importing Asian and Latin American labor). Today, U.S. imperialism rests on strategies of dominance in several, interconnected realms, such as "control over international bodies (the United Nations, World Bank, International Monetary Fund, World Trade Organization), covert actions, global surveillance methods, direct military interventions, political machinations, and deadly economic sanctions of the sort used against Iraq" (Boggs 2003, 6). American global dominance blurs the boundaries of "formal" and "informal" empire with this mix of imperial strategies of direct and indirect control (Burbach and Tarbell 2004, 65). This ambiguity and invisibility are the first and most important characteristics of U.S. imperialism I want to note, as it is these features that obscure the workings of imperial power and aid in its denial.

Despite the existence of amorphous forms of globalized power and capitalism and the discourse of U.S. exceptionalism, the dominance of U.S. military, economic, and political power—the three major aspects of imperial power—is still paramount (Joxe 2002). Theorists such as David Harvey (2003, 30, 54) rightly point to the need to balance an analysis of political imperialism and economic imperialism, bridging narrower Marxist approaches that focus only on global capitalism, on the one hand, and political analyses that ignore the economic logic of empire, on the other. In fact, Aijaz Ahmad (2004, 232–33) points out that informal empire is a strategic preference of the "current composition of global capital" and "disciplinary neoliberalism," not an "ideological preference" of the United States. The United States has long tried to crush "economic nationalism" in the Third World, from Iran, Egypt, Guatemala, and Chile during the

Cold War, to Iraq and Venezuela today.[4] With the fall of the Berlin
Wall, the presumed New World Order was premised on the United
States as the sole global superpower touting the victory of free-market
capitalism. This vision fueled the overt flexing of power by Republican
presidents, from Grenada to Iraq, in addition to covert actions in Central America and Iran, as well as Bill Clinton's doctrine of "full-spectrum
dominance" (Mahajan 2003).

"Informal" empire has been facilitated in the post–Cold War period
by advances in technology and travel that have enabled the United States
to conduct long-distance military interventions relatively quickly and
covertly, without necessarily occupying other states. The United States
has used covert operations and proxy wars, particularly after the defeat
in Vietnam, to avoid the public scrutiny of direct military interventions
and the criticism of assaults on the sovereignty of other states (Mamdani
2004). As Mahmood Mamdani (2004, 69–84) observes, "low-intensity
warfare" was a euphemism for paramilitary wars and mercenary fighters
used to crush leftist uprisings in the Third World that undermined U.S.
designs for dominance, from Nicaragua and Laos to Angola and Congo.[5]
The United States has also tried to avoid direct colonial administration
by outsourcing military, security, and administrative functions to private
contractors (Ho 2004, 239) and installing puppet regimes in order to
avoid the semblance of empire (a strategy that has failed to convince in
Iraq, still under U.S. military occupation and economic control).

Amy Kaplan (2005) points out that the U.S. brand of imperialism led
to the creation of new designations of overseas territories, under varying degrees of U.S. control, and new categories of persons and citizens
serving imperial interests while obscuring the nature of U.S. imperialism.
This process has continued to the present day and is illustrated by the
contradictory national space occupied by Guantánamo Bay, neither fully
under Cuban or U.S. sovereignty but clearly under U.S. control (Kaplan
2005). Spaces such as Guantánamo, Abu Ghraib in Iraq, and also lesser-
known sites such as Bagram Prison in Afghanistan—as well as the secret
planes used by the CIA to ship "ghost detainees" to prisons in Europe
and other countries—represent the "spaces of exception" that make the
empire's violations of international law the norm (Hansen and Steputat
2005, 1).[6] Legal ambiguity is exploited by the U.S. military in Iraq in its
outsourcing of "security," interrogation, and torture to private contractors who are not bound by the conventions applying to soldiers (Joshua

Comaroff 2007). The inhabitants of the American military prison at "Gitmo," who are classified as "enemy combatants" and not prisoners of war deserving of internationally recognized rights, live in a hellish legal limbo. Kaplan astutely observes that Guantánamo is a metaphor for the paradoxical form of "American Empire, a dominion at once rooted in specific locales and dispersed all over the world" (2005, 832). This nuanced analysis captures the simultaneous localization and dispersal of power that characterizes the United States as an imperial state. The deterritorialization and ambiguity of U.S. imperial control underlie the mythologies justifying imperial policies in the name of humanitarian intervention and obscuring the settler-colonial roots of the nation-state.

Dirty Secrets: Settler Colonialism and "Benevolent Imperialism"

In addition to the flexibility and secrecy of American imperial power as it has evolved, a second significant feature is that various imperialist doctrines have historically been embedded in the political vision of the United States as a nation-state. This has been true from the early founding of the nation-state as a settler-colonial project inflicting genocide on the indigenous Americans and the ambitions of the framers of the Constitution, such as Thomas Jefferson and James Madison (Williams 1980, 39–48), to the Monroe Doctrine of U.S. expansionism and the Cold War program of establishing U.S. supremacy (Aronowitz 2003, 19; Little 2002). Furthermore, a comparative understanding of empires shows that U.S. imperialism has existed in relationship to the decline and fall of other empires, while taking distinct form at various historical moments. For instance, the "special relationship" between England and the United States, some argue, is embedded in the legacy of British imperialism ("divide and quit") that the United States inherited in regions from Afghanistan to Iraq and Palestine (Hitchens 2004 [1990], xiv; N. Smith 2005). During the Cold War, the Nixon doctrine of proxy wars was devised to ensure that the United States, not the Soviet Union, gained control over regions newly freed from Portuguese and French imperialism in southern Africa and Southeast Asia (Mamdani 2004, 63).

A third important feature and an important element of continuity with other empires is the rhetoric of democracy and freedom that has been used to cloak the U.S. imperial project in a discourse of "benevolent imperialism." The imperial power of the United States shrouds itself in the language of human rights, so freedom becomes, paradoxically, the justification for dominance and neocolonial occupation. The hypocritical logic of "war for democracy" is questioned by dissenting observers and even young people like Nasreen, who pointed to U.S. interests in oil as underlying rationales for the war in Iraq and challenged the premise of attacking Afghanistan as retribution for 9/11. Nasreen was also able to counter the officially sanctioned narrative about Saddam Hussein, noting not only the earlier U.S. support for Iraq during the war with Iran, but also notions of Iraqi nationalism and sovereignty that were violated by the disingenuous inspections for "weapons of mass destruction" (see Ali 2003). Her comments, and also implicitly Osman's, reversed the logic of the War on Terror, suggesting that the idea that the nation, one's collective "home," could not be protected from aggression—inflicted by another nation-state, in the case of the U.S. invasion of Iraq—was problematic; it revealed the contradictions in responding to terrorism by presenting "violence as a weapon of reason and preservation of freedom of the citizens from threats by outsiders," if used by a (certain) state (Hansen and Steputat 2005, 8). The modern notion of national sovereignty is often taken for granted even though breached in reality, as Thomas Hansen and Finn Steputat (2005, 1–2) observe, for the right to wage war against external (and internal) enemies is still a "central dimension of how a state performs its 'stateness,'" especially imperialist states who are able to exercise unchecked "violence over bodies and populations" in the name of defending the "hard kernel" of territorial sovereignty.

Some argue that the paradoxical logic of "imperialism for democracy" serves to resolve the obvious contradiction for the United States between practicing imperial dominance and professing respect for national sovereignty, as the more overt logic of racial superiority did in a different moment in an attempt to justify the intrusions and ravages of the British empire (Harvey 2003, 50). This civilizational mission has been evident in the United States from the rhetoric of "civilizing" Native Americans to the "benevolent assimilation" of Filipinos in the brutal war of 1898. Almost a century later, Ronald Reagan portrayed the United States as the righteous cowboy of the "free world" fighting the "evil empire," the specter of Soviet Communism in the 1980s justifying various military and political interventions in other countries (Churchill 2003; Williams 1980). The imperial ethic of imposing democracy and freedom at the point of a gun has continued in the War on Terror: bombing families in Afghanistan in order to "liberate" Muslim women, occupying Iraqi towns and smashing historic buildings so as to free the people, imposing puppet regimes so as to bring democracy.

This inverted morality has been further bolstered during the Republican regime by the alliance of George W. Bush with the evangelical Christian Right, a relationship that bolsters George W. Bush's messianic imperialism (Barry 2003, 43). The vision that Bush Jr. has offered since September 11 has been based on a discourse of good versus evil that is both simplistic and apocalyptic (AbuKhalil 2002; Lincoln 2003). Sandra Silberstein's (2002) linguistic analysis of Bush Jr.'s public discourse after 9/11 shows that the president's consistent use of religious metaphors evoking an impending apocalypse and struggle to assert "goodness" and realize the will of God (which is one meaning of "jihad" in Islam) ironically echoes the discourse of the Islamic "fundamentalists" who are the enemy in this moral crusade.[7] The rhetoric of a holy war is not coincidental, for the Christian Coalition has mobilized masses of Protestant fundamentalists to support the Republicans, ever since Reagan's rise to power (Burbach and Tarbell 2004, 94). The evangelical imperialism of the Christian Right bolsters two important tenets of the current imperial formation: first, a capitalist ethic consistent with the free-market policies of the United States and economic globalization; and second, a Christian fundamentalist-Zionist alliance supporting Israeli colonial occupation in the Middle East, since some Christian fundamentalists believe the Bible calls for the settlement of Jews in Palestine before the "Second Coming of Christ" (Ahmad 2004, 263; Burbach and Tarbell 2004, 97). The U.S. role in arming and funding the occupation of Palestine is central to the politics of the Middle East and to the War on Terror; in supporting other colonialist projects in the region, the United States consolidates a network of repressive regimes that is opposed around the world for its hegemonic force.

The "special relationship" between the United States and Israel also helps shed light on the cultural premise of U.S. imperialism, for as Mahmood Mamdani (2004) emphasizes, both nations were founded as colonial-settler states—if shaped by different historical trajectories—and so share core foundational myths.[8] Both the United States and Israel share histories of suppressing indigenous people's rights and of dispossessing native peoples that are mystified and erased through national mythologies that deny the existence and claims of native peoples. Mamdani argues that the general discomfort in the United States with acknowledging the "original sin" against Native Americans is linked to a deep-seated American view of "settler projects," as "civilizing missions" taming an empty wilderness, which is echoed in Zionist founding ideology about Israel (see Beit-Hallahmi 1993; Said 1992 [1979]). These shared myths of a chosen people conquering new frontiers are not just a product of coincidence, as other comparative studies have pointed out that the Zionist founders of Israel drew inspiration from the policies of the United States toward its own indigenes (Salaita 2006b). The moral contradictions of U.S. imperial culture are resolved through an uneasy rationalization or denial of foundational crimes, such as slavery or genocide, but also through a cultural analysis that uses "democracy," if not "civilization," as a justification for imperial interventions and control.

In addition to recasting imperial power as humanitarian intervention, the achievement of Ronald Reagan and other right-wingers, according to scholars such as Donald Pease (1993), was to rewrite the history of the anti-imperialist movements of the 1960s and 1970s in the United States and elsewhere. Republicans and Christian conservatives portrayed critics of the Vietnam War as being on the wrong side of the battle for human rights and denounced the so-called Vietnam syndrome, or fear of military defeat that haunts U.S. debates about the "quagmire" in Iraq. In fact, there are now bumper stickers that proclaim "Iraq is Arabic for Vietnam," which is perhaps reductive as a simple analogy but makes an important link between these two wars (see Elliott 2007). The defeat in Vietnam was countered by the triumphalist discourse of Reagan's battle against the "Evil Empire" during the Cold War era, "reimagining Vietnam as a sanctified noble crusade," which is how both the first and second wars with Iraq were respectively framed by George H. W. Bush and his son (Gardner and Young 2007, 9).[9]

In historicizing an analysis of U.S. imperialism, I want to point out that the goal of "maintaining U.S. global military supremacy in perpetuity" and a proactive military "omnipotence," was crystallized, if not fully realized, during the Democratic regime of Clinton, supported by the Pentagon's post–Cold War plan for restructuring the armed forces, *Joint Vision 2010* (Bacevich 2002, 131). The plans for consolidating and extending U.S. imperial power were in the works long before 9/11 and go beyond the divide of Democrat and Republican politics—even though there are differences between Clinton's multilateralist, diplomatic approach and Bush's unilateralist, preemptive doctrine. This point is generally given less weight in the debate about the "new imperialism" which tends to highlight only the policies of the neoconservatives brought to power with the Bush regime, and far more attention is given to the fact that "neocons" such as Dick Cheney, Donald Rumsfeld, Paul Wolfowitz, Douglas Feith, Elliott Abrams, and Richard Perle had been waiting to promote a policy of global military dominance and unilateralist foreign policy—a "strategy of pure power" (Pozzano and Russo 2005, 211).[10]

This said, it is indeed significant that the Project for the New American Century (PNAC), which has promoted this neocon imperialist vision, is embedded in a growing network of right-wing institutions.[11] Well before 2001, the PNAC had a specific military-political project in mind—war on Iraq—and an interest in supporting Israel's occupation of Palestine, for Douglas Feith, Elliot Abrams, and Richard Perle are supporters of the Israeli right-wing Likud Party. Middle East politics have obviously played a central role in U.S. interventions in that region as well as in the domestic crackdown on Muslim and Arab Americans. September 11, 2001, provided the neocon regime with a justification for accelerating the plans for the "New American Century." At the same time, the globalization of the War on Terror and the targeting of "Muslim terrorists" also led to increased justification for regimes around the world, from the Philippines to India, to crack down on internal dissidents (Koshy 2003).

This has been a very cursory summary of the ideological framework and historical developments that undergird American imperialism and the targeting of Muslim, Arab, and South Asians in the United States in the "post-9/11" context. Imperial policies and histories shape the cultural form of U.S. imperialism that South Asian immigrant youth encounter when they come to live, study, and work in the United States. Immigrants from India, Pakistan, and Bangladesh come from a region which is already influenced by U.S. foreign policy interests in extending the War on Terror and building strategic alliances in South Asia (see Koshy 2003), and which has been penetrated by U.S. culture in various forms. Yet when South Asian immigrants come to the United States, they often have to confront the lack of awareness about U.S. interventions in their home

regions, or even around the world, and a resistance by some to acknowledging the imperial role of the United States.

The Empire That Dared Not Be Named

Why is it that the imperial might of the United States is so invisible that
it could not be widely named by its citizens, despite its global reach? This
knowledge was brought home most forcefully when rage against the empire exploded within the territory of the United States. One of the primary features of U.S. imperial culture is the consistent denial of empire
because unlike earlier European empires, the United States has tried to
distance itself from direct colonization and to shroud its interventions in
other sovereign nation-states in secrecy. Enseng Ho calls this an "empire
not knowing that it is one" (2004, 237), but it would be more accurate to
say that it has been, until after 9/11, an empire not *willing* to admit that it
is one. Ho and others argue that the mask partially covering "empire" was
ripped off by the attacks of September 11, 2001, bringing U.S. empire forc-
ibly into the realm of the visible. There is always at the heart of empire
a denial of knowledge of the workings of imperial power to suppress the
guilt that comes with the awareness of its impact while enjoying its benefits and privileges. Many Americans live not just in ignorance of political
reality based on a repression of this knowledge, but in a fictional uni-
verse where causality is reversed and the United States is seen only as the
victim, not the perpetrator, of terror. Charles Maier acerbically observes,
"The dirty little secret of empire is that for all the rhetoric of 'burden,'
it is often psychologically fulfilling for those who justify it" (cited in
Rosenberg 2006, B11).

Williams wrote, "from the beginning the persuasiveness of empire as a
way of life effectively closed off other ways of dealing with the reality that
Americans encountered" (1980, 5). This has led to a culture of repression
and denial of dark secrets, like the knowledge of ongoing abuse that cannot be spoken about at the dinner table. Family secrets leak out, however,
as they did during the Iran-Contra affair in the late 1980s or with revelations of the role of CIA and U.S. complicity in the "dirty wars" in Central
America, Chile, and Argentina since the 1960s. Yet some wars remain
largely forgotten, such as the bloody fifteen-year Philippine-American
War, which has legacies in the present war in Iraq, possibly even more

than the Vietnam "quagmire." The war in the Philippines was also fought under the pretext of liberating the natives from another regime (Spain) and bringing "civilization" and "democracy" to the ambiguously defined colony through the co-optation of local leaders and elites (Rafael 1993; Zwick 2002). However, resurrecting the "famously forgotten imperial adventure in the Philippines" (Bascara 2006, ix) would make the designs and doublespeak of U.S. empire in the Middle East only too clear, and so it has been completely repressed in discussions of the war in Iraq, as the Philippine government has itself joined Bush's "coalition of the willing" (Ileto 2005, 231).

While the word "empire" may be coming out of the closet in the United States, there is a tension that persists between two approaches: one that acknowledges that imperialist domination is linked to U.S. interests and aggression, and a second view that the United States has no choice but to reluctantly bear the mantle of empire as an inevitable outcome of global political and economic logics. This tension is captured by the euphemistically titled "American Century" formulation of Henry Luce in 1941, which, Neil Smith argues, used the notion of time rather than space to imply that U.S. global power was a matter of historical destiny—"beyond geography" and geopolitics (Smith 2003, 20, cited in Harvey 2003, 51). Similarly, the present-day Project for a New American Century developed a plan for absolute domination under the guise of protecting human rights and democracy (Barry and Lobe 2003, 42; Harvey 2003, 80). The myth of the United States as "the reluctant superpower" continues to this day and obscures the active role the United States has played in asserting its political, economic, and military interests through global interventions. In 1961, Ernest May pronounced glibly, "Some nations achieve greatness, the United States has greatness thrust upon it."[12] This myth has led to what is not just a "historical amnesia" embedded in U.S. imperial culture about its past crimes, but a collective repression of this memory supported by an apparatus of secrecy and enabled by a policy of covert actions (Rogin 1993). Secret U.S. military and economic interventions kept what the American people didn't want to know from them so that they could continue to support empire and enjoy its benefits without undue guilt (Williams 1980).

This historical amnesia and repression of empire have infused popular culture and become part of what Amy Kaplan and Donald Pease (1993) called the "cultures of U.S. imperialism" in their groundbreaking collection of the early 1990s. My work builds on their approach by excavating the cultural processes of imperialism that shape the everyday understandings of belonging and the state for South Asian Muslim immigrant youth after 9/11. The rationalization of U.S. empire occurs not just in the arena of policy but also in the domains of media and everyday popular culture, which do the work of representing or translating formal and informal state practices to the public. One of the contributions of a historical cultural studies approach to U.S. empire has been to show how collective amnesia is, ironically, accompanied by imperial spectacle. As Michael Rogin (1993, 508) suggests, political spectacle is intrinsic to the working of U.S. imperial culture, for it maintains "identification with the state" and "racial domination." The processes of erasure and visualizing actually work in hand in hand, for political spectacles enable a kind of political amnesia, a forgetting of imperial violence and the causality of wars and militarism.

Rogin's analysis demonstrates how U.S. popular culture does the work of justifying U.S. foreign policy and military intervention, for the covert foreign policy of the United States has been accompanied by televised wars or glamorized militarism, as evident during the first Gulf War.[13] The culture of militarism is bolstered by mainstream media portrayals of the War on Terror, especially with journalists officially "embedded" (a telling pun) with the U.S. military in Iraq. There were other kinds of embedded representations promoting national consensus for the war as well: a "Hollywood 9/11" committee was formed so film executives could produce public service announcements promoting patriotic volunteerism that were screened nationally on television and in theaters, and a Madison Avenue advertising executive was recruited to sell "the Bush message" to the American public, in coordination with the White House senior adviser Karl Rove (Thrupkaew 2003, 110).

Imperial spectacle was broadcast daily on television during the war in Afghanistan—"Operation Enduring Freedom"—and the invasion of Iraq—"Operation Iraqi Freedom"—through visual representations of a "specular foreign policy" (Rogin 1993), which aimed at avenging the attacks on the United States and also purportedly bringing "liberation" to West Asia. But in my view this spectacle was also, even more paradoxically, produced through invisibility. The wars were made visible only through

darkened photos from jet fighters on nighttime bombings of Afghanistan, avoiding the rubble and casualties on the ground, or presented from
the embedded perspective of U.S. reporters traveling on tanks invading
Baghdad, erasing images of bleeding or dead bodies. American television viewers are thus consumers of increasingly disembodied wars that
are scripted by the military-industrial-media complex (C. Kaplan 2006,
693–94). The mass media coverage of these wars elided the facts of U.S.
funding of and support for the Taliban in its proxy war in Afghanistan
against the Soviet Union, and U.S. support of Saddam Hussein during
the 1980s and sanctioning of his war against Kuwait—not to mention the
fact that the United States had, in effect, already been waging war against
Iraq for fifteen years through the sanctions, at the cost of a half a million
Iraqi children's lives (Mahajan 2002; Mamdani 2004, 189).

While the omissions and special effects of these televised war spectacles have received growing attention over time, I argue that the overt
spectacle of war is the split screen for another set of images that are both
hypervisible and invisible in the public eye, but are part of the same script
of spectacle and invisibility. These are the images of Muslim and Arab
men, who are "terrorists" or suspect citizens. On the one hand, the media
widely publicized the faces of the nineteen Muslim male hijackers—most
of them Saudi, not Afghan nor Iraqi—accused of perpetrating the attacks of 9/11. On the other hand, the faces of the over 1,500 Muslim men
detained by the government in the months following 9/11, without a
single proven charge of terrorism, were invisible to the public; their detention was secret and their names were not released until the government
was challenged in court. In addition, the hundreds of South Asian and
Arab Americans who were assaulted, harassed, and profiled beginning on
September 11, 2001, were largely invisible in the mainstream media, even
if their experiences lurked uneasily in the public imaginary. Consuming
war means imagining "the Muslim terrorist" based on viewing murky
mug shots of the hijackers and photos of Muslim and Arab men charged
in other terrorist cases, images that blur into the iconic photos of "Islamic fundamentalists," "militant Arab nationalists," and kaffiyeh-swathed
Palestinians that permeate the U.S. media and cultural imaginary
(McAllister 2001; Said 1981 [1978]). As Osman pointed out, the image
of the terrorist after 9/11 also became conflated with that of turbaned
Sikh men, dragging South Asians into the backlash of rage and suspicion

that, in effect, was directed at a range of individuals with head coverings, Sikh men or Muslim women in hijab, who were now symbols of "un-American" outsiders and suspect citizens in the War on Terror.

Domestic and Foreign Fronts of Empire

The War on Terror overseas and the war on terror "at home" are actually part of the same visual story: the spectacle of empire. A central premise underlying the experiences I document in this book is that empire works on two fronts: the domestic and the foreign. However, the link between the two realms of imperial power are obscured in everyday discussions and representations, which avoid directly addressing the links between domestic and foreign policies, even if they allude to them implicitly and sometimes problematically. This fissure between the two fronts of empire effectively prevents marginalized groups in the United States from understanding how their subjugation within the nation is connected to dominance overseas (Pease 1993; Young 2001, 28).[14] The national consensus for U.S. foreign policies is strengthened through historical processes of scapegoating "outsiders" and conflating internal and external enemies (Stoler 2006, 12). American foreign policy is linked to the "policing of domestic racial tensions" and disciplining of subordinated populations through gender and class hierarchies at home (Pease 1993, 31). This analysis is important for understanding questions of citizenship for immigrant youth after 9/11 because it has always been the case that imperial power maintains dominance outside the nation by maintaining dominance over subordinated groups at home, such as racial minorities, women, workers, and immigrants (Román 2002).

This book sheds light on the links between the domestic and foreign faces of empire through a discussion of citizenship for Muslim immigrant youth whose experiences of work, popular culture, or migration are shaped by U.S. state policies, both in their home countries and within America. Some suggest that the United States has created an "external state" that expands its "coercive apparatus" outside its borders, through regimes of surveillance and repression that extend into other countries, while using the same apparatus within its "internal state" (Laffey and Weldes 2004, 126). Barry Hindess (2005, 242) argues that the current form of empire dominates the "non-Western populations" through a "liberal world order" that uses the promotion, not denial, of citizenship for the recolonization of the "non-Western world." Institutions of citizenship are no longer just internal to the nation-state, but are "part of a supranational governmental regime in which the system of states, international agencies and multinational corporations all play a fundamental role" (Hindess 2005, 242). These institutions continue to discipline bodies and regulate labor through divisions between "citizens, subjects and non-citizen others" and communalized distinctions in group rights that were enforced by colonial regimes and that persist in late twentieth-century and postcolonial states (Hindess 2005, 254–56).

Citizenship in the United States has long been tied to practices of racial exclusion that were key to its settler-colonial project, for citizenship was initially only the "right of free white men, leaving Native Americans, African Americans, and women clearly outside the vision of nation" (Shanahan 1999, 83; Young 1990) and also excluding Asian and Latin American immigrants.[15] Yet members of these subordinated groups become drawn into a unifying national identity, even a militarized nationalism, especially at moments when they identify as parts of the national body that are presumably wounded by attack from without, and are not immune to being mesmerized by imperial spectacle. Lutz (2006) has shown how militarism is intrinsically part of U.S. culture and defines social values, ideas of citizenship, and (racialized) notions of gender and sexuality, offering immigrants and minorities an entry into dominant notions of national belonging and (heterosexual) masculinity. Later in the book, I will explore how the crisis of 9/11 unified minority groups behind a renewed American nationalism and support for the state's War on Terror, in some cases sharpening the divide between citizens and immigrants who are Arab and non-Arab, Muslim and non-Muslim, and weakening the possibilities for dissenting alliances. Internal dissent was criticized by ultranationalists after 9/11 as playing into the hands of the "terrorists" who wished to weaken the nation, as former attorney general John Ashcroft so infamously observed in his attack on those who dared to criticize his assault on civil rights as unpatriotic (cited in Chang 2002, 94).

After September 11, many Americans willingly sacrificed their civil liberties, or at least the civil rights of other communities if not their own, and accepted the surveillance state as being necessary for "national security," believing it was "security," and not imperial dominance, that their leaders were offering them. The notion of security, and its presumed opposite, terror, are ideological frameworks within which the American empire exercises its strategies of domestic and overseas dominance and exploitation (Bacevich 2002).[16] But there has also been a growing movement of Americans, constituted of individuals of various racial and class backgrounds and an array of political groups, expressing varying forms of dissent against the domestic and global War on Terror, most strongly against the crackdown on civil liberties that has affected U.S. citizens and that many on both the Left and the Right find too extreme.

One of the questions this book addresses is what it means to express dissent in a climate of political repression, and what this might look for those who are seen as outside of American national culture or citizenship, and who are most vulnerable to state surveillance. For example, Osman seemed reluctant to discuss the war in Afghanistan and post-9/11 politics more generally, perhaps due to the warnings of his father—a taxi driver with few resources to fight possible detention or harassment—while Nasreen, who had lived in the United States longer and was a citizen, was clearly outspoken and willing to share her outrage at U.S. policies. The contradictory relationships between citizenship and nationalism on the one hand, and the imperial state on the other, is addressed through a discussion of the various and often nuanced responses that immigrant youth and students of color expressed to the events of 9/11 and the War on Terror. The book situates the experiences of these youth within the political context of the aftermath of 9/11, but also within the broader cultures of U.S. imperialism in which empire is constructed through myriad interconnections between cultural representations, public discourses, state institutions, and social relations that shape identification with, support for, or dissent from imperial policies.

Imperial Feelings

Notions of national belonging and responses to the War on Terror, of Muslim immigrant youth as well as others in the United States, need to be linked to the collective denial and repression of knowledge of U.S. empire that underlie everyday imperial culture. Cultural critics and historians have pointed out the ways in which empire has long been a "way of life" in the United States (Williams 1980, ix), an intrinsic part of the fabric of society, a structure of feeling that underlies the relationship of the individual to society. This is what I call the "imperial feeling," the complex of psychological and political belonging to empire that is often unspoken but always present. The notion of imperial feelings draws on Raymond Williams's (1977) concept of "structures of feeling" that links individual subjectivity to planes of power. It follows in the genealogy of Edward Said's (1993) seminal work on "structures of attitude and reference" that are part of the "cultural topography" of empire. Said developed the idea of cultural attitudes and references inherent to metropolitan cultural identities in the contexts of British, French, and American literature that implicitly upheld a certain understanding and imagining of imperial identity (1993, 52). Similar work is performed by a range of American texts today—literary, journalistic, and popular—that convey this feeling, potent because it is not named as such, of being at the center of empire. In contrast, Paul Gilroy (2005, 118, 100–101) argues that the "nagging uncertainty" about what defines British national identity is shaped by Britain's postcolonial melancholia, an "inability to mourn its loss of empire and accommodate the empire's consequences," particularly the arrival of immigrants from the former colonies, who are "unwanted and feared precisely because they are the unwitting bearers of the imperial and colonial past."

For the United States, however, imperialism is not (only) in the past but in the present, as I have argued. Rather than nostalgia or mourning for the glory days of imperial domination that shapes the "melancholic outlook" underlying British racism and xenophobia (Gilroy 2005, 118), there are a range of sentiments associated with the United States' imperial role that have intensified after 9/11: anger, loathing, fear, uncertainty, ambivalence, apathy, and denial. But U.S. imperial culture also displays feelings of imperial guilt, the "self-scrutiny and self-loathing that follow among decent folk" (Gilroy 2005, 101) about the violence inflicted on others, both outside and within the United States. Susan Buck-Morss (2003, 24) rightly observes that the question "Why do they hate us?" repeated often after 9/11 was a rhetorical query that was presumed to have no answer and so became a "ritual act" that reinforced the notion of "American 'innocence,'" and perhaps, in the reiteration of those five words, defended it. I would argue that the ritualization of the question also protects those who ask it from situating the events of 9/11 in a larger analysis that would force them to confront the culpability of U.S. imperial power and the history of U.S. military and political interventions predating 9/11.

The viewing of the world through an imperial vantage point is always—even in more critical manifestations—structured by American concerns and an American language of empire. The discourse of U.S. empire is different from the European imperial projects studied by Said and other postcolonial theorists; however, the structure of cultural anxieties in the moment of empire as they emerge in discussions of liberalism, Orientalism, and feminism in relation to U.S. imperialism is remarkably similar, as I will show in chapters 5 and 6. Scholars such as William Appleman Williams, Amy Kaplan, Vicente Rafael, Donald Pease, Michael Rogin and others have done important work in mapping the cultural archive of American empire and examining its structuring themes, as Said (1981 [1978]) did in excavations of the work of Orientalism in British and European colonial literatures and cultures. My aim here is not to provide an overarching analysis of intrinsic structures of U.S. imperial culture; rather, I seek to point to some of the tensions that form the cultural landscape of the U.S. after 9/11 but that are not always explicitly linked to an imperial topography. Describing imperial knowledge and identification with empire as a "feeling" allows us to grapple with the contradictions that constitute living in and with imperial culture, and with the blurring of cultural and state processes that uphold imperial power.

This book focuses on the ways in which youth, in particular Muslim immigrant youth from South Asia, understand national belonging in relation to the U.S. imperial state and its imperial culture. It is based on an ethnographic approach that allows us to see how the subjective dimension of imperial feelings in the daily lives of individuals is inextricably linked to material and political structures of power. It is by exploring this link between individual biography and political structures that the imperial feelings of belonging versus disidentification, allegiance versus betrayal, and dissent versus complicity become apparent. These tensions are not binary oppositions but nuanced and graded expressions that structure imperial feelings, and that come in moments that lie on a continuum between feelings of belonging and alienation, between the clarity and obfuscation of empire. It is important to understand the depth of imperial feelings and the complexity of their contradictions, subjective and structural, if we are to oppose empire or even to think about how to do so.

The "War on Terror"

The global War on Terror waged by the Bush administration overseas, which provided a frame for the invasions of Afghanistan and later Iraq, was accompanied by a domestic War on Terror as part of a campaign that many describe as being, in effect, a war on those identified as Arab or Muslim as well as an ongoing war on immigrants. Muslim immigrant youth such as Osman or Nasreen commented on the fear and suspicion that affected them and also their parents, prompting Osman's father to fly an American flag from his cab and Nasreen to preempt questions about being Muslim. The state-sponsored War on Terror after 9/11 was aided by the USA-PATRIOT (United and Strengthening America by Providing Appropriate Tools Required to Intercept and Obstruct Terrorism) Act, which gave the government sweeping new powers of investigation and surveillance (Chang 2002, 29–32). A brief overview of the legal and political regime that was intensified by the War on Terror is important in order to understand the political and cultural climate in which these South Asian Muslim youth were living and grappling with ideas of citizenship, belonging, affiliation, and dissent. State practices of surveillance, detention, and deportation that were used to discipline and intimidate communities after 9/11 are part of the regime of U.S. imperial policies that have shaped the political expressions of Muslim immigrant youth. These Muslim immigrant students responded differently to the War on Terror: some, like Osman, were hesitant or afraid to openly discuss political issues such as the war, while others, like Nasreen, were quite explicit in their denunciations of the war in Afghanistan and Bush's rationale for the threatened invasion of Iraq.

It is also important to note that these state practices and legal regimes have long been used to target "aliens" and political radicals in the United States—from the Alien and Sedition Act of 1798, which criminalized dissent, to the Palmer Raids of 1919–20, which led to mass roundups and deportations of anarchists and union members, to the anti-Communist witch hunts of the McCarthy era (Hing 2004). Many observers compare the post-9/11 hysteria about an invisible "fifth column" to the internment of Japanese Americans, including U.S. citizens, in American concentration camps during the Second World War. However, the scapegoating of "aliens" and "subversives" extends back to well before this infamous mass incarceration and has historically been used to persecute those considered threats, not just to national security but to U.S. imperial policies and capitalist ideologies.

Contradictory to the notion that "the fate of justice during war is an aberration," Richard Delgado (2003, 80) observes that the recurrent pattern of suspension of civil liberties and use of the law to execute U.S.

Protest of post-9/11 racial profiling, Coney Island, New York, 2003.
Photograph by Irum Sheikh.

government policies suggests that these are not "exceptions to an otherwise scrupulously fair system" but, in fact, "the rule, the most obvious,
most visible case," for "all of law is a war zone." Like other critical legal
theorists, Delgado (2003, 80) suggests that the law is embedded in, not
outside of, the social system and is linked to a coercive state apparatus;
it is a mechanism for framing the terms of conflict that it is presumably
designed to mediate—for example, defining who is an "enemy combatant"
and who deserves habeas corpus. In the United States the law has historically been used to execute repressive government policies. The PATRIOT
Act was an extremely egregious shredding of constitutional rights, but
it was not an aberration. A 342-page document rapidly passed within six
weeks of September 11, it granted the government enhanced surveillance
powers and took away due process rights from noncitizens, who could
now be placed in mandatory (and in actuality, indefinite and secret) detention and deported because of participation in broadly defined "terrorist
activity," often for minor immigration violations and also in secret (Chang
2002, 43–44; Cole and Dempsey 2002, 151–53). It became quickly apparent that Attorney General John Ashcroft was reinstalling many of the
provisions of the FBI's Counter Intelligence Program (COINTELPRO),

that had surveilled and infiltrated civil rights groups in the 1960s, and had been challenged by the Church Committee (Chang 2002, 29–32). There was an additional sense of horrifying déjà vu for those who recalled the witch hunts and paranoia of the McCarthy era's targeting of "un-American" dissenters; suspects after 9/11 were labeled "terrorists" or supporters of terrorism, much as the word "Communist" was used during the Red Scare from the late 1930s through the 1950s (Schrecker 1998).

The PATRIOT Act violated basic constitutional rights of due process and free speech and, in effect, sacrificed the liberties of specific minority groups in exchange for a presumed sense of safety of the larger majority. Before 9/11, about 80 percent of the American public thought it was wrong for law enforcement to use "racial profiling," popularly used to refer to the disproportionate targeting of African American drivers by police for the offense of "driving while black." After the shock of the 9/11 attacks, public opinion shifted dramatically due to the climate of fear, and 60 percent favored racial profiling, "at least as long as it was directed at Arabs and Muslims" (Cole and Dempsey 2002, 168). While public hysteria about terrorism seemed to have waned somewhat over time, suspicion about Muslim and Arab terrorism seemed to have congealed; in summer 2006, a Gallup poll showed that 39 percent of Americans were in favor of having Muslims in the United States, including citizens, carry a special identification card.[17] Foreign policy interests were encoded in the PATRIOT Act, since its provisions principally targeted foreign nationals, especially from Arab and predominantly Muslim nations linked by the Bush administration to al-Qaeda, but not those from Spain, Germany, France, or Britain, all countries where alleged al-Qaeda suspects had lived.

The War on Terror was waged primarily against immigrants, heightening the distinction between citizens and noncitizens and making citizenship a crucible for the post-9/11 crackdown. Nasreen was like many other Muslim immigrant youth who were concerned about getting legal citizenship for themselves and their family members in a climate of repression and erosion of civil rights. Civil liberties granted to citizens came to be seen as a privilege, not a right, for noncitizens. In *Enemy Aliens: Double Standards and Constitutional Freedoms in the War on Terrorism*, the law professor David Cole (2003, 21) points out that since 9/11, "the government has repeatedly targeted noncitizens, selectively denying them liberties that citizens rightfully insist upon for themselves." Immigration law was intentionally used in lieu of criminal law to execute the domestic crackdown in order to avoid the constitutional requirements applied to citizens (Cole 2003, 24). The attorney general also used immigration law to detain individuals, without any evidence of connections to terrorism, because it provides the state with "extremely broad discretion in how and when to enforce immigration violations" (Cole 2003, 24). Sweeping powers have been given to immigration judges to detain and deport Muslim, South Asian, and Arab immigrants (Fernandes 2007). Critics point out that using immigration law to conduct the War on Terror gives the government a cover for religious and ethnic profiling that is similar to the use of traffic law for drug enforcement that encouraged racial profiling in the War on Drugs (Cole 2003; Nguyen 2005). Immigration violations became a pretext for rounding up noncitizens selectively after 9/11, for the state has in practice, despite its anti-immigrant rhetoric, largely turned a blind eye to the huge number of undocumented immigrants that provide cheap labor crucial for the U.S. economy (De Genova 2002, 438–40).

Cole observes that noncitizens are confronted with "double standards" in the PATRIOT Act's definition of "terrorism," which is more narrowly defined for U.S. citizens than it is for foreign nationals. "Domestic terrorism," according to the PATRIOT Act, is constituted by "acts dangerous to human life that are in violation of the criminal laws ... [and] that appear to be intended ... to influence the policy of a government by intimidation and coercion" (Cole 2003, 58). This is a rather vague definition as well, but foreign nationals can be considered guilty of terrorism for completely nonviolent activity, innocent associations, support of charitable organizations, and political speech. Noncitizens can be deported for association with political organizations deemed to be terrorist—as was the African National Congress until the 1990s—and are subject to unilateral executive detention indefinitely, without due process, and often in secret; as well as to secret searches without probable cause.

While the heightened repression of the Bush-Ashcroft era was one of the most troubling moments for civil rights in U.S. history, it is important to remember that the PATRIOT Act built on repressive and anti-immigrant policies that had previously been established under Democrat regimes. For example, the Anti-Terrorism and Effective Death Penalty Act and the Illegal Immigration Reform and Immigrant Responsibility Act passed under Clinton in 1996 narrowed the definition of the "civil community" in response to the "heightened sense of insecurity required to maintain a restructured, wartime regulatory state after the primary security target disappears," as Kathleen Moore points out (1999, 95).[18] Moore underscores that political repression at home is used to justify foreign policy and military campaigns and also to support the domestic priorities of the U.S. state, such as the battles over "welfare, affirmative action, and immigration reform" (Moore 1999, 87). This is even more true when the illusion of a "peacetime economy" is discarded for a nation at war as in the present moment, what Michael Hardt and Antonio Negri succinctly describe as the "warfare state" (2004, 17). Critics on both the Right and Left understand that it is the links between the domestic and foreign contexts that are key to the national agenda of the warfare state. Social conservatives frame the domestic "culture war" in the United States as linked to the global "moral and military crusade against evil" represented by George W. Bush's foreign policy; for example, William J. Bennett founded Americans for Victory Against Terrorism to galvanize U.S. public opinion into recognizing that "the threats we face are both external and internal," through campaigns for conservative moral values at home and patriotic support for U.S. policies overseas (Barry and Lobe 2003, 45). Thus the War on Terror has entailed a battle that has rested not just on policing the legal, but also cultural, boundaries of citizenship through defining the behavior required of "good" citizens in terms of a "coercive patriotism," which continues to be evident during the war in Iraq (Park 2005, 6).

Furthermore, the War on Terror is an extension of the "war on immigrants," revived by the Right and stoked by nativists since the late 1980s, because it has stripped civil rights from noncitizens and led to sweeps and mass deportations of undocumented immigrants, extending the assault on immigrant rights exemplified by the anti-immigrant Proposition 187 passed in California in 1994, the 1996 immigrant acts, and the ongoing policing and increasing militarization of U.S. borders (Fernandes 2007; Hing 2000, 2001; Nguyen 2005). The increased cooperation between immigration and the FBI for domestic law enforcement was evident not just in the War on Terror, but also the so-called war on gangs, which has led to the annual deportation of up to 40,000 alleged Latino and Latina gang members to Mexico and Central America for "aggravated felonies" since 1996, applying practices used for potential terrorists (Nguyen 2005, 87). The War on Terror thus connects U.S. foreign policy concerns with issues of citizenship, immigration, criminalization, and incarceration, exemplifying how the domestic and foreign faces of empire belong to the same beast.

Disappeared in the USA

South Asian immigrant youth were not always aware of the details of specific immigration policies or of the PATRIOT Act, but they were keenly
aware of the impact that these policies had on their lives, their families,
and communities in the War of Terror and particularly on rights for immigrants and citizens. The "war on immigration," the War on Drugs, and
the "war on gangs" have folded into the "war on terror," all of them providing a legal and rhetorical arsenal for one another and exemplifying what
it means to live in a warfare state where war is not just a pervasive cultural metaphor but is seen as crucial for the "health of the state" (Lutz
2006, 292). The state of preemptive and "perpetual war" (see Young 2005)
is built on the assumption that certain categories of citizens and subjects are criminal, undesirable, and unworthy of national belonging, and
so must be purged from the body politic. These groups of people must
be deported, "removed," or disappeared from the nation-state, a process
that could be rendered extraordinary were it not part of the ordinari-
ness of daily policies of detention and deportation that have long targeted
criminalized populations in the United States. After 9/11, Muslim families began experiencing the "disappearances" of their husbands, brothers,
and sons, for none of the detainees were identified publicly and the locations where they were held remained secret (Chang 2002, 69–87). As
part of the domestic "War on Terror," at least 1,200 Muslim immigrant
men were rounded up and detained within seven weeks in the immediate
aftermath of 9/11, none of them with any criminal charges, and some in
high security prisons (Cainkar and Maira 2006). The use of "the disappeared" by civil and immigrant rights activists was intended to evoke the
human rights violations associated with the (much larger scale) abduc-
tion, secret detention, and torture of innocent civilians (the *desaparecidos*)
during the "dirty wars" in Argentina in 1976–83, as part of the campaign
against left-wing "terrorism." By May 2003, the U.S. government had also
detained over 1,000 foreign nationals under the Absconder Apprehension
Initiative, which prioritized deportation of 6,000 Arabs and Muslims
from the pool of over 300,000 immigrants with outstanding deportation
orders (Cole 2003, 25).

These detainees began to disappear into the vast American prison-
industrial complex, and into "a vast system of immigration prisons that
had been detaining 150,000 people annually since the mid-1990s and

Rally against mass arrests, deportation, and disappearances, Middlesex County Jail.
Photograph by Irum Sheikh.

now hold more than 200,000 people each year" (Nguyen 2005, 7). In
American Gulag: Inside U.S. Immigration Prisons, Mark Dow (2004,
11–12) documents the workings of the vast but largely "invisible" prison
system run by the the Immigration and Naturalization Service (INS)
and its later manifestation under the Department of Homeland Security (DHS), along with the often brutal treatment of immigrant detainees,
who constitute a shadow "nation within a nation." The warehousing and
disproportionate detention of certain segments of the population have
coexisted with targeted polices of deporting, or threatening to expel,
certain groups of immigrants from the nation. Both these policies are
part of what Ruth Gilmore describes as the imperial state's "modus operandi for solving crises [through] the relentless identification, coercive control, and violent elimination of foreign and domestic enemies" (cited in
Rodríguez 2006, 16).[19] The INS, which has been restructured partly as the
Bureau of Immigration and Customs Enforcement (ICE) under the DHS,
has warehoused immigrants in local jails as well as privately run prisons.
There is evidence that detainees were often abused and even tortured
by prison officials and held in secret detention well before 9/11, within
a prison regime that Dylan Rodríguez describes as an "indispensable

element of American statecraft, simultaneously a cornerstone of its militarized (local and global) ascendancy and spectacle of its extracted (or coerced) authority over targeted publics" (2006, 44). The War on Terror has also drawn large numbers of immigrants who were not from Arab or Muslim communities into its dragnet. In just one instance, in November 2001 the government began requiring all airport screeners to be U.S. citizens and conducted a multiagency sweep of airports, called Operation Tarmac, which resulted in the detention and deportation of more than 1,000 undocumented airport workers, mostly Latino and Latina and Filipino and Filipina (Nguyen 2005, xx, 18).

After 9/11, the state created new policies to monitor and collect information on suspected populations that officially and openly targeted Muslim immigrants, particularly men. In June 2002, the National Security Entry-Exit Registration System (NSEERS) was established, requiring all male nationals over sixteen years of age from 24 Muslim-majority countries, including Pakistan and Bangladesh, as well as North Korea, to submit to photographing and fingerprinting at federal immigration facilities. Though outrageous, this program seems to be still unknown to many Americans (including most of the college students I teach in Asian American Studies).[20] Over 80,000 men complied with the "Special Registration" program and went to register, by groups of countries, even though information about the process was badly disseminated among the target communities, heightening fear and anxiety for Arab and Muslim immigrants. Many of these men, however, never came out; 2,870 were detained, and 13,799 were put into deportation proceedings (Nguyen 2005, xviii). After news broke of mass arrests of nearly a thousand Iranians complying with Special Registration in Southern California in December 2002 (Nguyen 2005, 52), some undocumented immigrants and those with pending immigration applications tried to flee to Canada, for they were worried about being detained and deported if they registered (Ryan 2003). The anxiety about Special Registration and the chilling effect of the mass detentions permeated the South Asian Muslim community in Wellford, causing particular concern for undocumented Muslim students whose legal status was rarely, if ever, discussed publicly in the school given the sensitivity of the issue.

The Justice Department stopped releasing numbers of persons detained in the post-9/11 sweeps in November 2001, as public criticism began to mount, so though the official estimate was 1,182 detentions, a conservative estimate of detentions until May 2003 is at least 5,000 (Cole 2003, 25). Nearly 40 percent of the post-9/11 detainees were thought to be Pakistani nationals (Schulhofer 2002, 11). There have also been mass deportations of Pakistani nationals on chartered planes, some leaving in the middle of the night from New York state, that were unreported in the mainstream media (Ryan 2003, 16). Pakistani immigrants were disproportionately targeted for detention and deportation even though there were no Pakistani nationals involved in the 9/11 hijacking, because although Pakistan has been a key ally of the United States in its War on Terror in the region, the U.S. government also views with suspicion the guerilla networks in northwest Pakistan—from the same areas that provided the mujahideen that the CIA had armed and trained to fight its proxy war in Afghanistan.

Muslim and Arab American men also began getting calls or surprise visits by the FBI for so-called voluntary interviews, initially from a list of 5,000 men from countries allegedly connected to al-Qaeda (Cainkar 2004, 246). As the United States geared up for its invasion of Iraq, the FBI began interviewing Iraqis living in the United States and, with mounting pressure on Iran, has been calling in Iranian immigrants for questioning (Nguyen 2005, 84). Increasingly, Muslim and Arab males are being questioned not just in their homes but in airports and border crossing points where they are subject to prolonged detention, intensive interrogation on personal and political issues, and even refusal of entry, regardless of citizenship status (Sinnar 2007). The surveillance, detentions, and deportations in the domestic War on Terror are clearly and inextricably linked to U.S. foreign policy in South Asia and the Middle East. As Nasreen astutely observed of the discrepancy in the War on Terror's focus, given that the majority of the 9/11 hijackers were from Saudi Arabia, "I heard in the news that Saudi Arabia has the most oil. So Americans may hate Saudi Arabians, but they still have to keep in touch with them because of oil." Thus she was able to piece together the links between the wars on Afghanistan and Iraq and the state's political and economic interests in the region.

The deportations and detentions set in motion by the "war on terror" had national as well as global impact, for they triggered a flow of Arab, Muslim, and South Asian immigrants back to their home communities or to other places. As news of the domestic crackdown spread quickly in South Asia and the Arab world, there was increased anxiety about migrating to the United States in this political climate (see Peutz 2006). As

Nasreen quipped, "If the rights are gone, then what's the point of living here?" Pakistani Americans increasingly talk of the "return migration" to Pakistan since 9/11, such as to cities such as Karachi that have a history of out-migration to the United States, while others suggest that South Asian and particularly Muslim migrants are turning to Europe. These shifts in global flows are just beginning to be documented (see Peutz 2006), but it is clear that imperial policy has rippled through local and global realms, altering immigrants' migration patterns, family networks, and economic futures, and in some cases heightening repressive forces and systems of surveillance and incarceration already in place before 9/11.

It is important to remember that while "antialien sentiments and tactics" were generally used to target noncitizens, political repression has eventually extended to citizens as well, breaking down the sanctity of the divide between citizens and noncitizens, as was the case with government surveillance of U.S. citizens who belonged to the Committee in Solidarity with the People of El Salvador (CISPES) in the 1980s (Cole 2003, 85). Cole points out that in "war on terror," citizens have also been affected by the PATRIOT Act's provisions for "new surveillance powers, strengthening of laws against domestic terrorism, and the easing of restrictions on FBI spying" (72). However, there certainly are racialized differences in the government's treatment of citizens. For example, Yasser Hamdi, a U.S. citizen who was captured in Afghanistan, did not receive a civilian criminal hearing unlike John Walker Lindh, a white Muslim convert who was also captured in Afghanistan. Hamdi was released without a hearing on the condition that he renounce his U.S. citizenship (Saito 2005, 55). José Padilla, also a U.S. citizen, was eventually transferred to the criminal justice system in 2006 after a grueling imprisonment in a navy brig in Charleston, South Carolina, which left him mentally disturbed, while Ali al-Marri, a citizen of Qatar, still remains in the same Kafkaesque situation as an "enemy combatant" held in solitary confinement since 2001 without the right to a trial.[21] Furthermore, the brunt of the repression and detentions was borne by noncitizens, and there was much greater public outcry against proposed programs that would target American citizens, such as the proposed national identity card, the infamous Operation TIPS (Terrorist Information and Prevention System) to enlist private citizens to spy on potential terrorists, and the Total Information Awareness project for mass technological surveillance of private transactions (Parenti 2003). All these programs were scrapped after being denounced by critics, on both the Left and the Right, who felt that they the assault on citizens' civil liberties was going too far. It took much longer for public criticism of Special Registration requirements to gain momentum, since it affected only Muslim and Arab immigrant men and many citizens were not even aware of this ignominious program. The program's requirements were softened after one year, but it was not completely eliminated.

Citizenship remains a linchpin of the war on terror, with the proposed PATRIOT Act II (the Domestic Security Enhancement Act), leaked in February 2003, providing that "citizens who are associated with 'terrorist' groups" would be "stripped of their citizenship"(Cole 2003, 69). Citizenship thus loomed even larger in the lives of Muslim and Arab Americans after 9/11 than it had before, and was associated with desire and mobility as well as anxiety and fear. Nasreen's concerns about changes in citizen rights in the United States are thus part of a much larger national debate about the meaning and limits of citizenship in a climate of fear and repression. The following chapter explores how theories of cultural citizenship can help explain the cultural boundaries, and political possibilities as well as limitations, of citizenship as articulated by growing movements for immigrant and cultural rights, and as performed and learned by immigrant students in a variety of contexts in their everyday lives.

Two

Cultural Citizenship

Sara

*I met Sara in Wellford a few weeks after she came to
the United States from India in the fall of 2001. She
and her sister, Rukshana, had just joined the public
high school, and they both knew virtually no English.
They were terrified, and the bilingual program teachers
in the school were worried about them. When I first
met them, they were both dressed in cotton salwar kameez, Sara in an orange salwar kameez and a* dupatta
*(scarf) with orange and green flowers that made her
brown hair look tinted gold and her large eyes gleam
hazel. Rukshana wore a blue salwar kameez, and a
dupatta that had the same printed design as her sister, in blue and yellow. It was September, but I could
tell they were cold in their thin cotton cardigans. They
looked tiny, standing next to Fred Ellery, the bilingual
program director, and the male students who towered
above them. They must have been four and a half feet,
much shorter than me. But I was struck most by how
overwhelmed they seemed by the anxiety of being thrust
into this new space, and by not knowing English. When
I began talking to them in Hindi, their faces dissolved
visibly into relief. Then it was time for the next period,*

and they went off to their ESL *class, disappearing into the throng of backpacks and sweatshirts streaming through the hallway.*

I got to know Sara and her family better than any of the other South Asian immigrant girls in the high school that year, partly because of Sara's openness and affection, which quickly cemented into a warm connection between us, and partly because of issues that were to spiral intensely over the next two years into her life and the lives of others.

Amin

Amin left India and arrived in the United States a few months after Sara, and entered the Wellford High School in the spring of the same academic year. He was quickly adopted by Ismail, an older Indian student who was from the same town in Gujarat, and who made it a point to look out for and mentor the new students from South Asia. Ismail told me about Amin, suggesting that I introduce him to SAMTA, *and offered to take me to visit him.*

I picked both of them up one afternoon from the high-rise apartment complex on the outskirts of the city where they both lived. Ismail met me downstairs and walked over with me to the building next door to meet Amin, who lived with his father. Going up in the clanking elevator, Ismail looked at the candy wrappers lying on the floor and whispered that his building had a different management company that took better care of the premises. Later, I found out that the complex of three apartment buildings in North Wellford was a mix of private and public housing; the residents were almost entirely nonwhite, African Americans as well as immigrants from Haiti, the Caribbean, and Asia. Interestingly, the buildings housed nearly all the Indian Muslim families whose children went to the Wellford public high school, and a few of the Bangladeshi and Pakistani students as well. Sara's and Rukshana's family lived in the same building as Amin, I was to learn afterward. When we knocked on Amin's door, he greeted us with a wide, open smile, his signature greeting.

Sara

"My family comes from a village in Gujarat near Valsar. I miss it because I liked living in the village. We all lived together, my father and his two brothers. One of my uncles had many sons; the other had one daughter and two sons.

*We all lived together in one house. It was so much fun. There was always fam-
ily around. We have twenty cousins! Whenever you came home, there were
people to talk to. We came here because my father's sister had come to the
U.S. She lives in Connecticut, and she sponsored my father. My abba [father]
came thirteen years ago, and lived in Hartford; then he moved to Wellford.
He sponsored my brother, who joined him here. They both lived together with
some other Gujarati men in one apartment. There were only two rooms, and
there were six men in the apartment. So my father used to work during the
day and sleep in the bed at night, and my brother used to work at nights and
sleep during the day. After a while, they both started working at an Indian
restaurant in Belltown. Then after a few months, they sent for us and we came
to the U.S. We have some relatives in Chicago too, but we hardly see them.
Before we came here, we didn't know Chicago was so far away. We thought
we would all be together, close by, but it is not like in India.*

"I didn't know much about the U.S. before I came. But I had heard about
it from my father and brother, and my brother sent us a video of the movie
The Titanic. You know that movie? It's very good. We saw American films
with my friends, and they all said, 'America is very nice, America is great.' So
we were really happy to come here. But then we came here, we began to cry
and cry, because we missed India so much, and we missed our relatives there.
We wanted to go back to Valsar. And they cried too there, and said maybe we
could come back. When we started at the school, it was very tough, because we
didn't speak English and we had no idea what to do. But Mr. Ellery helped
us—he was very kind. And Ismail met us, and he told us what to do, how
the classes are here. We had two cousins at the school, Yusuf and Shireen, but
they moved to Maine. There is no Indian store up there. They come here once
a month to get all the Indian things for cooking.

"Now Rukshana and I both work at the store in Belltown where my father works; it has Indian spices, food stuff, videos, music—everything! My
brother has his own business; he's married. He has a convenience store nearby.
My younger sister, Naseem, helps him there on the weekends. She's fourteen.
Rukshana and I are fifteen. You didn't know we are twins? Yes we are! Of
course, look at us, we're twins! She's a bit darker than I am, and her hair is short;
that's why people don't believe it always. But we're exactly the same height, and
we can wear the same clothes. She likes blue and green more, though, and I like
orange and pink. We both work at the store, but at different times. I go there
during the week, mostly, and Rukshana goes there on the weekends. Actually,
she doesn't go as much as I do. I'm not sure why. Also the weekends, we like

to spend time with our family and watch videos. No, we don't watch movies so much, we watch Hindi TV serials. You've heard of Kusum? It's great!"

Amin

"I'm from Billimoria, a village in Gujarat. It's about an hour away from Valsar. People don't know where it is, so sometimes I just say I'm from Valsar. But I'm really from Billimoria. I have an older sister and an older brother. My sister came here, because she married a guy who is living in Wellford. So she sponsored my father, seven years ago, and he came and was working out here. He works in Building Seventeen and a Half; it's this big store. I was supposed to come with my mother last fall. But my mother passed away in India, last summer. So I came alone. I was hoping to come here before Eid. My father said to me, 'You'll celebrate Eid with us in America.' We all thought we'd be together here, after seven years of waiting there. But you know what? It didn't matter. My mother couldn't come to America anyway. She passed away in September last year, right before that thing happened here. So my visa got delayed, because of what happened on September 11. I thought maybe I would never get to be with my family. Maybe I would never see my father again too. But then the visa went through in December. So I missed one semester of school; I started in the middle of the ninth grade.

"I was in an English medium school in Billimoria. It was a convent. No, they weren't any nuns, it was just in English. That's what we call English medium [schools], it's a convent school. There were both boys and girls. But we had uniforms, so it wasn't like here. My English isn't that good, but I can speak a little. It's hard for me to understand sometimes what people in the school say. I didn't watch a lot of American films, but my sister told me about America. Yes, I think it's what I thought it would be like. The only thing is the weather: it rains a lot here. Oh, that's because it's spring? Yes, I know that in the winter it snows. I'm glad it didn't snow too much here this winter. I think it's very cold in Wellford. I miss being outside every day. Here, I go home every day after school and do my homework. I want to work, but I am waiting for my social security number. Do you know how to get it? I've been waiting for a long time, no, and I need a job. I didn't know that they had an internship program at the school. I'd like to talk to you about that afterwards.

"My father has faith that things will work out for me, like my visa. My father is very religious. He always tells me, 'Just ask Allah for what you want, and he will give it.' He has done the Haj [pilgrimage to Mecca]. My mother

did it with him. He goes to the mosque in Prospect Square sometimes. I pray too, but it's harder here. On Fridays, I go with him to Prospect Square. There are some Indians and Pakistanis, Bangladeshis there. But mainly Arabs, people from Morocco, Egypt, Lebanon. Even China. Yes, I think there are some Chinese Muslims there! After September 11, my father was walking through Prospect Square and someone said to him, 'Are you from Afghanistan?' He has a beard, so maybe that's why they thought that he was Afghan. He said, 'No, I'm Indian.' And he just walked away. It was during the war against Afghanistan. So I think those men were suspicious, and they might have done something, but my father just walked away. He doesn't get scared easily. And he's a tall guy! No, no one at his work no one said anything. But he doesn't talk about it too much to me."

Cultural Citizenship

The stories by Sara, Amin, and other youth often touched on the question of national belonging, linking it to issues of race, religion, ethnicity, labor, and particularly to the War on Terror. The cultural dimensions of national belonging were apparent in their narratives of everyday experiences of inclusion, exclusion, and engagement with the school, workplace, and public sphere. Amin was one of several youth who alluded to the regimes of surveillance and profiling that categorized Muslim and Arab males as suspect immigrants and "un-American" citizens. Both Sara and Amin came from families that had been scattered across national borders, their fathers having lived in the United States for several years before being able to reunite with their children through family visa sponsorship. Amin's mother died before she was able to join her husband, who had been living in the United States for seven years, sponsored by his daughter who had gained citizenship through marriage to a Gujarati Muslim man already living in the United States. Sara's father sponsored his son, and they both shared a tiny apartment with several other South Asian immigrant men, taking turns sleeping and going out to work, until they were able to move out to Wellford and work in their own stores or family-run businesses. Sara herself worked in her uncle's store, which was also a source of the Hindi TV shows she loved to watch on video, so her work and leisure were intertwined, conveniently, since she had little time or money to go out with friends or see movies in the cinema. These immigrant youth understood national belonging and transnational identification in relation to cultural consumption and, also, labor. Young immigrants have to deal with the migration choices of their parents and with the demands of being both students and workers, and it is clear that their lives are deeply shaped by the state and economic policies that drive their parents to cross national borders. The narratives of family sacrifices and hardworking immigrants struggling for a "better life"—as told by Sara, Amin, and other youth in this book—may appear to reinforce the fable of the American Dream, of "good" immigrants participating in the "common American tale of heroes, enduring struggles, and happy endings" (Park 2005, 110). But this myth dissolved in the face of the persistent obstacles and the treadmills of work and school, deferring the prospect of "happy endings" and leading some youth to question the notion of the productive citizen-worker, as I will discuss in chapter 4.

Cultural citizenship was also tied to an awareness of the difficulties in obtaining legal citizenship, generally through discussions of the scattering and reunification of family members, establishing a trail of immigration documents and legal "papers" that never seemed to come soon enough. Most of these young immigrants desired and had applied for formal U.S. citizenship, since they came to the United States sponsored by relatives who are permanent residents or citizens, as illustrated by the stories of Sara, Amin, Osman, and Nasreen. These immigrant youth also spoke of legal citizenship in the context of wanting voting rights and freedom to travel, which I will elaborate on in the following chapter.

Citizenship has traditionally been thought of in political, economic, and civic terms, as articulated by T. H. Marshall (1950), but it is also a "normative ideology that dictates how members of a given nation-state should behave depending upon particular social markers including race and gender" (Park 2005, 5). Analyses increasingly focus on the notion of cultural citizenship, as multiethnic societies are forced to confront questions of difference that undergird social inequity. It is very apparent that the rights and obligations of civic citizenship are mediated by race, ethnicity, gender, sexuality, and religion, not to mention class (Berlant 1997; Hobson 2000; Miller 1993; Rosaldo 1997; Werbner and Yuval-Davis 1999). Saskia Sassen (2004, 184) observes that though citizenship is often discussed as a unitary concept and institution, it "actually describes a number of discrete but related aspects in the relation between the individual and the polity." She points out that more recent work on citizenship sheds light on "the tension between citizenship as a formal legal status and as a normative project or an aspiration" that remains unfulfilled, in countries such as the United States, despite the "formal equality" guaranteed to citizens. Citizenship has always been imbued with "sentiments and emotions of membership" that are based on ideas of social morality and cultural beliefs about what defines "civic virtue" and the "good citizen" (Turner 2001, 11); these ideas and beliefs, in turn, are racialized, gendered, and classed. For example, some theorists argue that if normative ideas of citizenship encoded in the law conceive of the citizen as white, middle-class, male or gender-neutral, and heterosexual, then "youth of color" in the United States "learn how to negotiate life as a minority as they learn about the limits of full citizenship" (Russell 2002, 260). It is this tension between the formal, legal dimensions of citizenship and the cultural practices of membership in the nation-state that has driven the development of the notion of cultural citizenship.

Cultural citizenship, according to Lok Siu, is the "behaviors, discourses, and practices that give meaning to citizenship as lived experience" in the context of "an uneven and complex field of structural inequalities and webs of power relations," the "quotidian practices of inclusion and exclusion" (2001, 9). Cultural citizenship is an important notion for South Asian Americans because legal citizenship is not enough to guarantee protection under the law with the state's War on Terror, as is clear from the profiling, surveillance, and even detention of Muslim Americans who are U.S. citizens. These dramatic enactments of exclusion from cultural citizenship are on a continuum of historical practices that have culturally and racially constructed nonwhite groups, such as Asian Americans, as "perpetual foreigners," despite legal citizenship (Tuan 1998). This notion of being "forever foreign," as well as the myth of the model minority that confers "almost white" status, are used to discipline and divide minority groups and uphold the racial order (Okihiro 1994).

The concept of cultural citizenship has been developed by some theorists out of concern with immigrant and civil rights, such as the work of Latino and Latina studies scholars Renato Rosaldo (1997) and William Flores and Rina Benmayor (1997). They propose a notion of citizenship that would support new social movements for rights based on class, gender, sexuality, ethnicity, and race. These scholars use cultural citizenship to analyze "how cultural phenomena—from practices that organize the daily life of individuals, families, and the community, to linguistic and artistic expression—cross the political realm and contribute to the process of affirming and building an emerging Latino/a identity and political and social consciousness" (Flores and Benmayor 1997, 6). For example, in a study of working-class Puerto Rican women, who developed a political and cultural understanding of their collective condition in relation to state practices through an educational program, the authors suggest:

> Bringing together culture and citizenship into a single analytic framework underscores the dynamic process whereby cultural identity comes to bear on claims for social rights in oppressed communities; and at the same time, identity is produced and modified in the process of affirming rights . . . in light of concrete obstacles and opportunities posed by the state, the economy, civil society, and the family. (Benmayor, Torruellas, and Juarbe 1992, 4)

Cultural citizenship theory and movements are based on critiquing the cultural dimensions of inclusion and exclusion; however, they address not just issues of cultural recognition, but also of economic and political rights. The mass-scale immigrant rights protests in 2006 in response to the proposed "immigration reform" bill, H.R. 3477, saw hundreds of thousands of immigrants, mainly Latinos and Latinas, marching in cities across the nation with slogans such as "No human being is illegal" and waving American flags. The general focus of this movement, at least in its mainstream manifestation, was that undocumented immigrants sought legal as well as cultural citizenship as hardworking members of the American nation who wanted inclusion in the national polity.

Clearly, there are a range of strategies in struggles for cultural citizenship: some challenge the notion of differentiated citizenship and argue for universalized rights and obligations, while others propose that the state should acknowledge difference as a basis for inequity in its treatment of citizens, or even that the state should guarantee cultural rights to protect diverse groups of citizens (Kymlicka 1995). In fact, the global discourse of children's rights has been extended by the United Nations Convention on the Rights of the Child to include an acknowledgment of children's rights to culture, particularly for minority or indigenous youth, yet theorists caution that these rights should not be used to promote an essentialized or exclusive notion of "tradition" or prioritize a universalizing, abstract notion of "culture" at the expense of material and political realities of war, poverty, and migration (Stephens 1995, 4, 37–39). Furthermore, while the "politics of [cultural] recognition" has converged with the growing discourse of human rights in what some call an "age of rights" (Bobbio 1996), the work of Michel Foucault and other scholars has expressed an increasing wariness of the imposition of rights that conceal technologies of domination (Hansen and Steputat 2005, 10). The limitations of a discourse or regime of rights will become apparent in discussions of civil rights and human rights that emerged after 9/11, as I will discuss later.

Theorists of cultural citizenship who are influenced by Foucault's approach, such as Aihwa Ong, view citizenship as a process that the state uses to discipline populations through notions of the ideal citizen and distinctions between those considered worthy or unfit for citizenship. Ong defines cultural citizenship as "a dual process of self-making and being-made within webs of power linked to the nation-state and civil society" (1996, 738). The state defines the "citizen" as someone who embodies values central to the national social order and economic system; for example, as productive, consuming individuals who subscribe to a capitalist ethos of work and meritocracy, as loyal subjects willing to bear arms for the nation, and as heterosexuals who will marry and reproduce the family as a unit of society. In her research on Cambodian refugees in California, Ong (2003, xvii) considers citizenship to be an "idiom of rights" but also a "social process" defined in relation to a "set of common (in this case American) values concerning family, health, social welfare, gender relations, and entrepreneurialism." This approach to citizenship is skeptical about transforming the identity of "citizen," since it relies on a politics defined by the state's disciplining power, not to mention the force of capital. Some scholars, such as Toby Miller (1993), are cautious about the possibility of using citizenship as the collective basis for political transformation, and perhaps rightly so. Citizenship has increasingly become individualized and privatized; being a citizen, some argue, is more akin to being a consumer of services or social goods offered by the neoliberal state (Cohen 2003; Schudson 1998). Ong (2006, 145) is critical of the technologies of "subjection" used by neoliberal citizenship in disciplining low-wage and immigrant workers in the United States, and challenges models of multicultural citizenship by political theorists, such as Will Kymlicka's (1995, 105), that are based on promoting values of "individual choice" central to Western "liberal democracy." Yet some Foucauldian critics are open, at the least, to the possibilities of using citizenship as the basis for rethinking the relationship between the individual and the state. For example, Ong's focus on "self-making" allows room for the production of citizen-subjects within the constraints of state and capital and for the emergence of political subjectivity.

My work bridges these two approaches, the social movement approach and the Foucauldian approach, for I am interested in the critical possibilities of cultural citizenship for galvanizing struggles for civil and immigrant rights. Yet in my view, cultural citizenship brings with it all the contradictions of liberal multiculturalism and the inequities of global capital in which it is embedded, and so it is necessarily politically ambiguous in its liberatory possibilities and cannot be idealized (Hutnyk 2000; Kymlicka 1995; Miller 1993). One of the chief contradictions is that movements for cultural citizenship critique the state while still remaining within the framework of engagement with the state or inclusion within it, even if they challenge or reject the notion of rights and identities as defined solely by the nation-state. As Inderpal Grewal points out, "concepts such as cultural citizenship and . . . new social movements based on racial, gendered, and ethnic identities have shown both their links to the American nation and their struggles with its affirmations of white supremacy . . . sometimes affiliating itself to [the nation] but also claiming a position outside it" (2005, 200).

The notion of cultural citizenship has by now been widely discussed and debated, but I think we need to map the different *kinds* of cultural citizenship and their tangible manifestations in everyday life, in all their subtlety and contradictions, and the ways in which issues of economic and legal citizenship spill over into cultural citizenship. We also need to understand better what cultural citizenship means for immigrant youth, particularly groups such as young Muslims and South Asians in the United States, whose experiences highlight the tensions of belonging and rights.

Learning—and Studying—Cultural Citizenship

This book offers a methodology for studying cultural citizenship for youth through an ethnographic lens that grounds theorization of youth and politics in a range of sites, thus providing instantiations of theories of state and empire. South Asian Muslim immigrant youth encounter the state in a variety of realms and are engaged in "cultural struggles" over what the state means at this particular moment "in the sphere of representation but also in the domain of the everyday practices of state agencies" (Sharma and Gupta 2006, 11). The research made it apparent to me that

South Asian immigrant youth learn about what it means to be a citizen and are exposed to ideas of national belonging and explanations of "political events" from different sources: school, family, work, friends, media and popular culture, and religious communities.

Theorists of citizenship observe that education is a "technology of power" that constructs the attitudes, beliefs, and skills, considered necessary for the national citizenry and workforce (Ong 2006, 139). Schools are viewed as a primary site of teaching informal and formal citizenship lessons to youth (Bejarano 2005; Buckingham 2000, 11) through cultural symbols and rituals as well as through civic education, history, and social studies courses. The public school, in both formal classes and informal conversations between teachers, staff, and students, inculcated ideals of civic engagement, pluralism, and liberal-democratic notions of racial justice and minority civil rights, as demonstrated in the following chapters. Discussions and events staged at the school about the War on Terror also addressed issues of U.S. militarism and post-9/11 policies, as Nasreen's experience suggested. Some teachers were critical of the state's policies and of the "war on terror," and the school was known to have a liberal political culture, which both supported and frustrated Muslim immigrant students, as implied by Sara's and Amin's narratives. At the same time, the school also maintained the authority of the police to maintain law and order in the local community and sponsored workshops with police on issues of crime and rights for citizen and noncitizen students, which I attended in the International Center. This is not unusual for a public high school, and the school's policing and security policies were generally not intrusive—there were no metal detector or body searches at the entrance, for instance, unlike other urban public high schools. My fieldwork showed that students received a range of messages about the role of the state and encountered different models of citizenship and dissent, which I will explore in chapter 5.

These youth also received messages about what it meant to be a good "citizen" from their immigrant parents, who often emphasized the connection of citizenship to spatial as well as class mobility, as I will discuss in the following chapter. Both Amin and Sara came to the United States because their parents thought their families would have a "better life" there. Here citizenship represents an "aspiration," to use Saskia Sassen's term (2004, 184), for economic advancement through investment in the education of the next generation and procurement of citizenship rights in another country. For example, Osman and Nasreen were both bright and highly motivated to go to college and to work in computer programming or banking. Yet neither student's family fit the profile of model minority citizenship associated with high-achieving Asian American professionals, even if they aspired to move into that class. Osman's father was a taxi-cab driver and Nasreen's parents both worked in service jobs in Wellford. But it seemed that most of these young people's parents emphasized, and modeled, the belief in hard work and education as the avenue for upward mobility and integration into economic citizenship, if not cultural be-longing, and the following chapters demonstrate how cultural citizenship is shaped by transnationalism and labor.

The workplace was a site for young people to grapple with ideas of national belonging based on neoliberal capitalism, as part of a class of young workers in low-wage positions in the service sector, as discussed in chapter 4. In their various work sites, they learned about the racialized hi-erarchy of jobs and the frustrations of having limited social capital, such as not being fluent English speakers and not having previous experience with the labor market. Some of these immigrant youth acted as mentors for those who were more recently arrived, as in the case of Amin and his older friend Ismail, who helped new students navigate their new environ-ment in the school and guided them in their pursuit of work and legal documents. These practices of youth mentorship at school and work also provided lessons in the meaning of citizenship and belonging.

The immigrant youth in this book are not just students and workers but also consumers, and even if their personal income was used less on consumer goods and more to support their family, they consumed dif-ferent forms of popular culture, as both Sara and Osman mentioned in their discussions of South Asian films and music and Hollywood movies. Nasreen was one of the students who was most engaged with U.S. news media, which she devoured to understand the politics of nation, state, and war. The media is a venue which produces a range of representations of "American" national culture, offering definitions of who is "American," what constitutes "politics," and how citizenship is performed. In chapter 4, I discuss the ways in which both American and South Asian American popular culture shaped these students' ideas about belonging in relation to consumption and subcultural citizenship.

These young people also learned about citizenship from their friends and peers in the high school, grappling with issues of racial and cultural difference in the context of local race politics. Some of them came to understand cultural citizenship through experiences of both interracial tensions and nationalist sentiment among their peers that produced expressions of multicultural, or what I call polycultural, citizenship. In some cases, these youth experienced suspicion or exclusion based on their identification as Muslim. This collective experience as "Muslim" became a key category through which they understood the state's power and issues of civil rights and cultural belonging. This is evident in the observations of Nasreen, Sara, and Amin about being singled out or viewed with suspicion for being Muslim, which was only one of many categories of belonging to which they were attached. These youth arrived in the United States shortly before or during a moment when their "Muslim" identities were highly politicized and intertwined with the War on Terror. Most of these youth did not go to the mosque, but many began to think about the political meaning of being "Muslim" and about the actions and ideal role of the state and of civil society after they migrated to the United States.

As my reflections in the book indicate, discussions of citizenship and politics also emerged in contexts in which I was involved as a volunteer with SAMTA, such as workshops or after-school activities. While most research is coproduced by the researcher and researched, in some sense, these traces of my presence are not completely erased in this account. Citizenship is, after all, embedded in social relations and micropolitics in which academics also play a role, impelled sometimes by their own histories and feelings about the subject. For example, at a workshop on the history of South Asian immigration to the United States that I participated in with other volunteers from SAMTA, a Nepali immigrant girl commented that when immigrants "don't have a green card, they do things that they don't want to do, take jobs that they don't want, or marry people they wouldn't otherwise marry." The remark about marriage was in response to a discussion of the antimiscegenation laws in the United States in the early twentieth century that led to marriages between Indian immigrant men from the Punjab and Mexican women who worked on their farms in California, at a time when immigration laws made it difficult for Indian women to migrate.[1] In the present-day context, immigration policies and citizenship law do not restrict marriages based on ethnicity or race, but these youth were aware of so-called green card marriages where immigrants enter into an agreement to marry a U.S. citizen, who is sometimes paid a sum of money and who can then sponsor them for citizenship. They understood that citizenship shaped the most personal of life decisions, such as whether to live as a family in one country or whom to marry. Citizenship, these young people were forced to realize, was a way in which the state intruded into questions of love, partnership, and family ties.

Forms of Cultural Citizenship

Based on my research, I propose that there are three ways in which South Asian Muslim immigrant youth understand and practice cultural citizenship: "flexible citizenship," "multicultural or polycultural citizenship," and "dissenting citizenship." These forms are drawn from the ways in which the young immigrants in my study expressed and practiced cultural citizenship, and build on existing theories—of flexible and multicultural citizenship—extending them but also suggesting new, critical forms, such as polycultural and dissenting citizenship, performed by these immigrant youth. These three primary modes of citizenship are not all encompassing of the range of ideas and performances of citizenship that these youth demonstrate in their everyday lives. In the following chapters, I show how practices of labor and economic citizenship, belonging in the city, cultural consumption, and subcultural affiliations are also threaded through the three major forms of cultural citizenship, lacing these categories together and connecting these experiences of citizenship to those of other urban, immigrant, working-class minority youth.

The forms of citizenship that emerged from this study are not static categories but responses that these immigrant youth simultaneously express to the condition of living a transnational adolescence. They do not exist in some kind of hierarchy of political or personal efficacy or a typology but as dynamic processes that cross overlapping spheres: social, economic, legal, and political. These practices of citizenship existed before the events of 9/11, but are heightened in certain ways for South Muslim immigrant youth because of the historical and political conjuncture in which they are living. The three major forms of cultural citizenship I discuss in the book point to the ways in which the questions facing these youth go beyond debates about cultural rights to broader questions of economic, civil, and human rights. It is important not to lose sight of the continuing salience of traditional bases of citizenship, even as they are being transformed. At the same time, the experiences and views of these youth point to the limitations of rights-based discourses and the guarantees of legal citizenship.

In the next chapter, I focus on the notion of transnational practices of flexible citizenship as they emerged in this study. In chapter 4, I discuss multicultural citizenship and propose the notion of polycultural citizenship through an analysis of work, leisure, urban citizenship, youth subcultures, and interethnic affiliations. Chapter 5 explores dissenting citizenship and the resistance, ambivalence, and alliances produced by the climate of repression and the War on Terror. Finally, chapter 6 reflects on the politics of fear and terror, complicity and solidarity, liberalism and nationalism and what has gone missing in this moment of empire.

The Rally

In the summer of 2003, a group of us from Wellford organized a rally in Prospect Square under a hazy gray sky. The idea for the rally had emerged at a meeting of our group, the South Asian Committee on Human Rights (sach), after a brutal attack that had occurred in June in New Bedford, Massachusetts. A twenty-two-year-old Indian graduate student, Saurabh Bhalerao, was attacked by two white youth while delivering pizza. His assailants beat him, burnt him with cigarettes, kicked him in the ribs until they broke, tried to stab him, and finally tied him up in the trunk of their car. Bhalerao broke free and escaped, through his sheer determination to live, surviving this post-9/11 lynching. His attackers yelled at him, "Go back to Iraq." The irony was that Bhalerao was Hindu, so this was an anti-Muslim and anti-Arab assault on a man who was neither Muslim nor Arab, something that happened quite frequently in the backlash after 9/11 that targeted many who "looked" Muslim or Arab. Indian American community organizations in the area were quick to condemn the attack, after having remained mostly silent in public for the past two years about the countless attacks on Muslim South Asians, let alone Arabs, since September 11, 2001. In fact, one Indian political organization in New England organized a joint protest in New Bedford with a chapter of the Anti-Defamation League (adl)—an organization whose anti-Arab and anti-Muslim policies, not to mention its little-known history of spying on Arab American and civil rights organizations, is belied by its misleading name and public programs emphasizing multicultural tolerance.[2]

Our group, SACH, consisted of a handful of Indian and Pakistani American students, educators, and professionals living in the Wellford area and had just formed a few months previously, built on the ongoing work of activists such as Simi (short for Naseem), a Pakistani American woman. We wanted to work on issues of civil and immigrant rights that we thought other South Asian community organizations were not adequately addressing after 9/11, and formed a coalition of immigrant and second-generation Pakistanis and Indians who were also involved with issues of human rights, communal violence, and economic justice in South Asia. Members of SACH decided to organize the public rally not just to protest the Bhalerao incident as a "hate crime," as some organizations in New Bedford were already doing, but also to highlight the ways in which the attack was implicitly sanctioned by the framing of Muslims and Arabs as the enemy, given that the United States was at war with Iraq. The mainstream media had been disturbingly silent about the incident, and our press releases to local newspapers urging them to cover the attack had not met with any response. So we agreed to call for a protest in a Wellford neighborhood where there were several South Asian families and other immigrant residents, close to the mosque, to show the larger community that we were concerned about this violence and to bring together different groups to protest the targeting of South Asians and Arabs both within and outside the United States.

I talked about the incident with Amin, Sara, and the other students; most of them had not heard about the attack. They were clearly troubled by the incident, but it had occurred outside their local orbit and since it had received no coverage in the mainstream media this was not really surprising. I also realized that it would be difficult for Muslim students such as Sara and Amin to attend the rally, not just because Sara's father would not be comfortable with it, nor because Amin worked in the dry-cleaning store all weekend, but because I knew they did not feel safe attending a public protest given the (justifiable) anxiety about political speech created by the suspension of civil liberties under the PATRIOT Act. Simi and I spoke to the young Indian American woman who worked as the outreach director of the Prospect Square mosque, Sabrena, and her sister, Asra, who happened to be a local volunteer with the Muslim American Society's Freedom Foundation, a national Muslim civil rights project. They had both agreed to speak, as had the vice-president of the mosque in the area where the hate crime had occurred. We also invited the director of

STOP THE ATTACK ON IMMIGRANTS AND PEOPLE OF COLOR!

Rally at ▓▓▓▓▓▓▓▓▓
4 pm, Sat. August 2

The assault on immigrant and civil rights continues with the detentions, "disappearances," and deportations of Arab and South Asian Americans, as well as ongoing racial profiling of African Americans and Latinos. The Patriot Act has not helped to make our communities feel safer.

We unite to protest recent hate crimes, such as the vicious anti-Muslim attack on an Indian man in New Bedford, and the anti-Muslim flier circulated by Mass. Senator Guy Glodis.

We demand our civil liberties and human rights, and an end to racial profiling and racist violence. Stop the silent war at home!

Remember to speak up before there is no one left to speak up for you!

SOUTH ASIAN COMMITTEE ON HUMAN RIGHTS (SACH)

Co-sponsored with: South Asian Center; Alliance for a Secular and Democratic South Asia; Civil Liberties Task Force, ACLU, Massachusetts; Muslim American Society–Freedom Foundation; Project Voice, American Friends Service Committee; Labor Council for Latin American Advancement, Mass. Chapter; U Mass Boston Human Rights Working Group.

For more information, contact: southasiancommitteeonhumanrights@yahoo.com

We will not be silenced! We will not be divided! We will not be removed!

Flier for rally, August 2003.

the state chapter of the American-Arab Anti-Discrimination Committee (ADC) to speak, as well as local Latino and Latina immigrant rights organizers and Palestine human rights and antiwar activists.

We worried that it was going to rain on the day of the rally and wash the protest out of the streets. The weather forecasts said there would be showers, and we were already concerned that there would not be many people willing to gather to protest attacks on South Asian and Arab Americans, even in a liberal city such as Wellford. I had been running around the city for a couple of days to get the police permit for the portable speaker, and we had been distributing fliers for a week. Our flier called for an end to attacks on immigrants and people of color and, echoing campaigns against deportation, stated, "We will not be silenced, we will not be divided, we will not be removed!"

On August 2, it was a diverse group of people who gathered in the middle of Prospect Square. The usual collection of local residents and shoppers were passing through, looking on curiously as we set up the sound system and distributed placards and signs. Women carrying bags of groceries from Caribbean and South Asian stores, groups of teenagers chatting and laughing in front of clothing and sneaker shops, smartly yet casually dressed professionals coming out of their urban condos, homeless vendors selling street newspapers, young hipsters with dyed hair— the usual mix of people in this rapidly gentrifying neighborhood where rent control had been abolished some years previously. There had been some local outcry by housing rights groups but not enough to prevent the influx of chain stores, high-priced loft apartments—and of course a Starbucks store—and the gradual flight of African American, Latino and Latina, Caribbean, and Asian American residents. The neighborhood still remained more diverse than other parts of the city, and on Fridays people streaming out of the nearby mosque could be seen strolling by, some by themselves, and others in small groups. Today, however, it felt like the only South Asians present in the plaza were those of us involved in the rally. I looked at Simi and we both hoped that the people we had spoken to at the Pakistani and Bangladeshi restaurants would come, but we both knew why they wouldn't. Fear and self-censorship had permeated South Asian, Arab, and Muslim immigrants due to the surveillance, detentions, and deportations targeting their communities since 9/11.

Sabrena and Asra, the two Muslim activist sisters, took the mike to talk about the ongoing FBI interviews of Muslim immigrants and the anxiety and distrust chilling the community that attended the mosque. This was the reason that not one of the people we had spoken to outside the mosque last Friday was present today. Syed Khan, the vice-president of a large suburban mosque on the South Shore, spoke movingly about the U.S. war in Iraq and the destruction of the historic Iraqi library, home to a much-revered collection of Islamic literature, as well as the assaults on Iraqi women and children and the humiliation of home raids and searches by the U.S. military. By the end of his talk, some people in the crowd seemed to have glistening faces and the circle of bystanders was thickening. A few women put down their grocery bags to listen, and a small cluster of teenagers joined the crowd. On the fringes, a young man wearing green sneakers and selling a socialist newspaper popped up, as if on cue. The rally was in full swing.

We had been told by the police at the Prospect Square station that if the crowd swelled and blocked the sidewalk, we would have to clear the pavement in order to comply with local ordinances that regulated public gatherings and protests. So when Simi and some of the volunteers designated to monitor the crowd noticed that people were jostling to get by, we picked up the portable speakers and started marching through the square. Tina, an Indian American college student, was walking in front next to me and began leading the chants. The women with shopping bags and a few of the teenagers dropped away, but as I turned back to look, I realized there must have been a throng of a hundred or so people who walked behind us. Simi and a few women in headscarves, including Ayesha and Mariam, were following in the rear. An older white man passing by tried to provoke the sisters by yelling offensive comments, but they ignored him and Simi took his photograph, just for the record.

I remember noticing then that there was a middle-aged white man with curly brown hair who was walking with us and who seemed to be taking a lot of photographs—of the speakers, of people in the crowd, even of the children walking with their parents—but whom I did not recognize. I did not dwell on it at the time because he did not really stand out in the throng with his NPR tote bag and scuffed jeans. I figured he was a freelance photographer, perhaps with Boston Indymedia or some independent media outlet, though Simi did not know him either. Only when a young man, who came up to Simi and me after the rally for an interview and permission to post photos on Indymedia's website, said he had no idea of the identity of the other photographer did it occur to me that the man might not have come as a supporter.[3]

Three

Transnational Citizenship: Flexibility and Control

Mohiuddin

"I came here from Bangladesh six months ago. I live with my sister and my brother here in Wellford; my parents are still in Chittagong. I have three brothers and two sisters, and I live with my older sister here. I have another brother who is in Bangladesh—he works in the civil service. My father works for Lever Brothers. My parents and other brother and sister couldn't come to the U.S., because they didn't get the visa. My sister's husband, who works here in a bank, he sponsored us, but only the three of us got the visa. I don't know why that happened. My other brother and sister are older. Maybe that's why they couldn't come. I would like to try to get a green card, so I can stay here. I don't know if my parents can come here. Yes, I miss them. It's very far, and they cannot visit us. Maybe I will go to visit them in Bangladesh, if I get a green card. Or maybe I will wait till I finish school and get a job.

"When I was in Chittagong, I saw some American movies. So I thought that maybe America would be like that. But when I came here, I thought the country is not too beautiful. Why not? I don't know. It's okay. I live behind the apartments on Lakeshore Avenue; my cousins live in the big building on Lakeshore. I think

there are some Bangladeshis in our building, but I'm not sure. There are people from India, China, Haiti; not too many Americans live there. After school, I work at the Star Market. My brother works there too; my sister doesn't have a job.

"I know about the war in Afghanistan. My sister wears a hijab, so some people said some things to her after September 11. It was at the train station. I wasn't there, but she said she feels afraid. I feel very scared because I am a Muslim. I see what they say about Muslims on TV, and I think it's wrong. Something is wrong in how they see us and what the government is doing to Muslims.

"I think of myself as a Muslim, and also I am Bangladeshi. Not American. I don't have an American passport. I don't think people think I am American. Sometimes they say I am Pakistani, Bangladeshi. But many times, they don't know Bangladesh. I know some people from India who are Bengali. They speak the same language, but their food, it is a little different. I don't know that restaurant in Prospect Square—Royal East it's called? It is Bengali? I think my sister's husband knows it. I have never been to a Bengali restaurant here.

"I like the school. It is much easier than in my country. I like math, biology, physics. After school, I would like to study physics, but I think I will just get a job. I want my parents to come here. I wish my brother and sister could come here. My brother who is married in Chittagong, he just had a baby. I don't know when I'll see her."

Zeenat

"I came to this country in January this year, just eight months ago. I'm fifteen years old. When I came to the United States, it was winter, and I never saw winter like this because in my country, it is not so cold. So I was not happy then! And when I came here, I missed my country. Everybody was speaking in English in the school and I never used English in my country, so I was very, very nervous. When I went home, I told everybody, I can't understand English so how am I gonna learn? And then I went to the bathroom and cried and cried—what am I gonna do if I cannot speak English? Then my father, like, gave me power and he said, 'Don't think like that, you can do it, you can do it.' And then I got a job in the McDonald's, so by speaking and speaking I learned some English. And then I saw TV everyday, and my father was right: I learned. I love biology—it is my favorite subject. And after I graduate from

high school, I want to go to college, and I want to do something in science, like, be a doctor or work in a pharmacy.

"My father came here to make extra money, for our education, for a better life. My uncles are here in Wellford; all my family is here from my mother's side. They all live in the Lakeshore apartments. First we lived in Lakeshore too, then we moved here, to Prospect Square. Yes, there are many Pakistanis in Lakeshore. My father and brother go to the mosque; it's pretty close. I do namaaz [prayers] at home. I don't like it that my religion has to be separate from school here; I would like things about Islam in the school. But I have different friends here, some Indian, some Haitian, some Puerto Rican, some from Pakistan, Bangladesh, Afghanistan. What do I think of myself, as black or white? I don't know, in India, we don't use black and white so I'm not sure.

"Our family is from Marori in Gujarat. There are lots of Hindus and also Muslims in the village. My father's family is all from Marori. I have many Muslim friends in school, from India, Pakistan, Bangladesh, Afghanistan. We all mix in the school with Haitians, Spanish people. In school here, we wear jeans or pants, jeans and T-shirts. I like to wear jeans! I never wore jeans in my country, but here I just like it. After September 11, the Pakistani girls who wear salwar kameez, they heard some Americans say some bad things about them. I heard that in New York, if someone wears salwar kameez, they hit them and fight them. Everybody hate the Muslims. I think they don't have any idea about the Muslims or Islam. Even in the school, I heard that some guys tried to push Farid, the Gujarati boy. There were two guys—they are being punished by the school. The teachers try to tell them, don't say anything wrong about the Muslims; September 11 has nothing to do with all Muslims. What do I think of the war there, in Afghanistan? I think it's wrong: they didn't attack the United States; they didn't bomb on this country, right? So why we are bombing on their country?

"Life here is hard and different. In my country, the women don't work and here you have to work. And here, life is so busy. My aunt worked in a company, but she got laid off. And my uncle works in a company, but I don't know what kind. They live in New Jersey; they've been there for twenty years. My father worked in a bookstore in Marori and now he works at Whole Foods store. My brother used to work there too but now he works on the weekends, all night, in a factory. He gets tired but he says he makes more money if he works at night. I work at the Dunkin Donuts, and I know other Indian girls who work there too. Fatima and her sister work there too. Ismail is my cousin, *but he is in a different Dunkin Donuts. I go from school to work every day, and on the weekend I work six hours on Saturday and on Sunday. But sometimes, I watch Hindi movies. I get them from the Indian store—Sara's uncle's store. And sometimes I go to the movies with my sister, or my relatives. I know some of the families in Prospect Square, I see them at Eid, we get together and have a party. But we don't have parties late in the night, and we don't go outside alone at night, like, go to English movies alone, with friends. We watch movies at home from the video store, and we play* antakshari *[singing game]. We sing Hindi movie songs. It's fun!*

"I learned about Islam from my father. What does it mean to be Muslim? Like in Islam, we shouldn't fight with each other; we can't say something about another religion, something wrong about other religions. We don't drink wine, and then everyday you have to pray to God, like don't forget to pray. But after September 11, I think Americans hate the Muslims, or the American government hates the Muslims, like they think all Muslims are the same, all Muslims are fighting them, or they hate the Muslim countries. I heard that George Bush is going to get some Muslim people to leave the country, like he is going to send them away, even if they didn't do anything, even if they have green cards.

"We got the green card after four months of coming here, and after five years we are going to become citizens. I want to be a citizen because if I am going to live my whole life here, I want to go to India easily; I want to vote for president. For me, still I'll always be Indian; it is the most important thing. Next most important is being, like, Muslim. Then, being Gujarati."

Ismail

"My relatives came to America twenty years ago; both my father's sisters are here, and they live in Medford. My father works in a factory—he makes car parts. My aunt's daughter is a lawyer, and the other is doing a Ph.D. degree, I'm not sure in what. I went to school in Dunbury for two months, and then I transferred to Wellford. My family is from Valsar, in Gujarat, and there are a lot of Gujarati people in these two buildings—they're all from Valsar. Now, there are a lot of people coming from villages around there. There is a lot of industrial stuff happening in Valsar so there are jobs, computer stuff and other things, but a lot of people want to come here because of the education.

"When I came, I was in the sixth standard, I was about to go into the seventh standard. When I got to America I was a bit shocked, I was confused; I didn't *know how I'd do in my studies. And no one here knew me. My brother came here too, and he is doing his second bachelor's, in information technology. My sister had already been to the high school for a year, so she told me about everything. She had been to* SAMTA *meetings too. She told me, You should do this, you should do that. And now all these new students are coming to the school, so they come to me in the same way, ask me questions. I've been at the school for four years, so I know everyone, and everyone knows me. So if there's a problem, they come talk to me. I take them upstairs to the tutoring center. I tell them how to get a work permit so they can get a job, help them fill out the forms.*

"We would like to come more to the SAMTA *meetings, but we have to leave school right after it ends and go to work. I do a phone card business with my brother, where I sell phone cards to these Indian stores and convenience stores, and I also work at the university doing tech support. One of my friends is working at Dunkin' Donuts; the other one has left and he's now working with his father in a store. The other boys—Pakistani boys work at security jobs, and they work from five to twelve at night. So we don't really have the time to do things: every one's busy with their own thing; no one has the time. We don't have the time to go to the Gujarati events in Billtown, or to do the* dandiya raas *[Gujarati folk dance]. Actually, it's been five years since I've done the dandiya raas, I've lost the habit. I'm just occupied with work, and with helping my mother. My sister's not at home much now since she's at college, so I have to do the housework, shopping, laundry. So there's not much time, but I listen to music and watch films for fun, mostly.*

"I'm thinking that after I finish school, maybe I'll go to India for six months and then I'll come back here for six months and work. Maybe I'll buy a gas station or a convenience store. I might do a business with my uncle, who works in McDonald's. My auntie works in a laundry. They're not very educated, but they have some money to invest. Actually, the thing is I'd like to stay here but this place doesn't need me more than my country, because in India there's a lot of poor people who need our help and our education. If we study here, then we'll go back to our country, open up some kind of company or something. That'll be really good for them there because our economy is really down right now, you know. So most people are unemployed in India right now. If I at least learn some computer stuff and my brother and me open up a company there, and one here, that'll be a great thing because people can work and they can come here. They can support their whole family.

"I don't really mind if I call myself Indian or American, as long as I feel comfortable with the people. So I'm going to become an American citizen next

month. You're not a citizen yet? How come, if you've been here seventeen years? I got my green card four and a half years ago so now I can apply for citizenship. My relatives were U.S. citizens, so that's why they called us here. They've been here twenty-two years. I have relatives in Florida, and my aunt is in London, my mother's sister. I think I'd like to go to California to see what it is. I like Wellford, but maybe I'd like to live there.

"Here, in my building—it's very international. There are Chinese people, Korean, Cambodian, Moroccan, black. In the last building, there are more blacks; in the middle, there are more Indian. Now there are more Indian families filling up this building. In the last building, people say there used to be shooting and cars being stolen, but now it's getting better. It's because of drug dealing; that's why you used to see police coming here night and day. It never happens in this building, because there are cameras everywhere. You know where you came into the building? There's a camera following you from the parking lot. This building is private, but the other ones are government buildings. Here, the manager lives upstairs, and if there's a problem, there's a girl downstairs you can talk to. Two or three times a year, there's a party downstairs, and all the people from the building come and there are games.

"But for blacks and others who live here, it's not a problem that we are Muslim. I had just come here to this country when I met a black person and he said, 'For me, it makes no difference that you are a Muslim, I don't care. It's crazy, what these white people are doing to Muslims after September 11.' That's the problem with the Bush administration. If they wanted to, they could try a nonviolent solution over there, in Afghanistan. Jesse Jackson came to our school one time, when there were people from the International Center and some lawyers and Muslims talking to us after September 11. And he was talking about peace and saying 'It's not right for the American government to go crazy after September 11; you should first understand what is happening in other countries.' I've talked to some friends of mine about the war, and they said this is all wrong—the American government is just causing more violence and we don't want this war—we should solve the problem peacefully. Whoever's done this, they should go and get them. Why are they bombing people and blaming all these other countries? See, if bin Laden has killed them, just get bin Laden. Why are they bombing Afghanistan and killing innocent people? They are starving there; they're dying anyway, and they are killing them. My black, white, Spanish friends: they all agree with that."

Flexible Citizenship

Mohiuddin, Zeenat, and Ismail all spoke about feelings of belonging in relation to several nation-states, such as India and Bangladesh; regional or linguistic identifications, such as Gujarati; and localities, such as the villages or towns of Valsar and Chittagong. Their stories moved between these places, threaded together by strands of family and desires for work and education. Their desires for U.S. citizenship and permanent residency were not seen as conflicting with their affiliations with their home nation-states but layered in a flexible understanding, embedded in mobility and migration. "Flexible citizenship" was the form of cultural citizenship most consistently evident in these young people's stories about their experiences of migration and citizenship. As a concept, it is used to describe the emergence of new uses of citizenship by migrants in response to the conditions of transnationalism, specifically, the use of transnational links to provide political or material resources not available within a single nation-state, as has been demonstrated for affluent Chinese migrants by Aihwa Ong (1999).[1] Saskia Sassen points out that practices of citizenship are no longer based in the arena of the nation-state alone, as the national state has been transformed, but also extend to "international arenas." Actors now make claims that express what some call "postnational citizenship," which is partly outside the national realm, or "denationalized citizenship," based on a transformation of the nation itself. Both forms coexist as the national state continues to be significant (Sassen 2004, 190–91).

Flexible citizenship, in my view, is a manifestation of both postnational and denationalized citizenship, for it emerges in response to changes in the institution of citizenship within nation-states as well as to shifts in power on national and global scales. This concept is different from traditional notions of dual citizenship, which imply an actual legal status as citizen of two nation-states; in contrast, flexible citizenship leaves open questions of national loyalty or strategic uses of citizenship status for legal and economic purposes. It is a form of citizenship that responds to the conditions of globalization and U.S. domination, although not in the romanticized sense of Hardt's and Negri's (2000, 399) "multitude" of immigrants resisting empire by crossing national borders. But it is also true that empire needs the labor power of the mobile multitude, so flexible citizenship has emerged in tandem with the flow of labor across national borders that benefits the U.S. economy, in some cases facilitating labor migration and in other cases developed strategically by migrants moving between different labor markets.

Ong (2006, 122) extended her work on flexible citizenship to develop the concept of "latitudinal citizenship" embedded in "horizontal spaces of market rights" and emerging from ethnic networks and labor relations that span national borders under neoliberal capitalism, thus tying together an analysis of Asian American communities and global capitalism. Ong (2006, 19) argues, "The neoliberal exception thus pries open the seam of sovereignty and citizenship, generating successive degrees of insecurity for low-skilled citizens and migrants who will have to look beyond the state for the safeguarding of their rights." As such, flexible citizenship does not only resist or only serve global capitalism but often manages to do both, as the stories of the youth above illustrate. They migrated to the United States with their families to try to avail themselves of perceived economic and educational opportunities, but ended up being low-wage workers in the service sector or in light manufacturing—with the exception of Ismail, whose family was slightly more affluent and educated, but whose entrepreneurial aspirations were still a distant vision.

Despite the interest in transnational movements, the liberatory potential of "postnational citizenship" (Soysal 1996) or "global citizenship" (Hardt and Negri 2000) remains an abstract ideal, given that individual and collective rights still remain largely tied to territorially bounded nation-states (Shafir 2004). Political movements, too, continue to address their claims for immigrant and civil rights to the nation-state as the guarantor of rights, as evident in the mass immigrant marches across the United States in spring 2006, in response to the proposed "immigration reform" bill, H.R. 3477. The American flag–waving segments of the rallies included undocumented (mostly Latino and Latina) immigrants proclaiming that they were "good, hardworking" immigrants desiring legalization so they could have a piece of the American Dream. This is perhaps a strategic rhetoric, but South Asian Muslim immigrant youth too understood that their transnational vision for mobility and collective advancement, as well as re-creation of family ties, was necessarily tied to formal citizenship and legal belonging in the nation-state. Mohiuddin's family was one of several that had been torn apart by immigration regulations of entry and citizenship, and so all these immigrant youth acknowledged the importance of nation-state membership in defining who could travel, work, or vote.

About half of these immigrant youth had green cards already; the remaining were a mix of citizens and undocumented immigrants. Nearly all of them desired a U.S. passport because of what they perceived as its civic and also economic benefits. A few, such as Zeenat, said that they wanted U.S. citizenship in order to vote, and several said that they wanted to be able to travel freely between the United States and South Asia, to be mobile in work and family life. After 9/11, of course, naturalization seemed to become less a matter of choice for immigrants—particularly Muslim, South Asian, and Arab Americans—than a hoped-for shield against the abuses of civil rights. In fact, some students were surprised that I had not obtained citizenship yet in the fall of 2001 and wanted to know why it had taken me so long. Ismail, for example, was concerned during my conversation with him that I did not yet have this vital document. I had to explain that by the time my own parents became naturalized and could sponsor me for a green card, I had already advanced into the category of adult children over twenty-one years, a low priority for permanent residency. Had I not been on a student visa while in graduate school, I may have had to leave the United States myself. I finally applied for U.S. citizenship after 9/11. This reflexive discussion of citizenship momentarily shifted my relationship with these young immigrants, as they perceived themselves to have advanced a small step farther on this legal road to official belonging to the state, and worried about my own vulnerability.

However, Mohiuddin seemed to suggest that even if he managed to get a U.S. passport, he would still not be perceived by others as American, pointing to the fissure between legal and cultural citizenship. Nearly all these youth understood flexible citizenship to be a form of cultural citizenship, shaped by racial boundaries that distinguished them from "Americans" as much as by legal and economic boundaries. All three of the young people above critiqued the scapegoating of Muslims after 9/11 as a form of collective punishment for the Twin Tower attacks and pointed to the state as responsible for profiling Muslims, as Mohiuddin and Zeenat observed of "the government." Ismail was one of several youth who also thought that waging war on Afghanistan as retribution for the 9/11 attacks was unjust and would only intensify the spiral of violence, an issue I will return to in discussing dissenting citizenship in chapter 5. These observations suggest a transnational analysis focusing not just on citizen and human rights within the United States, or India and Bangladesh, but also in other nation-states. Thus these young immigrants' experiences of flexible citizenship were necessarily layered with questions of work, class mobility, religious identity, war, dissent, and civil and human rights.

For these immigrant youth, flexible citizenship is part of a carefully planned, long-term, family-based strategy of migration in response to economic pressures on those living in, or at the edge of, the middle class in South Asia. Legal citizenship and immigration documents were understood by these youth as artifacts created by the state that they needed in order to move across national borders and to be reunited with their families, but they were also the source of disruption of family ties and cleavages of emotional bonds. Mohiuddin was living with his brother and sister but without his parents, who were still living in Chittagong, Bangladesh, and he could not visit them until he got his green card. There was some sorrow in his statement that his brother in Chittagong had had a baby girl, but he did not know when he would be able to see this new member of his own family. In some cases, these immigrant youth had fathers who had migrated alone many years earlier, as in the case of Amin and Sara. At least three students, Nasreen, Osman, and Faisal, had been separated from their fathers for twelve to fifteen years and so had basically spent their childhood years without them. For Nasreen's father, migration was supposedly an investment in his children's education, first and foremost, but this aspiration was ironically undermined in some cases by the difficult process of migration. For example, Faisal, who was from Pakistan, said his father had left Peshawar for the United States right after he was born and worked to support him and his family, returning only occasionally to visit, until their U.S. visas were approved. By the time Faisal came to the United States, however, his older brother was too old to enroll in high school and had to struggle to get a GED and find a job with his limited English skills.

Flexible citizenship is a strategy driven by family and based on family relationships, which are used to sponsor relatives for permanent residency and then citizenship, but it is also a strategy that divides and disperses families and radically alters the meaning of kinship ties. These youth seemed to take these transnational family arrangements as a fact of their lives and did not speak readily in public about the impact of these separations and reunions, but they did speak longingly of the friends and familiar places they had left behind, as Mohiuddin's and Zeenat's reflections suggest. Riyaz, a Gujarati boy who had just come to the United States when I met him in fall 2002, spoke with anguish and almost disbelief at his uprooting from his village, his companions, his daily life. He hardly spoke English when he first came and did not engage much in discussions at SAMTA workshops, but when we asked students to share an image they associated with the places they had left behind, he simply drew a broken heart on a sheet of paper. A Pakistani boy scribbled "India" and "America" next to each of the jagged halves of Riyaz's heart. Riyaz's uncle in Gujarat was an agent who helped people migrate to the Persian Gulf states from their hometown of Valsar, underscoring that the United States is just one node for labor migrants in the vast Gujarati diaspora (e.g., see Ho 2004).

There is a strategic dimension to flexible citizenship embedded in these histories of migration and dispersal, but there is also an affective dimension rooted in a geography of loss, sorrow, and memory, and in feelings of alienation or disorientation. The ambivalence and seemingly emotional responses of these immigrant youth suggest an implicit resistance, perhaps, to the narrative of migration as leading inevitably to self-fulfillment, achievement, and the American Dream, as will become clearer in chapter 4. There is, at some level, an ambivalence about the biopolitics of migration, or the ways in which migrants are "a form of human life upon which the sovereignty of states, of ethnic/religious communities . . . can be performed and 'natured'"; if migrant lives are considered anomalous, drawing on Giorgio Agamben's work, they are also the "spaces of exception" that help define notions of what is "'normal' citizenship and community life" (cited in Hansen and Steputat 2005, 35–36).

It is ironic that South Asian immigrants, and Asian Americans more generally, are held up in the United States as model minority citizens who embody exemplary "family values," presumably promoting stable family units with two parents, while one could also view these immigrants as the model citizens of global capitalism who are willing to scatter family members across the globe and separate parents from their children. These are the actual family values that the globalized free market engenders, even as "broken families" are paradoxically denounced by the Right. Immigrants rely on family ties and on re-creating extended families through chain migration and citizenship, especially as the decline in state-sponsored social services or inability to provide financial security, due to global economic restructuring and the pressures of World Bank and International Monetary Fund (IMF) policies on regions such as South Asia, drives people to seek new modes of livelihood and reshape family models (Cole and Durham 2007, 13). There are other, complex shifts in "cultural values" that the often reductionist debate about immigration and immigrant cultures in the United States fails to note. For example, Ismail spoke of how the pressure of trying to juggle school and work meant that he had little time to socialize with other South Asian friends, let alone participate in cultural events such as "traditional" folk dances. Zeenat spoke of the difficulties of learning what it means to work outside the home, which she did not have to do in India; she noted a shift in gender roles in an immigrant community where middle-class women may not have traditionally worked for wage labor outside the home—although this is changing in India—and where it is now common for immigrant girls and women to work because of economic pressures in the United States. These examples show how "tradition" in this South Asian Muslim immigrant community, which is perceived as conservative by some measures, is actually flexible in arenas linked to work and citizenship, challenging Orientalist discourses about immigrant traditions or "Muslim cultures" as somehow outside of the influence of global capital and media. As Jennifer Cole and Deborah Durham point out, "The changing world economy presses parents to seek new ways of preparing their children or of drafting their own parents into new forms of flexible labor" (2007, 6). Families adapt their cultural practices and ideals to the demands of neoliberal globalization, showing how "culture" in immigrant communities is enmeshed with practices of neoliberalism. Transnational labor networks and ethnic ties draw these immigrant youth and families into what Aihwa Ong calls "lateral spaces or latitudes," spanning national borders that promote ethnicization but also a persistent self-disciplining and flexibility in response to the demands of the market (2006, 121–23).

Working-class South Asian migrants, too, seem to be enacting a version of flexible citizenship, if at greater cost and with fewer immediate benefits to themselves and their children than for elite migrants (Ong 1999). Some of these youth in Wellford, such as Ismail, imagine their lives spanning national borders and speak of returning to South Asia in the future, at least temporarily, once they have become U.S. citizens and perhaps after their parents have retired there. Transnational marriages and social ties are common in their families, but this does not mean they happen easily or smoothly. For example, one of the first conversations I had with Ahmed, an older Gujarati Muslim man who worked as a bagger at the Whole Foods grocery store near the North Wellford apartments, was about how he could bring his children to the United States from India. I grew to know Ahmed the most of the three Gujarati immigrant men who were working there at the time, because he was friendly and always happy to have a little chat to break the monotony of his work. These exchanges with the Muslim immigrant workers in the aisles of Whole Foods were always instructive, not just of the lives of the men whose children I was interviewing at the high school, but of relations of production, consumption, and labor and processes of migration that led to their daily packing of expensive organic groceries in shopping bags that I took home. One day, standing among the rows of gleaming apples and shiny pears, Ahmed began asking me about how to obtain U.S. citizenship and where he could take English classes to pass the language test for naturalization. Ahmed only had a green card and was anxious to get his U.S. passport so that he could sponsor the immigration visas of his four children still living in Gujarat, who were already past the age of twenty-one years (so it could be several years before they would be allowed to join him). In the meantime, Ahmed kept up his cheerful face at the grocery store and watched Hindi and Gujarati programs at home on the satellite channel he had just obtained. Every time I saw him at the store, he reminded me that I should subscribe to the channel so that I could watch Indian news on television.

Ahmed planned to return to Gujarat after he became a citizen and once he was eligible for Social Security benefits, so that he could spend part of the year in India and return to Wellford in the summer. This was a common pattern of transnational living, especially for older South Asian immigrants who decided to retire on two continents, shuttling between warm weather in South Asia and children in the United States. Yet Ahmed was separated from his children, and I could feel his almost palpable longing to finally be reunited with them. Ahmed's story was the reverse of the growing pattern of parents living in India while their children are settled overseas, or of elderly parents who come to live with their adult children in the United States, which has led to new programs such as old-age homes in Indian cities and support services for retired parents in India as well as in the United States that allow the elderly to be "self-reliant" (Lamb 2007, 133).[2] Globalization has altered not only what it means to be "young" but also "elderly," as traditional models of aging and intergenerational relations are shaped by "new forms of biopolitics" and neoliberal conceptions of individualism (Cole and Durham 2007, 2)— even as these traditional ideals were always challenged by internal migration of the rural poor to seek work in urban areas in India, dividing and dispersing families. For middle-class South Asian families, or those struggling to stay middle class, global migration and flexible citizenship highlight the tensions in intimate relations generated by reconfigured relations between the state, global capital, labor, and family.

Despite their struggles to realize flexible citizenship, some of the immigrant youth I spoke to still expressed hope that they could create the transnational future they imagined, for themselves and their families, a future that is curtailed by restrictions in both home and host nation-states and is contested in debates about national allegiance in both places. For example, Ismail wanted to set up a transnational hi-tech business so that he could live part-time in Gujarat and part-time in the United States while supporting his parents. He saw this as a development strategy for diasporic Indians to fulfill their obligations to the home nation-state, using the benefits of U.S. citizenship. Official practices of flexible citizenship for the benefit of home nations has been encouraged by South Asian nation-states, such as the Indian government, which developed policies to encourage Indian citizens living overseas, or Non-Resident Indians (NRIS), to invest in the Indian economy, especially as foreign currency reserves were declining in the early 1990s (Sharma and Gupta 2006, 26). Persons of Indian Origin (PIO) cards were created in 1999 as an interim category of flexible citizenship that could be purchased for three hundred dollars and conferred the right to acquire property but not the right to vote; this is not available, however, to persons of Indian origin in Pakistan and Bangladesh, thus excluding Muslim populations who were displaced by the partition but are not officially recognized as part of the Indian diaspora.[3] The Constitution of India still did not allow dual citizenship at the time this book went to press, but in 2006, the government introduced the Overseas Citizenship of India (OCI) scheme to allow foreign citizens easier travel to India and limited economic rights (but no voting rights), continuing to exclude citizens of Pakistan and Bangladesh.[4]

In winter 2003, while I was visiting New Delhi, the Indian government hosted the first Pravasi Bharatiya Divas, a festival to celebrate the Indian diaspora from Fiji to South Africa and, primarily, to publicize the achievements of economically and politically powerful NRIS. I was struck by the fact that this celebration of the successes of flexible citizenship performed by Indian elites had little room for recognizing the struggles of those who were also a significant part of the Indian diaspora, such as guest workers in the Gulf or labor migrants in the United States and Europe. In fact, one could play on the title of the event and argue that this was a show-case for "diva citizenship," drawing on Lauren Berlant's (1997, 223) term for celebratory performances of citizenship. While Berlant focuses on dramatic testimonials by oppressed minorities, this diva citizenship uses the same form (first-person testimonials) but for a different purpose; the festival was staged as a spectacle feting the most successful "model minor-ity" NRIS and designed to court economic support for India's role in the global economy.

The then prime minister, Atal Vajpayee, "also cautioned against divided loyalties" in the diaspora, advising NRIS to be "loyal to their country of adoption" and suggesting that diasporic Indians should express their alle-giance to India economically but without risking accusations of not being fully loyal citizens of their countries of residence.[5] This was of course, in the post-9/11 context of the global War on Terror, when Indian Muslims in the United States (and later, Britain) were among those suspected of having transnational ties and political affiliations, and being profiled, and Indian Sikhs were also being assaulted, yet this was not a cause the Indian state was willing to take up. One reason for the lack of attention to the struggles of Indian Muslims abroad was probably that the ruling Hindu nationalist Bharatiya Janata Party (BJP) government at the time was us-ing the Bush administration's campaign against "Islamic terrorism" to bol-ster its own campaign of targeting Muslim minorities in India (Koshy 2003). An Indian critic pointed out that "the irony of Mr. Vajpayee's advice . . . is that it comes from the head of a political parivar [referring to the Sangh Parivar, or network of Hindu right-wing organizations of which the BJP is a member] which has long questioned the right of reli-gious minorities to their own unique culture in this country."[6] While on the one hand, the Indian government was issuing PIO cards to wealthy diasporic Indians, on the other hand, news media reported a plan to de-velop identity cards to identify and deport "illegal settlers" from Pakistan and Bangladesh to combat "terror threats" to the nation, using language remarkably similar to that of the U.S. government after 9/11.[7] So the chal-lenges to national belonging for South Asian Muslims, Indian Muslims in particular, need to be considered on both sides of the transnational terrain in which citizenship is claimed and contested, in the United States and also in South Asia itself. This is the historical context in which these youth and their families migrated from South Asia, and which probably played some role in shaping their responses to the profiling of Muslims in the United States after 9/11.

Practices of Flexible Citizenship

Extending the work already done on flexible citizenship, I found the transnational affiliations of these immigrant youth were based on at least two specific, and related, processes of "self-making and being-made" (Ong 1999), in relation to different nation-states. First, their everyday identification with India or Pakistan was based largely on transnational popular culture: on Bollywood (Hindi) films, South Asian television serials, and Hindi music that they accessed through video, DVDs, satellite TV, and the Internet. Many of the South Asian boys, for example, regularly surfed the Internet for Hindi film and music websites either at home or on computers in the International Center. Jamila, a Bangladeshi immigrant girl, talked of visiting Internet chat rooms for diasporic Bangladeshi youth as well as youth in Bangladesh, who are part of a transnational Bangladeshi community. She commented, Bangladeshis "in London, they're like, they're almost the same as me." Some of the girls regularly watched episodes of Hindi TV serials on DVD or cable TV, and everyone watched Indian films on video. Sara was a fan of *Kusum*, the Hindi TV serial, and knew all the details of the intricate family and social relationships of the extended families in the serial. These films conjured up an imagined India that was both remote and close, since she and other youth were themselves living in extended or "joint" families reconstituted in the United States, though these were now spread across apartment buildings and city blocks.

The home is an important site for consuming South Asian popular culture, since few of these youth had the money or time to go to movie theaters or other public spaces of cultural consumption, with the exception perhaps of shopping malls, where they strolled and browsed with their friends. In almost all of the homes I visited, large-screen televisions and entertainment centers seemed to be the point of pride in the living room, and some households also subscribed to AT&T's recently established satellite link with South Asian Zee-TV. It became apparent that national and transnational identities were explored and fashioned by these youth in private spaces, through the consumption of popular culture. Néstor García Canclini (2001, 5) argues that "for many men and women, especially youth, the questions specific to citizenship, such as how we inform ourselves and who represents our interests, are answered more often than not through private consumption of commodities and media offerings than through the abstract rules of democracy or through participation in discredited legal organizations." Flexible citizenship is constructed by these youth through popular culture practices, which is important to consider in the lives of immigrant youth and fills a gap in some of the existing literature (e.g., Ong 1999).

Second, flexible citizenship is necessarily intertwined with labor and education, issues that are interrelated for working-class, immigrant youth and that I will explore more in the next chapter. These youth have come to the United States with their families as migrant workers, in some sense, and work in low-wage, part-time jobs in retail and fast food restaurants. As such, these young workers provide the flexible labor that the globalized U.S. economy relies on for maximum profit, but they also find that the opportunities available to migrant workers through immigration and citizenship policies discriminate between U.S.- and foreign-born workers. These young people entered the labor market to support their families economically and saw education in the United States as an avenue to a "better life," as Zeenat remarked, expressing the same aspirations for class mobility that had driven their parents' migration across national borders. This "aspirational citizenship," a desire for economic advancement tied to migration strategies, is evident in the hopes and career ambitions of Mohiuddin, Ismail, and Zeenat. Yet these aspirations for upward mobility are tempered by their awareness of the many constraints in realizing their goals—their daily struggles to try to keep up in school, improve their English, find even an entry-level service job with low wages, learn about the American college system, and find financial aid to go to college.

It became clear to me that these young immigrants thought about citizenship in ways that were themselves flexible, shifting, and contextual. In some cases, religious identity actually prompted youth to think of themselves as belonging to the United States or at least identifying with its concerns, if not identifying as American. Ismail said to me in the fall of 2001, "Islam teaches [us that] what country you live in, you should support them . . . See, if I live in America, I have to support America, I cannot go to India." Interestingly, he seemed to be connecting Islam to a notion of territorialized cultural citizenship based on loyalty to the nation-state of residence. This, of course, is the same boy who said that he ultimately wanted to return to India and support its economic development, but his statements about national allegiances are not as contradictory as they first appear. Perhaps they reflect a consumerist approach of selectively drawing on various models of citizenship as appropriate, but they also reflect a deeper, strategic sensibility about belonging in relation to the nation-state. Ismail was able to frame his relationship to Islam in a way that would help him think through questions of loyalty at a moment in the United States at which Muslims were being framed as noncitizens *because* of a particular suspicion of Muslim identity as superseding all other national identities and loyalties. Ismail, instead, seemed to be drawing on the Koran and using Islam to counter this technology of exclusion and to support a flexible definition of citizenship. In his view, being Muslim required loyalty to the nation-state of residence regardless of national origins. His comments are one strand in a complex debate among Muslim Americans about the compatibility, and even centrality, of a new "American Islam" and of participation in American public and political life to the "evolving international umma," or worldwide Muslim community (Leonard 2003, 101). While Ismail did not speak directly to these larger debates about the "relationship between state, society, and religion" among American Muslims (see Mattson 2003, 199), he seemed to voice a pragmatic and also sophisticated understanding of citizenship as necessarily mobile, drawing on different ideological resources to respond to the exigencies of diverse moments and places.

Flexibility and Control

Flexible citizenship is clearly an economic and family strategy for these immigrant youth and also has a cultural, and affective, dimension as these youth try to manage diverse national affiliations and feelings of belonging and alienation. Flexible citizenship is a response to the conditions of immigration and relocation of their families, and it forces these youth to deal with the displacement and re-creation of their communities, and encounters with strangeness and familiarity. But after 9/11, flexible citizenship can be a tenuous or even potentially dangerous strategy for these South Asian Muslim youth, for transnational ties and shifting national allegiances are precisely what have come under scrutiny for Muslim Americans by the state in the era of the PATRIOT Act. After 9/11, ties to Muslim communities and organizations outside the nation cast Muslim immigrants as potential security threats to the United States, even if only through transnational businesses or charities, or at least as immigrants whose political loyalties were suspect. "The privilege of transnational identification," according to Sally Howell and Andrew Shryock (2003, 445), "has been, for Arabs in Detroit, the first casualty of the War on Terror." Travel across national borders; money transfers, including donations to Islamic charities; and transnational businesses and organizations have all been monitored and used to detain Arab and Muslim immigrants, as the state has broadened its definitions of involvement with "terrorism" in the PATRIOT Act.[8] In late 2001, U.S. Customs launched "Operation Green Quest" to seize currency and cashier's checks being sent out of the country by Arabs and Muslims, supposedly to fund terrorist groups, including those that had never threatened the United States.[9] Small businesses owned by South Asian and Arab immigrants in the United States were investigated on the suspicion that they were funding "militant" groups, leading to nationwide raids of Pakistani-owned jewelry stores and sweeps of Indian-owned convenience stores in California in 2002, although none of these were reported to be channeling funds to terrorists.[10] The impact of all of this, of course, is that Muslim and Arab entrepreneurs and workers have suffered economically for taking advantage of their transnational networks.

After 9/11, the Bush administration shut down "three of the largest Muslim charities in the United States, on the charge that they provided 'material support' for terrorist activity without a criminal charge or hearing" (Cole 2003, 76). The government used the International Emergency Economic Powers Act to ban all transactions with the charities and freeze millions of dollars, as President Bill Clinton had done in 1995 to block several political organizations in the Middle East, including ten Palestinian groups who were critical of the "peace process" (Cole 2003, 777). This selective clamping down of transnational flows of funds is clearly political, as it has restricted the donations that many Muslim and Arab Americans send to support relief for those suffering from war and occupation in Palestine and other zones of conflict in which the United States has strategic interests. The flow of money to the Middle East is now carefully monitored, and funding from overseas to organizations, businesses, and mosques in the United States is suspect, creating an additional layer of frustration and anxiety for Muslim, South Asian, and Arab American entrepreneurs, political advocates, and religious clerics. In Dearborn, Michigan, which is home to 30,000 Arab Americans and was subject to intense surveillance after 9/11, an imam commented tellingly, "The mosques that are suffering are the ones that receive support from the Middle East. Praise God, we do not receive support from outside this country" (cited in Howell and Shryock 2003, 454).

There is also greater fear among Muslim and Arab immigrants about sending money to support family members in their home countries, particularly through money-transfer agencies run by Muslim Americans. It is not just immigrant families in the United States who have been affected by the War on Terror, but also families overseas who depend on economic remittances from relatives working in the United States and, on a larger scale, their homeland economies. For example, one estimate suggests that at least 95 percent of Somali immigrants in the United States send money home, and over 40 percent of war-torn Somalia's GDP is from remittances from Somalis abroad (Nguyen 2005, 34). The family ties, immigration networks, financial connections, and political links that constitute Muslim and Arab diasporas have been constrained by monitoring and repression (Howell and Shryock 2003, 455). Increasingly, diaspora is not just viewed by these communities as a site of hoped-for cultural and economic flexibility and opportunity but a zone of increased state suspicion and repression.

According to Enseng Ho (2004), one way to describe the politics of the War on Terror is in terms of a confrontation between diaspora and empire. Ho argues that there is a tension between the transnational social, political, economic, and religious networks established by diasporic communities, on the one hand, and the imperial forces that try to suppress transnational political movements viewed as oppositional, on the other. Ho points out that diasporas often emerge from histories of Western colonization, trade, marriage and kinship, and religious ties that stretch across national borders and that bind together communities of resistance to empire. These diasporic communities form a context in which opposition to empire can be organized, in the case of al-Qaeda, through a transnational structure that developed over 500 years (Ho 2004, 221). It is the awareness of these transnationally structured movements that underlies the U.S. government's suspicion and monitoring of transnational economic, religious, and political ties of Muslim Americans after 9/11. Louise Cainkar (2004) and other scholars (e.g., Abraham 1983; Haddad 1994) also note that the increasing Islamicization of Muslim immigrant communities in the United States since the 1980s, coinciding with greater immigration of Arab Muslims, situated them in transnational networks that were shaped by the global Islamic revival and continued to be informed by political events such as the Iranian Revolution, the Israeli invasion of Lebanon in 1982, and the first Gulf War. However, the specific, regional or local, grievances that animate these transnational links are often not acknowledged by state officials in declaring the United States' War on Terror. Ho (2004, 234) observes that the resistance of many in these transnational communities is based on their opposition to imperial policies in the regions they inhabit or originate from, such as bin Laden's demand that the United States withdraw its troops from Saudi Arabia and end its support for Israeli occupation of Palestine. (Not to mention that bin Laden and his followers were, in fact, supported by the United States when they were helping it drive the Soviets out of Afghanistan, and so the transnational layers of the conflict are thicker and more complex than they are portrayed in U.S. mainstream discourse.) Ho does not condone al-Qaeda's methods or endorse their religious ideology, but he suggests that there is a historical, anti-imperial analysis evident in their actions that has a global appeal. This is the rationale, explicit as well as unspoken, for why the Bush administration views flexible citizenship as both an economic necessity in a global economy and a political threat to its designs to establish a new global order serving U.S. imperial interests.

The notion of flexible citizenship is, and always has been, politicized and has had disastrous consequences for immigrant communities in a time of national crisis. Berlant (1997) argues that cultural citizenship in the United States has become defined through the idea of crisis: the theme of a nation which is morally, culturally, and politically under attack and whose national identity must be defended, as has been propagated by conservatives for the past several decades and, even more dramatically, after 9/11 (see also Cole 2007). Flexibility in national loyalty is viewed as potentially threatening when national security is perceived to be at risk, and there is a fear that this threat is both from without—from foreigners who oppose the United States—and from within—from treacherous immigrants or "un-American" citizens. This theme was used to justify the internment of over 100,000 Japanese Americans during the Second World War who were considered inherently loyal to the Japanese government, even if they were third-generation U.S. citizens; the detention of 10,000 immigrants, who were also legal permanent residents, detained during the Palmer Raids of 1919 because of fears of ties to Bolshevik Russia (Brinkley 2003, 32–34; Chang 2002, 39; Murray 2004, 64–65); and the witch hunt by Senator McCarthy against Communists during the Cold War in the 1940s and 1950s (Schrecker 1998). In each of these cases, formal citizenship was not enough to guarantee the protection of civil rights by the state, but the idea of flexible national loyalties was highlighted and exaggerated in fanning xenophobia and national hysteria and targeting particular groups as scapegoats for larger national anxieties.

Much has been said in the academic literature, and also in popular discourse on globalization, about the movement of bodies, commodities, capital, images that is part of a "transnational" world (Appadurai 1996; Basch, Glick Schiller, and Szanton Blanc 1994; Ong 1999). But these discourses sometimes underemphasize how this movement and crossing of national spaces is also powerfully controlled, and coercive, especially as flexible labor is used to discipline and exploit immigrant workers. Ong's (2005, 274) recent work on immigrant labor in Silicon Valley suggests that there is a "splintering of cosmopolitan privilege" for low-wage or undocumented workers, as well as Indian "technomigrants" on HI-B visas who are "semi-indentured" through insecure contracts; some migrants enjoy the rights and privileges of sovereign subjects more than others. Mobility can feel powerfully, even painfully, constraining for those who are circumscribed by immigration laws, state documents, and racialized perceptions of those who belong and those who do not. Flexible citizenship is layered with this tension of immobility and with complex feelings—of ambivalence, anxiety, frustration, desire, fear, and fantasy. This does not mean that there is a stark dichotomy between the flexibility of transnationalism and the inflexibility of regulation by state and capital, but there is often an acute tension in the way time, not just space, is experienced by those who move and those who hope to stay. The struggles generated by migration and citizenship create a peculiar temporality that I call "immigrant time," a notion that I will return to later in the chapter and that encapsulates the convergence of generational, biographical, and citizenship-based passages of time that belie the notion of linear, individual or col-

Ansar Mahmood, detained
and deported to Pakistan,
wearing Free Ansar T-shirt.
Photograph by Susan Davies.

lective, movements toward "progress" and liberatory self-actualization through acquiring U.S. citizenship.

The paradox of flexible citizenship in the current moment is that it is considered desirable for some and dangerous for others, for the sovereign rights to "freedom" and "mobility" are unevenly distributed. Transnational ties have been encouraged, and produced, by global capitalism and global media and viewed as not just positive, but necessary, even glamorous. The question is for whom flexibility of citizenship is considered favorable and supported by the state, and for whom practicing flexible citizenship is seen as a threat, to be scrutinized and circumscribed by the state in certain moments. Even if all the youth in this study were not engaged in institutionalized transnational practices involving business or organizational ties, they felt the power of the state to limit their mobility across national borders and to interrogate their national allegiances, and also experienced the anxiety felt by their families and community as their businesses and immigration histories come under state scrutiny. Flexibility, then, is always in tension with *control*, and it is a strategy that is in practice constrained by the state and by ideologies of who can and cannot move or waver. This is a key tension as the aspirations of these immigrant youth because spatial and class mobility collide with the limits of immigration and citizenship policy, especially after 9/11, something I explore further in the next chapter.

Amin

"Now that I've been here three months, I like being in Wellford much more. I like the school much more too. Mr. Ellery is very kind; he asks me every time he sees me how I am doing, how my father is doing. I like going to the International Center room and talking to him. The other teachers are good to me too. No one else has talked about Islam much in class since Miss Daniels did that day. But I had to miss a few classes this month because I had to go to the INS office about my green card. I had applied for it when I had come to America, through my sister and her husband who have green cards. But I am not sure what is going on with the application. So I had to miss school a few days to go to the immigration office and wait in line. Every time I go, it takes the whole day. I have to catch the subway so that I can go downtown, then wait in line at the office for a few hours. Sometimes, my number did not come up in time and I had to leave to come back home and help my sister out. But I hope I get my green card interview soon, because then I can work. I know for Indians now, it takes a long time to get the green card. I think once I get the green card, I can apply for a passport and become a citizen. Then I won't have to worry about being able to work. But I still feel I will always be Indian. Why? The passport—it's a piece of paper. When people see me, they don't think I am American. They think I am Indian, maybe Pakistani, maybe Mexican. But at least I will be able to go to India and see my family, and not worry about whether I can come back to America.

"I think Sara has some relatives who have come from Gujarat. So I don't see her much in the building because she hasn't come downstairs much recently. I met her one time when I was waiting near the bus stop with Ismail, and he told me, 'Look, there's that new girl with her sister. Do you want to try to talk to her?' I said, 'Of course.' I wanted to know her name, but I didn't know if she would talk to me. I said hi to her, and she told me, 'Hi, I'm Sara.' Then she went inside with her sister. But after that I saw her in Miss Daniels's class every week and we talked a little every time. And during Eid, I gave her some sweets after school. I was worried a little because Rukshana saw me, so I told Sara to give some sweets to her sister too. I don't know if Rukshana likes me.

*Actually I want to give her a necklace for her birthday, with an 'S' for Sara.
Do you think that she would like that?*

"One day Sara told me, 'You know, my father is very sweet but he is very
strict. So we should be careful.' We don't talk outside the building any more,
only at school. I will give the necklace to her after class, maybe. The other boys
know I like Sara, and they also think she is pretty. But most of the time they
are too shy to talk to the girls. But I am not like that, because I don't think
there's anything wrong with that. I don't think my father would mind that I
like her. He is just worried about my green card, and he wants me to get it
soon so that I can live here. I want it too, but I also want to know if Sara likes
me as much as I like her."

Sara

"Now that my relatives are here from Gujarat—my family sponsored them for
the visas—I have been so busy every evening with them. I haven't been going
to the store as much, or even walking downstairs. I told Amin that we should
be careful because I am worried, a little, about what will happen if my father
finds out that I talk to him. My little sister, Naseem, knows, but she won't say
anything. I don't know what Rukshana thinks. Yes, I like Amin. I think he is
very nice, very good. But you know, there is a problem. His family is from a
different community. Yes, he's Gujarati, but he's from a different caste. We're
both Sunni, yes, but his family is Khalifa and I am Ganchi. Back home, some
people marry even if they are from different communities, but here, I don't
know. Khalifas and Ganchis pray in different places, and they don't get together much. No, I haven't talked about it with Amin. I don't think he cares.
But I think my father cares. It is like when we were watching Kusum, the day
you came to my house. You know, Kusum has a sister who wants to marry
a Muslim boy and her parents say no and his parents say no, but then they
get married anyway and go away together. Their parents don't talk to them,
but then she falls very sick, and he takes care of her and the parents come to
see her and see how much he loves her. Maybe my mother will feel that way,
I don't know.

"You know, my father seems very strict, but he is very soft inside. I know
he is very fond of me. Like that time you called him about the play about children in war that I wanted to be in but it was at the university?[11] I remember
that first he told me, 'No, you can't be in it. I don't care if it is at the college,

and if the other girls are going to be in it too.' He doesn't like us going out at night in the city; he is worried about us here. I was so glad you called him on the phone, because he knows you are a teacher—when you told him that the play was about people who come from different countries and that we would go there with other girls to practice, I think he felt okay. I know he told you on the phone that he didn't want us to go. But when I went home, I cried and cried and he told me if I really wanted to go, it was fine, because he didn't want me to feel bad. Then he said okay to Rukshana too, so we both went for the practice every day for two weeks. I was glad you came to see the play, because my parents were working, and they couldn't come. I showed my parents the pictures from the newspaper with the man who made the play, and they were very happy.

"In the play, there were many students from the school, and I went there in the van they sent for us every day for practice with other Indian, Pakistani, Bangladeshi, Nepali students. Also Haitian, Spanish, Brazilian. So I got to know them. I have a Pakistani friend, Maryam. She is going to graduate this year, but she is worried she will not be able to go to community college because she doesn't have papers. She came two years ago, and she is so smart. She is good at history, math, everything, even English. She was in the bilingual program when she first came to the school, then she was put in standard curriculum very soon. Maryam was working in a hospital after school. She wants to be a counselor; she said she would like to study psychology. But she is very afraid because of her papers. I am glad that we are okay, because our relatives sponsored us for the green card so it will come soon, insh'allah.

"Maryam wears a hijab, you know, and after September 11 someone said something to her on the street when she was coming home from the hospital. It was in Wellford, not far from the school. I think that her parents were worried about her, but she still works at the clinic and she still wears hijab. I tried to tell Miss Daniels that day that all Muslims don't wear hijab, like me or my mother or sisters. I really don't know why they care so much here about why we wear hijab, do you? They don't know very much about Islam. Now I don't explain it so much to Americans anymore. My father still goes to the mosque in Prospect Square sometimes, but mostly we pray at home anyway. That's what we do, here or in India. We're still Muslim. I always feel I am Muslim; I feel I am Indian; I feel I am Gujarati. The teacher tried to ask me how come we were sitting with the Pakistani kids in class, because she said our countries were fighting with each other back home. But we are not fighting with the Pakistani kids, so why does it matter? We feel the same as them, being here."

The Passport: Marking "Immigrant Time"

I lost my Indian passport after I had been in the United States for about
ten years. I had moved several times, from apartment to apartment, and
from Wellford to my parents' house in Lexington to New York, so I
figured it must just have gotten lost in the shuffle of relocations. I got
my passport when I was seven years old—unlike many Americans who
do not have passports well into adulthood and never leave the United
States—for my family left India to live in Malaysia for two years. My
parents traveled a lot; when I was nine, I traveled to the United States and
to England for the first time. My Indian passport became full of stamps
recording my comings and goings from and to India, including my entry
to the United States on a college student visa when I was seventeen years
old. When I applied for my green card, the application required me to
count the number of days I had spent in the United States; the only way
that I could calculate that was by poring through the passport's pages and
trying to decipher the dates of my entry and exit at various airports. The
markings were in different colors, and different scripts too sometimes. It
was strange to realize that in those pages, I only existed when I came and
when I left.

My parents had moved to the United States two years after I did and
were living in Lexington, Massachusetts, when I lost my passport. I was
planning to visit India that winter and suddenly realized that I could not
find my passport, despite having carried around for years my carefully
organized file box of personal documents in neatly labeled folders. I went
home and searched through all the boxes in my parents' attic but the passport was not there either, which left me feeling frustrated and also uneasy.
I was without a passport for the very first time after a very long while. I
had no choice but to apply for a new one, something I couldn't help feeling was symbolic—I would no longer have my black-and-white childhood
photo, taken in India at the age of six, and all the marks of my earlier life
and travels. So it was with some ambivalence that I traveled to New York
and went early one morning to the Indian consulate. Standing in line at
the visa office, I listened as my compatriots quarreled about who was really
first and who was jumping the queue, with an eagerness that seemed like
a rush into culturally familiar routines, both pleasant and stressful. Lines
in INS offices always felt different from this one. Inside the Federal Building in Boston, or the high-rise INS building in downtown Manhattan,

there was always a palpable anxiety, a tension that crammed the room as thickly as the bodies waiting, always waiting, as numbers were called out on the public announcement system for people to come up and talk to the INS officials sitting in their cubicles.

This is the world known to all of us who are or who have been immigrants in the United States, the ritual performance of the state that terrifies us and yet that we have to keep returning to, some of us month after month, some of us year after year. This is the marking of "immigrant time"—entries, departures, waiting periods, applications, letters, interview deadlines, petitions, searches. The state is experienced not just in certain spaces, but temporally, in the varied encounters with the state of different groups of citizens and noncitizens. "What the state means to people is profoundly shaped through the routine and repetitive procedures of bureaucracies" and "iterative practices" (Sharma and Gupta 2006, 11), which produce and perpetuate hierarchies of class, gender, and of course, citizenship. Citizens, too, must wait for state documents and wrestle with government bureaucracies, but immigrant time is not quite like citizen time. Immigrant time passes slowly, sometimes quickly, like the time of citizens, but it is always intensely bound up with distance, and with an incredible preoccupation with, and fear of, documents issued by the state. "Papers" determine how and where immigrants exist and loom large in their lives. Papers determine which line you must stand in at the airport for "passport control," whether you will be in the line of non-U.S. citizens who will look, often longingly, from within their maze of ropes at that other short line, as if across a border drawn within the airport. And letters that appear, as if magically, on your boarding pass determine whether you deserve a "special search," or to fly at all, whether or not you are technically a citizen. The "ssss" that links airline passengers to some secret watch list or list of names spilling out of an Arabic lexicon reminds you, yet again, that you need to wait while they search, and search, and search, and search. Why? The loop of questions is endless—Where? when? how? with whom? for whom? why? But the why's of immigrants are rarely answered.

Citizen time is also intertwined with the pursuit of documents, but for immigrants the banality of documents and government procedures is bound up with a particular experience of space, as well as temporality, which overlaps with that of other disenfranchised or marginalized groups in many ways. Immigrant time conjoins biographical life histories, generational passages, and collective identities that do not conform to the evolutionary model of progress but often circle back. Those citizens who were once immigrants remember this time, and it often shapes our experience of time ever after, so the memory of that "other" temporality slips unexpectedly, and sometimes uneasily, into our "present." Every once in a while we catch ourselves thinking: It is strange that these ten years since I got my green card have passed so quickly, unlike the five years I was waiting. Or, I cannot wait to go back to Bangladesh for one more month or even one more week, now that I can finally go whenever I want. Or, missing someplace else used to feel like a long, long time—and now, it still feels like missing *something*.

The tension between mobility and immobility—the in-between state of waiting, neither moving nor stopping—is what Amin seemed to be expressing in his reflection on the green card application. He kept returning to the INS office trying to apply for this document, but he did not know if and when he would get permission from the state to stay. In the meantime, he kept circling within his limited orbit in the city, circumscribed by work and school schedules. This is the contradiction of immigrant time which imbues the experience of space and nation with different layers of meaning for immigrants. These different temporalities and feelings of space coexist within the nation, but are often invisible to those who are not subject to the state's regulatory power in the same way as those who are, or once were, immigrants. It is often said in debates about immigration and race in the United States that all Americans were, once, immigrants. Yet the question of immigrant time is bound up with the history of settlement, slavery, and displacement within the United States and the violence of nation-state founding, for the presumed rootedness of indigenous peoples is juxtaposed with the mythologized movement of white settlers and the repressed history of the genocide and forced movement of Native Americans (Clifford 1997). Claims to citizenship are situated in this contested history, and embedded in other trajectories of movement and nation-making in the places that immigrants lived before.

I chose to apply for U.S. citizenship after the events of September 11, 2001. I always thought of a passport as a stapled collection of paper, as a material artifact that simply determined how I crossed national borders, and not how I felt about any of the nations in which I lived. Before I got a U.S. passport, I lived in the United States as a "nonresident alien," and then after getting a green card as a "resident alien," both terms reinforcing the science fiction–like nature of my outsider status. Like my uncle who had come to the United States fifteen years previously and who resisted becoming a U.S. citizen, remembering the draft during the Vietnam War, I was deeply ambivalent about swearing to bear arms in defense of the U.S. state, or any nation-state for that matter. But after 9/11, I thought about getting U.S. citizenship, paradoxically, because of my feelings of political dissent and desire to take as public a stance as possible. The Bush administration's rush to bomb Afghanistan, the partitioning of the world into those who were "with us" and who were with "the enemy," and the surge in patriotic nationalism in the wake of the tragedy pulled me into publicly expressing my alienation from these responses and the policies of the country in which I was living and working.

The signing of the PATRIOT Act gave me pause. In this climate of re-pression, I thought I needed to get a U.S. passport as a minimum shield for my participation in protest movements or activities. I didn't have any illusions that citizenship was a guarantee against being targeted; several cases had already involved U.S. citizens, such as the highly publicized ones of Yasser Hamdi and Jose Padilla,[12] as well as many other cases of detention, profiling, and persecution of citizens that went unpublicized. Americans I knew who had been involved in the 1960s civil rights move-ments, particularly those in groups singled out for surveillance by the FBI's COINTELPRO program, remembered these state tactics of using immigration and citizenship status to stifle dissent, and understood my deep ambivalence.

In an ironic twist on history, the day I became a U.S. citizen was August 15, 2002, India's fiftieth anniversary of independence—another one of those jokes that immigrant time plays on you. My swearing-in ceremony in Boston was in some ways a quintessentially New England event; it took place in the elegant, pillared assembly room in the historic Faneuil Hall building. Everyone in the hall that morning was brimming with a palpable excitement, and the ceremony felt like a mix of wedding ritual and debutante ball. However, the 346 new citizens that day were old deb-utantes. Most of the people being sworn in that day were in their thir-ties and forties, and each seemed to have traveled a long way to get here. As we immigrants always are when we confront the face of the state, we were all dressed in our immigrant-best. Most of the men were wearing neat button-down shirts, some in jackets and ties, and we women were in our most careful, most celebratory, and most alluring dresses, skirts, robes, saris, suits, and jeans. The African women sitting in the gallery in joyous accompaniment of relatives being sworn in below had wide head-dresses matching their printed robes. I wore blue, but with bright pink, Indian-style. A couple of people clutched flags or had stars and stripes on their sweatshirts.

But even though we were there to become citizens, we still had to wait. We sat in our seats for over half an hour, for no apparent reason. Like good immigrants, we waited and asked no questions. It was not for us to ask, only to sign our photographs and assert that we were indeed the real selves of our ghosts, and file up to the desk to collect our papers. We all had very different feelings, obviously, about the United States. For most, it was clearly a moment of celebration, and when we recited the oath, the congregation seemed to heave a collective sigh of relief. At least, I thought, this will hopefully be the last time I wait in an uncomfortable chair for an immigration-related ritual.

I did, however, feel a slight twinge of emotion in marking this passage. I have no nostalgia for INS waiting rooms, but I had grown instantly to recognize and even identify my time in the United States with this waiting, this air of patient desperation, this carefully dressed compliance with forms and lines and incomprehensible regulations. I-20, I-90, and finally N400. Immigrants speak not just in tongues, but in numbers, for our various tongues don't matter for citizenship in the land of English Only. For my citizenship interview before the naturalization ceremony, the examiner, a middle-aged Italian American man, had laughed about having to test my English, since I was teaching in an English department at the time. He asked me to write, as if partly in jest, "I drive a silver car." It was an easy test for me, unlike for many other immigrants who have to struggle to find time to learn English after work or pay for classes so that they can meet the citizenship requirements for English literacy; I did indeed drive a silver car, a Honda CRV. The wait at the INS for my interview that day was short. In fact, it was the shortest time I've spent in an INS waiting room in my entire fifteen years in this country; perhaps, I realized, the wait gets shorter as one moves closer to citizen status. I wonder if I'll ever again have that feeling of walking into that web of austere bureaucracy and seeing those faces, generally all shades of brown, all shades of waiting, and recognize that expression—perhaps it's the uncertainty that immigrants share that makes our presence tenuous, even if massive. We don't know if we can stay or who we will be, citizens or nonresident aliens or political refugees, until the state tells us. In the glare of official light, we're all specters, each with an identical brown file. So it's like recognizing other ghosts when all along you were trying to pretend that you lived in the world of the living.

That morning in Faneuil Hall at the naturalization ceremony, the judge, a middle-aged white man, swept in half an hour late. We rose to our feet when he arrived. It was like being in school assembly in India all over again, or perhaps in church. The judge delivered the homily. He was not quite eloquent, and seemed to be searching for a way to tell us that we had rights to perform as citizens. He stumbled on the mention of war, however: "Of course, you all are obliged to bear arms for the United States, if it needs to defend itself, though of course I hope you will not need to. But if there is a war, of course, you should all fulfill your obligations. I hope, of course, that there is no war that will cause you to do this, but if there is . . ." He was tortured by this discussion of military service, trying to move on to civic citizenship, the importance of the right to vote. But war, it seems, superseded civil rights. The ghosts in front of him didn't need to be told this, of course. We had lived through this before, and some of us had, in a sense, died because of this already. Many of us were here as testament to the wars that the United States waged, directly or indirectly, from the Philippines and Vietnam to El Salvador and Congo. And the judge must have known this, because he had adopted a child from Korea, a girl who was now a citizen. When he revealed this, the new citizens stood up and clapped. Why did we applaud this rescue, I wondered? Did we think the judge was a hero? Did we feel that the orphaning of generations of children in the countries the United States has fought in was connected to our own adoption of the United States as our new home, so we could be the adopted, not the orphaned, children? Or were we simply glad that he was finishing his sermon and getting on with it?

My mother was wearing white and waving from the balcony. She had become a citizen in this room five years before. My mother was annoyed that we had to wait for the judge without being told why. She could afford to be angry now, I thought. She could travel back and forth to India on her U.S. passport. Yet my mother was also outraged every time she was harassed at U.S. airports by security personnel opening her bags and, as she put it, asking her to spread her legs in front of strangers when pulled aside for "special security" searches after 9/11. I felt helpless and furious, too. That day, I remembered that becoming a citizen would not be the end of struggling with discrimination and indignity, but the beginning of a different phase of waiting for resolution, for something else.

Four

Economies of Citizenship: Work, Play, and Polyculturalism

Mumtaz

I spent a day with Mumtaz at the high school in September 2002. I had been trying to meet her for weeks, and as with some of the other students, it proved simply impossible to find the time to talk to her between her full school and work schedules. The only way I could spend time with her was to "shadow" her in her classes, which gave me a glimpse into what being a student in the high school was like, what the rhythm of the day was like, and what it felt like to sit in a high school classroom.

Mumtaz, who was related to Zeenat, was from a village in Navsari in Gujarat and had come to the United States a year and a half before I met her, sponsored by her uncle. She got her green card within a few weeks of her arrival, and now lived with an uncle in the North Wellford apartments rather than with her family in a neighboring town, so that she could attend high school in Wellford. Mumtaz worked after school at Dunkin' Donuts, as did many of the Indian immigrant girls at the school. She told me that she worked at a store in the suburbs and was on call for work on the weekends. Her job as a cashier paid seven dollars an hour, and she gave her paycheck to her mother. Mumtaz always struck me as quiet but focused, with a gentleness underlying her serious determination as she moved through the worlds of school, work, and family.

The first class I attended with her at the high school that morning was a business class, taught by a white, middle-aged, male teacher. The classroom had desks with computer monitors and posters and sketches on the walls proclaiming "How parties reach agreements," "Consideration," and "Take responsibility." The assignment for the day was to write a business letter to propose a business of the students' choice, the teacher warning that the proposal could not include liquor stores. A Haitian student sitting behind us was talking to a girl in Kreyol about starting a Haitian restaurant called "Cliffalicious." The teacher pointed out to the students that logos were really important, sometimes more so than text: "When you see the Golden Arches, you know what it is without the words, right?" The students all chimed, "Yes," in unanimous recognition of McDonald's global icon.

In the next class Mumtaz attended, which was English, I sat next to her friend Samira, who was also Gujarati, and a Bangladeshi girl, Nasreen. The three of them were good friends. On the blackboard was written the question, perhaps from an earlier class: "Define discrimination: Give one example (personal or made-up). Write it as a story." Next to the blackboard was a poster of Martin Luther King Jr. with the civil rights movement's credo, "I have a dream." Mumtaz and Samira chatted to each other in Hindi because there was a substitute teacher in the class, Samira commenting that the class was for "time pass," a typical Indian English student phrase that took me back to my own days of sitting through high school classes, waiting for them to end.

Samira and Mumtaz were also together in a banking class, a business elective for seniors. There was a training branch of a local bank inside the school itself, and Mumtaz had already done a three-week summer training session at a branch of the bank during the summer. The manager of the training bank was a white woman dressed in full business attire—suit, tights, and pumps. Her clothes accentuated the contrast with Samira and Nasreen, who were working at the teller's counter dressed in their salwar kameez, which they wore nearly everyday to school, whereas Mumtaz tended to wear slacks or jeans. A few customers, probably school staff, came in to get cash, deposit checks, and do other transactions at the bank, and the student trainees took turns helping them behind the counter. The teacher quizzed students on policies of cashing checks, two-party checks, signatures, and forms of identification. The other students in training were two African American girls, and the manager commented that the bank class seemed to attract female students. By the end of the fall semester, Mumtaz had been hired in a part-time job at the bank where she worked, so it seemed that the class had helped her find a better-paying service job. This was difficult for most of the South Asian immigrant students, whose English language skills were an impediment.

Mumtaz told me that she wanted to study pharmacy and was applying to the Massachusetts College of Pharmacy, as well as to four-year colleges in the area. Most South Asian students I talked to in the bilingual program planned to apply to two-year colleges, mainly because of their language skills and because teachers advised them that community colleges would be a good place to start and prepare for study in a four-year college.[1] Mumtaz was exceptionally focused in her plans to follow a different route, and navigated the guidance counseling system of the school with a sense of determined purposefulness to learn what she felt she needed to know. One of her teachers had told her that it would be a good idea to first get a job at a pharmacy near the school to see if she liked the nature of the work, but her guidance counselor had not given her suggestions for pharmacy programs. That day, Mumtaz left the banking class early so that she could try to talk to the guidance counselor about SAT forms. She was lucky in her quest because she managed to find her advisor in the counseling office, which was decorated with "Welcome" signs in Spanish, Portuguese, and French, and with college pennants hanging on the walls.

Eventually, Mumtaz did get into a four-year college, but it was a Catholic women's institution, not a pharmacy college as she had originally planned. Samira and Nasreen went to the same public two-year institution, and Mumtaz saw much less of her friends after they graduated and dispersed to different colleges in the area.

Samira and Shireen

Shireen had already graduated from the high school and had just been admitted into a four-year college by the time I met her, but her younger sister, Samira, was still in the high school. Both of them worked at their father's convenience store on weekends and in the evenings, after their classes. The store was in a residential neighborhood in a neighboring town, on a quiet tree-lined street off the main road. The two sisters generally took the bus to get there from Wellford, so Shireen was a bit uncertain when giving me directions for driving there.

When I visited the store one afternoon, Shireen and Samira were both there and their parents were on their way out. The store was spotlessly clean, newly painted, and incredibly neat. The goods on the shelves were lined up in flaw-lessly organized rows. The girls' father had just bought the store six months ago, but even then it was much more cheerful and sparkling than any conve-nience store I had been to before. Samira took me outside to see the little yard at the back, where she excitedly pointed to a rose bush they had just planted near the back door. There were a few weeds sprouting on the tiny plot of land, which they were clearing up. Her parents told the girls to offer me a drink or an ice cream. I don't speak any Gujarati, and they didn't speak any English, but I could understand their welcome completely. Samira and Shireen insisted that I have a cold drink or snack, as if I were visiting their home. I could feel that they were happy and proud to have this store, that they felt it was theirs.

Shireen was managing the cash register for the rest of the day, and seemed completely comfortable being in charge of the store. She ordered the inventory herself every week, something she had learned how to do from her uncle, who worked at an Indian restaurant in a nearby town. Samira laughed that they did not go to the restaurant often, because they would always be offered free meals that they could not refuse. Her father, too, had worked in an Indian res-taurant and then in a clothing store before he opened the convenience store. He had come to the Wellford area fourteen years earlier from Surat, in Gujarat, and sponsored his children two years ago after he got his green card. Now he was a U.S. citizen.

Samira and Shireen said that they had been happy in Surat, where they were surrounded by friends and relatives. Before they had come to the United States they had watched some American films, and Samira particularly re-membered the Hollywood blockbuster Titanic. After arriving in Wellford, they missed their high school in Gujarat, which had been co-ed but still very different from Wellford High. They missed wearing their school uniforms; Shireen said that it had made her feel "like a student." Both she and Samira were dressed in salwar kameez outfits that day, but remarked that their par-ents did not mind them wearing jeans to school. Shireen said that she was now happy living in the United States because she loved studying here; her favorite subjects were math and physics. Samira, on the other hand, hated math and liked literature.

The sisters said they had been scared to go out after the events of 9/11 be-cause they heard about the backlash and targeting of Muslims and Arabs. Yet they noted that they were sometimes identified as "Hindu" because they did not wear headscarves, as most Gujarati Muslim women in their community did not cover their heads. Both thought that people in the United States did not know much about Islam, but Samira's teacher had asked for her help in doing a project about Islam and South Asia, and Shireen recalled a woman from the local Islamic center visiting her class to talk about Islam. Samira commented, "If one Muslim did this, not all Muslims are bad; if one American did something, doesn't mean all are bad. . . . I think Bush wanted to get Osama [bin Laden]. But then why are they hunting all the [other] people?" She observed, "Some students seem to think that if people from other countries attack us . . ." and Shireen completed her sentence, " . . . we have to [take] revenge on their countries."

The sisters felt that their teachers in the high school didn't "want war" and that some of the other students had "different" views from the American mainstream, regardless of race or ethnic identity: "It doesn't matter if you're white or black or Latino," Shireen said. But they were concerned about the image of Muslim women in the U.S. media, for Samira observed that "they always show women don't have rights in Afghanistan." Shireen recalled Laura Bush's visit to Afghanistan to make a statement about the presumed liberation of Afghan women from the Taliban, justifying the U.S. invasion, and added, succinctly, "Everybody believes that America is a country where people have rights, and freedom." Both the girls, but especially Shireen, followed political developments by watching CNN and reading local newspapers which arrived daily in the store.

While I was chatting with them and sipping my soda, three or four customers came into the store. They were mostly slightly older, white men, reflecting the racial composition of the neighborhood, but also an African immigrant woman who was the only customer who knew the girls by name. She seemed to be a regular, for she asked how their mother was doing. Most of the customers bought lottery tickets, which Samira adeptly rang up on the lottery machine; she said afterward that their customers spent most of their money in the store on the lottery. Samira laughingly remembered that once a man came in and spent $200 on tickets at one shot, which she and her sister found incomprehensible.

Shireen was excited to be going to college, and was one of the few South Asian immigrant students who had gained admission into a four-year college immediately after graduating from high school. Though a bit quieter and less chirpy than Samira, Shireen exuded a sense of responsibility and thoughtfulness that made her seem older than her years. I left just as the afternoon sun was beginning to fade and cast shadows outside on the young rose tree, thinking that this was the only convenience store I knew that grew roses outside.

Walid

"I came here two and a half years ago from Lahore, in Pakistan, but my father came here sixteen years ago and lived here alone; then we came. My father worked in New York first with my uncle, then he moved here. My uncle worked at a hotel, but he got laid off so he moved here too. My father bought a grocery store, called Kerala Corner. Yeah, it's South Indian, but I think he bought it from somebody who was from Kerala. Now he works for security, like I do. I work for the same company in Wellford as my fiend Adil, but my father is a guard at the university, right near the school. My other friend works there too, as a security guard, and sometimes I go sit with him. It's funny, I never see students working while I'm there. I always see them going to parties, going out with someone. Yes, I've only been there on weekends, but still, I've never seen them study. It's hard if you go to high school here to get into the university because you need good SATs. But the students who come from India—they just give the university some money, and they get in. No, you don't think so?

"I want to do computer programming in college—that's what I'm thinking now. When I was in Pakistan, I was thinking of being a cricket player because I love cricket! I was in a cricket club in Lahore, but now there's no time to play. You gotta have to work here; we don't have no place to go besides movies and malls. I started going to the YMCA in Prospect Square to work out; I'd like to go every day but I don't always have time. And the other thing is, if you want to go meet someone, like your friend, you have a job and he has a different day off. Sometimes on Eid, we get together and we go and chill out. But back home, in Pakistan, you don't have to work and stuff. I work as security in a warehouse near the mall; I go there at nights every weekend. All you have to do is lock the gate and sit there' that's it. It's easy, but it's boring. It's very quiet there; sometimes, I call my friends from my cell phone. Do you have a cell phone? What service do you have?

"When my father worked in the store, he used to wake up at eight o'clock at night, go to the store, come home at four o'clock in the morning, and then go to a different job. Then my mother went to the store in the morning. After September 11 happened, I was worried about her because she wears a salwar kameez and I thought something might happen to her. But she was okay. A month after September 11, we sold the store.

"But something happened to me and Adil, in the school. We were talking in the class, I was showing a [magic] trick to Adil, and this girl was talking,

talking . . . She was saying things like, 'You are a Muslim, you kill people,' stuff like that. 'If you touch me, I'll call my brother and he will do this and that to you.' Adil called the security, but I was thinking, maybe she's high or something. She was saying crazy things. Mr. Ellery was very upset with the girl.

"The girl was black, but not all black people are like that. Actually, I think that a lot of black people don't feel like white people about that thing that happened on September 11. I've been thinking something else about white people after that thing happened. 'Cos I've seen a lot of black people talking about how one time they were slaves, so they don't really like white people either: why should they care what happened to them after they killed off so many people and made them slaves? But you know, I feel bad for Americans: this is their country. We are immigrants; if something happens back home and someone did something to us, we're gonna be angry too, right? So I can see how white people feel upset about September 11.

"I think Pakistanis are not white, but they're not black either. We're just in between. And some black people—they're not completely black either—they're standing somewhere in between too. I've seen a lot of different kinds of black. Some people come from Africa, Somalia, and people here call them black too even if they're lighter. And then someone who is the same color as me, but he's from Haiti, here they'd call him black but they don't call me black. I have black friends, Egyptian friends, Moroccan friends, Pakistani friends, Gujarati friends. Many of my friends are Muslim; some of them came by themselves. They live with their uncles and aunts here.

"For me, I feel no different about being a Muslim since the thing on September 11. Someone on TV said Muslims are terrorists, but what can we do about it? The first thing for me about being Muslim is that I was born in Pakistan; I was born in a Muslim community. It's a little bit hard for Muslims to live their life sometimes because you know, it's a strict religion, but it's okay—we can go with it. Sometimes people do things they're not supposed to do, like Muslims who come here from India and Pakistan. They forget everything from back home sometimes; they change their minds. It's not just about being Muslim; it's your culture. Like girls [who] start wearing pants: I think girls change more when they come here. But my cousin hasn't changed; she still wears a salwar [kameez]. American people, after eighteen, they can do whatever they want, but in desi [South Asian] families you can't. I can't go out with girls, but I could go out with boys; I just don't have time. I work till midnight on Friday, so I'm tired. My parents still have rules, so sometimes they don't know where

*I'm going. I tell 'em I'm going to a job or something. I think for Spanish people,
it's like that too; their parents are also strict with the girls.*

"My parents want to go back to Pakistan someday. They want us to get a
job first, get settled, become a citizen. My father sponsored us, so now I have
a green card but I get the same thing as with a passport, what d'you call it?
Rights."

Work, Play, and Culture

The experiences of immigrant students such as Walid, Samira, Shireen,
and Mumtaz bring to light the interconnections between leisure, labor,
and popular culture. Their attempts to find jobs in the city shape their
understandings of achievement, national belonging, and cultural difference as they struggle to find time to consume popular culture. The school
is one site where they learn about business models, careers, and service
jobs and are also exposed to notions of multiculturalism that are challenged by other students' own historical accounts of U.S. racism and the
contradictions of U.S. racial categorization. Thus cultural citizenship is
embedded in work, education, cultural consumption, and multiculturalism that drive intertwined expressions of neoliberal economic citizenship,
subcultural and urban citizenship, and multicultural and polycultural
citizenship.

WORK

Work is linked to young immigrants' aspirations for citizenship and
belonging and their pursuit of American cultural ideals of class mobility and the autonomous citizen-individual, a goal in tension with their
immigrant families' struggles to keep afloat and their efforts to help their
parents. These desires motivated all the South Asian immigrant students
to find part-time jobs after school, such as Mumtaz's banking apprenticeship, Samira's and Shireen's work in the store, and Walid's job as a
security guard. Mumtaz belonged to a Gujarati immigrant community in
which many of the families actually owned or worked in small businesses,
and it was common for children to work at family-owned convenience
stores, like Sara and Rukshana, who worked at their uncle's store after
school. Work was the primary motivation for migration for most of these
immigrant families, one of the major connections to local culture and

"multicultural" diversity for these youth, and a primary arena in which they realized the limitations of the American Dream.

Neoliberal Citizenship and the "Golden Cage"   Labor and neoliberal economic citizenship are critical for understanding the modes of belonging of South Asian immigrant youth, as the experiences narrated here suggest. However, both academic and popular discussions of Muslim American youth after 9/11, and even before 9/11, have neglected to examine the role of labor in shaping their experiences of difference or exclusion, and have also largely been uncritical in their perspective on racial, religious, and cultural difference and the ways in which these are connected to U.S. "multiculturalism" for South Asian immigrant youth.[2] Understanding the particular position of different groups of South Asian Muslim immigrant youth in the labor market and neoliberal economy is important for analyzing the processes that constructed South Asian, Muslim, or Arab Americans, especially undocumented and working-class immigrants, as targets of detention and deportation after 9/11. The assumption that certain groups are "alien" populations who can be expelled from the nation emerges from processes that are cultural and political as well as economic, and that extend back well before the events of 2001.

The South Asian Muslim immigrant youth I spoke to in Wellford, such as Mumtaz and Walid, all worked in part-time service-sector jobs, jobs that are rarely unionized and have few, if any, benefits. These are the low-wage jobs increasingly held by immigrants, especially with the decline of manufacturing and deindustrialization in the United States and the growth of what is known as the post-Fordist or hourglass economy—an upper strata of expanding high-skill jobs, such as in technology and information, and a lower strata of low-wage service jobs that has outgrown the stable, blue-collar factory jobs of an earlier era, including in New England. The increasing reliance on part-time, low-wage or flexible labor in the service-sector economy, fueled by immigrant labor, accompanied the rise of neoliberalism, or the reorganization of global capitalism according to free market principles, supposedly free of state intervention, that celebrated "individual freedom." In reality, neoliberal capitalism has shored up the wealth and power of economic elites, countering the threat of socialist policies and Communist parties after the Second World War, through a combination of political, military, and economic strategies to promote privatization since the 1970s, dramatically enacted in the U.S.-

backed coup in Chile on September 11, 1973, and continuing under Ronald Reagan in the United States and Margaret Thatcher's regime in Britain (Harvey 2005). While Bill Clinton used the IMF to liberalize and deregulate global financial sectors, the neoconservatives under George W. Bush have acted unilaterally to achieve their economic goals, using war to force privatization and the entry of American and multinational corporations, as in the "liberation" through economic liberalization of Afghanistan and Iraq (Harvey 2005; Smith 2005).

These neoliberal state formations are accompanied by neoliberal notions of citizenship that presumably enshrine the liberal-democratic ideals of individual freedom but that mask social inequalities and U.S. imperial policies. Neoliberal capitalism, which was consolidated in the 1990s as the post–Cold War "Washington Consensus" imposing free trade and structural adjustment globally (Smith 2005, 144), envisions citizens as productive, self-reliant individuals who are free of the dependence created by the welfare state, and as consumers of social services that are increasingly privatized (Miller 1993). The privatization of citizenship in the neoliberal state has diminished the right of citizens to public goods and services, which are now allocated according to individual "worthiness," and not by right. This is evident in the community service and "service-learning" programs at high schools and colleges in the United States where young people presumably learn to be responsible citizens by working for nonprofit or state-sponsored programs and programs for college graduates, such as Teach for America or AmeriCorps, which offer services subsidized by young labor instead of committing state funding to address problems of urban poverty and education. For example, George W. Bush founded the Citizen Corps Council in 2002 to tap into public anxiety about terrorism and provide a volunteer structure for patriotic citizens—defined as warriors defending the nation against terrorism—to "prepare their communities for potential terrorist attacks or other disasters" (Nguyen 2005, 76).

It should not be surprising that American youth today, who have generally grown up with this notion of neoliberal citizenship based on individual goodwill and virtue, and who do community service in order to better their chances of getting college admission or a job, should be more involved with volunteer work than in previous generations (Fields n.d.). Interestingly, I found that even some of the working-class immigrant youth in this book were volunteering at soup kitchens while their own families were struggling economically, since they had learned upon coming to the

United States that community service was a route to educational advancement and proof of virtuous citizenship. These experiences promote a certain understanding of citizenship in relation to the responsibilities of the state, for these community service programs, or even many nongovernmental organizations, are generally not linked to movements for social change addressing the roots of inequality.

Neoliberal citizenship in the United States is based on the legal and economic regulation of citizens and workers, and on the need for a low-wage, undocumented, or noncitizen labor pool. Undocumented immigrant workers are useful to the U.S. economy because the low wages and poor labor conditions that most are forced to accept, in the absence of rights for undocumented immigrant workers, allow employers to suppress wages and maximize profit. The state officially targets undocumented immigrants who are the scapegoat for national economic anxieties and xenophobic hysteria, while in practice it generally turns a blind eye to the illegal hiring of immigrants by employers, corporations and individuals alike, hypocritically supporting U.S. industries that want cheap, nonunionized labor (De Genova 2002, 438–40). The threat of deportation suppresses wages but also helps keeps undocumented labor compliant, a strategy that was used to maximum effect after 9/11 since the detentions and raids selectively targeted undocumented Arab and Muslim immigrants and simultaneously stifled political dissent in their communities, showing how practices of neoliberal citizenship and dissenting citizenship conflict and converge, as I will discuss in chapter 5.

Although the South Asian immigrant youth in this book were high school students, I and other volunteers in SAMTA quickly learned that work was a central concern in their lives. When I first began doing this research, I found it almost impossible to meet with the students and realized it was because they were so busy running from school to work. Acknowledging the salience of work for the students, SAMTA decided to do a series of workshops focusing explicitly on issues of employment and careers. In February 2003, we organized a workshop where we talked to the students about different kinds of jobs and asked them to guess the salaries associated with them. The experiences of work in these young people's lives were clearly very different from those of the SAMTA volunteers, who were mostly graduate students or young South Asian professionals and had never had to work to support their families, who belonged to the early wave of South Asian immigration after 1965.

In the workshop, it became apparent that many of the students were not sure about occupational income levels in the United States, for example, whether a small business owner could make more than an actor or whether a bank manager earned more than an engineer. Most of the students seemed interested in professional jobs, in technology or banking; none wanted to be teachers. It was clear that most of the students, and nearly all the boys, were aware that technology was a growing field—as was the case in Wellford—and wanted to have a "computer job." While medicine was traditionally a career favored by the middle classes in South Asia, the only one in the group of ten or twelve youth who wanted to be a doctor was Zeenat. Interestingly, two boys wanted to be airplane pilots, perhaps without really thinking about whether their Muslim names would be an obstacle—or perhaps assuming that anxiety about flying licenses for Muslim immigrant males after 9/11 would wane with time. Yet all the students in the workshop that day already worked in service-sector jobs. Only two of those present had found internships through school programs: Zeenat was working in a hospital, and Osman eventually found a part-time job in a library at a nearby university. Very few of them actually knew what an "internship" was, but three of them, including Osman, had already prepared their own résumés, possibly through business classes. Despite this uneven knowledge of work or the labor market, they all seemed to desire upward mobility, without being fully clear about what it would take to get there in the United States. Career decisions or desires may be deliberately unrealistic, for they are a way for youth from immigrant communities to display the "pursuit of legitimate social citizenship" (Park 2005, 112).

The workshops held by SAMTA provided a context in which ideas of cultural citizenship emerged and were debated, challenged, and legitimated at various moments. In May 2003, SAMTA held a workshop on budgeting that we had hoped would offer both practical financial education as well as lead into a larger analysis of capitalism and labor, clearly a lofty goal. This dual objective proved difficult to achieve and created contradictions we had not anticipated but that were interesting for reflecting on ideas of neoliberal citizenship and that infused our own approaches in the workshop. One of the SAMTA volunteers, Feroze, told the students the fable of the ant and grasshopper—the industrious worker who saved for the future and the lazy grasshopper who suffered because, essentially, he resisted long-term planning and investment. Feroze asked the students what the moral of the story might be. Sara and Mumtaz both responded, "You should save for the future." Mohan, a Nepali boy, commented that "you shouldn't listen to others who are trying to distract you from your goals." These responses may have been rehearsed over many years and inculcated in the school, and Feroze tried to use the fable to steer the discussion to concepts of interest and credit. It occurred to me during the class that we did not know if the Muslim students' families were opposed to interest for religious reasons. When I asked them if this was the case, only Amin raised his hand and said that his family did not believe that they should get interest as Muslims, and we talked briefly about Islamic banking alternatives. While not all of them knew the technicalities of interest and credit systems, these young people probably received messages about the meaning of money, income, savings, or credit from their parents, teachers, friends, and the media.

But the well-known fable of the ant and grasshopper is, after all, at core a story demonstrating the capitalist ethos of hard work and individual merit. How do some people become "ants" and some "grasshoppers"? We did not talk about issues of equity or class stratification that day, which was in retrospect a failure on our part, for it was surely clear to some of these immigrant students that some people could afford to save and others simply could not. One of the other SAMTA volunteers, who was critical of classical economics and of dominant models of globalization, introduced the notion of human capital and asked the students what they needed in order to invest in their education. Mumtaz answered succinctly, "Your mind." For some youth, ideas of individual merit were prominent and overshadowed economic or legal forces and notions of cultural and social capital—what Ong describes as "latitudes" of ethnicized labor networks and market power that shape immigrants' experiences of work in the global economy (2006, 123).

There is also unease and disillusionment among immigrants who find themselves trapped within these transnational or latitudinal "regimes of labor incarceration" (Ong 2006, 21). Immigrant youth from South Asia knew that their families had come to the United States to work, and that migration was their parents' strategy to try to invest in their futures through education in the United States. So to some extent, these young people may have believed that the American Dream held promise or could be realized for them and their families. But along the way, these immigrant youth also learned about class inequities and the contradictions of social capital through their experiences of trying to find work. Many of the students found jobs where their friends worked, combining social relationships with peer knowledge of workplaces, what Katherine Newman calls networks of "lateral partners" (1999, 162). In general, as in Newman's study, these "immigrant workers in the low-wage economy depend upon extensive family networks" to ease their entry into the new country but also to help them negotiate resources for housing, work, education, and child care (1999, 192). The costs of this ethnicized and collective economic strategy for working-class immigrant families are not always apparent to outside observers who are schooled in the "model minority" image and racialized divisions of American class culture. For example, an African American woman who lived in the North Wellford apartments once told me that all the South Asian families were middle class, if not well off, and she observed that they were quick to move out of the high-rise apartments and buy their own houses. What she did not see was that many of these family members worked, possibly even without wages, in family businesses and so did not earn much individually and that several family units were crowded into small apartments where they shared one or two bedrooms.

Compared to more affluent or highly credentialed South Asian immigrants, these working-class youth are more ambiguously positioned in relation to what Ong (1996, 739) calls the U.S. neoliberal ideology of productivity and consumption and are more ambivalent about its promise of "freedom, progress, and individualism." The shift from welfare to workfare schemes in the United States, marked by the 1996 Personal Responsibility and Work Opportunity Act passed under Clinton, was the culmination of a period of "government devolution" that shifted responsibility for social problems to those suffering most from those problems (Park 2005, 135). Neoliberalization has put even greater emphasis on the notion that economic rights for citizens come with individual self-reliance based on wage labor, with little regard for the extenuating circumstances of poverty. Neoliberal citizenship requires that the idea of the self-sufficient citizen-worker be inculcated in the young and in immigrant families so that they are less dependent on the state (France 1998, 108). However, these young immigrants see the limits of this model of the self-reliant "consumer-citizen" in their own lives and in those of their families, even if they are consumers of this notion of neoliberal citizenship in the contexts of school, media, or youth culture.

These young immigrants and their families came to the United States, in a sense, to consume the mythologized promise of the American Dream, but it was often shattered soon after their arrival. Soman, an Indian immigrant student, worked in his family's Bengali restaurant in Prospect Square after school and often waited on more affluent South Asian immigrant students from the prestigious university down the street. He said, "Here, you live in a golden cage, but it's still a cage. . . . My life is so limited. I go to school, come to work, study, go to sleep." Soman's comment about being imprisoned by the "golden cage" of the American Dream is profound because in a single image it points to the glittering appeal of American capitalism and the confining imprisonment, not just of the lifestyle it engenders—that of the worker "ant"—but also of belief in this illusion. Soman's insight suggests that young immigrants and their families may acknowledge the self-delusion, but continue to participate in it because for immigrant youth, at least, there is little alternative, especially now that they are in the United States. Soman's frustration with feeling like a hamster treading a wheel also reveals the paradox in notions of freedom and mobility that shape the golden cage of work under neoliberal capitalism.

In addition to part-time jobs in the service sector, South Asian immigrant youth also worked in their homes—doing child care or family chores—and for family businesses, work that sometimes fell into the category of unpaid labor and that is not uncommon for youth in general, particularly the children of immigrant entrepreneurs (McKechnie and Hobbs 2002; Park 2005). Lisa Park (2005, 103) points out that Asian immigrant entrepreneurs view the "small business as transitional mechanisms to greater mobility for the family, particularly the children." She astutely observes that Asian immigrants and their children who work in these family businesses contribute not just to the national economy, but also to upholding the "political ideology of the American Dream" and participating in "an already contentious debate about 'good' versus 'bad' immigrants" (Park 2005, 127, 135). Unlike "bad" immigrants and minorities who demand fair wages and labor conditions, "good" immigrants are assumed to work willingly in part-time, low-wage, "low-skill" service jobs. This flexible labor market is generally occupied by young people in the United States, for youth fulfill the need for cheap and flexible labor under the guise of gaining "work experience" and learning free market values of economic self-reliance (Newman 1999; Schlosser 2001). In fact, today, the gap between teenage and adult earnings in the United States is at its widest since thirty years ago (Tannock 2001, 3). However, unlike nonimmigrants who also provide part-time, low-wage labor, these immigrant youth can perform the model of economic citizenship required to be a productive worker-citizen, but cannot win cultural citizenship because they are nonwhite, immigrant, and, currently, also because they are identified as Muslim. This makes the situation of the working-class South Asian Muslim youth in this book particularly acute: they experience multiple levels of marginalization in the labor market and economies of citizenship.

South Asian immigrant youth learned cultural codes of belonging in the workplace at the same time that they were imbibing the meanings of class hierarchies and wage scales, as evident in Walid's frustration with his long hours as a security guard with low pay. Tasmeena, a Gujarati immigrant girl, told me that she and her sister, Fatima, both worked at the Dunkin' Donuts in North Wellford, and, while they only got paid seven dollars an hour, Fatima noted that the store manager owned two houses and that his son drove a "very nice" car. The sisters seemed well aware that there was a class hierarchy of employers and workers that seemed somewhat unjust to them. But Fatima also commented that working at Dunkin' Donuts had helped her learn English. Other youth, such as Zeenat, echoed this view that after-school jobs helped them with English language skills, as new immigrants with few other opportunities and little time to practice their English. Work was seen as a site that facilitated their advancement in education through acquiring language and cultural competencies that in turn would lead to hoped-for advancement in the labor market and justify their claims to "good" citizenship (Park 2005). Work, in a sense, would draw them to more work, if not to mainstream America. These youth had few options, and were disciplined by "neoliberal technology," which Ong argues is a "biopolitical mode of governing that centers on the capacity and potential of individuals and the population as living resources that may be harnessed and managed by governing regimes" (2006, 6).

Cultural citizenship is embedded in, and mediated by, work practices and ideas of productivity and merit under neoliberal capitalism. Young workers born in the United States understand their relationship to cultural and national identifications through work. However, for these young South Asian immigrants, work was not a part of their cultural experience before coming to the United States, and so they did not necessarily have a history of imagining themselves as part of a "working-class" culture or a class of young workers. Walid was one of many students who observed that the experience of youth labor was new for them, having come from lower-middle-class to middle-class backgrounds in South Asia.[3] Class relations and work practices affect the everyday experiences of these youth in relation to the state, education, family, friends, and popular culture. These are the sites in which cultural citizenship is created, performed, and contested daily, and labor is one of the key hinges linking these different arenas.

The cultural meaning of work is gendered, for as Zeenat commented, she was not used to women working in wage labor outside the house in her village in Gujarat, but part-time work was commonplace for both the South Asian immigrant boys as well as girls in Wellford. The only difference was that in the United States they entered a labor market that was itself gendered and so only boys worked at certain jobs, such as private security, but both boys and girls worked at other service jobs—and at home as well. Interestingly, Arifa, a Pakistani immigrant girl, remarked to me that "all the Indian girls" worked and seemed glad that she didn't have to find a job. This observation about national differences among South Asian immigrant youth was not borne out by the actual work experiences of the high school students I observed, but it perhaps reflected her own, or her family's, perception of the different cultural meanings attached by Pakistanis or Indians to the appropriateness of female labor, which could be shaped as much by class status and work experiences in the home country of origin, as by religious and social attitudes about gender roles. With the exception of Arifa, and perhaps one or two other girls whose families were more financially secure, I found that the female students were as deeply concerned as boys about finding jobs and supporting their families and did not express a sense of embarrassment or stigma about this, but rather frustration and fatigue.

Work was associated not just with financial but also political anxiety for these South Asian Muslim youth after 9/11, for the public sphere was a realm in which many no longer felt completely safe. The workplace was the venue of increased anti-Muslim and anti-Arab discrimination since 2001, as noted in chapter 6. Walid, for example, was intensely worried about his mother going to work in the store in her salwar kameez after the events of 9/11, and Shireen and Samira also remembered being afraid to go out in the city. The work of citizenship as a disciplining technology is very evident after 9/11 with the ongoing arrests and deportations of immigrant workers for immigration violations, given that the War on Terror, in effect, became a targeted roundup of undocumented or out-of-status Arab and Muslim immigrants, as well as immigrants from other communities. After 9/11, there has been a greater anxiety about work among undocumented immigrants and also noncitizens because of the regime of detentions and deportation of immigrant workers, as well as those who have transnational economic ties that are increasingly suspect when the "threat" to national security is attributed to specific foreign nations. Labor thus provides the hinge between the flexible citizenship discussed in the previous chapter and the dissenting citizenship I will examine in the following chapter: it connects questions of labor migration and globalization to U.S. policies for disciplining and repressing immigrants and workers.

The global security regime of the War on Terror has been extended to the domestic policing of immigrants and workers. Since 9/11, there has been greater cooperation of immigration and intelligence agencies to counter terrorism, and the former INS has been reorganized into new agencies separating enforcement and administrative services—Immigration and Customs Enforcement (ICE) and Citizenship and Immigration Services (CIS)—as part of the Department of Homeland Security created in 2003 (Fernandes 2007, 85). The border has shifted inland and it is no longer only at ports of entry and exit, or near the border with Canada or Mexico, that immigrants confront the arm of the state (Andreas 2003). Raids by the ICE and FBI have brought the border into people's homes, offices, and work sites (e.g., Maira 2007). These conditions facilitate a labor pool of potentially pliant workers who are even more vulnerable than before to hyperexploitation as part of the shadow economy of undocumented workers living with the specter of deportation.[4]

Economic Citizenship in School The high school was a site in which these young immigrants encountered the ever-present understanding of education as a route to a job and upward mobility and were also exposed to cultural notions of work embedded in economic citizenship. Through the academic curriculum, class discussions, extracurricular programs, social activities, and peer relationships, students are forced to grapple with racial divisions, class hierarchies, differences in social capital, and cultural aspirations for success. Mumtaz and her South Asian friends in the banking class were learning not just how to be bank tellers but how to look and act the part, how to perform the role of a worker in the service sector. Schools are an important site in which young people learn the meanings of national identity, multiculturalism, and neoliberal capitalism, in both formal and informal ways (Foley 1994), inculcating beliefs, attitudes, and skills considered vital for national citizenship as well as the neoliberal economy (Ong 2006, 139). The business class I attended with Mumtaz that day contained an implicit lesson in the values and approaches to business important to American capitalist culture. Such classes, as well as the banking program, introduced students to marketing strategies and work ethics considered useful in the neoliberal economy, such as branding or service skills. Some of these issues were probably already familiar to the immigrant students; the focus of the class that day emphasized the value of entrepreneurship, which was clearly evident in the South Asian immigrant community. Upon reflecting on the class later, it occurred to me that this formal discussion seemed largely divorced from the world of entrepreneurship as Mumtaz and her friends knew it, and perhaps others in the class as well who worked with their families in small businesses (see Park 2005). Some of these youth were already being schooled, informally, by their families in notions of entrepreneurial capitalism, even if the economic contexts that these young people's families migrated from were different from the U.S. economic structure and capitalist culture.

In addition to their experiences in part-time jobs outside the school, immigrant students also participated in a range of vocational education programs in the school, such as the banking program attended by Mumtaz and some of the other South Asian girls who were fluent in English. Such vocational education programs are based on the notion that youth need to be prepared for their entry into the labor market while they are in school; various school-to-work programs have been developed in the United States to train young people, especially those assumed not to be bound for higher education, to become workers in the restructured U.S. economy. Critics of these programs point out that they may involve racialized and gendered assumptions about who is "college bound" and who is not, and that some vocational educational programs are focused on improving national economic competitiveness and tracking certain groups of students into the low-wage, "low-skill" labor market (Lewis et al. 1998).

In the Wellford High School, immigrant students also encountered state-run or state-supported employment programs that positioned youth in relation to the local economy. The school was linked to youth employment programs that served the town's high school students, in conjunction with the mayor's Office for Workforce Development. These included Teen Works, for youth over the age of sixteen who met a minimum grade requirement, and Just a Start, a summer program for younger students and those with lower grades. These programs served two broad purposes: to provide part-time employment to youth who needed jobs and to give them training in skills they would need in the job market; and to provide part-time workers to local businesses as well as to nonprofit organizations. These programs were appealing, in theory, because youth who were eligible for these programs received a small stipend and employers obtained subsidized labor. Most of the students enrolled in these programs were from working-class families, according to a program coordinator in Just a Start, who observed that "kids whose parents have white-collar jobs" did not need such jobs. Yet, there was also an awareness among the staff in these programs and teachers in the school that young people were supposed to be focusing on their education, and an unspoken concern that youth should not be exploited as workers. According to the Fair Labor Standards Act, youth under the age of sixteen are technically not supposed to work more than twenty hours per week and not past seven o'clock at night during the school year (Schlosser 2001). However, it was clear that not all high school youth who worked complied with the regulations, either because they and their families needed more income or because employers did not follow the laws themselves.

For example, Osman, a Pakistani immigrant student, gave up his office job because it was only two hours a day. He was having difficulty finding a part-time job—even at the Star Market grocery store—in order to help his father, a taxicab driver who had to support a family of five. Osman was taking an automotive repair class in the school, but he had not chosen to take "garage"; it was the only elective available and one that seemed to draw mainly male students. One of the automotive repair instructors I spoke to seemed well aware that students needed to know more than just how to "change tires and fill air." He showed me the computerized teaching lab and emphasized that students learned science and technology while working on cars. Yet the "ideal" that vocational training will support young people's intellectual and social development as well as later entry into the adult labor market, as envisioned by theorists of youth and work (e.g., Lewis et al. 1998; McKechnie and Hobbs 2002), is not always matched by the realities of the labor market and the limited opportunities for immigrant youth.

Teachers in the Wellford public high school had a range of views about the issue of youth employment. Some teachers I spoke to offered classes through the school's recently restructured vocational educational program, which was based on a sequence of courses for students interested in technical education, such as automotive repair, culinary arts, and electronics technology. Through these classes, teachers also introduced students to varying views about work, success, capitalism, national belonging, and citizenship. For example, Roxanne Anderson, who taught computer programming, began her class one day by asking students if they had heard of a "layoff." I was shadowing Osman in his classes that day and he and the other students listened intently to their teacher as they sat at their computer monitors. Anderson responded to her own question:

> Companies are firing people. In the 1980s, there was gentrification, and there were many homeless people . . . I had a good student who stopped coming to school because he was homeless and the government put him in a shelter in Lynn. We fought for him to come back to school. Layoffs have hit the computer industry. . . . Do you know how much a two-bedroom apartment costs to rent?

A Haitian student raised his hand and ventured, "$1200?" Anderson responded:

> That's for a *one*-bedroom in Wellford. And that's just the rent. You have to pay for other things, like utilities. I want you to come into the real world, for this stuff is going to affect you. . . . I have a friend from the South who called to say that her son just came back from Afghanistan—in a body bag. So this is affecting me too, for I remember during the Vietnam War that neighbors were dying. The media is under a clampdown and doesn't talk about the war. Bush is going to Iraq, but we're not talking about what is happening in Afghanistan. So I want you to be understanding with your parents because they may not be telling you what is happening financially. So if you earn money, help them. They don't have deep pockets.

Anderson, a middle-aged African American woman from North Carolina with a frank, confident manner, was a mesmerizing speaker whom students seemed to like. Her discussion of work linked economic issues such as gentrification, the abolition of rent control in Wellford, and recession to larger questions of war, history, and international politics but also to personal issues of family and economic hardship. On the wall behind her desk was a vintage poster—which did not seem like her choice of artwork—with an image of a U.S. soldier and a white woman wearing a red bandana, and the slogan: "The girl he left behind is still behind him. She's a WOW (Woman Ordinance Worker)." Anderson challenged the militarism and gendered nationalism of the poster in her discussion with the students in a single comment: "Women have fought for the right to hold a gun and kill people." Below this poster was another one that proclaimed, more philosophically, "What am I working for? I guess I'm working not to fail. I want to succeed. But what are the things that will make me successful? A promotion? More money? But what is that getting me? . . . What is my dream? I guess that's what I'm WORKING FOR?"

These contradictory messages and philosophical statements about war, gender, labor, and achievement were not out of place in the school; some vocational education teachers I spoke to had a critical attitude toward labor and capitalism. "Chef Danny" offered popular classes in culinary arts and spoke of the link between culture, family, and food in explaining his approach to cooking as an aspect of ethnic identity. I was particularly interested in talking to him because I wanted to know why so many of the high school's students worked in fast food restaurants, and found that he was very critical of labor practices in the fast food industry. Chef Danny even recommended that I read Eric Schlosser's *Fast Food Nation* (2001); I did, and was indeed horrified by the exposé of gross safety negligence and hormone use in the beef industry. I also learned that the fast food industry employs more young workers than any other, fully two-thirds of its workers being under twenty, exploiting low-wage and immigrant labor (Schlosser 2001, 68). Other teachers, however, were less inclined to take such a critical stance on youth labor and capitalist culture. One of the technical arts labs featured a poster with aphorisms by Bill Gates such as "Don't complain about flipping burgers to make money, because your grandparents did it and they called it initiative/industriousness."

Regardless of their stance on neoliberal capitalism or youth labor, most high school staff acknowledged the shrinking labor market in Wellford and the obstacles facing students who were trying to juggle part-time jobs after school. A few of the immigrant students I spoke to had parents or relatives who had been laid off as the city struggled with the impact of economic recession. The director of a youth employment program that worked with the high school, Judith Brown, told me that the recession had affected the youth as well as adult labor market, and it had become difficult to place students in jobs over the past year, even in fields where there were generally more employment opportunities in Wellford, such as science, research and technology, biotechnology, and medicine. In Brown's view, immigrant students were "very committed to making it work," but she knew of only a couple of South Asian students who had found jobs in research and technology, an underrepresentation she attributed to their limited English language skills.

Brown seemed to think that South Asian students had a better work ethic than other immigrant and minority students, due to their cultural background, echoing wider assumptions about the achievements of model minority immigrants as opposed to less successful minorities. She commented, "Not everyone is [just] getting jobs at Dunkin' Donuts"; the reality, however, was that some of the South Asian immigrant students I talked to were, in fact, working at Dunkin' Donuts, which hired many immigrant and South Asian workers in low-wage jobs, who then recruited their friends. In Ellery's view, South Asians were more likely than other immigrant students to come from middle-class backgrounds, and there were fewer undocumented immigrants from South Asia than from other regions of the world. Both assumptions were generally true because migration to the United States from India tends to require greater financial resources than needed for migration from Haïti or El Salvador. Ellery also thought that most South Asian youth had received more years of education and had higher literacy levels than students whose families were fleeing war-torn countries or were displaced from rural communities in Latin America or the Caribbean. These views drew on Ellery's long years of experience at the school and were based on the realities of immigration patterns but also reinforced dominant perceptions of so-called model minorities, which shaped the broader perception of South Asian immigrant students within the microsociety of the high school.

Yet the coordinator of the Just a Start program also observed that university and office jobs in Wellford were shrinking and most youth in the city were now working in retail stores; he estimated that half of the high school's students had some kind of job but that some were more privileged and did not work until their senior year, getting a job as part of the middle-class American "rite of passage." There was a clear class stratification within the high school reflected in youth employment trends, and also a hierarchy of jobs in the views of the teachers and program staff, with more skilled "office jobs" ranking above retail positions, and with fast food and grocery store jobs considered the least preferable. While the immigrant students generally were concentrated in these last two categories, they generally seemed much less concerned with these work hierarchies than with pragmatic issues such as salary and schedules, which often led them to dead-end jobs.

Teachers and program staff had varying views about the "skills" and cultural knowledge of work possessed by immigrant students. Some commented that immigrant students lacked the experience and information about work, while others observed that U.S.-born students also did not fully understand what it meant to find or keep a job. In part, their opinions seemed to reflect a desire to mold students to become better workers, or at least to be more successful in finding the "right" job for them, though the assumptions and cultural expectations held by adults about youth and work were often not fully explored. It is true that young immigrants do not have the tacit knowledge of what it means to work in the United States—this knowledge is part of the norms and assumptions that make up cultural citizenship, the understanding of how one is supposed to function within a neoliberal capitalist state.

Studies of youth suggest that less is actually known about the experiences of working youth in North America than in developing countries, partly because there is a denial of the realities of youth employment in the United States (McKechnie and Hobbs 2002). However, existing studies of youth and work in the United States generally do not make connections between work, national identification, and cultural belonging, especially for young immigrants. Most studies of young workers focus more on the relationship between work and schooling, reflecting adult and policy concerns about the impact of work on young people's education and their future role in the labor market, or the relation between work and social and psychological development (Lewis et al. 1998; McKechnie and Hobbs 2002). What is needed is an approach that takes into account both domestic and global dimensions of the experiences of young immigrants in the labor market, acknowledging the role of foreign policy, immigration, and the national political context, as well as local and generational factors.

One of the most pressing issues wrestled with daily by the immigrant youth in this book was the increased scrutiny of immigration status and employment of Muslim immigrant communities, and its effect on their need for work and desire for education, making economic citizenship a highly politically and culturally contested issue. The heightened suspicion of immigrants and intensified nativist sentiment in the United States after 9/11 played a role in a local campaign that highlighted the stakes of education as a venue for inculcating cultural citizenship, linking immigrant education to national identity and culture. During the year that I was doing fieldwork in Wellford, the city was embroiled in a controversy over a statewide referendum to ban bilingual education. The euphemistically named "English for the Children" proposition had been barreled through onto ballots in four states with funding from the right-wing millionaire Ron Unz. Many bilingual education advocates themselves concurred that bilingual teaching could be improved but argued that it was important not to eliminate it entirely, to ensure that immigrant students could continue to learn subject areas while learning a new language; they protested that the Unz initiative was based on an anti-immigrant ideology of assimilation. The English for the Children campaign was heavily couched in a nativist rhetoric about un-American immigrants not wanting to learn English at all, playing into the anxiety about undocumented and nonwhite immigrants and xenophobia after 9/11.[5]

Contrary to these images of immigrants desiring cultural segregation, and confirming the research documenting the intense desire of immigrants to learn English and get better jobs despite facing many obstacles (e.g., Orellana, Ek, and Hernández 2000), most of the immigrant youth in the high school struggled to improve their English and continue their education. Arnoldo Vásquez, a Latino teacher in the bilingual program, observed of immigrant students, "It's cool to speak English, unlike what people think." But he also observed, "In the country right now, perhaps because of 9/11 and because of the war, there is a very conservative wave penetrating within the political agenda . . . , penetrating every aspect of our lives and trying to do away with bilingual education . . . By doing away with services for immigrants, they are guaranteeing an underclass of cheap labor." Despite an intense campaign by supporters of bilingual education and Latino and Latina activists across the state, the ballot initiative against bilingual education passed in the state and succeeded in replacing the existing bilingual education program with one-year, English immersion classes, although the state later conceded that students could use waivers to stay in bilingual classes and that two-way immersion programs could continue.[6] High school teachers in the bilingual program, such as Ellery and several others I spoke to, were very concerned about the impact of this measure on their students—anticipating increased paperwork as students sought waivers to stay in bilingual classes—and some students wrote letters themselves to state legislators and signed petitions supporting bilingual education.

Recently arrived South Asian immigrant students were new to bilingual education and were just beginning to learn about its implications for their education, let alone the controversies surrounding it, so they were not sure what the English for the Children campaign was all about. However, they were anxious about navigating the American educational system and immigration law to get educational credentials and find work. Several of these students found this an uphill struggle, not just because of the tenuousness of bilingual education but also in the face of measures excluding undocumented immigrants from financial aid for college, and of the labyrinthine web of immigration and work regulations. Amin's anxiety about getting a Social Security card so he could work legally as soon as he could after he came to the United States was shaped by these regulations and restrictions. A more complicated story was that of Sara's friend, Maryam, an extremely bright young woman who radiated purposefulness and who had worked at a dental clinic while at the high school. However, after she graduated, she was unable to go to college or study psychology as she had hoped, because she was still undocumented and so got caught in the growing net of work and immigration policies ensnaring undocumented immigrants. Economic citizenship was thus tied to the regulation of immigrant labor and debates about national belonging, and knitted into notions of cultural citizenship.[7]

Some South Asian immigrant youth were skeptical about the notion of merit in American higher education, as Walid seemed to imply in his comment that international students were able to get into elite colleges because they could buy admission, despite low SAT scores. While Walid may not have been accurate in suggesting that South Asian students literally buy their way into U.S. colleges, he was right in suggesting that international students from elite backgrounds often come to the United States with better academic skills than working-class immigrant students from urban American public high schools and in noting the inherent class inequity in U.S. higher education. Children of wealthy alumni often get admission into competitive colleges despite inadequate academic credentials, and the price of college education has increased so that educational degrees with varying values in the job market are a commodity to be bought and traded for class advancement. Walid's remark pointed to the experiences of South Asian students from urban public high schools in the United States compared to those of international students from elite South Asian families who managed to get admitted to prestigious universities in the area. In the year I was doing this research, one South Asian immigrant student who graduated from Wellford High School got entry into Harvard—a young Tibetan woman who was not in the bilingual program. Aspirations for educational credentials and class mobility underlying neoliberal economic citizenship shaped these young immigrants' understandings of national culture, social inequity, and racial difference.

The South Asian Muslim immigrant youth in this book understood work to be tied to the law, and to the regulatory powers of the state as it defined them as immigrants, aliens, or Muslims, but they also experienced work culturally and socially, in relation to the city and the public sphere. Work constrains these young immigrants' leisure time and social relationships, as Walid and many other students observed. Work affected young immigrants' sociality and access to popular culture, but they also forged relationships and understood cultural citizenship through work. Walid's reflections on his life in Wellford underscored that work schedules made it difficult for these immigrant youth to socialize with one another, to go out into the city, and to consume popular culture in public spaces. The participation of these young immigrants in American public culture, in fact, was largely based on work, and their relations outside the school and community were primarily with other immigrant or young workers and with employers, often of diverse ethnic and national backgrounds. Fatima and Tasmeena observed that the other workers at the Dunkin' Donuts store where they worked were Indian, Brazilian, and Haitian—the communities that comprised the bulk of the immigrant population in the city.

"Work" and "play" are not necessarily in polar opposition to each other, from a critical perspective on citizenship and consumption, for they are

not dichotomous spheres of confinement and discipline (work) and freedom and spontaneity (popular culture), but overlapping processes of constructing relationships to society and to the state. This does not deny that
confining work or flexible labor is exploitative, but it does point to the
ways in which young workers, especially, struggle to find meaning in work
and access to the consumer culture that they are told represents "freedom."
Paul Willis (1990, 15) points out that young people create an "informal
culture" infused with what he calls "symbolic work." This is performed
not just through the use of cultural commodities but also in the realm of
wage labor, where creativity is often stifled in low-skill, deadening service
jobs but in which young workers still try to invest their "own 'unofficial
meanings,'" which is perhaps a form of creative play. At the same time, the
informal cultural politics expressed through popular culture may subvert,
but also mirror, the structural exclusion young people confront in institutions. Cultural citizenship is embedded in processes of exclusion as well
as affiliation that are forged in the realms of work as well as play, both of
which are considered zones of individual self-actualization and achievement while deeply marked by national as well as economic ideologies.

PLAY

Work and "play"—the latter a process that I view as broader than that of
"leisure," with its implications as being distinct from labor—are processes
that link mobility and confinement, discipline and dissent, difference and
affiliation. Work is linked to play through experiences of urban culture,
youth subcultures, and popular culture, for these are not mutually exclusive arenas. The implications of labor and popular culture for citizenship
are multilayered and shape different modes of citizenship that are intertwined and simultaneously expressed through consumer-citizenship, urban or subcultural citizenship, multicultural citizenship, and polycultural
citizenship. These are the different facets of relationships to the state for
urban, immigrant youth of color that emerge in their daily experiences of
work, education, popular culture, and consumption.

Consumer Citizenship and Popular Culture Labor and leisure are linked,
for popular culture increasingly functions as an arena in which individual
consumer-citizen identities are constructed, a process clearly applicable
to youth as they grapple with the meanings of the state and citizenship
in their everyday lives. If youth are supposedly alienated from traditional,

public forms of political participation, so is the vast majority of the populace in a country such as the United States. This does not mean idealizing the possibilities for political expression available to youth through the consumption of media, but simply acknowledging that popular culture offers "symbolic resources" to young people to engage with questions of politics outside of official institutions and political parties and to produce their own understandings of cultural citizenship (Willis 1990, 131, 149). The production of cultural citizenship through the use of cultural commodities is still embedded in relationships with the state and market, both of which are heavily invested in the meanings attached to citizenship by the younger generation. The notion of "youth" itself, as a set of generational groupings that has particular social interests and consumption patterns, is after all a marketing category created by the cultural industries to target young consumers.

Cultural consumption is linked to neoliberal citizenship; and young people, like adults, practice consumer citizenship where turn-of-the-millennium American neoliberal nationalism is closely tied to a culture of consumption, on many levels. On one level, consumption practices are central to defining the "self" in relation to a collective identity, as well as to national culture, and to class, racial, and ethnic hierarchies (Maira 2000; Park 2005). On a broader level, theorists of citizenship point to the emergence of the model of the citizen as consumer with the increasing privatization of services previously offered by the welfare state. Liberal conceptions of individualized citizenship mesh well with the notion of individualized consumption in capitalist democracies, where citizen rights are a form of possessive property (Holston and Appadurai 1991, 11; Miller 1993, 129–30; Isin 2000, 2–4). Jean and John Comaroff (2001) argue that the neoliberal mode of "millennial capitalism" increasingly obscures the workings of labor and highlights instead processes of consumption, so that citizenship is re-created as consumer identity. The United States as well as other states that are "consumerized republics" place mass consumption at the center of nation-building, so increasingly "self-interested citizens . . . view government policies like other market transactions, judging them by how well served they feel personally," thus assuming the combined role of citizen-consumer (Cohen 2003, 9).

"Consumer nationalism," according to Grewal (2005, 197, 219–20), collapses classical liberal distinctions between civil society and the market, "promoting endlessly the idea of choice as central to a liberated subject and enabling the hegemony of both capitalist democracy, American style, and the self-actualizing and identity-producing possibilities of consumption, American style." The immigrant youth in this study understand themselves as consumers of not just commodities or media but also of educational opportunities or the promise of a way of life that compelled their parents to migrate from South Asia. South Asian immigrant youth have limited resources to purchase commodities, but they also engage in the ideological consumption of notions of democracy, representation, or belonging. Grewal observes that the notion of freedom, key to Bush's global War on Terror to defend the American "way of life," is marketed through American popular culture that circulates globally, and that "'freedom' as a specific kind of 'choice' was created as a symbol of [American] nationalism" (206) through the spread of American consumer culture. Many of these youth had encountered the United States first through Hollywood films; interestingly, a few students, such as Shireen and Samira, specifically remembered seeing the blockbuster *Titanic* in their villages and towns in South Asia before they embarked on their own journey to the United States. This film, imagining the United States as the destination of immigrants' dreams and the desires of the young protagonists, in particular, is an example of how the ideology of the American Dream is consumed by young people around the world. The notion of "choosing" freedom and democracy, presumably over other ways of life and in opposition to those who "hate" the United States, is a central tenet of U.S. imperial culture.

South Asian immigrant youth consumed U.S. popular culture and ideas of the "American way of life" that shaped their understandings of American national culture even before they arrived in the United States. After moving to Wellford, immigrant youth continued to engage with various forms of U.S. popular culture and media in the space of the city, though in limited ways given the constraints of time, access, and language, and so the school and workplace were the sites where they primarily consumed understandings of cultural citizenship. As suggested in the discussion of flexible citizenship in chapter 3, these South Asian immigrant youth also relied on transnational popular culture, such as South Asian films, music, and television serials, to bolster their South Asian identifications. Thus, at first glance, it might seem that these young people constructed their relationship to belonging in the United States in the public spaces of work and education, and that they performed South Asian cultural citizenship and expressed their feelings of belonging to South Asia through transnational popular culture, consumed privately at home. This dichotomy between ethnicization in the private sphere and "assimilation" in the public sphere has often been upheld in the traditional paradigms of ethnic identity and immigration in the United States, The dichotomy of private versus public national identifications is itself a very American notion of immigrant incorporation, or even assimilation, which assumes that national loyalties are spatially split between the private and public sphere (Abraham and Shryock 2000).

However, work was often a site where these South Asian youth socialized not just with other immigrants or with other Americans, but also with their South Asian friends and relatives. Work itself was often understood as an extension of their family obligations, a practice supported by economic motivations that were themselves not simply "South Asian" or "American" but also deeply intertwined with family ties, as in the case of Shireen's and Samira's work at their parents' store and the phone card business that Ismail had with his brother. Lisa Park's (2005, 65) research on Asian American youth who work in their immigrant parents' businesses shows that "the business provides an intense connection to their parents and community," redefining family relationships and shaping children's attitudes to work, ethnicity, and gender.[8] At the same time, home and community had become, after 9/11, spaces that were vulnerable to intrusion and investigation by the state. There was an underlying anxiety among South Asian, Muslim, and Arab immigrants that the "private" was no longer completely private in the era of the PATRIOT Act. For example, a few months after I began doing my fieldwork, I visited Ismail's house and noticed something that had not been there on my last visit: a U.S. flag draped on the living room wall next to the cloth painting of Mecca, which seemed to be the standard decoration in the homes of most of the South Asian Muslim families. The domain of home was not simply a place for connecting with South Asian popular culture, but also for staging different aspects of "American" life and loyalty that were juxtaposed, if not connected to, religious and ethnic identity. The division between "private" and "public" is, in actuality, blurred by the intrusion of the surveillance state into the private spaces of home, mosque, or community after 9/11, as I will discuss in chapter 6 (see also Parenti 2003). The boundary between private and public spheres is reconstituted in the lives of immigrant families who must re-create "community" and reimagine the relationship between work and culture.

Subcultural Citizenship: Scripting "Tradition" and "Freedom" These immigrant youth understood American cultural citizenship through their consumption of an array of cultural forms—including elements of local or urban U.S. youth culture—linked to larger imaginings of national belonging. Immigrant students were drawn to U.S. popular culture, often before they had set foot in the United States, not just due to transnational media but also because of transnational ties created through immigration that introduced them to new cultural forms or subcultural styles while living in South Asia. Faisal learned basketball while growing up in Pakistan, a country where cricket is by far a more popular national sport, because his father was living in the United States and introduced him to basketball on his visits home. So some of these immigrant youth had grown up with one foot tenuously planted in subcultures from another part of the world where their family members lived, as a result of the globalization of popular culture and its intersections with the South Asian diaspora. After Faisal came to Wellford, basketball became his entry into the subculture of nonimmigrant boys in the high school and facilitated his belonging to local youth cultures. Sports is an important arena in which American masculinity, not to mention national identity and cultural difference, is shaped and performed in relation to race and class (Martin and Miller 1999).

However, other South Asian immigrant boys, such as Walid, Ismail, and Osman, who were fans of cricket did not have the same connection to the local, urban culture of young males via basketball, nor perhaps to a national culture based on the intersection of sports, media, and racialized bodies (see Miller 1999). Instead, these immigrant boys tried to find the time to play in the weekend cricket games organized by international South Asian students from local colleges, as Walid observed, for cricket was also a basis for forming their own South Asian immigrant, male subculture in Wellford. One of the early requests that the boys had for SAMTA volunteers was, in fact, to help organize a cricket club, but unfortunately, there were not enough students interested in playing cricket to form a team. What became apparent was that there were different, overlapping youth subcultures into which these youth tried to gain entry and which had varying implications for their imaginings of belonging and difference within the school, city, and the nation.

Affiliation with U.S. subcultures varied by the kind of exposure South Asian students had to American popular culture, either indirectly through transnational cultural lives or directly, by growing up in the United States, and created boundaries between youth based on cultural consumption. South Asian youth who had come to the United States at a much earlier age, such as two Gujarati students, Farid and Ayesha, were more engaged with hip-hop and more likely to identify with U.S. youth culture styles than were immigrant youth. Vásquez, who had himself migrated from Central America at a young age, commented:

> Some South Asian youth are adopting what it means to be a young man of color in this society, their body language . . . young people from other groups also adopt that, for they seem to think that's what it means to be a young person in this society, the gangsta-ghetto look. . . . What seems to provide the window into this culture is black role models.[9]

While I was talking to Vásquez in his classroom one day, Suhail, a young boy who was Pathan (Pashto-speaking, from northwest Pakistan) and who dressed in punk style, walked into the room. Suhail was the only South Asian student I had seen in the school who visibly identified as punk; he was often alone and did not hang out with many other South Asian immigrant youth, seemingly removed from their cultural tastes and orientations. When I complimented him on his chunky steel necklace, Suhail seemed pleased but remarked that he was "bored"; he talked about trying to create his own Web page with a friendliness that belied his alienated image in the school. Suhail never articulated to me what had drawn him to punk, chatting instead about his website and job at a shoe store, but the visual statement he made was enough to set him apart from the other South Asian youth.

After Suhail left the room, Vásquez insightfully observed that the high school's subcultures seemed to provide "pockets of culture" within the larger society that allowed immigrant youth to "cross over in the new culture" and to combat isolation and marginalization as newcomers to the United States. The understanding that youth of a particular generation cluster around certain forms of popular culture, through which they define themselves and negotiate their relationship to the "parent culture," was most famously developed by the subcultural theory of the Birmingham school. In their seminal analysis of youth subcultures, *Resistance through Rituals*, Stuart Hall and others argued that subcultures provide youth with a set of "social rituals" associated with a "collective identity," in response to the personal, political, and economic contradictions that youth confront on the brink of adulthood (Clarke et al. 1976, 47). Despite the later critiques, some of them well deserved, of the Birmingham school's theoretical approach and methods (e.g., Cohen 1997; Frith 1997; McRobbie 1994), this framework provides an important analysis linking the cultural consumption, and production, of young people to larger political, economic, and cultural relations at a given historical moment. Subcultures can also promote the notion of individual freedom to "choose" an identity based on style, through purchasing certain kinds of fashion, music, or other commodities, and learning codes of subcultural belonging, thus performing various kinds of consumer citizenship within the landscape of neoliberal capitalism.

In this research, it became apparent that subcultures provide a microcultural realm for "subcultural citizenship," a space where youth learn codes of belonging based on style, body language, and cultural interests, and adopt different orientations to the adult world and larger society (see Gelder and Thornton 1997; Thornton 1996). Second-generation South Asian youth in the high school more commonly became involved in subcultures that connected them to local and national cultures, moving between listening to hip-hop and discussions at the mosque as Farid did. Immigrant youth, however, generally gravitated toward their own subcultures within the school based on common national or regional identities, such as Pakistani, South Asian, Haitian, Central American, Latino and Latina, or Brazilian. Immigrant youth in this study also formed a subcultural connection with one another based on their shared identification as immigrant, South Asian, and Muslim. They hung out together inside and outside school and shared similar cultural interests in South Asian films and music, though some of them found themselves drawn to American pop, as Zeenat did, or crossing over into rock, as in Faisal's case. All immigrant youth had experiences of negotiating their relationships with new cultural institutions, such as the school, and their immigrant families, as suggested by the narratives of Mumtaz, Walid, Shireen, and Samira. Yet theirs was not a subculture formed out of choice, but rather born of their cultural displacement, and it was not centered primarily on cultural consumption, but rather on managing their precarious economic position and cultural and political alienation from post-9/11 America.

There is a perception, in mainstream media, public discourse, and, even implicitly, in some academic research that what binds immigrant youth together is the presumed culture clash between traditional family values and American public culture, suggesting that intergenerational conflict is a key element of immigrant youth subcultures. Much has already been written about Muslim immigrant youth straddling "two worlds," a trope which frames Muslim and American identities in binary opposition and that is pervasive in the academic literature on immigrant and second-generation youth and in general public discourse, as well in debates within Muslim American communities (Abu-Laban and Abu-Laban 1999; Ajrouch 1999; Eisenlohr 1996; Swanson 1996; Sarroub 2001). Some teachers in the Wellford High School used this binary frame to empha-size the cultural conflict they believed immigrant students experienced between the values presumably associated with their ethnic community and with mainstream American culture. This was not a completely irrel-evant approach: cultural tensions certainly exist for South Asian Muslim immigrant youth. For example, Walid spoke of the differences between "American people," who had freedoms "after eighteen" that were culturally sanctioned, and "desi families," who had certain restrictions for daughters and also "rules" for sons which curtailed his own social life. Yet the immi-grant youth in this study responded to these tensions of cultural transi-tion in ways that were far more complex, even fluid, than acknowledged in mainstream discourse, especially in discussions of Muslim American youth that are generally tinged to varying degrees with Orientalist no-tions of binding traditions.

Walid seemed to have a more complex notion of cultural "freedom," for he was conscious that adult rights and lifestyles were shaped not just by formal citizenship, but by the particular cultural scripts of belonging and obligation within families and ethnic groups, which shifted over time or with migration. He also observed a similarity in these gendered cultural scripts between South Asian and "Spanish people"—the term commonly used to refer to Latinos and Latinas by high school youth—implying that some of these tensions in subcultural citizenship were shared among different ethnic and immigrant groups. Therefore, there were certainly community-specific notions of the meanings of "freedom" and "adult-hood," rights and responsibilities, which were tied to subcultural belonging. Discussions of subcultural citizenship for Muslim immigrant youth also need to be situated in relationship to ideologies of U.S. cultural citizenship and nationalism that construct any incipient Muslim American youth culture as potentially opposed to Western modernity and questioning of the "American way of life" or, at least, vulnerable to political movements that are viewed as a threat to the American nation.[10] Especially after 9/11, the mainstream media in the United States played on this theme of conflicting identities to question the political allegiances of Muslim American youth and confine them to a subculture against which the so-called American way of life could be defined in opposition.

The fashioning of Muslim American youth subcultures also has a gendered meaning, but one that is often distorted in the public imagination through the linking of youth, Islam, and popular culture and the conflation of modernity with a particular definition of Western individualism and freedom. Much of the discourse in the mainstream media about Muslim youth in the United States, after 9/11 but also well before, has tended to dwell on the image of fanatical boys and girls wearing hijab (the headscarf), generally producing an Orientalist notion of Muslim youth bound by an unchanging religion and completely outside of modern (i.e., "Western" or American) youth culture. Yet only one of the South Asian Muslim girls in the high school that I interviewed wore a headscarf— whose meaning itself is more complex than that ascribed by Orientalist frameworks about Islam and gender (see Ahmed 1992; Mernissi 1991; Yegenoglu 1998). Furthermore, these girls' engagement with U.S. popular culture and also with work outside the home contradicted the perception of Muslim immigrant youth alienated from mainstream American culture, a belief that is outdated given the global penetration of U.S. popular culture. I found that the South Asian Muslim boys had varying perceptions of the relationship of Islam to commercialized popular culture, of women's clothing styles and what would be "appropriate" or culturally familiar, engaging in lively debates which expressed a range of views that defied the dominant image of "Muslim youth." While some came from families that could be considered socially conservative in the context of Wellford, none of the youth followed a "fundamentalist" interpretation of Islam, a term that has been misused in the War on Terror and that has long been politically and culturally contested (see Moallem 1999). If these young immigrants affiliated with one another as "Muslim youth," it was largely based on a common minority identity, rather than through a common understanding of Islam or what it meant to be Muslim. Little room exists, in academic research or in mainstream media or public discourse, for youth who are South Asian, Pakistani, Pathan, and Muslim in background, and punk in style.[11]

There were many youth subcultures in the high school that borrowed elements from one another while still carving out distinctive codes of belonging and claiming space in the high school, as visible during lunchtime, when students in the cafeteria generally sat together in ethnic or linguistic groups. In this sense, it becomes apparent that cultural citizenship for immigrant youth is most immediately defined in relation to specific, localized subcultures, created in certain geographic and cultural spaces, which provide a conduit into understandings of a larger "national culture" that is powerful, but largely abstract, and becomes tangible in these micropolitical realms. As Vásquez insightfully observed, "The sense of community that these young people find is within their own group. It is their own group that helps them assimilate. . . . Kids who have been here longer become the connection between the new arrivals and the dominant society."

The young immigrants in this book seemed to be crafting an immigrant subculture in the making that was not defined solely based on being Muslim, South Asian, urban, or working-class immigrants, but rather on a combination of *all* these elements as understood differently by each of these youth, who still collectively identified and socialized with one another. It is a subculture based on a hybrid notion of cultural belonging that challenges the dichotomy of tradition and modernity, but in ways perhaps more subtle and less obviously commercialized than the cultural rituals of middle-class or affluent South Asian immigrant youth. Second-generation South Asian youth who can afford to go to South Asian parties in clubs or restaurants have created their own highly visible public culture, which I explored in my earlier research and which has its own codes of subcultural belonging and authentic membership based on gender, sexuality, religion, and ethnic "purity" (see Maira 2002a). The creation of subcultural citizenship and cultural consumption is certainly a gendered process, and many theorists of youth culture have observed the different ways in which girls and boys engage, or are expected to engage, with cultural consumption and production (McRobbie 1994; Willis 1990, 13). However, I found that these young people's experiences challenged the traditional assumptions about immigrant girls being confined to the home by expectations of performing domestic care and consuming popular culture only in private spaces, in contrast to boys who presumably have more freedom to engage in public cultural consumption. The girls certainly watched films and television serials at home, but Mumtaz, Samira, Shireen, and other girls also traveled around the city to work. As the stories of Walid, Amin, and Ismail attest, many of these boys felt unable to consume popular culture because of their work—and they also spent time at home helping their mothers and sisters with domestic chores. The gendered differences in cultural consumption were not as stark as conventional images of immigrant youth, particularly Muslim youth, seem to suggest.

South Asian immigrant girls engaged with popular culture in ways that defied stereotypical assumptions about the cultural tastes of "traditional" Muslim females and the expectations that immigrant youth are either fully Americanized or ethnicized in their cultural consumption. A vivid example of this was one evening when I was in a car with a group of South Asian girls from the high school, driving them to a South Asian culture show at a local university, an event they were eager to attend. I had given rides to girls from the school before, and they knew I always liked to play music in the car, so this time they came prepared. Tasmeena had brought her own CD of Hindi remix music and requested I put it on and turn up the volume. We drove through the streets of Wellford blaring Indian film music, the girls piled on top of one another in the car, laughing and chattering in Gujarati, Hindi, and English. Driving around with loud music pumping into city streets is something one might associate with teenage boys, but it was clear that the girls got immense pleasure from blasting Hindi music into the night (and I must confess, so did I!). These girls rarely got a chance to drive around the city in a car, and it was by no means common to hear Bollywood music in the predominantly white, public spaces in Wellford. Tasmeena's small, sonic gesture seemed to be claiming the city for her own, if only for a few minutes, while in motion through its streets.

Urban Citizenship: A Dialectical Approach García Canclini (2001) observes that youth increasingly access ideas of national belonging through the form of popular culture, rather than through more traditional avenues based on formal institutions of citizenship or political organizations. But what is the content, not just form, of this national belonging and its relationship to the spaces in which it is produced? How do youth understand the nature of the nation-state (or nation-states) to which they think they belong, or want to belong? It became apparent to me that for many of these South Asian immigrant youth, belonging in the United States meant belonging in the city, and that Wellford provided a specific, local context for their ideas of what being in the United States meant. Coexisting with transnational forms of flexible citizenship are localized, territorialized understandings of belonging that emerge in specific places (Sassen 1999). James Holston and Arjun Appadurai (1999, 3, 10) argue that cities have been "challenging, diverging from, and even replacing nations as the important space of citizenship—as the lived space not only of its uncertainties but also of its emergent forms," due to the role of cities as "specialized sites for the operations of more globally oriented capital and labor" where different groups of citizens and immigrants, workers, and elites engage in struggles over the rights and claims of citizenship (see also Sassen 1991). Theorists of urban citizenship argue that the "work of modern nationalism" is done in the city, the sphere in which people engage most immediately with ideas of rights and belonging through their relationship with "local governance," if not local government. While this does not mean that the nation-state is obsolete and no longer operates as the context for ideas of "loyalty" and "discipline" for citizens (Isin 2000, 9–10), nor does this mean that it no longer regulates immigration and labor, it is clear that globalization has made cities the "spaces where the very meaning, content and extent of citizenship are made and transformed."

Engin Isin (2000, 6) suggests, "Being at the interstices of global networks of flows and commodities, services, capital, labour, images and ideas, the global city, both as a milieu and object of struggles for recognition, engenders new political groups that claim either new types of rights or seek to expand modern, civil, political and social rights." Even if Wellford cannot be considered a "global city," it is still a globalized, small city and a diverse urban context in which different social groups shape collective identities, enact claims of belonging, struggle for rights, and make demands on the state (Isin 2000, 15). In fact, Saskia Sassen argues that secondary cities, such as Wellford, are emerging as strategic sites for the transformations of citizenship by immigrants, among other marginalized groups, where "claim-making is not confined to formal citizens" (2004, 176). However, these analyses of the potential for immigrants to enact informal citizenship in cities need to be reconsidered and taken with more caution after 9/11, for the ongoing campaign to limit the political or economic rights of immigrants and constrain their struggles to claim cultural rights was only intensified with the War on Terror, particularly in the case of South Asian, Arab, and Muslim Americans.

My point is not to idealize or privilege "local" or "urban" practices of citizenship, but to understand how the city, not just the nation-state, is a site that shapes practices of citizenship. For young people in particular, cities are sites where struggles over their inclusion in national projects are often waged through moral panics over "law and order" that criminalize particular groups of youth and through discourses of cultural difference, tradition, and "modernization" that focus on young people (e.g., Diouf 1999). The experiences of immigrant youth make it clear that the city is a space in which ideas of loyalty, discipline, civics, and virtue are practiced, to draw on Isin's framework for urban citizenship (2000, 9–10). I would argue that, in fact, each of these "rationalities of modern local government" that Isin identifies is in a productive tension with a force that counters the rationality itself. It is this dialectic that makes urban citizenship useful to think, along with flexible citizenship. "Loyalty" is in tension with expressions of dissent, "virtue" with practices of demonization, "civics" with disenfranchisement, and "discipline" with complicity. In the next chapter, I explore further the notion of dissenting citizenship and why I think it is complicity that is the other face of discipline—rather than anarchy or even resistance—in the post-9/11 surveillance state.

These dialectical modes of urban citizenship are embedded in the concrete, everyday ways individuals, including immigrant youth, practice politics. The city provides not a "singular, abstract public sphere" but "intensely concrete" and "plural public spaces" (Isin 2000, 18); indeed, it is the context for constructing, engaging with, or being rejected from public spheres by South Asian Muslims after 9/11. The rally in Prospect Square organized by SACH to protest the hate crime against a young South Asian man was an instance of the activity of "assembling and protesting" by citizens in the space of the city (Isin 2000, 18), of physically expressing dissent and challenging the demonization and disenfranchisement of groups targeted by the state after 9/11. Yet that many members of the targeted communities were absent from the demonstration because they were afraid of openly expressing political dissent also shows the limitations of focusing only on politics in the "public sphere," which is in reality shaped by exclusion, fragmentation, and policing. The possibility of surveillance at the rally, perhaps in the form of an innocuous photographer penetrating the crowd, powerfully conjoins state discipline to complicity, and also the suspicion of complicity. The public sphere is not an inclusive "public," and after 9/11, even the notion of competing or subaltern counterpublics constituted of minority communities (Fraser 1997, 74) has been curtailed by surveillance, self-censorship, and distrust, as I will discuss in the following chapter, forcing us to rethink the meaning of counterpublics for targeted groups in a climate of repression.

This tension between loyalty and dissent, between petitioning and rejecting the state, and between local and national modes of belonging runs through all the chapters in the book, for these dialectics of citizenship constantly underlie the experiences of citizenship for immigrant youth. The diverse social groups that encounter one another in the space of the city forge collective identities as a basis for expressing rights and obligations, but are also divided by the notion of cultural citizenship that the city offers, for the idea of difference—cultural, racial, ethnic, gendered—is a component of imagining citizenship at both national and local levels. The notion of cultural difference is the basis for inclusion and exclusion by the nation-state and is apparent in the local, everyday practices of work, education, and popular culture in the daily lives of South Asian immigrant youth. Isin (2000, 15) argues that this difference leads to fragmentation and the weakening of struggles for rights in the city, and rights to the city. However, other theorists of cultural citizenship argue that citizens who are excluded on the basis of cultural, racial, or gender difference can also seize the idea of difference as the basis on which to contest the idea of who belongs to the national, or local, polity (e.g., Flores and Benmayor 1997; Rosaldo 1997). The notion of multicultural citizenship, and the contradictions of cultural difference and political exclusion that it generates, is an issue that I explore in the section that follows.

The interplay of cultural and class difference in the city was heightened for these working-class immigrant youth in Wellford, which was home to some highly acclaimed colleges. The public high school, in fact, was within a stone's throw from one of them, and the students often walked through its elegant campus after school. Yet an incident one wintry afternoon made me think of how far, in a sense, the university really was from the local public high school. It had begun to snow earlier in the day, and by the time classes were over, the lawns of the university were covered in a soft white that seemed to muffle sound and wash the stark silhouettes of the tall trees against the brick facades of the buildings. I was walking through the campus myself on my way home from the school, and spotted a group of young people laughing boisterously and playing in the snow. At first, I thought that they were just another group of Wellford High students, and then I realized that the sound of their voices seemed to strike an unfamiliar chord in the snow-filtered silence, but one that was familiar to me, for they were speaking and shouting to one another in Gujarati and Hindi.

I saw Sara and Rukshana, who always seemed so demure and quiet in the school, packing snowballs and hurling them at the others. Both sisters were dressed in jeans and sneakers, and while Sara was wearing make-up and had her hair coiled in a graceful, grown-up bun, Rukshana's hair was flying loose as she screamed and laughed and played with the snow, an unrestrained small bundle of energy and excitement. I saw a group of South Asian boys, including Riyaz, his brother, and Walid, who were walking a little farther ahead and trying to evade the girls' assaults. Samira and her friend Nasreen, who were often inseparable, were standing together, laughing but not joining the fray. They saw me and asked where they could buy a disposable camera to take pictures of the snowball fight, wondering if they should go to the drugstore to get one to capture this winter ritual.

I suddenly noticed a white projectile coming toward me and tried to duck, but it was too late. Rukshana's snowball hit me on my arm and my bag fell off my shoulder, shaking me off balance so I almost fell. Rukshana was tickled by her excellent aim, but I could see that Sara and the other boys and girls were slightly concerned and not sure how I would respond. Samira rushed to me and began packing a ball of snow for me to retaliate, but I laughed and said that I was in the company of competent girls—I wasn't sure my own aim was that good. Sara looked somewhat relieved to hear my response and picked up my bag, while Samira muttered something about the sisters being "a little crazy." The boys looked slightly amused, and we all walked past the library together as students carrying mounds of books and white-haired professors in tweed jackets passed by, whiffs of academic shoptalk floating on the air. Some of the older white passers-by looked at us with a mix of surprise and puzzlement, probably wondering where this group of noisy youth were from and how they had appeared in the middle of the campus. A couple of college students who had paused to watch the snowball fight walked by and looked at us curiously, asking each other what language was being spoken. I knew

already that few of the public high school's graduating students got admitted into this elite university, even though they ironically passed through its
world often, but I think it was this moment that made me feel viscerally the
tension of belonging to very different, contiguous but not fully overlapping, cultural and class worlds in Wellford.

CULTURE: MULTICULTURAL AND
POLYCULTURAL CITIZENSHIP

For South Asian immigrant youth, it is apparent that cultural "difference" is one of the ideas they associate with belonging in the U.S.
nation-state and living in Wellford, and that they understand ethnic, racial, national, or religious difference through the lens of multiculturalism.
Multicultural citizenship, as discussed by Will Kymlicka (1995), is based
on the idea of minority cultural rights, the rights of minority groups
within multiethnic nations to express their cultural identity (see also
Pakulski 1997, 74). Others suggest that collective cultural rights within
a multiethnic national culture, such as "access to educational institutions,
the possession of an appropriate 'living' language, the effective ownership
of cultural identity through national citizenship membership" are necessarily embroiled with political histories of inclusion and exclusion and
need to be linked to the obligations of the state and private media to de-
mocratize access to the public sphere (Turner 2001).

Since multiculturalism is such a pervasive discourse of cultural belonging in the United States, particularly in education, it is not surprising that
some of these youth talked about ideas of difference and relationships
with others in terms of multicultural citizenship, even if only implicitly.
South Asian immigrant youth expressed a vernacular multicultural citizenship based on everyday understandings of pluralism emerging from
their social relationships. For most of these immigrant youth, it was important to emphasize that they had friendships that crossed ethnic and
racial boundaries, as Walid did in commenting on his black, Egyptian,
Moroccan, and Gujarati Indian friends. In their daily lives, these students
did, in fact, hang out with Latino and Latina, Caribbean, African American, and Asian students and with Muslim African youth, especially, who
were from Somalia, Ethiopia, or Egypt, forming cross-ethnic affiliations
and an incipient pan-Islamic identity. But it was also apparent that most
students in the school, as in most American schools and even colleges,
tended to cluster by ethnic group in the cafeteria and on the playground.

For instance, Ismail commented that his friendships with non–South Asian students were sometimes questioned by other desi youth, but he defended this crossing of borders by arguing for a more expansive conception of community:

> I hang out with different kids but even I heard it from a lot of desis who say, "Why you go with them?" They don't like it, but I say if you want to live in a different world, you have to exist with them. . . . Sometimes you have to go outside [your group] and say, yeah, alright, we are friends too, we are not going to discriminate [against] you, because you are white, we don't look like you. . . . Your relationship is gonna be bigger, right. But if you're gonna live in the desi community, you're only going to know desi people, not the other people.

Ismail implicitly comments on the racialized boundaries within the school between white and nonwhite students, a boundary whose meaning is different from most schools because students of color were actually the majority in Wellford High. Interestingly, Ismail seemed to trace the value he placed on multiculturalist coexistence not just to the liberal pluralism of the school but also to his belief in India as a multiethnic nation, observing "India is a really good place to live in . . . because they've got a lot of religions, different languages, different people." But this was before the massacre of Muslim Indians by right-wing Hindu militants during the Gujarat riots in spring 2002 intensified debates about Indian secularism and communal divisions for many Indians, especially Muslims, already critical of the "Hindutva" notion of a nation essentially for Hindus that has also permeated Indian diasporic communities (see Kurien 2003; Rajagopal 1998; Visweswaran and Mir 1999/2000).

The problems with liberal multiculturalism in the United States—as well as in other countries such as India—is that it highlights the idea of belonging in "diversity" in constructing groups of citizens in relation to the nation-state, while evading discussions of political inequity. Multicultural citizenship expresses some of the contradictions of consumer-citizenship, for it suggests that the consumption of cultural difference can promote mutual recognition and respect between different groups, the notion of multiculturalism itself having been absorbed by capitalism in marketing to different groups of consumers (Hall 1997). Racial difference has been largely detached from biological notions of race and has come to reside in ideas of cultural difference that are equally entrenched in the new "cultural racism" and underlie multicultural policies for managing "diversity." Modern nation-states that promote a multicultural rhetoric of racial inclusion and pluralism, such as the United States, simultaneously use state technologies such as immigration law to exclude, based on racial difference, and, as David Goldberg (2002, 9) argues, this exclusion becomes internalized by the nation-state. The "new managed" multiculturalism effectively erases the connections between the impact of colonialism and present-day racial inequities, in the United States as well as in Canada and European nation-states (Goldberg 2002, 218).

In France, for example, the public controversy about Muslim girls of North African origin wearing headscarves is linked by critics to the "universalist Republican principles" of French citizenship that make it difficult for France "to come to terms with its own multi-ethnic reality" (Freedman and Tarr 2000, 5). The figure of the veiled Muslim woman became a signifier of the threat of the fanatical Muslim and militant terrorist and evoked a growing "moral panic" about Muslims and Arabs as the "enemy within" and immigrants as invaders of France and of Europe since the 1980s. Neil MacMaster (2003, 301–2) suggests that the anxieties about students, in particular, centered on education as a bastion of republican values of universalism and assimilation, as Arab youth who had grown up in segregated *banlieue* (public housing estates) expressed their outrage over their exclusion and alienation from French society in confrontations with the police. The hostility to multicultural citizenship expressed by right-wing, nativist movements drew on the "Jacobin tradition of France 'one and indivisible'" and also on a "deeply rooted and racist hatred of 'Arabs' and of Algerians in particular" (MacMaster 2003, 299, 302). Some argue that the multiculturalist policies under François Mitterrand failed to resolve the legacy of France's "bloody recent colonial past" in Algeria for the "Beur" generation of French-born Arabs, who experienced rising unemployment and ongoing racial discrimination, particularly in the context of the "second Algerian war" and post-9/11 hysteria about "Islamic terrorism" (Bowen 2007, 20). In contrast, Canada has an official multicultural policy that envisions an "ethnic mosaic" of national belonging and provides state funding to promote expressions of "ethnic heritage," though Will Kymlicka (1995, 14) observes that these "polyethnic rights" may promote "diversity" but not necessarily "justice" for minority groups living in a society historically dominated by the culture of French or English colonial settlers. Sherene Razack's important work (2004, 13; 2007) has shown how the "everyday experiences of eviction from the national," from political community, and from Western law for Muslims (and other people of color in Canada) is underwritten by civilizational mythologies of a "kinder, gentler nation," in the shadow of its superpower neighbor, that mask its settler-colonial past. She argues that Canada's own War on Terror demonstrates that the "neo-liberal management of racial-minority populations who are scripted as pre-modern," requiring "regulation and surveillance," relegates them to "camps," or spaces of exception created for "abandoned or 'rightless people'" (2007, 6, 148).

Britain has its own headscarves affair and ongoing problems of economic marginalization and social alienation of youth from South Asian and Caribbean immigrant communities.[12] British multiculturalism is blamed by some conservatives for the emergence of radical political Islam and even for the attacks in London on July 7, 2005, while British Asian Muslims struggle with the shifting meanings of multiculturalism since the Salman Rushdie affair of 1988–89 (see Abbas 2005; McCabe et al., 2006; Modood 2002). Yet the anxieties about multiculturalism and immigration from Britain's former colonies are entangled with the legacy of British colonialism; as Paul Gilroy (2005, 100–101) observes, in postimperial Britain "the body of the immigrant . . . comes to represent all the of the discomforting ambiguities of the empire's shameful but nonetheless exhilarating history. . . . [They] may be unwanted and feared precisely because they are the unwitting bearers of the imperial and colonial past." In the United States, too, there is deep ambivalence for both the Right and Left about the meanings and limits of multiculturalism, which in its popular liberal incarnation evades histories of settler colonialism, cleansing of natives, slavery, and immigrant labor and focuses attention instead on the perceived assimilability of certain groups, such as Arab and Muslim Americans.

It is important to understand why multicultural citizenship is appealing to postimperial or neoliberal states: it encourages citizens to turn to a politics of representation rather than of systemic change, by fostering a cultural, rather than structural, analysis of social inequity. While Goldberg acknowledges the limits of a politics of recognition for marginalized citizens (2002, 253), he and other theorists underemphasize the ways in which liberal-democratic notions of universal rights and multicultural inclusion suppress debates about political injustice and economic inequity, as I will explore in the next chapter, on dissenting citizenship. As

Nancy Fraser points out, "pluralist multiculturalism" fails "to connect a cultural politics of identity and difference to a social politics of justice and equality . . . to link struggles for recognition to struggles for redistribution" (1997, 186).

The discourse of multiculturalism is readily absorbed by immigrants, students, and youth in the United States, for the state uses education, the law, bureaucratic processes, media images, and official rhetoric to propagate and celebrate this official doctrine of inclusion. The high school, implicitly and explicitly, promoted this notion of multicultural citizenship through visual symbols and support for ethnic-based student activities that mixed a political as well as cultural recognition of difference. Some teachers displayed posters in their classrooms, such as that of Martin Luther King Jr. and his dream of ending racial segregation, and outside the high school's main office was a display case with changing exhibits which often focused on the theme of cultural diversity, among other issues, acknowledging different ethnic groups in the school through artistic products and cultural symbols. The International Center was a visual shrine to multiculturalism, with posters on the walls of Puerto Rico, India, and Haiti. Multiculturalism was not simply symbolic in the center, however. The bilingual student population was incredibly diverse, and about a hundred languages were spoken by the high school's students, who mingled and interacted with one another in various ways in the center and in other spaces inside and outside the school. Ellery himself spoke at least four languages fluently, switching effortlessly between Spanish, Portuguese, French, and English when speaking to students or their parents. So multicultural policies as enacted in certain spaces within the school were embedded in practical, not just ideological or superficial markings of boundaries.

The International Center also acknowledged other kinds of difference, for there were charts on the wall displaying statistics on social stratification in the United States. The school officially hosted various ethnic clubs, which were very popular, such as the Black Student Union, Asian Club, Haitian Club, Portuguese Club, and Spanish Club, and support programs such as SAMTA and Ahora, for Latino and Latina students, as well as other kinds of more political groups. such as Free Tibet, a United Nations Club, and a progressive, antiwar student group (which did not seem to be very visible at the time). It seemed that institutional multicul-

turalism in the school coexisted with what Gilroy (2005, 120) calls a "multiculture," which is based on an everyday cosmopolitanism that emerges in
"heterocultural" urban spaces such as London. Gilroy (2005, 67) suggests
that in these metropolitan spaces, diverse racial and immigrant groups
interact and produce an ordinary hybridity, or vernacular cosmopolitanism that goes beyond multicultural consumerism; however, one cannot
idealize this multiculture, which is still influenced by market-driven and
state-produced ideas of diversity.

Many teachers and parents I spoke to in Wellford acknowledged that
there were class and racial fissures in the school's politically liberal culture
and in Wellford at large. One white American parent—an academic—
who had sent three children to the school, commented that the school's
"party line" was "pluralist coexistence," reflecting the generally liberal tenor
of the city's political culture. But he also observed that the "dominance
of black youth culture" at the school "masked structural inequities" that
were less visible, for example, the underrepresentation of African American students in advanced placement courses. Ellery, who was a veteran
teacher at the high school, said that the school's population had changed
as a result of the abolition of rent control and of escalating gentrification
of the city, squeezing the lower-middle-class population that was not eligible for public housing into less expensive towns and leaving Wellford a
"have or have-not kind of city" with "either fancy condos or public housing." Vásquez, who came to Wellford as a young refugee from El Salvador
in the 1980s, noted that the major issue facing the Latino and Latina community was the "housing crunch in the city," which had driven many out
to nearby towns with more affordable housing, curtailing the growth of
the Latino and Latina population in the high school. African American
students were overrepresented in the school; their proportional presence
in the school was more than double what it was in the city. While whites
made up almost 70 percent of Wellford residents in 2000, they comprised
only 40 percent of the student population. Overall enrollment in the
school had declined, according to Ellery, and some in Wellford said that
many white parents who could afford it, as well as academics teaching in
the area, were sending their high-school-age children to private schools.
In fact, in the years since I did the research, the immigrant student population at the high school reportedly began shrinking considerably, due to
escalating housing costs that drove struggling families out of Wellford.

The high school's liberal multiculturalism thus coexisted with issues of class difference that were discussed openly by teachers and staff, who seemed quite aware of the tensions between idealized cultural pluralism and structural inequity in the city's changing social landscape.

Students and teachers also spoke of moments of racial and ethnic tension between different groups of youth, similar to those in any school or community, tensions that had affected South Asian students well before 2001, though in different ways. Some of the second-generation South Asian students who had grown up in Wellford talked about being picked on for being South Asian, or a different kind of "brown" student than the recognizable Latinos and Latinas. Mary Alexander, who was from a South Indian, Christian immigrant family, remembered being punched by other children in kindergarten, labeled a "teacher's pet," and ridiculed in high school because her parents didn't allow her to wear tank tops and shorts. It is no surprise that antagonisms between children tend to be expressed in racial and cultural terms in the United States, in keeping with the pervasive discourse about racial difference that is imbibed by minority groups, dividing groups and turning immigrants against more recent newcomers. A Tibetan girl in the high school spoke of being harassed by other students for being "Chinese," which was ironic given her political involvement in protests against the Chinese occupation of Tibet. She recalled hearing the word "Gandhi" being used as a racial epithet against other Asian students in the school, a practice common in urban American schools where the Indian anticolonial icon strangely has become a racial slur, to be replaced after 9/11 by the more politically charged, if equally racist and also Islamophobic, label of "bin Laden."

The stories that these students tell are indicative of the ways in which racism against South Asians and other Asian Americans before 9/11 was often couched in model minority stereotypes of overachieving Asian Americans whose academic success or class mobility was attributed to cultural values, rather than to their economic or educational handicaps. The War on Terror, however, shifted the image of South Asians, particularly those identified as Muslim or Arab, from being "good" minorities—although with "foreign" cultural traditions—to potentially "bad" or militant minorities who could be a threat to the nation. Mary talked about feeling afraid as she walked through the city on her way home from school and noticed that people gave her "weird looks," for although she was Christian she realized she "might look like a terrorist." The War on

Terror has ruptured the thin veneer of protection afforded to so-called model South Asian citizens by multicultural pluralism in the United States. Victor Bascara (2006) links this change to a "model-minority" imperialism that is used to absorb Asian American difference into imperial frameworks of multiculturalism and global capitalism; the image of the model citizen is ruptured when the connection of Asian immigration and labor to U.S. empire and nation-building is revealed. For South Asians, this connection was apparent in the early nativist attacks on Punjabi laborers in the Pacific Northwest in the early twentieth century (Jensen 1988), and has resurfaced at various moments of economic anxiety in the United States, but none so strongly as when nativist and Islamophobic sentiments coalesced after 9/11.

For some Muslim Americans, the post-9/11 backlash shattered their belief in American multiculturalism as a framework that would accommodate a critique of civil rights for religious, not just racial, minorities. Syed Khan, an Indian immigrant who was on the Board of Religious Directors of the Islamic Center of Sharon, in Massachusetts, was the founder of Muslim Community Support Services, an organization that held forums on issues of civil rights and cultural citizenship for Muslim Americans after 9/11. He grappled with the failure of liberal multiculturalism to address the profiling of Arab, Muslim, and South Asian Americans after 9/11 and reflected in fall 2002, "If this had happened to some other religious or ethnic group, which professors would speak out? How many rallies have you seen? How many protests? None of those traditional forms of response have happened. . . . Everybody is scared to speak up about basic values that are enshrined in the U.S. constitution or psyche." Khan and other Muslim civil rights activists expressed disappointment that the promise of civil rights by the state did not live up to the American promise of equality that they had previously believed in, or hoped for, as immigrants.

Yet, as in the case of Britain or even France, the racism of the domestic War on Terror is not simply a problem of religious difference or multicultural tolerance within the nation, but is linked to histories of imperial policies and U.S. involvement in the Middle East and South Asia. These overseas wars are, paradoxically, fought in the name of bringing human rights and democracy to people supposedly suffering under intolerant regimes, Islamist (Afghanistan) as well as secular (Iraq). As Wendy Brown argues (2006, 6, 8), the universalizing discourse of "tolerance" at the turn of the twentieth century is at root a practice of "imperial liberal governmentality" that "regulates the presence of the Other both inside and outside the liberal-democratic nation-state"; "often," she notes, "it forms a circuit between them that legitimates the most illiberal actions of the state," justifying the U.S. War on Terror by distinguishing "Occident from Orient, liberal from nonliberal regimes, 'free' from 'unfree' peoples."

Regimes of tolerance and intolerance legitimizing U.S. foreign policies are linked to supposedly apolitical understandings of tolerance and intolerance in everyday life that produce essentialized notions of "cultural difference" and "civilizational conflict" (Brown 2006). This was evident in the discourse of intolerance that was used in the targeting of Muslim and Arab Americans after 9/11, including the South Asian Muslim high school youth in this study. Accusations such as "you're a terrorist" or "bin Laden's your uncle" entered into what might otherwise have been just an outbreak of youthful aggression among boys. These epithets were now part of an Orientalist discourse about Islam as essentially antidemocratic and antimodern that was deeply gendered, portraying Muslim males as militant and Muslim females as submissive and oppressed.

One of the anti-Muslim incidents in the high school occurred when an African American girl accused two Pakistani students, Walid and his friend Adil, of "killing people" and reportedly called them "Muslim niggers"—another new racial epithet after 9/11 that suggests that "Muslim" is one of the most degraded identities because of its "blackening," if somewhat ironically used by a black student. The girl was eventually suspended, but Adil was actually a friend of the girl's brother and said he tried to intervene to soften her punishment. Both Adil and Walid emphatically refused to portray the incident as a black versus South Asian or a black versus Muslim conflict; they insisted that this was the case of a lone individual who, Walid half-jokingly said, must have been "drunk" or "high." Adil, in fact, thought African Americans were less likely to have an uncritically nationalist response to the events of 9/11 than white Americans, even though he was hesitant to extend this generalization to their responses to the U.S. war in Afghanistan.

For Walid and Adil, the aftermath of 9/11 prompted a heightened self-consciousness about racialization that seemed, if anything, to reinforce the black-white racial polarization. Walid felt that African Americans were not as shattered by the attacks on the United States the preceding fall, because, in his view black Americans feel alienated from the nation-state due to the legacy of slavery. While this racialized difference after 9/11 is more complex than Walid suggests, what is important is that he *believed* that African Americans shared his experience of marginalization within the nation. But Walid did not completely dismiss the renewed nationalism of Americans after 9/11, saying "The first thing is they're born here in the USA, so that's their country. . . . We are immigrants . . . If something happens in back home, like, and someone else did something, we're gonna be angry too, right?" Yet it is also apparent that 9/11 seemed to have drawn him into an understanding of citizenship that is based on racialized fissures in claims to national identity, and affiliation with other youth of color.

For Walid and Adil, the response of African Americans seemed more significant than that of Latinos or even Arab Americans because on the one hand, they were the largest group of students of color in the school that these immigrant youth encountered, and on the other hand, they symbolized a contested U.S. citizenship for these youth. The responses of these Pakistani boys suggests to me a potentially "polycultural citizenship," based not on the reification of cultural difference that multiculturalism implies, but on a complex set of political affiliations and social boundary-crossings. Robin Kelley's (1999) notion of polyculturalism suggests that "we were multi-ethnic and polycultural from the get-go." A polycultural approach to difference suggests that cultures are inevitably already hybridized, and that there are no discrete, "pure" cultures. Vijay Prashad (2001, 40) uses Kelley's idea to emphasize the "inherent complexity of cultures" that challenges the "pretense of universal, and nonembodied values" and argues for a polyculturalist history that shows "the world constituted by the interchange of cultural forms."

Polycultural citizenship suggests a more complex, less culturally essentialist notion of difference that allows for political, not just cultural, conjunctures between different groups and is situated in the realm of power relations (Maira 2000; Prashad 2001). The nascent polycultural citizenship of South Asian immigrant youth is embedded in the messiness and nuances of relationships of groups with one other and to the state, and in cross-border affiliations emerging from particular historical and material conjunctures. These young people are not involved in formal political organizations or in traditionally defined activism, but their deepened understanding of racism and cross-racial identification is based on a political, not just cultural, resonance with other youth of color in the school based on shared experiences after 9/11.

These young immigrants simultaneously invoked a multiculturalist discourse of pluralist coexistence and a polyculturalist notion of boundary crossing and affiliation, embedded in political experience but also in popular culture practices shared with youth of color. Multiculturalism has attempted to subsume the assault on the civil liberties of Muslim and Arab Americans into a racialized framework of minority victimhood. "Muslim Americans," or the trio of "Arab, Muslim, and South Asian Americans," are constructed as belonging to just another, culturally distinct ethnic category whose problems can be contained within a discourse of domestic racism and addressed by inclusion within the multicultural nation. However, the War on Terror has highlighted the limitations of multicultural citizenship as a response to state policies targeting Muslim and Arab Americans after 9/11, for these were based not just on racial but political profiling, as I will discuss in the following chapter.

It was striking to me that some of these immigrant students articulated a sense of affiliation with other youth of color after 9/11 while simultaneously pointing to the social constructedness of race in the United States. Partly this is because the American concept of race is new to South Asian immigrants; Zeenat, for example, commented, "We don't [use] like, black and white to think of ourselves." Walid went further, noting that Pakistanis were neither black nor white, but "in between" these dualistic racial poles. He astutely observed that "some black people" are "not completely black either," for there were "a lot of different shades of black." Walid's remark underscores the limitations of pigment-based racial identification, for he called attention to the fact that some East Africans who were relatively light-skinned were still called black, and noted that he himself was as dark as some Haitians who would be readily identified as black, though he typically would not. Walid seemed to have figured out that race was a cultural construction through experiencing the contradictory labeling of U.S. race politics. His affinity with African American youth was based on a shared political relationship to the nation-state rather than on a shared identity based on culture or color.

While some South Asian Muslim youth expressed a polyculturalist understanding of race and nationalism, antiblack racism did indeed exist in the South Asian immigrant community as it does elsewhere (see Prashad 2000), and immigrant youth were not impervious to the racialized antag-

onisms and suspicion in the school. One of the second-generation South
Asian students spoke to me of tensions between the Asian American and
African American girls that sometimes manifested themselves in physical fights. I also heard of conflicts that had existed between older and
newer minority groups in the school, such as between Puerto Ricans and
recently arrived Central American refugees or between African American
youth and Haitian immigrant students. These conflicts among minority
groups in the school reflect the larger landscape of tensions that erupt,
and are fostered, in U.S. race and ethnic politics when groups adopt a
politics of recognition that pits them against one another, rather than addressing the roots of economic and political inequity. There is room in the
notion of polyculturalist citizenship to acknowledge the resentment and
competition bred by these daily struggles over shared turf or limited resources. Polyculturalism critiques the idea of "pure" culture, or even "pure"
hybridity, so I argue that it would not also envision a pure or idealized
politics of interracial solidarity, without any tension or negotiation.

Muslim immigrant youth sense a connection with other youth of color
and with African Muslim youth in the city, based in common social and
political experiences of cultural citizenship, but after 9/11 it also became
apparent that minority groups who had traditionally borne the brunt of
racial profiling were not completely resistant to the anti-Arab and anti-
Muslim suspicion and paranoia of the War on Terror. Solidarity between
South Asians, Muslim Americans, or Arab Americans, and African
Americans or other communities of color is not, and has not been, fully
realized after 9/11. There are many reasons for the failure of interracial alliances between these groups, historically and politically, which could be
clarified in a longer discussion (see Davis 2005). Such a discussion would
have to include the resistance of some South Asians to affiliate with marginalized groups of color in their desire to achieve model minority status,
within Bascara's framework of model-minority imperialism. Post-1965
South Asian immigrants have generally been unwilling to affiliate with
marginalized groups of color in the United States, although they have
benefited from the gains of the civil rights movement, and many are unaware of the civil rights struggles of racialized minorities and even express
antiblack racism (Prashad 2000; Singh 1996). U.S. empire uses multicultural difference and neoliberal citizenship, in its domestic subordination
of marginalized groups, to divide struggles against racism at home from
movements for justice and against imperialism abroad.

Polycultural citizenship explains the gaps in affiliation that are produced at certain historical moments between groups that might otherwise be assumed to be in alliance, because it highlights the notion that identification across group borders is embedded in the negotiations of power and relative privilege that complicate easy expectations of political convergence. Polyculturalism, unlike multiculturalism, also explicitly acknowledges that the state plays a role in constructing, unifying, or dividing groups by determining what benefits accrue to different groups that play varying roles in supporting the national agenda. For example, minority groups expressed mixed responses to the racial profiling of Muslim and Arab Americans after 9/11 and to U.S. military interventions in the Middle East. On the one hand, there were accounts of the kind proffered by Walid and some other students in the high school about African American youth who objected to the profiling of Muslim and Arab Americans as part of a larger critique of the state's pretensions to equal citizenship. On the other hand, there were reports of more ambivalent responses by African Americans, Latinos and Latinas, and other minorities—racial, religious, and sexual—who might have in principle opposed racial profiling but also believed, to varying degrees, in the premise of the War on Terror to defend national security, as I will discuss in the following chapter. A polyculturalist approach takes into account the shifts in racial formations and nationalist sentiments after 9/11 and helps to lay the foundation for a discussion of the possibility of varying modes of dissent in a climate of repression.

Sara

I went to Sara's house one evening so we could watch episodes of her favorite Hindi television series, Kusum. Sara regularly brought home videotapes of the show from her uncle's Indian grocery store in Waltham, and since I had never seen the show before, she took on the role of introducing me to it. When I arrived at Sara's apartment, her mother and sister-in-law were in the kitchen neatly packing mounds of rotis, or Indian bread, in plastic bags, which I guessed were for sale in the family store. Sara took me inside her family bedroom, where there was a television and VCR, smaller than the giant-screen TV in the living room. We sat on the bed, blankets piled high for family members to spread on the floor to sleep on at night, as Sara lived with her married brother and his family.

The series Kusum *is ostensibly about a woman who marries a rich man and lives with his extended family and about the conflicts and dramas that emerge between family members, but it also highlights issues of work, class aspirations, and globalization. One episode we watched was about an affluent couple who had returned to India from London, and the conflict emerging between them because the woman worked for a multinational company whose products were competing with those of her husband's Indian-owned corporation. Another episode portrayed a highly successful businesswoman talking about financially selling out her husband. It seemed that most of the female characters in the series who were successful career women were depicted as being excessively devious, callous, and scheming; as Sara put it, they were simply* kharab *(bad). The morality of the series seemed to have a gendered message: women who were financially successful and powerful are morally questionable.[13] But the episodes I watched could also be a commentary on the injustices and paradoxes of globalization for the recently liberalized Indian economy that was opened to multinational corporations since the 1990s, as it was reshaping family and gender relations, and the increasingly acute inequity between the cosmopolitan upper classes and everybody else in India. Sara did not comment on these issues while watching the series with me, but these economic factors and pressures had undoubtedly motivated her family's migration, and that of most of her friends.*

Watching the Kusum *episodes with Sara in her home was interesting because the series also dealt with the tensions of living together in an extended family. In one scene, a woman is accused of flirting with a married man by another woman who is a member of the "joint family" household. When I commented to Sara that there seemed to be no privacy for* Kusum, *in her family, she looked at me rather uncomprehendingly while her toddler cousins ran in and out of the bedroom. It occurred to me that I was making assumptions about the meaning of "privacy" that were culturally or class laden, not comprehending myself the ways in which families negotiate living in small or shared spaces.*

Sara was adept at following the complex chain of events in the TV *series and knew the intimate details of the intricate web of relationships among the characters. There was both a nearness and distance between the film and Sara's own life in Wellford that was striking. While watching a scene in which* Kusum's *brother is sitting in his plush office and talking to a woman he's having an affair with, I asked Sara if she wanted to work in an office. She said that she didn't know. Sara's sister, Rukshana, was working in the family store until eleven that night. Sara was not going to work at the store any more, and while I initially assumed she was happy about this situation, she later told me she was at home because her family already had four members working in the store and there was simply not enough work for her. Sara was looking for a job at Dunkin' Donuts and also going to the school employment office, but had had no luck so far.*

Amin

Amin worked at a dry cleaner in a suburban town, about half an hour from Wellford, for ten hours a week. Since his family did not have a car, he had to take a bus to get to the store after school and on weekends. The dry cleaner was owned by his uncle, and both his older sister and Ismail's aunt had previously worked there. The store was clean and bright, with a long red Indian carpet laid out on the floor, and a fake marble counter. The family was struggling to make the business successful; there was a dry cleaner just across the street that was the most popular in the town, and a third one down the street. Amin used to have more customers coming into the store but said that recently it had become more quiet. Sometimes there was nothing to do at work, and he would lie down and take a nap on the floor. The clothes were sent out for dry cleaning to a facility in a nearby town, but Amin did all the pressing of clothes in the store, using dummies and ironing stands for shirtsleeves and tablecloths. Amin said he was happy to get a paycheck, but wished he could work in a place that was more lively.

While I was visiting the store one afternoon a customer came in to pick up her dry cleaning, a white woman who realized she did not have enough cash to pay her bill. Amin explained to her politely that he could only accept cash or a check, and pleasantly wished her a good weekend. His uncle had coached him on how to talk to the customers, who were mostly white or East Asian. Amin said that the customers generally knew he was Muslim, but were very nice to him and often asked about his sister, who used to wear a hijab when she worked in the store. But he admitted that he had encountered anti-Muslim sentiments from some American customers, which he chalked up to the stance of President Bush: "Their leader says such things, and so they think it's okay to think that way about Islam." His math teacher, who was Chinese American, had asked him one day in class if he talked to Osama bin Laden on his cell phone. Amin must have been flouting classroom etiquette if he was, in fact, talking on his cell phone or checking his messages in class, but he clearly felt the Islamophobic sting of that remark. Sara was not in the class that day, nor was the other new Pakistani student in the bilingual program: Amin was the only Muslim student in the room. He said that he replied to the teacher, "Do you think all Muslims are terrorists? You shouldn't say such things!" The other students seemed shocked by the teacher's comment, according to Amin. When Ellery heard about the incident from another teacher, he asked Amin if he wanted to file a complaint. But Amin told him he would rather not complain officially because he did not want the teacher to lose his job.

"In India," Amin said, "it is not a problem to be a Muslim." I pressed him on this point a little, because in spring 2002, hundreds of Muslims had been massacred and many more turned homeless in the bloody riots in the state of Gujarat, instigated by Hindu fundamentalists with the complicity of the Hindu right-wing government, the Bharatiya Janata Party (BJP). Amin acknowledged that Muslims had been targeted in India, but pointed out that at least there was more knowledge of Islam and Muslims in his home country. Amin said he came from a Gujarati Muslim caste called Khalifas that he associated with the Tablighi Jamaat, an orthodox Muslim missionary movement originating in South Asia. He said they had different prayers from Sunni Muslims and did namaaz [prayers] at the house of a Khalifa man who lived in Prospect Square; most Khalifa families lived farther away from the city in the suburb of Billtown, which was home to a significant Gujarati community.

Sara's father had forbidden Amin from seeing her because her family was from the Ganchi caste, and he believed that they came from a superior community. Amin rejected these caste hierarchies, as did Ismail, who stopped by the store to talk to his friend while I was there one day. Ismail called these divisions "backward" and thought it was wrong that Sara's father was opposed to his daughter being with a Khalifa boy. Apparently, in earlier times, Khalifa and Ganchi families in the area used to socialize together, but there had been a conflict between the communities and now each group congregated separately for social and religious events. Amin seemed critical of these hierarchies and divisions, but he respected the religious spirit of his community and spoke of going to Maine with other Khalifas where they had met some Somali Muslims while doing da'wa [outreach].

When I saw Amin in the store, he was reading a Gujarati book about the lives of those who had tried to teach and spread Islam. He said his father was very religious and prayed five times a day; Amin seemed to respect his religiosity and discipline and wanted to try to be more devout like his sister and brother. In Amin's view, his family was actually more religious than Sara's, and so her father should respect them for being pious and should not care that his family was less well off financially. "After all," he said, "I can work and earn money." Sara's father was apparently talking of getting her engaged to her cousin in Gujarat and threatening that if Sara did not agree to the marriage, her uncle would be upset and it would tear the family apart. Amin was worried about this threat, for he probably knew the power of family ties, and was concerned about her father's disapproval if he found out about the gold necklace he had given Sara. He told me had saved up to buy a used computer and cell phone so he could privately communicate with Sara via e-mail and phone.

The Job

After several months of talking to the students about work and their frustrations with finding employment, there was an unanticipated shift in my own views and I found myself imperceptibly absorbing their anxiety about getting a job and their notions of what constituted desirable work. Work was not just the rhythm of their daily lives, but also the meter of our conversations. When I spoke to Farid, I would ask if he had finally found a job at Star Market. When I met Walid's friend Samir, I would check to see if he had been to the school's employment resource center. Every time I spoke to Fatima and Tasmeena, I inquired how their work at Dunkin' Donuts was going. Often I found myself acting as a semiofficial mentor for the students on academic and work-related issues, although I did not officially play that role in the SAMTA program (which matched individual students with older mentors). I would urge students to investigate internship opportunities arranged by the school, for initially I assumed that these work experiences in offices or libraries would be better for them in the long term. But after talking to some students, I also began to realize that these jobs were often not very regular and sometimes did not offer enough hours of work to meet the students' financial needs. Although I was acutely aware of the class differentials between me and these immigrant youth, after a while I also began to realize that I was beginning to view part-time, low-wage, contingent jobs through these immigrant students' own eyes—as something necessary, if not desirable, and even preferable as an immediate solution to their economic struggles than less easily attainable jobs in technology, business, and education. It was a disconcerting feeling, given my own critique of flexible labor and the exploitation of young, immigrant workers, but it also forced me to understand the pragmatic realities that drive those who have no other choice into this labor market.

The students often asked me about my own job, and while it impressed them that I was a professor, they generally did not know what academic work entailed or what doing research meant—like most other people outside the academy. They were pleased that I was writing a book about them, but I sensed that it often seemed unreal or abstract to them, which was not surprising. It seemed unreal and abstract to me a lot of the time as well, especially in the midst of the political climate after 9/11 and the crisis in the South Asian Muslim community. How was my research going to be useful to these young people or to their families? How could it respond to the intensified targeting that was exacerbating the economic struggles and adjustment issues they already faced as working-class immigrants?

As part of my work with the South Asian Committee on Human Rights (SACH), my fellow organizer Simi and I began contacting local immigrant rights activists and community leaders to learn about how the PATRIOT Act and other post-9/11 policies and practices were affecting immigrant communities in the area: Arabs, South Asians, Latinos and Latinas, Brazilians, Somalis, and Haitians, among others. We organized immigrant and civil rights forums and workshops bringing together people from different communities who became part of a loose network of local political groups and nonprofit organizations working with immigrants and refugees. So to a large degree, my research and activism dovetailed in ways that were mutually revealing for my own work, if sometimes in uneasy ways. For example, I had lunch one day with Imran Hussein, president of a local Pakistani community organization. Hussein was cordial, friendly, and happy to try to help me with my research. He told me that most of the 2,000 Pakistani families in the area lived in the suburbs, and it was "single people" from Pakistan who lived in or close to Wellford. Most Pakistani immigrants, he said, came from cities in Pakistan, mainly from the Punjab region, and about 10 percent had moved to Wellford from other locations in the United States.

Hussein was particularly concerned about the experiences of young Pakistanis growing up in the United States. He even sympathized with the predicament of Pakistani youth whose parents expected them to marry other Muslims even though they spent "day and night" with friends from school who were not Muslim, and at most saw other Muslim youth only one day a week at an Islamic Sunday school. I had visited one of these programs at the mosque in Quincy, a city where Hussein said there was an older South Asian immigrant community that included many working-class Pakistanis. His comments confirmed what was quite apparent in the Wellford area: that the South Asian immigrant community was spatially and socially segregated by class. After talking over lunch, Hussein took me to his office in Prospect Square, an architectural firm that had designed a local mosque as a way of "giving back to the community." I talked to Hussein about Osman, who did not have a part-time job yet and who had been trying to find an internship in the school, as an example of the issues facing Pakistani immigrant youth. Hussein said he enjoyed helping people in the community, especially young people, and volunteered to talk to Osman to see if he could find him some work, possibly even in his own office. I had not expected this personal offer of assistance, but I was glad that he was so ready to help, and I offered to bring Osman to meet with him.

Hussein was eager to talk to Osman alone, saying that it would help build his confidence and that he wanted to make sure that Osman had a job where he would not be scarred by working for a "difficult boss." It occurred to me then that Hussein, though well intentioned, was probably not fully aware of the class schism that might make the boy hesitant to meet with him alone, or could make having a difficult boss the least of Osman's concerns about finding work. Osman did end up meeting with Hussein a few weeks later, though I accompanied him to the office. However, the job did not materialize and after repeatedly asking Osman about what was happening for several weeks afterward, I realized that Osman himself did not expect Hussein to come through. Looking back on that episode, I wondered if I had done more harm than good. I felt I had wasted some of Osman's time and prolonged his frustrating job search for him.

But perhaps, at some level, Osman already understood what to expect from those who were from his community, but not from his class, and it was I who expected more and was naive. Even if I was skeptical about "ethnic solidarity" and understood, intellectually, that coethnic exploitation is often acute in immigrant communities, I had thought I could somehow "help" him by using contacts from my research; I had hoped that maybe one of these South Asian professionals would allow working-class South Asian immigrants to benefit in tangible ways from their economic and social capital. Without any help from me or anyone else in the South Asian community, Osman eventually got an internship, through a high school program, at the business school library in a local university. This experience proved to be a refresher lesson in class and culture, for me, more than anyone else.

Five

Dissenting Citizenship: Orientalisms, Feminisms, and Dissenting Feelings

Jamila

"*I came to America when I was seven or eight years old. I lived in Bangladesh before, in Dhaka. My uncle, who lives in Lexington applied to come here, and then we came. He's been here more than twenty years; he's a doctor. My parents wanted to come to America too. I don't know why—they just came. When we came here, my uncle rented us a place in the Prospect Square apartments. I thought Wellford was small when we first came here. My uncle had told us some stuff about America: he talked about it when he came back. I like living here. Why? I'm not sure, I just like it. Oh, you know what was so cool? It was my birthday the day we moved here.*

"*My father works at a place that is kind of a like a doctor's, but not really; they make things that go in the veins. But he just got laid off. I have three sisters and one brother, but one sister is over eighteen so she couldn't come with us to America. She's still in Dhaka; she has one daughter and one son. I didn't see her for seven, no six, years, but I just went back in November. I went to some places in Bangladesh, saw people we knew. When I went back Dhaka seemed dirty, because after I came here, I got used to places here being clean and stuff. We all live together, but one of my sisters just had a baby*" *and she is waiting to get her own apartment so she can move out. We're the only Bangladeshi family in our building; the rest are all black. I know some of the girls that live there, that are my age.*

"There are two other Bengali girls in the school; both are Bangladeshi. I have two of my cousins in the school; they're from my mom's side. They came with us the same day. I'm not sure what their dad does—I think he got laid off too. Her mom baby-sits now. My other cousins used to live in Wellford too, but they moved to Saudi Arabia. I don't have any classes with other Bengali or Indian people. I don't really hang out with Indian people. Some of my friends are black, some of them are Spanish, some white; they're all mixed. Some of them are from Somalia, from Ethiopia; some are African American, whatever. What do I like about them? I just like them as a person, and they were with me in my middle school. But I see Indian people, they'll be, like, hanging out together and having lunch together. And like, black people, they'll be together. And Hispanic people, they'll be like talking Spanish. And white people, I just don't know. I hang out with everybody. I tell my Hispanic friends, 'How come you all speak Spanish and I don't?' Yeah, I'm the one saying that 'coz I want to learn Spanish.*

"My friends and I talk, hang out; we go to malls and stuff. I like the mall because there's a lot of different stores and things there. Sometimes we pick out clothes for each other and stuff. Where do I shop? I dunno . . . the Gap? Old Navy too, I guess. I don't really listen to music that much, but I like to be on the Internet. What do I like to do? I dunno, chat, find out stuff. There's an online chat room where all the Bengali kids come and chat, from all over the world. London, Switzerland, and all these places. And even kids from Bangladesh. My sister found out about it and told me. In London, they're like [Bangladeshi youth], they're almost the same as me! They listen to the same music and stuff. No, I don't know—Joi or any Bengali groups from England. DJ State of Bengal? No, I never heard of him. My parents wouldn't let me go to dance parties anyway.*

"If I'm at home, my parents don't let me go out. But if I go somewhere straight from school, and go home afterwards, they don't care. Yeah, I know it's funny, if I went home right now and asked my mom, 'Can I go out?' she'll be like, 'No.' I'm not allowed to date boys. It was like that with your parents too? I think I'm not allowed to date till I get married, I don't know. I would listen to my mom. I think they wanted my sisters to marry a Bengali boy because they knew my sisters would like Bengalis and stuff. I would like to marry a Muslim guy too, because I don't want to be left out! I think my parents would* *want me to marry a Muslim guy, but if it was just dating, they wouldn't care. But I can't date anyway, so it doesn't matter to me right now. I speak Bengali at home with my mom, yeah, but with everybody else, no.*

"My family's Muslim—my parents pray five times a day but I'm too lazy to pray. I can read the Koran, but I don't understand it. I went to Buffalo to learn about my religion. My parents sent my brother to a school there, and he didn't want to stay because there was no TV or anything, and he likes playing video games. So my parents sent me too. The school was in a big building, with a lot of Indian and Pakistani people. I was there for a whole year. I had, like, regular classes and classes about my religion. We had to cover our face and stuff. It was so embarrassing! We went to Niagara Falls and we were all covered up; people were staring at us. I was like, 'Don't look!' My mother wears a hijab sometimes, not always. My sisters don't wear it ever. After I came back from Buffalo, I wore it for, like, a week to school and then I'm like, forget that! No, my parents didn't say anything. But if I do something really bad, my father would say, like, 'You're going back to Buffalo if you do this or you don't do that.'

"What is being a Muslim for me? Yeah, all that stuff—my family is Muslim; it's my culture. I think I felt differently about being Muslim when I was in Buffalo, but when I came back, it was the same. No, it didn't change for me after September 11. Other people didn't even know I was a Muslim. I don't think my brother and sister got any weird looks. Everyone thinks my sister is Spanish, so it doesn't matter for her. Spanish people are always talking to her in Spanish. No one in my family looks Indian, except for me; I'm the only one who's dark.

"I know this girl—her family is Sikh and she moved to Granville, so now she goes to high school there. Her brothers used to wear that thing on their head, and I was like, 'Why does he wear that?' I thought he had a big bump. But she explained it to me, and she told me that girls had to keep their hair long too. And she told me her brother had to wear a bracelet. What religion are you? Oh my God, you're all mixed!

"My parents were worried after September 11; they were saying, if something happens, we would have to go back to Bangladesh. My friends were worried that someone might actually bomb the harbor or the university. But I felt safe in school. Something happened to Adil and Walid? I didn't know that. I don't talk about things like that with my friends; we talk about other stuff. What did I think of the war in Afghanistan? I felt bad for those poor people there.

Because America didn't have no proof that they actually did it, but they were killing all those innocent people who had nothing to do with it.

"I want to be an American citizen because then I can go any place. I want to see other countries. But if I become an American citizen, I won't be Bangla anymore. Right now, if other people ask me what I am, I would say I'm Bangladeshi because I'm born there. I don't call myself Asian, because when people say I'm Asian, I feel like I'm Chinese. My parents wanna go live in Bangladesh. You know why? Because they don't have to, like, work there. They can just relax and other people do all the work. I don't know if I want to live in Bangladesh; maybe when I'm really, really old. I wanna go to college; I wanna be someone that helps doctors. And I wanna go somewhere where I can live in a dorm. My parents want me to stay at home when I go to college.

"Are you interviewing only Muslim people? Oh, not all, okay. Sure, I can ask my cousin if she wants to talk to you, but I'm not sure she'll want to. No, I haven't been to the Bengali restaurant in Prospect Square but we can go there. Sure, we can have Chinese food too. I can't have meat though. No, I'm not vegetarian, but it has to be halal. You know a Chinese halal restaurant? No, I didn't think so!"

Adil

Of all the South Asian immigrant boys in the high school I met that year, Adil was perhaps the most outgoing and gregarious. It seemed to me that this was not just because he had lived in the United States longer and so was more fluent in English and comfortable in the city, but also because of his self-assured and friendly personality. I had been trying to talk to him for some weeks after I heard about a couple of post-9/11 incidents involving him and his friend Walid, including one in the school, but he was always rushing off to work when I tried to meet him after classes. Finally, one afternoon, we managed to have a conversation after school had ended.

Adil said that on September 11, 2001, his mother called him on his cell phone at 2:30 PM, the minute that classes ended. She told him, "I want you to come home RIGHT now. Don't go anywhere; don't stay at school. Come right home and stay inside!" Adil remembered how worried his mother was about him, especially because she knew that Adil did not like "sitting at home."

One day, after the events of September 11, Adil and Walid had been fooling around in class with a book that was "like a magic trick." A girl in the class began to "get in [their] business," making comments about "box cutters" and Muslims. Adil talked to the school's security afterward because he didn't want her to be dismissed; he thought she was simply a "troublemaker." He had, in fact, been a friend of the girl's brother, who apologized to him soon after the incident occurred. It was clear that, like Walid, Adil was bothered by the incident but did not feel any general animosity toward African Americans after the exchange. But one Friday night in fall 2001, when he went downtown, he had an encounter that disturbed him much more. It was late at night, and he was driving with Walid, his cousin, and some Pakistani and Indian friends through an area known for its clubs and bars. "Six white guys" in an Explorer accosted Adil and his friends, and one young man got out of the car and threatened him. Adil clearly had his wits about him, for he said he "knew they'd be cops" around the corner and so he immediately reported the incident to the police, who later came to his house to follow up on the complaint.

I asked him, "Did you feel afraid or freaked out after the incident?"

"A little freaked out," Adil replied, "But I wasn't afraid. When Walid and I are together, we are not afraid."

"What about the other Pakistani kids? Were they afraid after 9/11?"

"Well, you gotta understand that there are two groups of kids in the school. I'm cool with everybody; everybody's my friend. I have black friends, Spanish friends, white friends. Like that [African American] girl's brother—he came to say sorry to me, because he's my friend. And he's a BIG *black guy, really tall!"*

I asked him what the other students in the school thought about the events of September 11. Adil seemed to feel that the tragedy had traumatized white students much more than black Americans. "I think the black people are not so into it," Adil responded. "It's the white people who are really into this thing, because more white people got killed in those buildings." But Adil was cautious to qualify his statements about the war in Afghanistan, for when I asked him if he thought that blacks supported the war as much as white Americans, he replied, "It depends. Because black people have different feelings. Like you and I have different feelings about things."

When I pressed Adil on what he thought about the invasion of Afghanistan, he responded in an equally nuanced way, "You have to look at it in two ways. It's not right that ordinary people over there, like you and me, just doing their work, get killed. They don't have anything to do with the attacks in New York, but they're getting killed. And also the people in New York who got killed—that wasn't right either."

Adil and I were talking as he walked out of the school to his car, a gleaming gold Toyota parked on a nearby street. "Do you like my car?" Adil was clearly excited about it, saying that it was a used car bought by his sister, who worked in a biotechnology firm. He laughingly said he worked everyday to "stay out of trouble," remarking, "If I'm not doing anything, I'll be driving around in my car, playing music, and getting into trouble. Like today, I wasn't meant to be going into work, but my friends are going to Foxwood[s] Casino, so I decided to sign up for more hours [at work]." Adil slipped a CD into the car's audio system to show me the kind of dance music that he liked, explaining as he did so why he hadn't participated in the bhangra [Punjabi folk dance] lesson we had arranged for the students at a recent SAMTA workshop. Some of the students had been shy and hesitant to dance in a mixed group, but Adil had laughed and apparently held back mainly because he didn't like traditional bhangra music. The music pumping out of Adil's car, which he apparently got from an Indian friend, definitely had a faster, club tempo. Adil had to go straight to work after school, so he got into the car and sped down the street, dance music pounding.

Ayesha

I had lunch with Ayesha at a new Indian restaurant that had just opened in Wellman Square, a neighborhood in Wellford known for its eclectic restaurants and ethnically mixed population. The restaurant was called, playfully, Punjabi Dhaba (a Hindi and Punjabi word for "roadside cafe"). It was actually a small, takeout restaurant in the middle of the square, with a couple of tables and chairs near the full-length glass windows. Ayesha attracted a lot of attention from the South Asian waiters when we went in, perhaps because her make-up accentuated her large eyes and fair skin, or perhaps because she was dressed in hip-hugger jeans and a tight, pink shirt under her denim jacket. Ayesha had blonde highlights in her hair and wore large hoop earrings—in other words, she dressed like most of the other U.S.-born girls in her high school.

Ayesha was nineteen years old and had come to the United States when she five. She and her family now lived in the Prospect Square apartments. Over lunch, we talked about the local Punjabi and Gujarati communities in the area. Ayesha's family was Gujarati, and she had never eaten Punjabi food before. As we munched on rotis and vegetables, she told me that she knew some Punjabi girls in Granville, a town bordering Wellford with a large Punjabi *and Sikh population. Ayesha had met some of the girls from the high school at parties but said, "I really wouldn't want to hang out with those kind of girls, you know why? Because they're too out of control."*

"Why do you think they're out of control?" I asked her.

"Trust me, they're out of control," she replied. "Going out, hanging out, they have, like, boyfriends. I don't mind that, but they're too outgoing. I can be a wild kid too when I go out, but there's a time when you can do that, and there's a time when you gotta be serious."

Ayesha's Gujarati boyfriend was a college student from the neighboring town of Granville, and she was open in discussing their relationship with me. As one of the few Gujarati, and Indian, girls in the high school who had grown up in the United States and identified with local urban youth culture, there seemed to be a cultural distance between her and the more recently arrived immigrant students. The South Asian boys sometimes raised their eyebrows when I asked if they had seen Ayesha around. Ayesha herself seemed to be aware of the suspicion with which she was viewed by other South Asian youth, particularly girls: "They don't like me, to tell you the truth." But she was emphatic in claiming her South Asian, or desi, identity, saying "They want me to go and talk to them, which is fine, but then they think that I'm going to be all American, and for me, I'm like proud to be desi, to tell you the truth, to be Indian. But if you grew up here, it's kinda hard to be Indian like them, you know what I'm sayin'?" Ayesha seemed to be able to balance her assertion of national pride with a clear acknowledgment of her diasporic identity, challenging her dismissal by other desi youth on the grounds of cultural authenticity.

Part of Ayesha's discomfort with the desi girls who rejected her seemed to stem from the monitoring of female sexuality in the community, a common issue in sexual politics for teenage girls, or even for adult women, and one that crosses national and religious backgrounds.[1] Ayesha spoke of a female friend who she felt had betrayed her by telling her other friends that her "name is not good." But she was also frustrated with desi boys who had grown up in America and who were sexually aggressive with girls they saw as "available." Ayesha made it clear that she did not think that desi boys were inherently sexist, but suggested that they had learned the "virgin/whore" dichotomy from "American culture." She remarked that boys who had grown up in India seemed to be "more polite." Her parents did not know she had a boyfriend, but Ayesha seemed to be free to "hang out in Boston" with her "girls." She had been to all the big dance clubs in the city, and though she listened to Hindi film music on the Internet, she was not a big fan of Hindi movies. She loved shopping and clothes, and we chatted for a while about the outfits she was going to wear at her sister's wedding in Gujarat. Ayesha said she had about a hundred Indian outfits in her closet at home, most sent by relatives in Gujarat every year, and was up-to-date on all the latest salwar kameez styles in India.

Ayesha defied the stereotypical representations of South Asian American girls, and Muslim girls more generally, as portrayed in the U.S. media, and her comments gave me much to think about even as we spoke. Her national, religious, and cultural affiliations were complex and layered, if not uncommon among urban South Asian and Muslim youth. She belonged to the black student club in the high school, and had been involved with planning Black History Month. She stated this very matter-of-factly, probably because she had African American friends and also because her affiliation with black and African students seemed very much embedded in the multiracial culture of the high school. She also identified unequivocally as Muslim and said she had finished reading the Koran twice and had studied Islam at a local mosque. When I asked her what she felt about being Muslim in America after September 11, she replied, "I'll always be Muslim. I think religion always stays with you. I'd rather have religion with me, because you can change the culture any time you want, but religion is going to stay with you while you're still alive." She seemed to acknowledge the dynamism of culture, even as she adhered steadfastly to religion. Perhaps this insistence on the constancy of religious identity was also prompted by the aftermath of September 11. A week after the attacks in New York, Ayesha chose to write the words "INDIA + MUSLIM" on her bag. She said, "Just because one Muslim did it in New York, you can't involve everybody in there, you know what I'm sayin.' Just because a couple of Muslims did it, they gotta blame everybody for it." For her, this was a conscious gesture of defiance, for she knew well the possibility of repercussions for those publicly identified as Muslim after September 11 but was not afraid of backlash. She said staunchly, "I'm hardheaded, that's how I am."

Dissenting Citizenship

The critique of the anti-Muslim backlash after 9/11 and of the U.S. war on Afghanistan, expressed by Jamila, Adil, and Ayesha, was pervasive amongst the South Asian Muslim youth to whom I spoke. Their dissent was driven by two factors: they had been forced to deal with the impact of state and civil society discrimination targeting their communities soon after arriving in the United States, and they were from a region that was now experiencing a U.S. military invasion. All three of these youth were critical of the war in Afghanistan and the attacks on innocent civilians who had nothing to do with the events of 9/11, framing it as a question of human rights and justice. These and other South Asian immigrant youth voiced a political critique of the War on Terror while simultaneously noting their shock and sadness at the attacks on the Twin Towers. While not all the students were as bold as Ayesha in challenging the profiling of Muslims and publicly claiming a Muslim identity—which Ayesha did without wearing a hijab, contrary to expectations of what religious identification looks like for Muslim girls—they still affirmed a Muslim identity which crossed national borders.

The school was one of the few, if only, public spaces where these Muslim immigrant students felt comfortable expressing their political views, mainly because of the liberal political climate and the support of progressive teachers and staff at the school. Students who had grown up in Wellford expressed polycultural affiliations that crossed ethnic boundaries; Ayesha, for example, moved between the black student club and desi friends, engaging with Black History Month and Bollywood music without any seeming contradiction, even if she felt judged by some of the South Asian immigrant girls for dressing and behaving "inappropriately" by their standards. Yet these polycultural identifications with other youth of color, particularly African American youth, also led some youth to absorb a discourse of racial identity and civil rights that shaped their dissenting stance after 9/11, especially in the high school.

After the anti-Muslim incident in the high school involving Adil and Walid in fall 2001, the International Student Center organized a student assembly featuring two Arab American speakers who criticized the War on Terror and the attack on civil liberties. Adil, Walid, and Shireen delivered eloquent speeches condemning racism to an auditorium filled with their peers. About being threatened by some young men in Boston, Adil said, "I could have done the same thing, but I don't think it's the right thing to do." Adil was a muscular young man and his call for nonviolent response was a powerful one at that assembly, especially at a moment when the United States was bombing Afghanistan in retribution for the attacks of September 11, and it implicitly spoke to the larger question of violence and war. Shireen stood up in her salwar kameez and said, "We have to respect each other if we want to change society. You have to stand up for your rights." Shireen later told me that she was "scared and nervous" about making a public speech in front of such a large audience, but was encouraged by Ellery's support.

Other students who did not express their views as publicly as Adil and Ayesha voiced their dissent in private discussion. For example, Zeenat thought that the bombing of Afghanistan in response to the attacks of 9/11 was "wrong" because the United States was attacking people who were not involved in the terrorist attacks and, echoing Ayesha's remark, observed, "After September 11, they [Americans] hate the Muslims. . . . I think they want the government to hate the Muslims, like, all Muslims are same." Zeenat seemed to be distinguishing between civil society and the state, while pointing to both as Islamophobic and responsible for constructing Muslims as a category of collective guilt. Issues of innocence, culpability, and punishment were uppermost in the minds of the South Asian Muslim students when discussing this topic, even of new immigrants such as Zeenat.

Muslim immigrant youth in the high school—such as Adil, Walid, and Shireen—were being visibly drawn into political and civil rights debates in the local community, although it is not clear what the impact of this politicization would be over time. But a year later, on the anniversary of September 11, the International Student Center organized another student assembly, and Samira (Shireen's younger sister) and Mumtaz voluntarily made similar speeches. Mumtaz spoke of her sadness at the events of 9/11 and also commented that "it's not right to go after Pakistan and Afghanistan and all Muslims who had nothing to do with it." Samira mentioned that a reporter from the local media was videotaping the event and asked the girls for their permission to quote their speeches. Samira seemed pleased by this request but also slightly hesitant, given the targeting of Muslim and Arab Americans for political dissent and political speech after 9/11. She said to me, "I'm asking you, should I do it?" The article eventually did appear in the local paper.

Even though these working-class immigrant youth did not have the support of, or time to participate in, community or political organizations, they seemed to have become spokespersons in the public sphere willing to voice a dissenting view. Other Muslim American youth have also been forced to play the role of educators for the American public, giving speeches at their schools and in community forums about Islam. A coordinator of a Muslim youth group at the Prospect Square mosque pointed out that it is a role that has brought a certain pressure and fatigue to young Muslim Americans. Becoming a "native informant" about one's religious or national background for the dominant culture makes members of marginalized or targeted communities responsible for compensating for the Eurocentric focus of the American educational system, and the racism and ignorance of the media and civil society. The explosion of talks, television programs, and books about Islam after 9/11 may have in some cases dispelled ignorance about Islam, and occasionally about the Middle East, to a certain extent. However, in many cases it has affirmed a neo-Orientalist perspective on the "Muslim world" and evaded the politics and histories of the Middle East, focusing on selected issues such as gender oppression, religious fundamentalism, and (certain) repressive regimes.

The spotlight on Islam also reinscribes the multiculturalist presumption that political injustice can be resolved simply by awareness of religious or cultural "difference," an Orientalist approach that ignores the larger national and international analysis of the War on Terror. Asad Abu Khalil (2002, 29) points out that much of this neo-Orientalist discussion spotlighting Islam after 9/11 contains a virulent strain of "theologocentrism," making a "direct connection between Islamic theology and the political conditions of the Arab and Muslim world," and providing a problematic explanation for the presumed causes of "Muslim terrorism" in the pages of the Koran or reductionist portrayals of the Muslim world. Furthermore, the hunger for native informants about Islam and the Middle East has led to the recruitment of what Hamid Dabashi (2006) calls a "new breed of comprador intellectuals," or native Orientalists, who provide authenticity and credibility to reports of atrocities, particularly the oppression of women, "justifying the imperial designs of the U.S. as liberating these nations." Native spokespersons such as Azar Nafisy, the Iranian author of *Reading Lolita in Tehran* and subject of Dabashi's trenchant critique; Ayaan Hirsi Ali, the controversial Somali Dutch author and politician; Fouad Ajami, the Iraqi scholar-pundit; and Kamal Nawash, the Republican founder of the Free Muslim Coalition Against Terrorism, are just some of the many "moderate" Muslims trumpeted by the mainstream U.S. media for endorsing a civilizational view that champions the freedoms of Western democracy and global capitalism. Yet the increasing visibility of these Muslim and Arab native informants who stage public testimonials of their "liberation" in the West has been accompanied by the silencing of many of their own compatriots in the United States who remain largely invisible in the public eye, except as caricatures of "radical" Muslims or alleged terrorists.

After September 2001, Muslim immigrants across the United States were increasingly hesitant to speak publicly about political issues, and even U.S. citizens were worried about expressing political critique or dissent. As the state acquired sweeping powers of surveillance with the USA-PATRIOT Act, discussed in chapter 1, there were numerous incidents of FBI and police investigations of "unpatriotic" activity that have been variously frightening and absurd (see Rothschild 2007, for a compilation of cases). In the face of such repression, I found some South Asian Muslim immigrant youth to be engaged in a practice of dissenting citizenship: an engagement with the nation-state that is based on a critique of its politics, and not automatically or always in compliance with state policies. Jamila was one of several students who spoke of the need for the U.S. government to provide "proof" of who was really culpable in the terrorist attacks and who condemned the killing of "innocent people who had nothing to do with it," holding the state accountable for offering its citizens evidence to justify their response to the terrorist attacks. Adil and other youth emphasized the importance of political justice and respect for international human rights, denouncing both the terrorist attacks and militarized state aggression as a means of retribution. The expressions of dissenting citizenship by these youth means they stand apart from the dominant perspective within the nation at some moments, and also identifying with others outside the borders of the nation who are affected by U.S. foreign policy. However, the notion of dissenting citizenship that I propose is not meant to suggest that dissent by South Asian Muslim immigrant youth, or South Asian or Muslim Americans more generally, was overt, consistent, or public, let alone that it is inherently guaranteed. At this moment of U.S. empire, dissent is difficult to express given the intensified climate of repression and surveillance, and the targeting of South Asian, Arab, and Muslim Americans and critics of the government's policies as potential "traitors."

Dissenting citizenship is still a form of citizenship, and so it still engages with the role and responsibility of the nation-state and the question of belonging and rights for subjects, however marginalized. Thus it encapsulates the contradictions of challenging the state while seeking inclusion within it. As "transmigrants," or migrants with transnational ties (Basch, Glick Schiller, and Blanc 1994), these young immigrants strategically use citizenship and the framework of immigrant and citizen rights, trying to advance from one category of protection and entitlement to the other. Dissenting citizenship captures some of the ambivalence toward the United States that these youth experience, for it is simultaneously a place invested with their parents' desire for economic advancement and security and their own hopes for belonging in a new home, and also the site of alienation, discrimination, fear, frustration, and anxiety about belonging. A few young immigrants, such as Shireen and Samira, had expectations that the United States would live up to its ideals of freedom and equal rights, but most seemed to emphasize simply that American actions should be held to an international standard of justice that should apply to all nation-states, including India and Pakistan.

Between Home and Empire

The process of dissenting citizenship is not without important tensions that animate its expression, for these young immigrants implicitly understand the limits of a state-based notion of citizenship, in its economic, cultural, and political senses, and the limits of "rights" afforded by the state. Muslim immigrants from India, in particular, have had to consider the failures of both home and host states—India and the United States—to guarantee protection and equal rights to Muslim subjects (Glick Schiller and Fouron 2001, 3). The anti-Muslim massacres in Gujarat in spring 2002, and the military standoff between India and Pakistan that preceded it, reinforce for Indian Muslim youth a sense that they are in an ambiguous zone between religious and national identification, between an Islamic state and a secular state turned Hindu nationalist. It is possible—although at the time not many of the Indian Muslim immigrants seemed comfortable or willing to speak about this—that the state-condoned anti-Muslim massacres in Gujarat also raised questions about their belonging and their rights for equal protection under the law in India. One Indian Muslim immigrant told me that in "private spaces" there are expressions of the vulnerability that Muslim immigrants have felt, both in the United States and at "home." This was understandably a difficult subject for Indian Muslim immigrants to speak about, and it was not generally discussed in my conversations with the youth or their parents, given the raw emotions in the wake of the Gujarat pogroms and also the unwillingness of many mainstream Indian American community organizations to oppose Hindu fundamentalism, in India or the United States. Right-wing Hindu American organizations have produced a virulently anti-Muslim rhetoric and hysterical generalizations about "Islamic terrorism" and Pakistani militants that have overlapped, often intentionally, with the Bush regime's rhetoric in the War on Terror (Kurien 2003; see also Menon 2006).

When India and Pakistan were on the brink of war in 2002, Ismail spoke to me of the suspicion Indian Muslims felt about their national loyalty and their willingness to support India in a possible war: "In India . . . they were asking Indian Muslims what we should do, right, that should we kill them because they [Pakistanis] are Muslims too." Ismail pointed to the precarious ways in which Indian Muslims are positioned between nations: they are viewed as potentially betraying not just India but also Pakistan, by not being a part of its Islamic nationhood: "Pakistan is getting stupid right now . . . they don't think that all Muslims who live in India are Muslim; they think they are Hindu." Ahmed, an older Gujarati immigrant man who worked in a local grocery store, was the most willing to speak openly to me about his feelings about the Gujarat massacres and about being Muslim in India. He recalled that a communal riot had almost happened in his home village in Gujarat, but it was averted— tellingly, without any help from the police, who have been notoriously complicit with the perpetrators of anti-Muslim violence in Gujarat. In Ahmed's view, Gujarati Muslim immigrants were more reluctant to return to India after the anti-Muslim riots in the state instigated by Hindu fundamentalists and implicitly sanctioned by the state's right-wing BJP government under the chief minister, Narendra Modi. "There is no compassion in the hearts of those fanatics," he said to me one day. Ahmed noted that thousands of Muslims had left Gujarat, and many had "disappeared." There was a cruel resonance between the events in his home state and the targeting of Muslims in the United States after 9/11, where many hundreds of Muslim men had also disappeared in secret detentions and deportations.

Though Ahmed was more willing to speak of the atrocities in Gujarat than the other Gujarati Muslim immigrants I talked with, he was equally insistent on the inherent religious tolerance of Indian national culture, simultaneously lamenting its decline. He firmly believed in the Indian tradition of pluralism, attributing the communal tensions to the insidiousness of "politics," and specifically to the BJP government that came to power in 1988 on a platform of Hindutva, or Hindu supremacy. "In our time," Ahmed reminisced, "relations were good between Hindus and Muslims. Even now, our children have friends with Hindus . . . Those children who grew up there say, 'India is great.' But right now, India is not so great.'" Ahmed might have been waxing somewhat nostalgic for an idealized era of secular coexistence in India and not willing to acknowledge that communal tensions predated the BJP regime, though they clearly reached shocking levels with the destruction of the Babri mosque in Ayodhya by Hindutva followers in 1991 (Ahmad 2000). Yet interreligious friendships and amicable relations were, indeed, embedded in the fabric of many communities in India, even if identities were always communalized in India since the partition of the subcontinent along religious lines.

What was striking to me was that while voicing his dissenting critique of the Hindu nationalist government, Ahmed seemed sorrowful that he could not express the nationalist pride he was once able to uphold more wholeheartedly—the belief that India represented a "great" ideal of interreligious harmony and diversity. Dissent against exclusionary policies in the United States as well as those of South Asian states coexisted with nationalist sentiments for Indian Muslim immigrants such as Ahmed, and youth such as Ismail and others, who applied for U.S. citizenship but also identified strongly with the Indian nation. It is also probable that these affirmations of nationalism by Indian Muslim immigrants were a defense against potential accusations that Muslims were not really loyal to the Indian nation, an attempt to preempt further cultural exclusion. Hindu nationalism has increasingly permeated Indian diasporic communities in the United States as well, supported by a network of organizations including the Vishwa Hindu Parishad of America and Hindu Students Council, and Hindu NRIs (Non-Resident Indians) have helped finance Hindutva organizations in India and sent funds to build a Hindu temple on the ruins of the Babri mosque destroyed by Hindutva militants in Ayodhya (Prashad 2000, 146; Rajagopal 1998). In both the United States and India, Indian Muslims have been targeted by the War on Terror, and the national allegiances of South Asian Muslims and Arab Americans, in general, have been culturally and politically suspect, so that cultural citizenship rests precariously on fault lines connecting home and empire.

Some Pakistani Americans were also critical of the fact that the Pakistani government had not more publicly protested their treatment in the

United States after 9/11, continuing instead to support the United States in its War on Terror in South Asia and assisting U.S. military campaigns in Afghanistan and Pakistan. One Pakistani American journalist from Coney Island Avenue in New York, home to a large Pakistani immigrant community, said, "People blame not just Bush but President Musharraf. He has helped the U.S. all he can, but he did not take a stand for Pakistanis in America. We are deprived of rights and justice from both sides. It's a very sad story" (Nguyen 2005, 17). Immigrants are generally hostage to the relations the United States has with their home nations, as in earlier moments when Asian immigrants who were discriminated against in the United States were unable to get support from their homeland governments, such as the case of Chinese immigrants before the Second World War and Japanese Americans who were imprisoned in concentration camps during the Second World War. The post-9/11 moment has highlighted the gap between what the state can presumably guarantee, through citizenship or constitutional rights, and what a specific political project such as the War on Terror actually puts into effect, as the experiences of these Muslim immigrant youth demonstrate. This gap is not random but consistent, a stable feature of the state of exception, as discussed in the introduction, which is constitutive of U.S. democracy and the regime of rights, repeatedly suspended for groups in order to legitimize the sovereign power of the state to police its internal and external enemies (Hansen and Steputat 2005, 1; see also Comaroff 2007).

Some might argue that South Asian immigrant youth were opposed to the War on Terror and particularly sympathetic to the plight of innocent civilians in Afghanistan during the U.S. invasion because they were from South Asia and Muslim and, as immigrants, were more likely to think about justice beyond the borders of any one nation-state. In this sense, their dissenting citizenship could be linked to a vernacular cosmopolitanism, as suggested in the previous chapter, or the belief in a global citizenship that transcends national borders and emerges from "experiences of movement among cultures, politics, and economies" (Clifford 1998, 367). Some have argued that such experiences potentially give rise to a "cosmopolitics" that counters a "dangerously reinvigorated U.S. nationalism" through an internationalist humanitarianism (Robbins 1998, 13). However, the vernacular, nonelite cosmopolitanism of the urban youth cultures that Gilroy (2005) finds hopeful, is not always what it appears, and cannot be reified or idealized. Cosmopolitanisms are always partial and contingent. As James Clifford (1998, 367) points out, these "discrepant cosmopolitanisms"—echoing chords of polycultural citizenship discussed in chapter 4—describe how "people have understood their fate, negotiated with difference, preserved a dignity in confrontation, survived as cultural/political subjects through complex tactics of separatism *and* accommodation." Clifford reminds us that these responses offer only "a chastened hope associated more with survival and the ability to articulate locally meaningful, relational futures than with transformation at a systemic level" (Clifford 1998, 367), as is also the case with polycultural citizenship if divorced from political mobilization.

South Asian Muslim immigrant youth are not part of organized political movements, but they necessarily resist the profiling of Muslim, Arab, and South Asian Americans as potential "terrorists" or disloyal citizens and also understand that it is linked to U.S. military incursions in South Asia and the Middle East. The perspective of Muslim immigrant youth is very much rooted in their identities *as* Muslims, for they are targeted as Muslims by the state, and it sheds light on the links between U.S. policies at home and abroad. Bruce Robbins (1999, 14) suggests that a transnational humanitarianism rooted in religious affiliation could be a form of internationalism, contrary to many liberal theorists who look for secular expressions of cosmopolitanism. In my view, this makes for a particularistic Islamic internationalism that focuses on selected human rights issues—Afghanistan, Kashmir, Bosnia, Chechnya, and Palestine. The more useful point that follows from Robbins's critique is that these theories of cosmopolitanism are themselves rooted in specific cultural ideals, generally linked to liberal Western political theory, based on particular understandings of nationalism, secularism, and citizenship (see Asad 2003).

The critique of these Muslim immigrant youth is far more attached to regional and religious identity than a universalizing ideal of cosmopolitanism suggests, and yet at the same time it is far more critical of U.S. nationalism and state powers than liberal theorists of cosmopolitanism allow (e.g., see Nussbaum 2002). What these theories of cosmopolitanism generally do not stress enough is that if we want to understand dissent in the face of human rights violations today, we need to focus more on the ways in which neoliberal humanitarianism is harnessed to what Paul Gilroy (2005, 60, 62) calls "armored cosmopolitanism": a U.S. imperial order that justifies its assaults on sovereign nation-states in the name of humanitarian ideals, framing a "cosmopolitical agenda in the co-alitional coming together of willing national states oriented by the goal of enforcing a desiderata of peace, privatization, and market mechanisms on a global scale."

The political responses of these South Asian immigrant youth go be-yond the debate between idealistic and skeptical appraisals of cosmo-politanism's possibilities (see Nussbaum and Cohen 2002) because their critique of the U.S. state raises the issue of armored cosmopolitanism as linked to an "imperial feeling." As I proposed in chapter 1, the growing public acknowledgment of U.S. economic and military dominance has led to increasingly overt "imperial feelings" about the United States' role as the sole global superpower—often mixing anxiety, ambivalence, fear, guilt, hope, assurance, desire, or denial—that infuse the habitus and everyday dispositions of life in post-9/11 America (Bourdieu 1977).[2] These impe-rial feelings troubled some of the youth and, as in the case of Walid, drew them closer to other minority youth who felt alienated from a dominant nationalism that dismissed self-critique and evaded acknowledgment of the nation's origins in genocide against the natives and enslavement of black peoples.

South Asian Arab and Muslim Americans also had a range of deeply affective responses, both to the attacks of 9/11 and to the often humiliat-ing treatment of their communities, but their responses were more often described in mainstream discourse in terms of victimhood and fear, rather than as recognized as unspoken dissent—although the dissent of tar-geted communities has become increasingly explicit in the public sphere since 2001, despite the state's repressive measures. The dissent of South Asian Muslim youth—and indeed of others who were not South Asian, Muslim, or Arab—responds in part to this imperial feeling, the intensi-fied nationalist sentiment of the post-9/11 United States. Dominant re-sponses to 9/11 in the United States were infused with passionate feelings about the nation and emotional empathy with its victims, leading some to support a global War on Terror that would crush those who "hated" the United States. While feelings of "anti-Americanism" in the "Middle East" or "Muslim world" were often discussed in the mainstream media as an irrational pathology, driven by antimodern religious and national-ist sentiments, and clearly misplaced, the hypernationalism that emerged in the United States after 9/11 was not similarly recognized, in general, as excessive or misguided (see Grandin 2004, 22–23) or, recognized, at least in the mainstream, as an "imperial feeling."

For example, Muneer Ahmad (2002, 108) argues that the five murders of Arabs, South Asians, and Muslims in the United States after 9/11, which were officially classified as hate crimes, were generally viewed as "crimes of passion" by public discourse and the mass media. He argues that these murders were attributed to "love of nation, the crimes a visceral reaction born out of patriotic fervor," and so received less attention from the mainstream media than other violent hate crimes committed in the past, and much less coverage of the victims themselves. Ahmad argues that while violent scapegoating to avenge the attacks against the United States was not condoned by the American media, it was still understood as expressions of anger committed in the heat of passion and sorrow and so was a comprehensible, if regrettable, aberration. Thus racial violence is implicitly justified by situating it in an affective landscape in which the United States is at the center and historical memory is selective, and where the occasional irrationality of American nationalist fervor is understood as an excess of nationalist love, an inherently worthy emotion.

The dissenting views of Muslim immigrant youth implicitly critique the imperial feeling of U.S. nationalism after 9/11 through their linking of warfare *within* the state to global war waged by the United States. It is this link between the domestic and imperial that makes their perspective an important mode of dissent because the imperial project of this new "cold war," as in earlier times, works by obscuring the links between domestic and foreign policies. The dissent of some Muslim immigrant youth—or of Muslim, Arab, and South Asian Americans more generally—does not mean that they should be considered the vanguard of critique of the U.S. empire. These young immigrants are simply, but not merely, subjects of both the wars on terror *and* the war on immigration. Their dissent is not always expressed as overtly or publicly as political dissent is imagined to be, but it tells us something about the nature of dissent at a time of political repression.

Dissenting Feelings

The politicization of these South Asian Muslim youth seemed to have been intensified by the events of 9/11 and the subsequent wars in South Asia and the Middle East, which forced them to develop a political stance on issues of war and civil rights and to confront the discrepancy between multicultural rhetorics of tolerance, state policies and legal rights, and everyday experiences of suspicion or profiling. I did not know how these young immigrants expressed their political subjectivity while growing up in South Asia, but none of them came to the United States with histories of formal political involvement in their home countries, even if they may have grappled with issues of national belonging and the limitations of citizenship there, as Ismail's observations suggest. There is also a developmental factor here related to age, for theorists suggest that cognitive and social development as well as moral reasoning are linked to the development of political subjectivity, even if the definition of this term varies and often carries normative assumptions related to liberal-democratic conceptions of citizenship (Sigel and Hoskin 1981). These immigrant students were in their adolescence, a period when concern with the social order and social morality is assumed to be growing, although this cannot be overgeneralized. Political socialization has to be placed in the context of historical events, cultural and social expectations, and individual subjectivity.

Given the intensified politicization of Muslim identity in the public sphere after 9/11, some wonder if this will lead to the emergence of a new "political generation" of Muslim, South Asian, or Arab American youth. At the time that I did my research, it was too soon to predict whether there would be a heightened politicization of some of these youth, and there was not enough evidence to make a generalized statement about this, but it is apparent that Muslim American youth who are U.S. citizens or who have lived longer in the United States, and those who grew up in larger, better-established Muslim immigrant communities, are more likely to be engaged in overt forms of political activism.[3] In the aftermath of 9/11, the surveillance, detentions, and deportations of Muslim, Arab, and South Asian Americans crushed political dissent in these communities and made it difficult for young people, especially those who were immigrants and struggling, to say anything that would depart too radically from what was considered acceptable political critique at a given moment. As Corey Robin (2003, 47–64) points out, repression historically works on two levels to silence dissent: on a state level, but also on the level of civil society, where individuals internalize repression and censor themselves. Robin astutely observes that there is a "division of labor" between the state and civil society for "fear does the work—or enhances the work—of repression"; the daily internalization of fear and self-censorship is evident today in immigrant, Middle Eastern, and South Asian communities, as I too found in Wellford (Robin 2003, 48, 53). Practices of racial profiling and detention that have long targeted other groups, such as African Americans and Latinos and Latinas, similarly represent "political technologies of the body" whose disciplining effects are not restricted to those bodies actually detained within prison walls, but (not unintentionally) extend to others who internalize these disciplinary regimes (Hansen and Steputat 2005, 12).

Since 9/11, there has been a self-censorship in Muslim American communities of any political discourse other than that voiced in the register of the "moderate Muslim," affirming American democracy and Islam as a religion of peace. Young Muslim immigrants, too, quickly became attuned to the registers in which political dissent is expressed in a repressive political climate. For youth in general, notions of dissent necessarily take forms that may be different from those expressed by adults, for their notions of the state, resistance, or politics are embedded in different developmental and social contexts. Youth are also generally more vulnerable to the state's disciplining power, and do not have all the legal rights of adult citizens. An incident with a Pakistani immigrant student, Samir, helped me think about the ambiguity of modes of political dissent expressed by South Asian Muslim youth and the complex possibilities of popular culture and humor as sites of dissent. This is an excerpt from my field notes in September, 2002:

> I'm in the International Student Center one morning when Samir comes in and sits down at one of the computer terminals. I ask him if he has a webpage and though Samir is generally a bit quiet, he calls me over excitedly and pulls it up on the screen. It has links to "Lollywood" [Pakistani] films, Bollywood film music, and also to "funny pictures." I ask him if I can see the funny pictures, and when he clicks on the link, pages and pages of pictures of [George] W. [Bush] appear, a row of him wiggling his hips, a row of him looking like a chimp, a row looking like Superman. I start giggling profusely, and Samir is clearly tickled that I'm enjoying the images.
>
> "This is great," I say, "So you and I think the same thing about Dubya!"

Samir doesn't seem to understand the reference, and he also doesn't respond.

"So you don't like George Bush?"

"No," he says, "I just saw these, and I thought they were funny."

Then he scrolls down and there's a digitally produced photograph of a bearded Bush looking like Osama [bin Laden]with a white turban coiled around his head, and a picture of the Statue of Liberty draped in a hijab. I had seen these after 9/11, both in the context of anti-Islamic humor and recirculating as irreverent/dissenting trivia on the Internet. I ask Samir what he thinks of these images and why he chose to put them up, and he simply replies that someone sent them to him. He has nothing to say about their meaning or his political views. Yet these are the only "funny" images he has up, and also the only images related to America or to politics. They are clearly, grotesquely, about 9/11 and about George W. Bush. So what does it mean that he has them on his Web page?

I spent a long time thinking about Samir's choice of these images, his response to me, and the political thinking it could imply: was this a vernacular mode of dissenting citizenship? Despite his verbal denial, was Samir placing these images on his website as a way of expressing a nonverbal critique of Bush? The images, obviously, did not collectively produce a consistent critique. The veiled Statue of Liberty reified notions of gender and Islam and evoked anxieties about the transformation of cherished symbols of "American freedom" and infiltration of American culture by Muslim fundamentalism, suggesting that what Muslim terrorists or al-Qaeda wanted was to attack not just the Twin Towers but the American way of life. In contrast, the image of George W. Bush grinning in a bin-Ladenesque turban played visually with the question of who the "real" terrorist might be. This image, reproduced on a by-now iconic postcard, digitally "mashes" together signifiers of the president and "the terrorist"; it superimposes Osama's signature white headscarf and white beard on Bush Jr.'s wryly smiling face emerging from a tweed jacket. In a single image, it implicitly questions Bush's own civilizational discourse of a clash between "Western" modernity and democracy, and Islamic fundamentalism and antimodernity, suggesting that the two are not as sharply dichotomous as this framework for the War on Terror suggests. On a

Bush as Osama: Do we know
the terrorist? Photograph by
"Mister Hepburn."

deeper level, the image could also challenge the presumed binary between
the rational violence and "just wars" waged by the United States and the
irrational violence and militant fanaticism associated with the 9/11 attacks
by fusing the two symbols of this clash between "good and evil." Bush
looks mischievous and knowing, not stern or sorrowful. Perhaps the image asks us to consider: Is the face of "terrorism" so unfamiliar to us? In a
less subtle way, the caricatures of Bush as chimp or Superman certainly
challenged the president's intellectual capacities and his heroic crusade
against "evil."

I wondered if the website was Samir's way of grappling with the anti-
Islamic caricatures pervading American popular culture by responding
with caricatures of his own choice, resituated on a Web page that was visibly pro-Islamic, swathed in green with greetings of *alsalamalekum?* Or was
it simply that Samir thought these images were amusing? Either way, the
choice of these images did not seem completely accidental but suggestive
of an attempt to play with the images of Islam, terrorism, and U.S. power
circulating in public and popular culture. "The political" seeped into his
translation of these images via technology and popular culture, wrapped
in his nostalgia for Pakistan, his national pride, his Muslim identity, and

possibly his own unvocalized feelings about Bush and the War on Terror. The seemingly contradictory juxtaposition of Samir's Pakistani pride and the images of bin Laden and the hijab may not express an explicit or consistent political critique, but they hint at some unease with the dominant discourse about Islam and "terrorism" and, certainly, a dissenting humor.

This incident was one of the moments involving youth in the study that gave me the most pause, for it made me think about the ways in which young people engage with the political, and the often subtle ways in which they may express a range of responses to questions of power, the state, and resistance. Clearly, these images are subversive, in some way, even if it is not clear exactly how they function politically for Samir. Yet it is these kinds of moments of ambiguous dissent, potentially expressed from multiple locations and against various forces, that are important to consider when thinking about the political subjectivity of youth, especially of Muslim and immigrant youth who cannot speak out and are increasingly afraid of doing so. This form of dissent illustrates what James Scott (1990 137, 152) describes as techniques of resistance of subordinate or repressed groups that infiltrate the "public transcript" of political discourse in ways that are "intended to be cryptic and opaque" to escape retaliation by the powerful; Samir's images are perhaps a form of "hinted blasphemy," testing the limits of what is permissible by a subtle manipulation of political meaning that exists on a continuum of challenges to dominant interpretations of "terrorism" or "fundamentalism" by targeted or dissenting groups.

Samir was not one of the students who expressed overtly political views; his family was religious and conservative, but he had never talked to me before about politics and was generally quieter than the other boys. While I understood his silence about politics to be primarily an expression of his own more taciturn personality, rather than due to fear of speaking out, this moment forced me to think about the difficulties and subtleties of studying the political subjectivity of a group, and especially of young people, whose political speech was being targeted for censorship by the state after 9/11. These young people's views about the school, their local environment, mass media, American and international politics express a political critique, even if they do not use an explicitly political language. The refusal or lack of verbalization of political critique by those who are South Asian, Muslim, immigrant, or young—or all of these as in this study—is important because it shows the many ways this silence is layered with the quiet but charged nuances of "dissent" and "complicity."

If the imperial is a feeling, it is also worthwhile to consider dissent as a "feeling," as something that is not simply caught in the binary of resistance and complicity but that is expressed in ambiguous and hard-to-identify ways, such as Samir's funny pictures. Recognizing this does not mean giving up on the tangibility of dissent, nor on the ever pressing need for resistance in the face of state terrorism and violence, nor on the difficult and ever lurking danger of complicity. On the contrary, thinking of dissenting feelings allows us to acknowledge the continuum of responses of resistance, especially among those who are coerced into silence by repressive state measures and who are outside of traditional organized movements; we can try to understand dissent without falling prey to a romanticization of heroic protest or passive victimhood based on easy rhetoric or familiar tropes.

Working-class South Asian Muslims in the Wellford area were generally not involved in Muslim American activist initiatives or community organizations—they tended to draw on the suburban, middle- and upper-middle-class South Asian community—but the youth I spoke to learned about politics in the high school as well as in other sites. For example, Farid, identified the most with hip-hop culture among the students in SAMTA and was also a practicing Muslim. At a SAMTA workshop at which we were discussing the U.S. invasion of Iraq, he said that the war was "messed up" and also spoke forcefully and eloquently against the U.S.-backed Israeli occupation of Palestine, commenting that his tax dollars were being used to kill "his people." Farid's vocal opposition to the occupation of Palestine was a stance that was not explicitly shared with other South Asian or Muslim immigrant students. In fact, at the same workshop, Farid ended up arguing with a Pakistani boy who defended U.S. attacks on Afghanistan because he believed they liberated the Afghan people from the Taliban. When I asked Farid later how he knew about issues such as U.S. economic and military aid to Israel that helps fund the Israeli occupation of Palestine, which are generally absent from the mainstream media, he simply commented that these topics were discussed at the mosque.

Clearly, there was no one position on U.S. military interventions among these South Asian Muslim immigrant youth but rather a range of political views, and varying ways in which they framed their solidarity, including an empathy based on Muslim identity and Islamic internationalism, with all its implied gaps I alluded to earlier. However, when Israeli human rights violations in Palestine are discussed in mosqued communities—or in American church congregations concerned about the "Holy Land"—more than in the U.S. mainstream media, which has historically failed to document Israeli atrocities or U.S. support for Israel, then issues such as the occupation of Palestine become for some a cause inflected by religion, although this can still lead to broader bases for solidarity and a widening public critique of U.S. power. Farid was indeed more openly critical of U.S. military interventions under the guise of liberation than other students, whose opposition to U.S. wars was based more on concerns about violence and the loss of civilian lives in "unjust" wars, even if they exposed the hypocrisy of this "benevolent" imperialism. Farid may have expressed this political critique more overtly than other students because he had grown up in the United States and so was less constrained by the vulnerabilities of being an immigrant. But he also seemed to be expressing a slightly different politics, one more explicitly concerned with the culpability of the state and the complicity of citizen-taxpayers supporting U.S. wars and client states overseas.

Farid was perhaps aware of this difference in political orientation, for in his view most other students in the school did not seem to care as much about global politics. He acknowledged that teachers in the school tried to talk about current events, and indeed I found that teachers in the bilingual program, as well as other teachers, often seemed to link class topics to contemporary political issues and encourage critical discussion in the classroom. For example, here is an excerpt from my field notes when I visited classes with Osman one day in fall 2002:

> In Osman's computer programming class, Roxanne Anderson asks the students to run "www.dictionary.com" on their individual monitors. She asks them to look up the word "terror." The first definition, which she reads aloud, is "intense fear." She then asks them to look up "war." She turns to the students, a diverse group of white, Latino, Caribbean, Asian and African American youth, who are quiet in the fluorescent light of the computer lab, and asks: "Is this country at war?" The students are silent; a couple say "no."
>
> Ms. Anderson pulls no punches: "They've declared a war on terrorism. And the U.S. is at war. I don't know how it's going to play out in terms

of the fighting, but it's going to affect M-A-L-E-S [she spells it out, as
if it were a family secret]. I don't know if it's going to affect females.
Have you heard of the draft?" Ms. Anderson remembers the draft. She
grew up in the South of the 1960s and remembers the antiwar movement and the civil rights struggles. "We're at WAR. So if there's a draft,
where are you going to go?"

"What about Haiti?" asks a Haitian boy, hopefully, in the front row.

"Well, the U.S. is searching for allies, and they say, if you're not with
us, you're against us, so there'll be no place to hide."

Osman likes Ms. Anderson, and he also likes Mr. Smith, whose U.S.
history class is the second one that morning. His class is bright and
sunny and has a framed flag and vintage Coke poster on the wall. Mr.
Smith tells them that today's local newspaper is "disheartening" because
it has reported that "Mr. Bush" is asking the UN to support a declara-
tion of war against Iraq, even though Saddam Hussein has agreed to
allow the UN inspection team into the country, as Mr. Bush had just
demanded. Mr. Smith says, "We're studying the Constitution, the Sen-
ate and the House, the powers of the President. Has the president gone
beyond the powers of the constitution? There are some things that he
or she can and cannot do. If you or I were asked, do you want war or
peace, what would you say?"

"Peace," all the students mumble. It's still early in the morning, but
they are listening attentively.

Mr. Smith presses them further: "Where do you think the president
gets his powers?" He talks about the Constitution as "a living document," and discusses a case in which an African American man was
wrongly accused of a crime in a largely white town. He comments, "If
we're going to make the Constitution relevant to you guys as future
citizens, we have to understand how this guy was denied a fair trial."

These and other moments I witnessed in the classroom demonstrated
the ways in which some teachers helped the students' shape an understanding of dissenting citizenship as an obligation to question state
power, the law, and militarism. These teachers may have had varying
views about the possibilities and limits of constitutional or citizen rights
as a framework for resistance, for some of them were products of the civil
rights era and so brought their own political histories and critiques of
U.S. imperialism to issues of dissent, civil rights, and social movements,

as I realized when I talked to teachers such as Anderson. The political discussions I happened to witness in the classroom were reflective of the generally liberal climate of the city: while Wellford had its internal class and racial fissures, it had a reputation as a haven for sixties radicals and hippies. This was a contested image, however, and the city's refusal to endorse the PATRIOT Act was viewed as un-American by right-wing communities in other towns in the state, as the question of dissent became a hotly charged issue on local as well as national levels. As one high school parent pointed out to me, not all the teachers in the high school shared Wellford's liberal politics and expressed varying responses to the events of 9/11. One teacher I spoke to seemed concerned about whether the increasing number of "Muslim" and immigrant students showing up in his classes would assimilate into "American culture" and was frustrated with the political correctness of Wellford. Yet another teacher said that some of her colleagues put up American flags in their classrooms, but she did not allow them to do so in her room because she thought this might reinforce the message of "us" against "them" to immigrant and Muslim students. She preferred instead to put up a poster saying "peace" in different languages on her door. These underlying differences and tensions about the meanings of nationalism, war, and citizenship were exacerbated after 9/11, as in other workplaces or communities.

Dissenting citizenship was contested within the local community of Wellford as well as at regional and national levels. It is possible that South Asian Muslim immigrant youth in other, more conservative towns might have been even less willing to publicly voice their political views to me. Teachers at Wellford High pointed out to me that while the high school had given them explicit instructions to allow students room to discuss the events of 9/11 in classes, and even provided sample lesson plans, other schools in the area mandated that teachers not talk about the event at all but leave it for private discussion at home. This mandate may not necessarily imply less concern about students, but such decisions do restrict spaces for public discussion by youth and create a different understanding of what constitutes appropriate "politics" within the space of schooling and what roles schools can and should play in relation to civil rights and academic freedom. For example, in contrast with Ellery's strong support for the Muslim students who were harassed after 9/11, I heard a very different story from a Pakistani immigrant woman, living in a suburban town about forty-five minutes from Wellford, whose family was the only

Pakistani family in the town at the time of 9/11. Shahnaz Chowdhury, whose children were the only Muslim students in the public high school, said that her son, Saleem, was accosted by a group of boys in the school who threatened him after 9/11, saying "What the f—— did you do over there?" Saleem asked his parents not to talk to the principal but went to talk to his counselor. A few days after the incident, Saleem was again confronted by the group of boys at a friend's house; the boys surrounded Saleem in the basement, saying "So, you think we're racist or something?" Apparently they had discovered that Saleem had complained about the episode to school authorities. This incident may be a relatively minor one, for it did not actually involve any violence, but it sheds light on the local contradictions of liberal multiculturalism and political racism after 9/11. While Chowdhury was asked by the school to give talks about Islam and "diversity," the school never responded to her son's complaint. This lack of concern left her feeling frustrated and worried about her children, even as she was called on to talk about Islam for the local church and embody cultural and religious difference to affirm the school's tolerance. The tensions between multicultural "inclusion" and dissenting citizenship were thus rife in a range of local political contexts, in and out of the school.

Gendering Dissent

In some ways, with the overexposure of "Islam" and "the Muslim world" in the mass media after 9/11, Muslim, Arab, and even South Asian American youth began to confront representations of themselves everywhere they turned, in the media or school or community. This made for a complex looking-glass effect of images of Muslims that were both familiar and also distorted and unrecognizable. Amin's and Sara's puzzlement about their teacher's preoccupation with the hijab, narrated in the introduction to the book, shows the strangeness of encountering these views of Islam or South Asia in public spaces such as the classroom. Some of these representations of Islam were performed by Muslim Americans themselves, but these self-presentations of Islam or South Asian culture generally had to fit into a limited slot that could not include a broader political critique of U.S. multiculturalism or of Orientalism.

Chowdhury's experience of being asked to speak about Islam in the local public school as well as church was not uncommon for Muslim American women after 9/11, many of whom did indeed become spokespersons for Islam and Muslim or Arab communities, as did the South Asian immigrant girls in the high school, for example, at the assembly mentioned earlier. A particular space has been constructed for Muslim and Arab women in the post-9/11 debate about the War on Terror that is very revealing of the ways in which Muslimness, and also Arabness, is gendered in the public sphere. In the high school, for example, more South Asian Muslim girls than boys spoke at public events, at least during the time of the research, even though the boys were the most visible targets of profiling. This may or may not have been an intentionally gendered pattern, but beyond the question of numbers what is striking is the differently gendered representations of Muslim and Arab females and males and underlying discourses of Orientalism and liberal feminism. Muslim and Arab women played a particular role in the American mass media and public discussions that both challenged and supported Orientalist perspectives on Muslim and Arab "culture" and on the status of women, in particular. Arab and South Asian women authors and spokespersons, such as Irshad Manji, Brigitte Gabriel, Wafa Sultan, or even Asra Nomani—began appearing frequently in the American mainstream media after 9/11, extolling the individual freedom offered by the "democratic" West and the United States, in particular, and denouncing the backwardness and repressiveness of "the Muslim world," some more shrilly than others.[4] Dissenting citizenship is gendered in ways that are often subtle but problematic, for it is bound up with a liberal feminist discourse about Muslim and Arab women that is Orientalist, and sometimes imperialist, as will become apparent later in this chapter.

The subtle contradictions of gendered dissent became apparent to me during an overtly political discussion with a group of South Asian Muslim youth in the high school. In May 2003, the students watched a documentary film, *Bridge to Baghdad*, at a workshop organized by SAMTA. The workshop was also an example of how I was myself, at certain moments, helping to shape the context in which the research questions I was interested in were emerging, and films are also a pedagogical tool that gives students and adolescents an opportunity to express and debate political views with which they are grappling but that may not otherwise be made explicit. *Bridge to Baghdad* was filmed just before the invasion of Iraq occurred and focused on an exchange, via satellite TV, of a group of college-age youth in New York and Baghdad. The students were mesmerized by the film and a few boys were particularly excited by the interview with Walid, a young Iraqi man who had a heavy metal rock band and an irreverent persona. A Nepali student claimed he had watched some "Iraqi rock" on MTV that sounded just like the music played by the young musician, suggesting a very different image of Iraqi culture or Arab youth culture, for that matter, one that was familiar rather than exotic or "traditional." The girls in the workshop giggled when an articulate young Iraqi woman in hijab swore in response to a question from the American youth that she had never dated anyone before. Interestingly, the film brought up discrepancies of race, class, and education as well, for while the Iraqi youth explained that they had the right to a free education, a Korean American student spoke of struggling to fund her college education as the daughter of a postal worker and of facing racism in the United States, something that the South Asian Muslim youth had experienced as well.

The documentary also brought to light the tension and fear these Iraqi youth felt, steeling themselves for the impending U.S. invasion while trying to discuss the war on film. The young rocker's father was in the Iraqi army and he was clearly anxious about the war, pointing to his father's military uniform hanging on the wall. In another poignant image, a stylish young Iraqi woman, who was a fashion designer, showed viewers the supplies stocked in her basement and freezer in preparation for food shortages after the invasion. The debate about the imminent war turned into a heated exchange among the Iraqi and American youth in the film, for a young white American man aggressively insisted that Saddam Hussein needed to be "removed" because he was harboring weapons of mass destruction. An Iraqi woman retorted with equal force that Iraqis were actually cooperating with the nuclear weapons inspectors, and a young Iraqi man asked the American youth where the evidence was for the existence of WMDs. Finally, the young woman in hijab asked the American students how they would feel if an army, "say an Iraqi army," came to invade their country and remove their leader. A young white woman responded that many Americans were actually opposed to the war, and an antiwar activist of color in New York went even further, remarking that she would be happy if an army came to get rid of Bush.[5] The students laughed. Later, in a discussion between the SAMTA volunteers and the students about the film, an Afghan student said that he liked the Iraqi woman's response. Zeenat made a similar remark, saying "It's not right that the war will affect innocent people." But the Afghan boy also wanted to know what happened to the Iraqi youth, or to their fathers in the military, now that war had begun. We, of course, simply said we did not know. The question was particularly pointed because it was voiced by the Afghan student, who was himself a refugee and personally understood the meanings of war and invasion.

The film brought home the tangible realities of youth facing an imminent war and challenged many of the stereotypical images of Iraqi and Arab youth, and of Muslim females in particular, countering representations of Arab and Muslim youth as hostages to unchanging tradition and religious fundamentalism. But what of the gendered responses of the South Asian Muslim youth to the film, and what these tell us about their views of Muslim identity or national belonging? One way to look at the responses of the South Asian students to the film would be to focus on the identification of the girls with the issues of dating and the boys with the young metal rocker. On the face of it, these responses fit neatly with the dominant way in which issues of gender among Muslim American youth have been discussed in U.S. mainstream media and public discourse, pinning the question of hijab and social control onto young Muslim women, and the image of rebelliousness onto young Muslim men. But the film also evoked more complex responses that challenged gendered stereotypes of submissive Muslim girls and angry Muslim boys, for the girls were drawn to the young Iraqi woman in the documentary who voiced the strongest dissent against the U.S. occupation, as evident in Zeenat's remark. At the same time, the boys were both fascinated by the young Iraqi musician's rock-star hairdo and moved by his anxiety about the impact of war on his future, identifying both with fashion and fear.

Gender inflected understandings of cultural citizenship for these youth in ways that were not immediately obvious, because boys and girls themselves showed very little difference in their expressions of dissenting citizenship. Yet it is certainly apparent that the scrutiny of Muslims in the United States after 9/11 has a deeply gendered shade, a preoccupaotion with women in hijab or presumably "oppressed" Muslim women requiring liberation from their tradition in order to be brought into the fold of the nation. At the same time, there is a deep anxiety about young Muslim men as potential terrorists and religious fanatics disloyal to the nation and, unlike women perhaps, ultimately inassimilable. As Jasmin Zine (2006, 8) points out, the gendered ideology at the "heart of the war on terror" is "to repress the Arab Muslim male on the one hand and to 'liberate' Muslim women on the other." The gendering of cultural citizenship is linked to Orientalist images of submissive Muslim women and fanatical Muslim men that are defied, if not overtly in explicit statements, then by the actions and self-presentations of Muslim immigrant youth in this study—the girls who spoke publicly about racial profiling and the boys who offered a reasoned analysis of anti-Muslim racism and state violence.

South Asian, Arab, and Muslim American youth are the subject of legal initiatives, organizing campaigns, and social scrutiny permeated by ideological representations of Muslim and Arab "others," male and female. It was in a peculiarly reflexive moment in my research that I realized the extent to which the everyday gendered representations of Muslim identity after 9/11 perform a classically Orientalist role in the present moment. Although this incident did not involve "youth" directly, it forced me to grapple with the limitations of liberal dissent. It is clear that these young immigrants were responding to social forces in relation to adult actors in the larger political context in which they were embedded, which was also shaping my own understandings of their expressions of dissenting citizenship. In fact, it was in the process of my own political engagement with issues of civil and immigrant rights in the city that my views of dissenting citizenship were challenged, especially by the many contradictions of resistance to the U.S. wars in the Middle East.

In spring 2003, I was at a meeting of the New England Immigrant and Detainee Response Network (NEIDRN), a coalition of immigrant and civil rights activists that was training volunteers to monitor the Special Registration process then under way in Boston and to be on hand to assist immigrants who registered. Toward the end of the meeting, a white American woman wondered aloud what it meant that the largely female group of volunteers from the South Asian community were working on behalf of Muslim men. Some participants laughed at this comment, and one person said that this might challenge the Muslim immigrant men's conceptions of gender roles, but I was unsettled by this question for I did not fully know what it meant and was uneasy with the response. At that moment, I understood that the question might also translate as Is this a feminist move? How do you feel about working "for" men? Maybe I was wrong about this. Later, it occurred to me that there was a deeper issue implied by this exchange that had troubled me. I realized that it was the identity of the observer who raised the question that was important in understanding its implications, that is, her position as a progressive, white American activist commenting on South Asian, Muslim, and Arab Americans and the larger politics of race and gender in Muslim immigrant communities. The question forced me to grapple with the broader intersections of liberal feminism and Orientalism at this particular moment, a complex issue that has not been sufficiently critiqued after 9/11 or acknowledged within feminist debates.

The role of female South Asian or Muslim activists after 9/11 is complicated, certainly, because there are ongoing contestations of gender relations within every community, immigrant, Muslim, or otherwise. Yet, further thought needs to be given to the implicit Orientalism that underlies dominant constructions of Muslim (or Arab) masculinity and that seeps into even progressive or feminist sites where state policies are being challenged. While the person who made this comment at the meeting may not herself have shared this view, there is a liberal American discourse that frames Muslim/Arab men as victims of the state's War on Terror and simultaneously assumes that Muslim/Arab women are, in turn, victims of these men's patriarchal beliefs. Within this framework, Muslim/Arab women are compromising, or bracketing, their gender politics while engaging in campaigns against detentions and deportations to defend Muslim or Arab American men, who are their oppressors. The deeper assumptions here are, first, that "Muslim" or "Arab" culture is inherently oppressive to women, and second, that the basis of post-9/11 political organizing among South Asian or Arab Americans is a shared religious or ethnic affiliation.

Yet for me, and for most other South Asian American women I know who have been doing immigrant and civil rights work after 9/11, we were not simply working on behalf of "our men." It is true that the vast majority of post-9/11 detainees were men; the June 2003 report released by the Department of Justice's Office of the Inspector General was based on 762 detainees, who were all men (Sheikh 2003, 72). It is also the case that many of the Arabs and Muslims targeted by the FBI for surveillance and deportation because of alleged associations with terrorism were men, with a few exceptions, and that the dominant linkage of Muslim men with terrorism was reinforced by the Special Registration policy, which only applied to Muslim males. But while I and other South Asian women felt we had a particular responsibility to work in our communities after 9/11, many of us also felt strongly about organizing on behalf of men, or women, of other communities, and some had already done so in various

"Stop the Disappearances," post-9/11 protest at Middlesex County Jail.
Photograph by Irum Sheikh.

immigrant, civil rights, and feminist campaigns. This was not simply an
ethnicized politics of working for "our men."

In fact, emphasizing the connection between gender and ethnic or
national community in discussing detention—the women on the outside helping "their men" on the inside—implicitly sets up an Orientalist
framework of emasculated Muslim, South Asian, or Arab males, helpless and impotent in prison, subjugated by U.S. imperial and state power.
Within this liberal Orientalist view, the relationships of these immigrant
men with "their women" are presumably imprisoned by tradition but are
liberated in a (colonially) perverse way by the crisis created by U.S. state
power and the agency of women who are empowered in the West. This
liberal Orientalist framework is part of a prevailing mainstream, state-
sanctioned discourse of Muslim/Arab masculinity and femininity that
dovetails with what I consider an imperial feminist perspective.

Susan Akram (2002, 62) observes that liberal Orientalist assumptions
about gender and Islam that presume to defend the rights of "Muslim
women" are linked to what Edward Said called the "neo-Orientalism"
of the present moment, infusing "modern feminism and human rights"
discourses in both their universalist and culturally relativist variants. A
liberal neo-Orientalism that is couched in the framework of women's

rights is evident in the discourse about oppressed Muslim women—from Afghanistan to Iraq and now Iran—who must be liberated by the "benevolent imperialism" of the United States. Zine (2006, 9) observes that "historically the category of 'Muslim woman' has been a malleable construct constantly redefined to suit particular political, cultural, or ideological purposes." For example, some analysts suggest that the U.S. military devised strategies to win the "hearts and minds" of local populations and crush insurgencies, from Vietnam to Iraq, by taking lessons from colonial strategists in other wars that used the "emancipation" of "subjugated" women as a wedge to undermine resistance (Elliott 2007, 28; see also Lazreg 2008). That women in many parts of the world—not just in the Muslim or Arab world—face many kinds of social, economic, and legal discrimination is undoubtedly true, but there are women's movements in all these regions that work to address these issues. Imperialist feminism assumes that it is the United States, or Western culture, that must bring "freedom" to certain areas of the world, if necessarily with a military or occupying force, ignoring these indigenous feminist movements—another case of white men (and white women) trying to save brown women from brown men (Nader 1989; Spivak 1988, 296), a familiar trope in Western colonial history.

Liberal feminists in the United States unfortunately fall prey to this Orientalist feminism as well and participate in imperial spectacles focusing on Muslim female victimhood. To give just one example, the playwright Eve Ensler, whose much-publicized performance, *The Vagina Monologues*, focused on issues such as sexual violence and female genital mutilation, organized a campaign showcasing oppressed Afghan women after 9/11 ("Afghanistan is Everywhere"), through performances and political conferences (see Cooper 2007). These spectacles stage a Western missionary feminism that detaches violence against women from its historical and political specificity and evades the complicity of the United States in global conflicts. This is just one dramatic example of a resurgent U.S. imperialist feminism that indirectly justifies support of colonialist projects through a universalizing discourse of women's rights. This "human rights feminism" aspires to an internationalist outlook but contains at it core a nationalist outlook that supports U.S. interests, which is never directly acknowledged as such (Barlow 2000). A critique of this imperialist and Orientalist feminism needs to situate questions of Muslim and Arab women's rights in a layered analysis that takes into account factors

of nationalism, race, religion, class, and immigration. It must resist letting the issue of gender rights becoming either a "pawn" to justify U.S.
interventions in the Muslim and Arab world or an apology for Islamic
fundamentalism (Zine 2006).

Liberal Orientalism or imperialist feminism distorts the nature of the
work of female South Asian and Muslim activists or men involved in post-
9/11 organizing, and the gendering of the political responses that emerged
within these communities after 9/11. Irum Sheikh's research (2003) documents the range of roles that South Asian and Muslim American women
played after 9/11 in response to the detentions and deportations targeting Muslim men. She notes several cases of South Asian Muslim women
who were "activated" by the disappearance or removal of their brothers,
husbands, or partners, in a variety of ways, from organizing campaigns
to speaking at public protests to taking over their husbands' businesses.
While these responses may appear to fit the model of women helping
their men or finding their agency as political actors in the West, Sheikh
suggests that this was also a form of women's resistance to the U.S. state's
war on terror; clearly, South Asian Muslim women, too, were affected
by these policies and opposed them in concrete and visible ways. The
experiences she documents not only counter the Orientalist notion of
submissive or voiceless Muslim, South Asian, and Arab women, but also
represent the dissenting citizenship of immigrant women who are "not
recognized as political subjects" and not "authorized" to speak as citizens
(Sassen 2004). In fact, in many cases, South Asian immigrant women
who were not citizens were making claims for civil rights that U.S. citizens were afraid of losing, petitioning the state but also implicitly challenging the presumed guarantee of rights within liberal democracy.

In the instance of the local immigrant rights coalition in which I was
involved, these unexpected conversations forced me to think more critically about how civil rights issues were being connected to state power
and local acts of resistance in gendered ways, and about the uneasy conjoining of liberalism, feminism, and nationalisms. The reflexivity of the
research process also highlighted the ways in which I was implicated in
these processes by contributing to, or challenging, a neo-Orientalist por-
trayal of post-9/11 activism. The liberal Orientalism that emerges in the
spaces of civil rights organizing is one layer of the social, political, and
legal fields that shape the experiences of Muslim immigrants and youth,
male and female, in the United States and is also an element of the do-

mestic and global frame for the War on Terror, as I will explore in the following chapter.

"Racial Profiling"—and Why It Isn't

Jamila, Adil, and Ayesha were perhaps some of the most outspoken South Asian youth I talked to in their responses to the U.S. War on Terror, at home and overseas. However, all the Muslim immigrant students were grappling, in some way or the other, with the implications of the state's framing of Muslims as the enemy after September 11, 2001, and had varying responses to the question of "racial profiling" and Islamophobia. Most of them spoke of racial profiling as an assault on Muslims, as Ayesha and other students did, and over time I came to realize that as a descriptive and explanatory term, "*racial* profiling" did not quite capture the particular practices of state and civil targeting of Muslim, Arab, and South Asian Americans in the War on Terror. Racial profiling works on multiple levels and through contradictions between official rhetoric, public policy, and individual actions (Robin 2003). George W. Bush tried to deny in his public rhetoric that the crusade of "good against evil" was a war against Islam, and made symbolic gestures of inviting Muslim Americans to the White House during the festival of Eid to stress a public rhetoric of multicultural tolerance (Ahmed 2003). However, ongoing state policies of intelligence gathering, security profiling, and immigration control that targeted Muslim, Arab, and South Asian Americans pointed to the hollowness of multicultural politics based on symbolic recognition. Syed Khan commented to me in the fall of 2002: "Initially leaders including Bush had spoken up [against racial profiling], but afterwards, when it wasn't as critical, outreach to Muslim Americans has stopped completely. Now, it's bashing time."[6]

Some South Asian Muslims were quick to point out to me the outpouring of support offered by neighbors and friends after 9/11. Imran Hussein, the president of the local Pakistani community association, repeatedly told me that his daughter, who was the only Muslim student in her suburban high school, felt that she was surrounded by supportive and caring friends—even though he himself recalled that he was called a "bloody Arab" while walking through Prospect Square after 9/11. It is true that individual acts of solidarity coexisted with acts of discrimination, private and state-sponsored, on a mass scale, as Hussein Ibish of the national American-Arab Anti-Discrimination Committee pointed out in 2002 (also see Hing 2002).[7] Hate crimes, and many more occurrences of harassment, suspicion, and xenophobic paranoia targeting Muslim Americans, have also continued well after September 11, 2001. In my view, the multiculturalist inclusion of Muslim Americans or Islam as a category of "difference" has allowed the official and unofficial targeting of Muslim, Arab, and South Asian Americans to operate in a sphere seen as "exceptional," occupied by "bad" Americans who are unrepresentative of American tolerance for "diversity." In fact, defining the anti-Muslim backlash as a rash of hate crimes suggests that such violence can be attributed to the hateful action of an individual who can be criminalized and punished by the state, rather than to a political and ideological campaign of state actors, thus letting national and imperial policies off the hook.

Speaking of hate crimes as a failure of multiculturalism allows for an evasion of the systemic racism and violence directed against Muslim Americans and Muslim and Arab populations in the United States and also overseas, through military interventions, intelligence operations, surveillance, deportations, and detentions. After 9/11, liberal multiculturalists attempted to absorb Islam as a marker of cultural difference, sponsoring talks on Muslim identity and including token Muslim American representatives to expand the rainbow spectrum of diversity, as evident in various programs organized by academic institutions and community organizations. However, a multiculturalist discourse that attempts to fit the profiling of Muslim, Arab, and South Asian Americans into a racially based framework of domestic civil rights fails to address the political connections of Islamophobia and "racial profiling" after 9/11 to imperial policies that are tied to the global War on Terror. This is perhaps a classic instance of how U.S. multiculturalism suppresses antiracist, materialist critique of the state and co-opts political injustice as cultural difference, encouraging a politics of representation rather than resistance.

The construction of Muslim, Arab, and South Asian Americans as the enemy is more akin to a form of "Green McCarthyism," as Vijay Prashad (2003) observes, than to the common domestic form of racial profiling, however ambiguous the concept of race has always been in the United States. The image of the Muslim terrorist has come to replace the threat of the Communist that was used to fan the Red Scare. Leti Volpp (2002, 1584) argues that the post-9/11 moment "facilitated the consolidation of a new identity category" that conflated "Arab, Muslim, Middle Eastern" with "terrorist" and "noncitizen." This identity category is obviously not new, but Volpp is right to point out that a "national identity has consolidated that is both strongly patriotic and multiracial." This multiracial nationalism simultaneously excludes and racializes Muslim identity, although Muslim is not a racial category at all, even in the slippery sense of race in the United States. "Muslim" identity has certainly congealed as a marker of exclusion and marginalization, in relation to white or mainstream America, which is subjected to similar processes of racialization, and racism, that operate for racial minority groups. It is also important to note that the racialization of Islam is embedded in much longer histories of Western colonial projects that can be traced to the domination of Muslims and Arabs in fifteenth- and sixteenth-century Spain and, later, of indigenous peoples in the New World by settlers in North America, that were based on "imagined biological racial differences" (Dunbar-Ortiz 2004, 34), and so are intertwined in complex ways with modernity, racism, religion, and imperialism.

However, the racial identities of Muslim Americans are ambiguous, for both Arabs and South Asians have experienced contradictory and shifting legal classification in the United States as variously white and nonwhite. This ambiguous racialization made their claims to citizenship rights tenuous during the era when nonwhites were not eligible for U.S. citizenship. For example, in 1923, the Supreme Court ruled that an Indian immigrant, Bhagat Singh Thind, was technically Caucasian but could not be considered white in the understanding of the "common man" and so was ineligible for naturalization. When Arabs began migrating to the United States in large numbers at the turn of the twentieth century, they were officially considered "white" but their eligibility for naturalization was disputed in certain locations, because they were "Asiatic" and sometimes on the grounds that they were Muslim.[8] Even when Arabs won the right to legal citizenship in U.S. courts, Suad Joseph (1999, 258) argues, historically "a more subtle and in some ways damning designation of difference is affixed to the Arab—as a non-independent, not-autonomous, not-individual, not-free person" that cast Arabs (and today, Muslims, due to similar perceptions) outside of liberal Western conceptions of citizenship.

The paradoxical racialization of Muslim identity, which is itself not racial, is what Moustafa Bayoumi (2001/2002, 73) calls the "tragic irony" of "racial profiling" after 9/11. I want to point out that this profiling is at root a form of "political racism" that is often couched in Orientalist cultural suspicion of violent and devious outsiders to Western culture and democracy. The political racism against Muslims and Arabs bleeds into a broader form of cultural racism that has replaced modern racism, based on a biological notion of race with a less primordialist, but equally essentialist, racism that discriminates on the basis of culture. In the case of Arabs and Muslims, this focus on cultural and religious "values" is embedded in a historically evolving Orientalist discourse about the "clash of civilizations." Samuel Huntington's (1996, 40–47, 207–18) theory of the clash between "Islam" and "the West," in his view the primary global conflict today, rests on the notion that the world is divided into civilizations, or distinct "human tribes" based on the "overall way of life of a people," corresponding generally to the major religions ("Sinic," Japanese, Hindu, Islamic, Western, and—"possibly"—African). He argues that "Western" civilization in the United States, representing a unique modernity based on "Christianity, pluralism, individualism, and the rule of law," must consolidate its power by warding off the internal threat of American multiculturalists and the external threat of Islam—not just Islamic fundamentalism—as a civilization that is inherently and violently anti-Western (Huntington 1996, 217). This is an example of what Hardt and Negri call "imperial racist theory" or, strictly speaking, "racism without race" (2000, 192), which has seeped into American public discourse about the War on Terror, even if officially denied by the Bush regime.

An understanding of imperial racism helps to clarify how religion, nationality, and race get conflated in the discourse of racial profiling, making the term even more problematic. Much of what gets framed as simply anti-Muslim sentiment contains a core of Islamophobia, which certainly exists in the United States and was heightened after 9/11, but also a kernel of historic "anti-Arab" feeling that undergirds U.S. military interventions or support for colonialist policies in the Middle East, but that is hardly ever named as such (Davidson 1999; Doolittle 2002; Said 1992 [1979]; Salaita 2006a). "Muslim" is often used to stand in for "Arab," ignoring the fact that the majority of Arab Americans are Christian and that only 23 percent are Muslim (Marvasti and McKinney 2004, 26), reinforcing Orientalist conflations of Islam with the Arab world. Muslims themselves are not a monolithic group: they have varying ways of expressing their religious identity and responding to conditions in the United States, as evident in the experiences of the two girls discussed above: Jamila, whose family sent her to an Islamic school for a year but did not expect her to follow any religious precepts after that; and Ayesha, who went clubbing and had a boyfriend but who distinguished herself from girls who were "out of control" and identified strongly as Muslim—without wearing a hijab (see Ajrouch 2004; Haddad and Smith 1996; Shyrock 2000).

More importantly, the roots of the War on Terror do not lie in a religious crusade or civilizational conflict between Islam and the West, as Huntington and contemporary Orientalists would have us believe. The War on Terror is a political struggle about the role of U.S. power and the nation's economic, political, and military interventions in various parts of the world, from Saudi Arabia and Iraq to Palestine and the Philippines, which have provoked resistance from a range of movements, including Islamist groups but also from other, secular political formations. Viewing the War on Terror as a conflict based solely on religion obscures the geopolitical underpinnings of the conflict that are tied to imperial domination of the world order, obscured by Bush's rhetoric of a Western crusade against "the axis of evil." For all these reasons, I think it is essential to complicate the discussion of racial profiling by including a larger analysis of Islamophobia and anti-Arab racism, as expressed historically in public culture and state policies.

The political racism against Arab and Muslim Americans has to be understood by placing it in the historic context of U.S. relations with the Middle East, as I discussed in chapter 1. As a result of U.S. strategic interests in the Middle East, Arab Americans and Muslim Americans have been targeted by the state for many years, well before 2001 (Abraham 1994; Marshy 1994; Saliba 1994; Shaheen 1999). Surveillance of Arab American communities has been closely tied to the ongoing U.S. support of the Israeli occupation of Palestine and repression of those who have protested U.S. policy in the Middle East at various moments since the 1967 Israeli-Arab War: from the FBI's monitoring of the General Union of Palestinian Students in the 1980s, to the attempted deportation of the pro-Palestinian activists known as the "L.A. 8," to the nationwide monitoring and interviews of Arab American individuals and organizations before and during the first Gulf War (Cainkar 2002; Cole and Dempsey 2002, 35–48; Green 2003). The profiling of Arab Americans was not a new phenomenon that began on September 11, 2001, but it was greatly intensified and publicly sanctioned by state policies in the War on Terror. What was new was that after 9/11, South Asian Americans were similarly framed as objects of intensified suspicion and surveillance, particularly those who were Muslim, which belied for the more privileged the assumed shield of their "model minority" status and forced on some an acknowledgment of U.S. racism. There has been a shift in race politics in the United States after 9/11, particularly in its immediate aftermath, where the primary fault lines are no longer just between those racialized as white Americans versus people of color, or even as black versus white Americans, but between those categorized as Muslim/non-Muslim, Arab/non-Arab, and citizen/noncitizen.

Muslim American Citizenship, "Good" and "Bad"

Modes of dissent and conceptions of citizenship after 9/11 also highlighted various tensions that I found myself grappling with in conversations with Muslim immigrant youth, as well as in my involvement with local civil rights organizing initiatives. Communities of dissent were formed in the Wellford area that, as in all moments of organizing, had shifting boundaries and bases for alliances. After 9/11, Muslim civil rights have become the focus of organizing initiatives, which have created unique coalitions and forced questions of secularism, the racialization of religious identity, nationalism, and class, into discussions of war, civil rights, and racial discrimination. The politicization of Islam could mean the greater adoption of a religious or political Muslim identity among a younger generation of Muslim Americans in response to their profiling by the state, as happened for an earlier generation of South Asian Muslim youth in Britain (Jacobson 1998). In the wake of attacks on British Muslim youth by the right-wing British National Party in the summer of 2001, the events of 9/11, the London bombings of 7/7, and the crackdown on civil liberties, a new generation of British Muslim activists has emerged in movements protesting the war in Iraq and challenging British policies that discriminate against Muslims (Akhtar 2005; Birt 2005). While there is intense concern in the United States about so-called radicalization or Islamization, there is little in-depth work that has carefully examined this issue. Around the nation, however, there are numerous instances of second-generation Muslim and Arab Americans who are actively engaging in civil rights or antiwar movements, as was evident in coalitions in Wellford and forums organized by SACH, which included local community organizers and immigration lawyers of diverse backgrounds (Arab, South Asian,

Latino and Latina, Brazilian, African American, Ethiopian) as well as Muslim activists. It was too soon to say whether this politicization was occurring for the Muslim immigrant youth in Wellford, though I sensed edges of this politicization of Islam among some of the high school students I spoke to, such as Farid and Ayesha, who had grown up in the United States and identified with other urban youth of color.

Those in Muslim and South Asian immigrant communities expressing dissent after 9/11 had varying views about the role of religion in relation to citizenship and the value of electoral politics as a strategy for resistance. As in all minority communities, some Muslim Americans organizations focused on encouraging political participation in the electoral process and believed that Muslims needed to become U.S. citizens and represent their interests at the national level through a liberal democratic notion of "active citizenship," but this notion sometimes also spilled over into other modes of dissent. Anwar Kazmi, an Indian Muslim immigrant, was president of the Massachusetts chapter of the American Muslim Alliance (AMA), a national organization that sponsored voter registration drives and whose members were mainly middle-class Muslims from the suburbs, citizens or permanent residents. After 9/11, Kazmi said that the AMA began getting involved with the peace movement, and its members attended rallies protesting the war in Iraq. His niece, Salma Kazmi, who was in her twenties, was outreach director at the Islamic Society of Boston at the time and spoke at civil- and immigrant-rights events and protests. She commented on the "desire to know what are the true limitations and restrictions in terms of being Muslims and citizens" after 9/11 and the perceived need, within the Muslim American community as well as in the mainstream, to have "a newer generation of Muslim civil rights leaders at the forefront, who are without an accent, or women in hijab." Salma Kazmi felt that she herself had become a poster child in this project of defining Muslim American citizenship, which seems to rest on a need to prove allegiance and assimilation into the nation based on a staging of cultural familiarity and translation of cultural unfamiliarity (particularly the "hijab"). This is visually demonstrated by the first issue of *Muslim Girl* magazine, which showcases a diverse range of Muslim American girls and young women—both with and without head scarves—playing sports, pursuing careers, excelling in education, and generally looking like other American teenage girls. The cover, which features a Pakistani American teenager wearing glitter eye shadow and a red-and-white-striped headscarf

First issue of
Muslim Girl
magazine, 2007.

emerging from her parka jacket and with small red, white, and blue stars on her cheek, matching the American flag in the lower corner, seems to suggest an all-American Muslim "cover girl"—patriotic, Muslim, and modern. Publications such as these signal the emergence of a younger generation of Muslim Americans who have increasingly assumed leadership of national Muslim organizations in the United States, with the growth of the Muslim American community and formation of national civil rights organizations that encourage participation in mainstream U.S. politics, especially after 9/11 (Al-Sultany 2007; see Hasan 2000).

"Good citizenship" was performed in a variety of ways after 9/11 by Muslim Americans who testified loyalty to the nation and asserted belief in its democratic ideals. There were different degrees of self-defense in this performance of good citizenship by those who felt that their political views were being monitored by the state and were afraid to openly express their dissent. Sometimes dissenting citizenship blurred into "good" Muslim citizenship as antiwar critics who were Muslim made public testimonials that emphasized that Muslims were peaceful, loyal, American citizens while critiquing aspects of the government's policies. For instance, in November 2001 I attended an antiwar rally in Boston, where I marched through the streets with thousands of protesters who congregated on the Boston Common in the heart of the city. Imam Talal Eid of the Islamic Center of New England proclaimed, to loud applause from the crowd, that Muslims "want to be a part of the U.S." and contribute to its "civilization." His statement appealed to the protesters because it was implicitly a twist on Samuel Huntington's (1996) infamous anti-Islamic argument about the "clash of civilizations"—"Islam" versus "the West." However, his statement still upheld the idea that what is at stake is the relationship between cultural "civilizations," and defended Muslim Americans on the premise of assimilation through U.S. citizenship. Public statements such as his implicitly reinforce the notion of good Muslims who are willing to be made into loyal citizens of the United States and believe in its democratizing mission—or at least participate in the discussion of citizenship on the state's own terms—as opposed to bad Muslims, who critique the United States as an imperial power and oppose its expansionist policies. This distinction has been notably critiqued by Mahmood Mamdani (2004, 15), who observes that after 9/11

> President Bush moved to distinguish between "good Muslims" and "bad Muslims." . . ."Bad Muslims" were clearly responsible for terrorism. At the same time, the president seemed to assure Americans that "good Muslims" were anxious to clear their names and consciences of this horrible crime and would undoubtedly support "us" in a war against "them." But this could not hide the central message of such discourse: unless proved to be "good," every Muslim was presumed to be "bad." . . . Judgments of "good" and "bad" refer to Muslim political identities, not to cultural or religious ones.

Mamdani's analysis clearly points to "good" versus "bad" Muslims from the perspective of the state's War on Terror but does not distinguish between the responses of individual Muslims themselves, so I am extending his notion here to the strategies and discourse chosen by Muslim Americans. In using this framework more broadly to think about various modes of dissent after 9/11, I am not suggesting that a public stance such as that of Imam Talal Eid's necessarily means that he supports U.S. foreign policy. He and others who publicly emphasize the peacefulness of Islam and who reject the association of Islam with terrorism may, in fact, privately oppose U.S. imperial projects in the Middle East and South Asia. In many cases, there is also a justifiable degree of fear or anxiety among Muslim Americans when making public statements opposing the United States, given the surveillance and repression of political speech in the PA-TRIOT Act era. What I am arguing here is that such public statements, if not accompanied by an acknowledgment of the root causes of terrorism, create new distinctions not just between "good" and "bad" Muslims but between "good" and "bad" Muslim *citizenship*, which implicitly reinforce the desirability of complying with the state's disciplining power, even if they challenge specific aspects of the law or particular state policies.

Most statements made by "good" Muslim (or Arab) citizens about the War on Terror or U.S. foreign policy in the Middle East are accompanied by a mandatory disclaimer condemning all acts of terrorism and violence. All acts of terrorism, state sponsored or otherwise, are morally reprehensible, but Steven Salaita (2006a, 51) points out that the compulsory disavowal of terrorism by Arabs and Muslims after 9/11 has become their "prerequisite to speaking" in the public sphere. Salaita rightly observes that the default attachment of the word "terrorism" to Arabs and Muslims is embedded in Orientalist cultural stereotypes and a decontextualized focus on violence, evading discussions of political grievances as well as state-sponsored violence. When Arab and Muslim commentators deny associations with Islamic terrorism, they implicitly reinscribe this set of cultural and political assumptions about Arab, and Islamist, politics and cultures. Salaita (2006a, 50–51) suggests that this mandatory statement about Muslim terrorism should not be invoked at all, neither in affirmation nor in dismissal. He proposes an ethics of refusal of this disclaimer, rejecting the very premise that Arabs and Muslims are supporters of terrorism, unless they insist otherwise.

Not all Muslim or Arab American commentators would agree with this tactic, but it is clear that there are varying responses and interventions by Muslim and Arab Americans that inform their notions of dissent and citizenship in response to the War on Terror. The desire to perform so-called good Muslim citizenship has inevitably altered the identities produced in Muslim American communities after 9/11. Sally Howell and Andrew Shryock (2003, 456) argue that Arab Americans and community leaders who want "to reassert their status as 'good' and 'loyal'" citizens of the United States have tried to distance themselves from "a strong identification with religious beliefs, political ideologies, or cultural practices that are genuinely alternative to those present in America today" and "from the people who are most likely to suffer from these images and their consequences." This has heightened cleavages within the targeted communities and reinforced distinctions between "good" and "bad" Arabs, similar to those between "good" and "bad" Muslim citizenship.

Yet in other spaces, local and national, I also heard dissenting speeches by Muslim civil rights activists who were very critical of the U.S. state and rejected its founding national myths as a premise for citizenship. At the July 2003 annual convention jointly held by the Islamic Circle of North America (ICNA) and the Muslim American Society (MAS) that I attended in Philadelphia, Imam Khalid Griggs, an African American Muslim, spoke passionately about how racism was the "elephant standing in the living room of America since its formation" and lamented that too many Muslims had "chosen to ignore for too long this beast that has stood in the living room." It was evident at the conference that some Muslim American organizations were trying to highlight the connections between religious identity and U.S. race politics, which Imam Griggs implicitly suggested had been ignored by foreign-born Muslims. There was also an attempt to reach out to Muslim American youth by packaging Islam in the language and look of hip-hop. This "marketing," quite literally, was apparent in the products displayed by the Young Muslims group at their table, such as T-shirts with graffiti-inspired designs and DVDs of speeches about Islam with titles such as "Thugs in the Mosque." Also on display were aspects of the "Islamic internationalism" that I alluded to earlier, with workshops, materials, and banners at the conference focusing on the plight of Muslims in Kashmir, Chechnya, Afghanistan, Iraq, and Palestine.

International and domestic human rights issues were linked in a large panel I attended featuring a representative of the national antiwar coalition, ANSWER (Act Now to Stop War and End Racism)—which has been involved in organizing several large antiwar demonstrations across the United States after 9/11—who spoke of the need to oppose the War on Terror, making visible the growing alliances between Muslim civil rights organizations and secular, antiwar, and progressive and Left groups since 9/11. Clearly, there was a developing strand of Muslim American activism that expressed an antiracist politics connected to the experiences of people of color in the United States and, in some cases, an antiwar and antioccupation politics implicitly critical of U.S. militarism. However, this activism was still based on the notion of a universal Muslim *umma* (worldwide community) and on a politics driven by faith-based ideals, which raises interesting questions about the new alliances being formed between Muslim American communities and U.S. political movements, from left to centrist.

These alliances were explicitly part of the conference's agenda; for example, I attended a workshop on "Outreach and Coalition Building" by Mahdi Bray, the charismatic African American Muslim President of MAS and director of its civil rights program, the Freedom Foundation. Bray had been shaped by the civil rights struggle in the United States, describing himself as an "NAACP baby," and he linked a critique of American racism to the post-9/11 profiling of Muslims. The thrust of his workshop was that Muslim Americans should get involved in mainstream civic and political life, from local to national levels, and should participate in everything from voter registration drives to school board meetings, with "a commitment to engage America in the laws of Allah." This message reflected the overall theme of the conference's political message: Muslim Americans should be more involved "citizens" in the public square of mainstream U.S. politics and promote Islam's vision of tolerance and justice, a version of "good" citizenship that could potentially challenge U.S. state policies from within, by accepting the participatory premise of liberal democracy.

Many speakers at this convention did explicitly denounce the War on Terror being waged against Muslim Americans, but at the panels I attended there were few calls to oppose it through actions other than documenting instances of profiling and surveillance and sending aid to families affected by detentions and deportations. Perhaps the only speech I heard that raised the level of political urgency a notch higher was that by Nahla Al-Arian, who spoke about the detention of her brother, Mazen Al-Najjar, a Palestinian activist who had been arrested by the FBI in November 2001, and her husband, Sami Al-Arian, a Palestinian professor arrested in February 2003. Al-Arian had been outspoken in protesting the Israeli occupation and was fired by the University of South Florida and detained indefinitely, without a lawyer, by the Department of Justice on charges of supporting "terrorism"—but alleged terrorism in Israel, not in the United States.[9] Nahla Al-Arian eloquently asked the audience what they were doing for her husband, who was suffering for their cause, and called for support of these "political prisoners."

The ICNA/MAS convention, even though primarily a gathering of the faithful, highlighted the forms that the growing politicization of Muslim American identity was taking after 9/11 in these organized spaces, and the debates about the national mobilization of Muslim Americans as emerging political constituencies that have their own agendas and internal debates, as do Christian or Jewish American constituencies. The convention also highlighted some ongoing questions for me and other activists, who are not themselves religious or involved in faith-based organizing, about the role of religion and secularism in political dissent. In Wellford and around the nation, Muslim civil rights activists forged, or strengthened, alliances with immigrant and civil rights activists to address the profiling of Arab, Muslim, and South Asian Americans after 9/11 and oppose the assault on immigrant and civil rights more generally. These coalitions raised issues that were not always easily resolved, because they brought together a range of views about strategies for political protest, the broader analysis of the War on Terror and Middle East politics, and the relation of (Western as well as non-Western) secularisms and religion to civil rights organizing. Work on Muslim politics in Britain has already addressed these questions and contradictions for antiracist and antiwar movements, given the greater visibility of British Muslim communities and the longer history of these debates, as crystallized in the controversy over Salman Rushdie's *Satanic Verses* in 1988–89, where religion emerged as a key site of difference (see e.g., Birt 2005; Modood 2006).

In the United States, immigrant and civil rights activists and antiwar organizers who found themselves working with religious communities—including Muslim Americans who had not been involved with religious communities before 9/11—grappled with potential tensions between secularist and faith-based or Islamist understandings of the nature of the crisis and its possible solution (see Zine 2006). While I did not experience these tensions in any of the coalitions in Wellford at the time, some South Asian leftists and progressives who strongly support secularism clearly had different views about the relationship of religion to state and society than the faith-driven activists with whom they were working. But it is also important to note that there were many secular Muslims from South Asian and Arab American communities involved in civil rights and antiwar organizing as well, and so secularist politics were expressed by Muslims and non-Muslims alike.

In general, I think potential tensions in these coalitions were resolved, in the short term, by a shared understanding among both secular and religious activists that the state was using religion, in addition to national origin, as the basis of its profiling. Furthermore, the primacy of racial discourse in the United States has meant that discrimination against Muslims has in some contexts become subsumed into a framework based on race that bridged alliances with other minoritized communities, as the talks by some African American Muslim speakers at the ICNA/MAS convention suggest. It is possible that as in Britain, there are Muslims who find the slippage of religion into race problematic and who do not think that their concerns translate easily into antiracist or civil rights frameworks, especially as coalitions forged in the 1980s among British Asian and Afro-Caribbean communities based on a shared "black identity" have dissolved (see Modood 2006). But it is true that in the post-9/11 United States, "Muslim" has in some sense become a shorthand to refer to a range of movements and actors, not all of them actually Muslim or Islamist, targeted by the U.S. imperial project as the "enemy." It is important to note that Islam is functioning for the U.S. state as a political, not just religious, category. The construction of the "Islamic threat" is part of broader policies that are also anti-Arab, and are tied to U.S. interests in the Middle East and South Asia as part of the larger vision for the New American Century. In reality, not all enemies are Muslim, and not all Muslims are enemies. In the War on Terror, defined famously by Bush after 9/11 as the battle waged by "us" against "them," there were "good" Muslim (and Arab and Asian) states and nonstate actors who supported U.S. interests and "bad" Muslim (and Arab and Asian) ones who did not, as observed by Mamdani (2004).

Furthermore, the "secular" state's management of religion and citizenship is rife with contradictions and ambiguities in the United States, as is apparent from the Bush administration's evangelical imperialism, religious crusader rhetoric, and support from the Christian Right—not to mention the historic use of various religious symbols and references in U.S. state rituals and institutions, including public schools, that continue to be contested for violating the presumed separation of church and state (see Asad 2003).[10] South Asian activists in Wellford, and other communities around the nation, who had long worked against the rise of Hindu fundamentalism and persecution of Muslims and other minorities in India, understood that despite the different political language in the United

States, and Bush's attempt to disguise the nature of the War on Terror, racial profiling after 9/11 was actually based in part on communal politics—as it is known in South Asia—for it targeted communities based on religion and ethnicity as well as on the basis of opposition to U.S. domination in the Middle East and South Asia. Dissenting movements resisting the imperialist premise of the War on Terror work in the slippery space where antiwar, antiracist, civil rights, immigrant rights, religious, and secularist politics intersect and sometimes collide.

Mixed Imperial Feelings

The boundaries of dissenting citizenship shifted slightly in the aftermath of 9/11 and realigned different minority groups in relation to one another and to the nation-state. There are several contradictions of imperial culture that complicate an easy understanding of political dissent in the United States after 9/11, for a resurgent American nationalism has permeated many groups or movements previously assumed to have a dissenting stance. The nationalism of "homeland security" spilled over historic fault lines of inclusion and exclusion, drawing in groups that had long been subjugated by the state to secure the civic consent of the majority to the War on Terror. Angela Davis (2005, 120) observes that "African American communities were certainly interpolated into this new racism" directed against the "terrorist enemy," defined as Muslim, Arab, or South Asian, and that "many previously excluded communities experienced—if only momentarily—a sense of national belonging" and integration into the multicultural nation. The climate of fear and demonization of an "enemy" population shifts attention away from the ways in which the "war at home" and the war abroad actually work in tandem with each other, at the expense of ordinary people whose only benefit tends to be their symbolic upgrading as more fully "American" after 9/11.

For example, a poll conducted by James Zogby on September 30, 2001, "showed that almost sixty percent of African Americans favored special scrutiny of those who look like terrorists" while another by the Boston Globe found that "just over seventy percent of African Americans it polled favored discriminatory checks at airports on all Arabs, including those who are U.S. citizens" (cited in Prashad 2003, 73). The Congressional Black Caucus supported Bush's post-9/11 security measures, and Representative John Conyers (D-Michigan), who had introduced the

Racial Profiling Act of 2001, cosponsored the PATRIOT Act in the House (Prashad 2003). However, there were other African Americans who made statements condemning the premise of post-9/11 racial profiling that went unreported in the mainstream media. Hugh Price of the Urban League commented that the polls mentioned above were "evidence of the perniciousness of racial profiling," and Bobby Rush, a congressman and former Black Panther, remarked, "Once this crisis is over, they're not going to be looking for Osama bin Laden or people who look like Arabs. As usual, they're going to be looking for you and me" (cited in Prashad 2003, 73–74). Barbara Lee, an African American Democrat from Oakland, became famous—and vilified by the Right as unpatriotic—for being the lone voice in a historic 420-1 vote in Congress on September 14, 2001, when she opposed giving the president blanket authority to wage a global War on Terror; she later went on to sponsor an unsuccessful measure in October 2002 to block a unilateral U.S. attack on Iraq.[11]

I think these varied responses by U.S. minorities to the War on Terror are instances of "mixed imperial feelings," attitudes and sentiments of nationalism and dissent that are layered in contradictory and unpredictable ways. They arise, in part, because the state has effectively used the politics of fear to foster a collective paranoia about terrorism that has hypnotized many into believing that the nation was at risk because of a nameless, faceless threat present in their midst. The Bush administration's crusade of "us" against "the terrorists" stoked a hyperpatriotism that drew into the national consensus groups that had until then felt marginalized, but were needed as foot soldiers, literally, for U.S. wars overseas. Minorities who had challenged the limits of liberal democracy before 9/11 came to believe that the United States did need to wage war and curtail (other people's) civil liberties in order to defend "American values" of freedom and democracy. For example, Tram Nguyen (2005, 72–75) notes that there were Central American refugees who had themselves fled U.S.-backed terror and repression in El Salvador but were moved and shaken by the tragedy of 9/11 and commented, "We're part of this too. We're as patriotic as anybody. We want to raise American flags."

These imperial feelings are mixed because they are unevenly shared among and within minority groups in different local contexts; as Adil's and Walid's comments point out, they depend on a range of factors such as class, immigration history, political experience, religious affiliation, and relationships with Muslim and Arab Americans. Many minorities were willing to believe this threat to national security could be eliminated by surveilling Arab and South Asian Americans and by waging war in South Asia and the Middle East, especially in the initial period of shock and mourning after 9/11. In the South Central district of Los Angeles, an African American woman volunteered to form a local Citizen Corps council to defend the community's "homeland security" because, she said, "We all felt vulnerable. . . . I think terrorism can happen anywhere, at any time" (cited in Nguyen 2005, 78). Partly, too, the "mixed feelings" of minority groups within the imperial nation arise because those who have long been targeted by the state, in some instances, experience a bitter vindication that another group has replaced them as the state's primary bull's-eye, and may even relish their new status of acceptance into cultural citizenship, however temporary. This is a complex and delicate topic, given that the Muslim population includes African Americans (the largest and only "indigenous group") and white as well as non-white converts, with a growing Latino and Latina Muslim community (Leonard 2003). These issues are made even more sensitive by the fact that, in a few cases, the attacks on Muslim, South Asian, and Arab Americans involved individuals from other minority groups.[12] This was also true in Wellford, where there were incidents in the high school such as those experienced by some of the South Asian Muslim students, as well as a controversial incident in a high school in a nearby city, where some Somali girls wearing hijab were harassed by African American girls after 9/11.

These mixed imperial feelings have sometimes been evaded in discussions of the shifting racial and cultural landscape after 9/11, because they are discomfiting for liberal notions of immanent political empathy. However, these mixed responses and nationalist feelings are not incomprehensible if the political context of class inequity and histories of racism, as well as the culture of U.S. militarism, are taken into account. Nguyen (2005, 75) notes that Latino and Latina immigrants often provide cheap, undocumented labor for South Asian and Arab American entrepreneurs, feeding a class resentment that underlies intergroup tensions and that heightens the suspicion of Arab and Muslim Americans. Yet other minorities resisted the premise of integration into the homeland's fight against terror, as an African American woman from Los Angeles commented wryly, "They ain't going to come here and bomb us, because we ain't got nothing. . . . They can't stop the Crips and the Bloods from killing each other right here, so how are we going to stop terrorism? . . . What they're doing to Arabs and Muslims, it's like how they do [to] us out here in South Central" (cited in Nguyen 2005, 79). Clearly, there is skepticism about homeland security policies and rhetoric about law and order in communities that have been criminalized and subject to police brutality but do not feel a sense of security themselves. Certain minorities will not be warmly welcomed into the fold of patriotic American nationalism overnight and will continue to be suspect as "domestic terrorists."

Mixed imperial feelings are important to consider because they highlight the numerous contradictions of class, nationalism, and cultural citizenship that were in place before 9/11 but were intensified, shaken up, and sometimes reconfigured by the War on Terror. In some cases, people of color saw the connections between poverty, the War on Drugs and gangs, and the War on Terror, questioning *whose* "homeland" was being defended and for what purpose. The metaphor of war has become an alibi for state force and repression of vulnerable communities, since the "war on poverty" receded with the conservative shift in U.S. politics, and the image of a nation at war is used to justify the targeting of internal enemies who must be cleansed from the national body politic (see Comaroff 2007). For some right-wing supporters of the War on Terror, different immigrant and minority groups merged into an imagined common campaign to undermine the United States. Representative Ed Royce, a Republican from California, described the U.S.-Mexico border area as a "war zone," thus justifying its militarization: "Al Qaeda has considered crossing our Southwest borders. . . . It may already have happened" (cited in Lovato 2006). Roberto Lovato (2006) observes that the "newly reconfigured national security culture that is wiring us for war" has merged the threat of "bad" Latino and Latina immigrants with "bad" Arabs through an "Al-Qaedization of Latino identity." One commentator described "radical Chicano activists" as "'America's Palestinians' [who] are gearing up a movement to carve out the southwestern United States . . . meeting continuously with extremists from the Islamic world" (cited in Mariscal 2005, 43). Ironically, there is a germ of analytic truth in this paranoid view, for the phrase "America's Palestinians" indirectly links the shared subordination of indigenous peoples around the world living in occupied homelands, including Chicanos and Chicanas and natives of the Americas, and expresses similar feelings of dissent against empire.

After 9/11, and contrary to the fear of a "minority intifada" uniting Arabs and immigrants, many Latinos and Latinas and new immigrants be-

gan signing up to join the U.S. military in greater numbers. The civilizational discourse of the War on Terror pits "'loyal,' 'civilized,' God-fearing,
pro-war Latinos" against "undocumented immigrants, gangs, anti-war
and anti-recruitment activists" (Lovato 2006). As Catherine Lutz points
out (2006, 291, 292), the culture of militarization in the United States
shapes the "social geography" of race and class and affects "general societal
beliefs and values," including notions of gender, sexuality, citizenship, and
national belonging, that are imbricated with ideas of "freedom" and "civilization" that make violence legitimate, in not banal. There is a historical
pattern in the military's recruitment of minorities, including some Asian
American groups such as Filipino Americans, who are overrepresented
in military service, especially at the lower ranks—it is ironic that those
excluded from full cultural citizenship in the nation are most likely to die
fighting its wars.

Jorge Mariscal (2005, 46) points out that the lure of the military is not
just a product of patriotic fervor, but of strategic military recruitment
policies that have historically used economic and educational incentives
to target disadvantaged youth, with Latinos and Latinas being recruited
at "about twice their rate in the general population." These policies include
the presidential Executive Order signed in 2002 that expedites naturalization for noncitizens in the military. Over time, however, and especially
as the increasingly unpopular war in Iraq dragged on, there was a slump
in military recruitment and young African Americans became increasingly unwilling to enlist in the army and Latino and Latina *movimientistas*
resisted assimilation into the national security culture (Lovato 2006).[13] In
fact, the U.S. military has tried to compensate for its shortfall in recruitment by doubling recruitment in its poorest colonial territories—American Samoa, Guam, and the Northern Mariana Islands.[14]

Military recruitment initiatives have targeted minority and working-
class youth through programs such as Junior ROTC, designed to "present the idea of the military life style to High School students . . . and
to create better citizens"; recruitment of teachers and counselors as "in-
fluencers" to unofficially recruit high school youth; and the Troops to
Teachers program (funded by the No Child Left Behind Act of 2001)
to place military veterans in the classroom and to expose children to
"military values" (Mariscal 2005, 46–48). The No Child Left Behind Act
mandates that any school getting federal tax dollars must give its students' names and contact information to military recruiters. In response, a

national campaign called "Leave My Child Alone" was created by a coalition of groups to advise parents on the option of not releasing their
children's' information, so that their children would not get calls from recruiters.[15] Education is a battleground for military recruitment campaigns
and antimilitarism efforts by parents, students, and counterrecruitment
activists who reject the military's false advertising for an "easy" route to
college and seeing the world.[16]

The Wellford High School had long opposed military recruitment, but
according to school staff, a few years before 9/11 it allowed ROTC to work
with the career center and advertise the military as an optional route
to college, although individual teachers were still critical of recruiting.
Nasreen, who immigrated from Bangladesh with four brothers and three
sisters, said that one of her brothers joined the army after graduating from
high school; although he really wanted to be a doctor, "he wanted the education" promised by the army, which he had heard about in school. None
of Nasreen's brothers were citizens, unlike her, and she was aware that
getting financial aid for college was easier for U.S. citizens. Her brother's
decision to join the military seemed embedded in pragmatic concerns of
citizenship and education, which are directly addressed by the military's
slogans of "Aim high" and "Be all you can be." Recognizing these concerns,
some U.S. legislators tried to make the Development, Relief, and Education for Alien Minors (DREAM) Act, first introduced in Congress in 2001
but not voted on yet, into an amendment of the 2008 Defense Appropria-
tions Bill.[17] The DREAM Act was no dream solution, however: it would
allow undocumented high school students to attend college and work legally for six years—although by registering they would likely reveal their
parents' status—and require them in that time to either graduate from
community college, finish two years at a four-year university, or serve two
years in the U.S. military; they would still not be eligible for certain federal financial aid to support their college education.[18]

The targeting of immigrant and working-class youth by the military is
part of the so-called poverty draft or economic conscription, promising
poor and working-class youth a supposedly easy route to college education and economic stability through military service, which in reality is
not easy at all.[19] As the need for more foot soldiers in Iraq increased with
the growing toll on American lives and drop in army enlistment, military
recruiters stepped up recruitment efforts targeting youth, producing more
television advertisements with incentives such as free watches, creating

video games to draw young males into a fantasy culture of battle bravado, and in some cases pressuring youth to make appointments with recruiters and threatening them for not complying.[20] Military recruitment programs are based on a racialized and class-based strategy to attract economically vulnerable, minority youth and promote a culture of militarism based on patriotic citizenship.

Like other notions of cultural citizenship, this militarized citizenship is introduced both through state-sponsored programs and private media. Popular culture has been infused with images of American military bravado, from the reporting of embedded journalists in Iraq to the war films made in consultation with the Pentagon. Contemporary Hollywood films reflect a "powerful nostalgia and desire for war in a new generation," and, as Catherine Lutz (2006, 292) points out, U.S. popular culture asserts that war is associated not just with "freedom" but also grants "supercitizenship to those who wage it." These media images support the idea that citizens must go to war to defend the "American way of life" and justify brutal attacks on enemy nations and civilian populations. South Asian Muslim immigrant youth are uneasily positioned in relation to this militaristic nationalism, viewed by others as having suspect or divided national loyalties, and some find support for their dissenting views in communities that offer a different perspective on citizenship and belonging.

Complicit Dissent and Armored Multiculturalism

The practice of dissenting citizenship may seem potentially contradictory because it juxtaposes challenges to state power with an approach that, implicitly or explicitly, uses the framework of rights that can be given or withheld by the nation-state. The ambiguity of dissenting citizenship is important to explore, for many dissenting approaches after 9/11 fall back on a liberal, democratic framework that evokes the rights and obligations of citizens to the state. Dissenting citizenship is a notion that has inherent political limitations, for it is yoked to a relationship or engagement with the state, however oppositional. It often falls short of a desirable framework for those who wish to envision a more radical mode of resistance to empire that challenges the conceptualization of the imperial state and its economic, political, and military regimes of governmentality.

Expressions of "dissent" by immigrant students were at some moments decoupled from nation-based ideas of citizenship, or more distanced from notions of loyalty to any one state, while at other moments they were attached to the nation-states to which they felt belonging: India, Pakistan, Bangladesh, or the United States. For example, in some instances, these youth critiqued the militaristic jingoism of both the United States and India; in other cases, they expressed a sense of affiliation with African Americans in Wellford or with Afghans and Palestinians overseas. The more time I spent with youth in the high school and in the city, the more I was forced to realize that dissent for South Asian Muslim youth, and for Muslim Americans in general after 9/11, could not conform to ideas of what critiques of the state should look like from a traditional activist or liberal-democratic perspective. This is also true for the population at large, for resistance necessarily has to respond to historical patterns of repression under the ongoing "state of emergency" of U.S. empire, as discussed in chapter 1, and subvert the tactics of surveillance, infiltration, and misinformation that are used to divide and destroy insurgent movements (as documented in Schultz and Schultz, 2001; see also McCarthy and McMillian 2003).

The question I want to raise here is: Does citizenship always exist in tension with complicity, even in the mode of dissenting citizenship? Conjoining dissent and citizenship draws attention to the fact that forms of dissent represent an engagement with the state, rather than a break from it. I would like to argue here, as alluded to in the previous chapter, that "complicity" is in tension, not just with dissent but with the state's power to discipline, locally and nationally; it is this disciplinary power that different strands of dissent attempt to resist or subvert in varying ways. The state's disciplining power attempts to co-opt the very notion of dissent itself, as is evident in the new McCarthyism after 9/11. This is not in the simple sense of state repression of dissent; rather, the state attempts to contain dissent by anticipating and allowing for particular, limited modes of resistance—even while implementing repressive measures—that sustain the illusion of an inherently democratic state that can be reformed. There is also skepticism and debate on the Left about the contradictions of expressing political dissent in the United States after 9/11, as at other moments, for public marches and antiwar demonstrations are implicitly sanctioned by the state. Political rallies are approved and regulated by the police and their permits, as in the case of the rally that I and others SACH organized in Wellford. Some argue that antiwar rallies do not really represent a threat to state power, especially if they are not truly on a mass scale or do not disrupt the economy, and are held up as proof that the state is inherently democratic, rather than repressive, since it allows protest in the public sphere; this echoes "Frankfurt School theorist Herbert Marcuse's notion of 'repressive tolerance,' where the state licenses a degree of dissent in order to defuse anything more threatening" (Williams and Chrisman 1994, 6; see also Churchill 1998). It is certainly important for citizens and residents of a nation-state to voice their dissent of unjust policies and to be able to engage in public protest in a variety of ways. Questions of strategy and vision for dissenting movements after 9/11 must address the issue of to what use their dissent will be put by the state.[21]

At the same time, those who are from nations resisting U.S. military forces and those being politically profiled after 9/11 remain largely absent from the public protests that have been organized against the domestic as well as global Wars on Terror. In Wellford, there were groups of youth from the high school who did attend antiwar rallies after 9/11, but there were many reasons that South Asian Muslim immigrant youth did not participate in public protests, in addition to their newness in the United States, such as the pressures of work and school and the fear justifiably felt by their parents and families in expressing political dissent. Partly because of these reasons, the U.S. antiwar movement generally remains led by white peace activists with a token sprinkling of Arab, Muslim, and other immigrant community leaders. However, the problem is not simply one of a politics of visibility and recognition: critiques of racism within antiwar or civil rights movements cannot be reduced to issues of multicultural representation, for this implicitly succumbs to liberal notions of multicultural citizenship by focusing on belonging within these dissenting movements in terms of identity, rather than understanding what the production and regulation of those identities reveal for a politics of resistance or for modes of organizing.

Many from immigrant and minority communities do not necessarily feel they belong in the antiwar movement or are comfortable with its tactics, even if they support its larger goals, but they do often carry histories and traditions of political resistance, as well as familiarity with U.S. political and military interventions, in other countries and regions—from the Philippines and Pakistan to Okinawa and Palestine—that infuse movements in the United States (see Maira and Shihade 2006).[22] This is just the tip of a much larger discussion about resistance and organizing that I cannot do justice to here, but I wish to acknowledge the thorny political

debates in which the idea of dissenting citizenship is inevitably embedded. Complicity—including the complicity of dissent—is not enacted in
the simple sense of conceding to or collaborating with government repression or official racist policies. It is a more subtle process by which
progressive dissent is in some instances tolerated by the very state that
is presumed to suppress resistance, or absorbed into liberal discourses of
multiculturalism and representation.

Dissenting citizenship is harnessed to multicultural citizenship by the
state, for multiculturalism was one of the political and rhetorical strategies used after 9/11, as well as before, to absorb Arab, South Asian, and
Muslim Americans into a discourse of difference and belonging to the
"pluralistic" and tolerant nation-state, as discussed in chapter 4. State-
sponsored multiculturalism is a strategy that officially co-opts the notion
of diversity and cultural sensitivity—a velvet glove that hides the iron
fist of imperial policies. For example, after 9/11, FBI agents were given
cultural sensitivity training to deal with Muslim and Arab Americans,
suggesting that their interviews, raids, and arrests could be intrusive and
sometimes illegal but, at the same time, culturally customized—to make
them go more smoothly for the agents. During their interviews of Muslim Americans, some "FBI agents began showing up on their early morning visits bearing head scarves for the women of the house, to save them
time as they got ready to be questioned and searched" (Nguyen 2005,
85). Nearly all the FBI field offices, and many local police departments,
invited Muslim Americans to serve on "multicultural advisory boards"
and teach classes on Islam to agents and police to facilitate their "counter-
terrorism" activities (DeYoung 2007). This is the cruel absurdity of imperialist multiculturalism—if Gilroy suggests that the United States stages
an armored cosmopolitanism, there is certainly an "armored multiculturalism" that "puts a Koran in every cell" in Guantánamo (Gilroy, in
MacCabe 2006, 41).

Furthermore, maintaining the image of respect for cultural or religious
difference allows the state to symbolically suggest that those targeted by
the state are included in multicultural citizenship, even if their political
and legal rights are denied and they are surveilled by the government,
thus drawing dissent into the cultural terrain. One of the aims of the
FBI's "cultural diversity outreach" programs and town hall meetings, from
Los Angeles to Albany, is to establish friendly ties with Muslim, Arab, and
even Sikh American communities and leaders in order to enlist members

of these communities in "reporting" and presumably "pre-empting" terrorist plots in their communities, recruiting potential "insider" informants.[23] The FBI now openly has recruitment booths at community events such as the annual Pakistan Day festival, as I noticed in San Francisco in August 2007. As a result of such tactics, ideas of multicultural belonging become laced with questions of complicity and complicate notions of dissent for Muslim and Arab American communities, who are divided over strategies of co-optation and cooperation, as are other communities targeted by state repression. A controversial issue is that some Arab and Muslim organizations have participated in the cultural sensitivity training and outreach programs for the FBI and local law enforcement, in an attempt to make smooth the implementation of policies targeting their communities or out of fear of government suspicion, or both. Some are critical of the cooperation of community and religious organizations as enabling the profiling of their own communities and helping produce an illusion of respect by the state that masks the underlying racism of the War on Terror, as was evident in the many discussions I had in Wellford with local groups and in debates on the Internet about organizing after 9/11.

The "War on Terror" Becomes Normal

Moments of contradiction, confusion, and uneasiness in spaces of political dissent in which I participated raised several questions for me about the scope, purpose, and strategic effectiveness of dissent against empire after 9/11. My own involvement with SACH also provoked questioning about my own potential complicity with the multiculturalist co-optation of dissent; Simi and I began getting several invitations by organizers of local forums on "post-9/11" issues where we were asked to speak about the experiences of South Asian and Muslim communities. Apart from our discomfort about the usual issues of representation and tokenization under the rubric of "diversity," we also noted the ways in which we and other activists were, perhaps unintentionally, beginning to normalize post-9/11 policies of surveillance and repression. Not all activists or nonprofit organizations accepted this normalization, of course, but in some sense we, and others, were redirecting our attention and resources to this new crisis and responding with familiar tactics, often in ways that were necessary but also sometimes slipped into an acceptance of this reality as comprehended through particular political frameworks.

For example, a year after the introduction of the Special Registration program requiring male citizens of predominantly Muslim nations to register with the government and reveal personal information, Simi questioned our strategy of assisting immigrants in complying with the program by publicizing it in the community and facilitating registration. Our initial response to Special Registration, such as our work with NEIDRN in providing legal information and translation of the requirements, had emerged from a sense of urgency about informing people who were confused and anxious about the program, and also outrage at the spectacle of throngs of Muslim and Arab men being herded into government facilities. The Special Registration interviews involved questions about personal information, movies, friends, and personal contacts—questions designed to supposedly mine for intelligence on "terrorist cells" and "anti-American" activities and that were intrusive and unnerving. Some immigrant men who complied with Special Registration ended up in detention or deportation without legal counsel and without being able to inform their families or friends. This image was frighteningly reminiscent of other moments in history when minority populations have been rounded up by religion and then whisked away by totalitarian states to secret prisons or camps. But we also wrestled with the question: Did those who opposed the Special Registration simply end up helping the government do its job better by educating Muslim immigrants about the process?

The NEIDRN coalition did stage public protests outside the federal immigration office in Boston, carrying placards opposing Special Registration, with slogans similar to those used at other protests of Special Registration held around the country condemning it as a racist assault on civil rights. However, we also realized that the immigrant men waiting in line felt anxious about being associated with political protest, a justifiable fear since the reason they were standing in line in the first place was that the government viewed Muslim Americans as politically suspect. As we handed out fliers with information about lawyers and free legal aid hotlines to the men in line, some of them seemed visibly uneasy about the placards challenging the government. The response network tried not to overwhelm or jeopardize the immigrants going in for Special Registration—taking care not to carry too many signs or stand too close to the men, or to create the misperception that the men were part of the protest—an uneasy but perhaps pragmatic compromise. In other cities

Protest against "Special Registration," Federal Building, Manhattan, New York, 2003.
Photograph by Irum Sheikh.

around the nation, activists shared our strategic ambivalence about how
to organize around Special Registration.

Simi and others pointed out that in retrospect, our protest would
have been more principled if we had tried to resist compliance with the
program altogether, by urging a program of mass noncooperation with
Special Registration on the grounds that it was racist and discriminatory.
This, of course, would have been possible only with a national movement
of mass civil disobedience requiring a well-coordinated campaign connecting groups around the nation that did not happen after 9/11, partly
because of the lack of time and the suddenness of each new government
program and, equally important, because of the lack of a grassroots organizing base in many of the communities that were targeted around
the nation, not to mention the divergence in political approaches within
these communities and among activists. In some cities, such as in the
New York / New Jersey area, there were South Asian organizations that
organized long-term campaigns with the working-class South Asian immigrant communities most affected by 9/11, such as DRUM (Desis Rising Up and Moving), Families for Freedom, the Taxi Workers Alliance,
and Manavi, and continued this grassroots mobilization well beyond

9/11. In the San Francisco Bay Area, organizations such as the Alliance of South Asians Taking Action (ASATA) worked with several other groups, including the American-Arab Anti Discrimination Committee (ADC), the Asian Law Caucus, and the National Lawyers Guild. In the Wellford area, however, the government's civil rights assault on Muslim, Arab, and South Asian immigrants caught us off guard: there was no organization focusing on immigrant issues in the South Asian community or based in working-class communities at the time of 9/11, and the ADC was a tiny organization with few resources at the time. Apart from the legal support provided by lawyers from the ACLU and National Lawyers' Guild and coordinated by NEIDRN, and the political protests staged by groups such as SACH and others, there was no effective mobilization of those most affected by the state's War on Terror.

Those confronting the fear or surveillance of their communities as well as those involved in organizing in response to the domestic War on Terror also began to normalize War on Terror's impact on daily life in other ways. I noticed that Simi, I, and other activists we worked with had begun developing strategies to manage the unspoken anxiety about the intrusion of state powers into everyday life, by self-consciously drawing attention to this constant possibility of surveillance. We made jokes about FBI videotaping and wiretapping, dressing for the camera, and possible informants in our midst that became "normal" at organizing meetings, antiwar protests, and events related to the Middle East, and also in Muslim communities at large. These jokes implicitly acknowledged the existence of a surveillance state and perhaps echoed responses from an earlier generation that experienced the COINTELPRO program of infiltration of the civil rights and antiwar movements in the 1960s and 1970s (see Schultz and Schultz 2001). This was not simply a paranoid response but a way of dealing with the many cases of government surveillance of Muslim and Arab Americans (e.g., Maira 2007), as well as the brewing controversy over warrantless wiretapping of e-mails and telephone calls of U.S. citizens; the FBI's covert acquisition of personal phone, bank, and credit card information; and the less publicized government dossiers of "political enemies" who criticized the Bush administration.[24] Our humor, I think, was a way to grapple with the unknown and ever-present reach of state powers in the era of the PATRIOT Act and the creeping knowledge that state surveillance could be an intimate part of our everyday lives, not unlike the ways in which people have written about the dark humor employed by those living in police states.

Interestingly, 9/11 has brought into the spotlight a growing generation of Muslim comedians on both sides of the Atlantic, such as the Palestinian American comics Dean Obeidallah and Maysoon Zayid, who cofounded the first Arab American Comedy Festival in New York in 2003; the Axis of Evil tour featuring the Arab and Iranian American stand-up comedians Ahmed Ahmed, Maz Jobrani, and Aron Kader; the Bangladeshi American comedian and actor Aladdin; and the British Pakistani stand-up comic Shazia Mirza. In general, as with other forms of racial comedy, this emerging genre of humor walks the fine line between addressing the absurdity of post-9/11 profiling and surveillance and producing cultural caricatures of Muslim and Arab Americans.[25] Some of these productions seem to use well-worn devices of liberal multiculturalism, such as that of "inter-faith dialogue" (e.g., in the show A Muslim, A Mormon, and a Jew Walk into a Bar: A Comedy of Religion), which implicitly suggest that in the current moment the primary identities that need to be staged, if through satire, are that of religion and that having a Jewish and Muslim comedian on stage together has something to do with resolving the political conflict underlying the War on Terror, by "bridging" religious difference.[26] There has also emerged a rapidly expanding genre of cultural production—including theater, visual art, film, music, spoken word, and creative writing—that critically addresses the issues of 9/11 and their aftermath by artists from these communities, as well as the larger public.[27]

In conclusion, it is important to note that while this chapter focuses on dissenting citizenship as specifically expressed by the communities targeted after 9/11, there has no doubt been growing dissent among ordinary Americans of various backgrounds. Though protest of state policies within the United States was engulfed by the overwhelming patriotism and fear of being labeled "anti-American" immediately after 9/11, it has burgeoned over time and especially since the growing frustration with the war in Iraq made criticism of the government's policies mainstream. Many city and town councils across the country, included Wellford, have passed local resolutions against the PATRIOT Act as part of a national Bill of Rights Defense campaign; residents have formed peace groups and held vigils against U.S. wars and the assault on civil liberties at home; librarians and booksellers have protested the government's scrutiny of lending records and book purchases; community organizations have held talks and screened films about Afghanistan, Iraq, Palestine, and global politics; online commentators have created blogs and websites; and artists have circulated independently created videos and music to contribute to a dissenting conversation that continues to grow and swell, joining other voices and movements around the world. The various dissenting movements that have emerged have engaged with notions of dissenting citizenship to varying degrees and in different ways, as I will show in the last chapter, sometimes participating in performances of multiculturalism and at other moments staging the limitations, and possibilities, of transnational networks that facilitate, re-create, or rethink the resistance of the "multitude."

Sara and Amin

If this book were a seamlessly linear narrative, this chapter would predictably end with a section on how Sara and Amin overtly expressed their political dissent and evolved progressively into explicitly political critics of citizenship and empire. Such a conclusion would suggest an activation into traditional modes of resistance, defined as public action or speech, as the desired end point of a political narrative about immigrant subjects experiencing repression or marginality. This is an assumption that is problematic for youth, as well as for South Asian Muslim immigrants after 9/11, because of the many, real reasons Muslim American youth might have been hesitant to express explicitly "political" views after 9/11 but also because of the implicit definition of what defines "politics" or dissent more generally. Sara and Amin did, of course, speak to me at different moments about racial and religious profiling, war and nationalism, gender and class relations, and they expressed a daily resistance to cultural stereotypes and Orientalist assumptions in the classroom and elsewhere. But they did not participate in traditional modes of political action or speech; nor were they as outspoken in their political views as some of the other South Asian immigrant youth in this study. What their stories reveal is the way young people grapple with larger forces such as the War on Terror in the details of their everyday life and speak about politics or express dissent in subtle ways that are important to consider. The voices of Muslim, Arab, and South Asian youth have generally been missing from political analyses after 9/11, partly because it has not been easy for them to publicly express their political views, and partly because their perspectives and their forms of political expression are not always fully understood or given serious analytic attention.

This is what makes Sara and Amin an important part of this story. They are two young people who were grappling with questions of school, work, family, citizenship, belonging, love, and war in a moment of empire. I grew closer to them than to the other boys and girls I came to know, perhaps because they were more open to me; I became like an older sister to Sara and particularly to Amin, who called me periodically to talk about his relationship dilemmas. But on some level, I also found that their struggles to deal with the issues in their daily lives in the face of the larger crisis resonated with me, for I shared many of the emotions and anxieties that they and the other immigrant youth were experiencing at this moment. If dissent is a feeling, it is an emotion that is often driven by outrage at material realities and the desire to oppose powers that are not always tangible. It can make you feel terrifyingly alone and yet also powerfully attached to a longing for something other than what exists.

Six

Missing: Fear, Complicity, and Solidarity

Fatima

I first spoke to Fatima in November 2001, in the teacher's resource room at the high school. Mr. Ellery's assistant had arranged for us to meet there, in the quiet reading area. Fatima had silky brown hair that flowed over her shoulders, and was wearing blue eyeliner. She had come to the United States from India when she was thirteen years old, in 1998, and wore jeans and sweatshirts, unlike most of the more recently arrived immigrant girls. Fatima's aunt had come to the United States many years earlier—Fatima wasn't sure if it was in 1969 or 1979—because she had married a Gujarati man who was a U.S. citizen and she had then sponsored Fatima's grandfather. Fatima's family came from Billimoria, a city about an hour from Valsar (in Gujarat). Several of the Gujarati Muslim families in Wellford had migrated from Valsar, including Amin's family, to whom she was related. When I asked her how she felt when she first came to the United States, Fatima replied, "I was scared. 'Cause I didn't know all of the American peoples and I don't want to leave my old friends that I had there. I didn't like it at beginning because I didn't have any friends. And like, after that I like it, [after] making friends."

Fatima's parents used to work at a factory in a nearby town, but had been laid off recently. She and her sister Tasmeena both worked at the Dunkin' Donuts store that was close to the North Wellford apartments where they lived and where her aunt had worked earlier. Fatima worked there three days a week after school, and noted that many of the other workers were Brazilian, though the owner was "Italian," probably Italian American. Her friends were Indian and Pakistani, but also Ethiopian and Egyptian. Fatima seemed hesitant to claim a shared Muslim identity as the basis of her friendships, but for her being Muslim was an important identity. She recalled that after the events of 9/11, "First I was scared. And after that, like, it's okay 'cause . . . the people were helping us." Fatima was upset that "Muslim people" were being blamed for 9/11 and characterized as "bad." A week after 9/11, a girl in her chemistry class declared, "We should kill Muslim people." Apparently none of the other students in the class challenged this remark. Fatima seemed hesitant to engage with others openly about issues related to September 11, perhaps simply so she could get through her day without confrontations: "I was like, 'Er, I don't want to talk about that.' And I didn't talk to anybody about that." Fatima said she felt "bad" for the people of Afghanistan "because they didn't do anything, and they're being killed."

As with the other South Asian Muslim immigrant youth I spoke to, the events of 9/11 and their aftermath had not weakened her identification as a Muslim; on the contrary, Fatima said she identified first and foremost as Muslim, rather than as ethnically Gujarati or Indian. When I asked her why this was important to her, she replied simply, "I'm so happy that I'm Muslim. And it's good for me." For her, being Muslim meant respecting her parents and praying five times a day. Like most other families in the Gujarati Muslim immigrant community in Wellford, Fatima and her mother and sister did namaaz at home, and only the men in her family went to the mosque. But she also commented that life was much busier for her in Wellford than it had been in India and she did not often have time to pray regularly, commenting "In America, it's really hard to be a Muslim."

Fatima said it was "strange" for her, at first, to be in a school with male and female students, for she had studied in an all-girls' school in Billimoria. She echoed some of the other South Asian immigrant girls' uneasiness about dating, and awareness of their parents' discomfort. However, Fatima also challenged her parents' expectation that she should get married after high school, because she wanted to go to college and said that she would prefer to get married when she was twenty-five. Fatima seemed respectful of her parents'

cultural expectations, but clear about where they departed from her own incli-
nations or ambitions. She wanted to study math and commented that her co-
workers at Dunkin' Donuts seemed to think that "Indian and Chinese people
are really smart at school." I was not sure what Fatima thought about this
perception of Asian Americans as the model minority, but she certainly did
not seem to believe in this image herself.

A little less than a year later, in September 2002, after Fatima had gradu-
ated from high school, I met her at her new workplace. She was now working
full time in an Egyptian-owned travel agency in the city, a long subway ride
from her home. She looked a little older already, dressed in a short orange
kurta [shirt] and slacks with her hair pulled back in a sleek ponytail. Fatima
was not going to college; she was now working seven days a week, and told
me she was receiving no benefits. Apparently, Tasmeena was still working at
the same Dunkin' Donuts store. Fatima was planning on attending a local
community college in the spring but said that for now, she liked working at the
travel agency and felt comfortable there because everyone who worked there
was Muslim. The agency dealt mainly in booking flights to Egypt, and her
job was to answer the phones. The other men and women working there all
seemed to be Arab and, like any business serving immigrants, they had to deal
with a variety of needs for their customers. While I was talking to Fatima,
an older Egyptian man came in who did not seem to speak much English. He
asked to talk to someone in Arabic about some documents he had previously
dropped off for translation. A young Arab woman, fashionably dressed and
with make-up, said that they were unable to help him with the translation and
he left, looking disappointed.

Fatima was one of the students who was most critical of her own community
and remarked that "things were getting worse" in the Gujarati community at
the North Wellford apartments. When I asked her what she meant by this
alarming statement, she said that "young girls" were "running away"; when
pressed for details, she only offered one story—that of a twenty-three-year-old
woman whose marriage had been arranged and who had left her husband to
be with another man in Wellford. Perhaps this scandal loomed large for her
because it reflected her own concerns about marriage and the future. We talked
about instances of Gujarati Muslim women in Wellford who had married
non-Muslims, white Americans, or Punjabi Indians. Fatima was unaware
if there had been as much drama in these cases but perhaps the looming ques-
tion of marriage provided the context for the scrutiny, and anxiety, of young
women, as in many immigrant communities. Fatima said that her parents

would not expect her to be in an arranged marriage, and that she herself did not want to get married until she was at least twenty-five, but she also said that they had become more concerned about her going out of the house since she had started working in the city. She said that she was not missing the Wellford high school very much.

Faisal

"I came to the U.S. in 1999 because my father sponsored me. I'm from a village in Peshawar, in Pakistan. My father had come to the U.S. right after I was born; he's been here sixteen years now. Me and my two brothers and two sisters were waiting for him to sponsor us since I was born. I think he came back to Pakistan once, when I was six years old. He was working in a pizza store in Wellford when he first came. My father thought that it would be good for us to go to America to get an education. He has an American passport. I am going to be an American citizen too, in one month. You know, there's a law that says that if your father is a citizen, you can get an American passport too. Yes, I definitely want to be a U.S. citizen. Because previously, when you would go to Pakistan, then you could only stay there for six months on the green card. But if you go with a passport, you can stay for six years, that's why. But my brother is over eighteen, so he couldn't get citizenship. You had that problem too? Do you have a U.S. passport yet? Oh, you should get it soon. They didn't let my brother into the high school, because he was over eighteen, so he is trying to get into a course to get the GED. He was in the Jobs for Youth program for one year, but he left because he found out they won't give him a GED. Do you know how he can get a GED? No, I haven't talked to Mr. Ellery; I will ask him.

"I like living in Wellford; I think the school is good. I like playing basketball. I learned it while I was in Peshawar, because my father taught me after he went to America. He brought a net when he came back, and I taught some of the other boys in my village. Here I play with a few Indian, Pakistani, Afghani, and black boys. I would like to be on a team, but I don't know if I can. Sometimes, the other boys get mad if we win and they even throw eggs at us. Once they stole my bike from in front of my house. I had just won a basketball match and when my brother and I went home, we found our bike was missing. Some boys had come and taken it while I was in school, because I saw it with them the next day. I told Mr. Ellery and he called the police, but I didn't want to tell the police their names, because they would harass me in school. I didn't get the bike back. They were bad boys, but I know some black guys who are very, very good. I have many black friends who are very nice. I have Haitian friends, Spanish friends. I think the biggest group of students in the ESL program is Haitian. Some of them are Christian, five or six are Muslim. Yes, Muslim.

"What do I think about 9/11 and the war in Afghanistan? I think that the U.S. should show Afghanistan and Pakistan the evidence; they should show them who did it [the 9/11 attacks]. I don't think it's right for America to attack Afghanistan. My friends in school don't think it's right either. I think a lot of people think that, and they know it is not a problem with Muslims. But I think that some people have a serious discussion about it, and other people are not telling the truth—they are afraid to say it. No, nothing happened to me after 9/11, or to my sisters. But when my sister goes out of the house, I go with her.

"My sisters don't work, but I work on weekends, both Saturday and Sunday, at a gas station. It is where my cousin from Pakistan works, but it is owned by a Lebanese guy. He is Christian, and my cousin has worked for him for twelve years. My cousin has never been back to Pakistan since he came, but he went back three days ago because the owner got him a green card. Yes, that was very good of him. I have to take the commuter train to go there because the gas station is in Sharon. So I can only work on the weekends, because it takes a long time to get there.

"When I have time, I like to listen to music—rock music, Indian rock, Pakistani music. Which bands? I don't know; I just listen to the Bollywood websites, and sometimes I get music tapes from the Indian store in Prospect Square. My father put up a satellite dish for us, so I sometimes watch cricket matches on TV. Do you know that yesterday Pakistan beat Zimbabwe? That was good! There are many Pakistani families in Prospect Square: I think there are maybe forty or fifty families, so like a hundred people or more. They don't have good jobs, because they don't speak English well. Most are Punjabi, some Sindhi, and a few Pathan like us. I speak Urdu, Pashto, also Kabuli. I can write Pashto and Kabuli. At home we speak both Pashto and Kabuli because there were many people from Afghanistan in Peshawar.

"What do I call myself? I'm Pakistani, and Pathan. Being Pathan means being brave. But other people are brave too—Sindhis, Punjabis. I know people say that Pathans are brave, and Punjabis are good at school, but I don't think it's like that.

"Actually, yes, I do have a question: when will this interview be over?"

Missing

Mohiuddin had to leave the country after he graduated from high school because of complications with Special Registration. He applied to study in England.

Osman's sister got engaged to a Pakistani man who was undocumented. She left the United States to marry him so they could live together in Canada.

Zeenat got admission into the University of Massachusetts, Amherst. She called me a month after she moved to campus to say that she was missing her family so much that she cried for two weeks after she left Wellford.

There were many other young South Asians and Muslims who were missing, and missing others in their lives, after 9/11. This is a place marker for them, whose names are missing as well.

The Invisible "War at Home"

The events of September 11, 2001, were clearly devastating for Arab, Muslim, and South Asian communities in the United States. Many of the young people, like Fatima and Faisal, spoke of the fear and anxiety they felt for themselves and their families. Both these youth opposed the war in Afghanistan because they thought it was unjust and affected those who had no connection to the tragedy of 9/11 or for whom there was no "evidence" of culpability, expressing a dissenting citizenship. These youth also had to grapple with the uncertainty about those they could speak to openly about war and politics and those they could really trust, while learning to navigate a new cultural and political environment. Fatima left the high school to enter an adult world of work that was structured by the transnational business activities of Arab and Muslim immigrant communities. In a sense, she was moving farther away from the sphere of her family and into a different community, but one with a shared Muslim identity linked to immigrant entrepreneurship. The travel agency depended on the flexible labor of young workers even while the global migration and transnational networks, travel, and ties of Arabs and Muslims became suspect. Faisal worked at an Arab-owned gas station, and spoke of the kindness shown by immigrants across national backgrounds in helping one another with the arduous citizenship process as they struggled to find work and reconstitute their ties to family and home country, inflecting multicultural belonging with the challenges of state-driven immigration and citizenship policies. Like Fatima, Faisal had connections with Arab immigrants largely in the world of work, where—as immigrants facing similar legal, economic, and political dilemmas—they engaged in a common struggle for formal as well as cultural citizenship as they grappled with the realities of neoliberal economic citizenship.

Faisal ventured into social activities with young people from different backgrounds and resisted racializing conflicts among boys in the school or expressing a reified ethnic or regional identity. He moved between being Pakistani and Pathan, between rock music and South Asian music, between basketball and cricket, and took pleasure in these different worlds without seeming concerned about the boundaries between them, occupying various kinds of subcultural citizenship simultaneously. In contrast to Fatima's reflections on being Gujarati and Muslim, Faisal did not seem particularly attached to an identity based on religion, or any other single identification for that matter, even after 9/11. This stance was expressed in his own declarations, but it was also borne out by his cross-border relationships and subcultural interests. The varied narratives of Muslim immigrant youth illustrate the different ways in which they fashion identities—crossing, reinforcing, or challenging boundaries—in response to constructions of "Muslimness" after 9/11. The stories of Fatima and Faisal, like most others I have narrated, encapsulate the three themes of cultural citizenship described in the book: flexible, multicultural or polycultural, and dissenting.

Faisal seemed worried about his sister experiencing the backlash after 9/11, though nothing had happened to him, but he also spoke of a different kind of fear: a fear of not publicly speaking the truth about the War on Terror. The War on Terror infused South Asian, Muslim, and Arab American communities with feelings of fear, anxiety, disillusionment, betrayal, and loss, as people struggled with the emotional and social impact of racial profiling, surveillance, detentions, and deportations. The South Asian immigrant community, like other migrant groups, had already experienced the displacement and separation of families scattered across continents through migrations before 9/11, as attested to by the stories of youth such as Fatima and Faisal. The detention and deportation of Muslim and Arab immigrants after 9/11 intensified and accelerated this dispersal of families, creating ruptures that were not voluntary nor, in many cases, reversible and blurring even further the already ambiguous boundaries of voluntary and involuntary migrations.

The War on Terror affected the composition of Muslim and Arab immigrant communities and transformed the social relationships within them. The fabric of the community was, in some ways, both shredded and strengthened by the disappearances of immigrant men and the climate of fear, suspicion, and secrecy. News of detentions and deportations spread through Muslim and Arab immigrant communities like chilling currents, both binding the community to one another and to the ghostly presence of the disappeared, and dividing it through fear and growing distrust. Asra, an Indian American woman who worked with the Freedom Foundation of the Muslim American Society in the Wellford area, said that Muslim Americans realized that someone in the community was missing, possibly detained or deported, when they stopped "showing up for mosque." Fear of detentions and deportations also affected unmosqued Muslim Americans and Arab Americans more generally. Nguyen reports one Pakistani immigrant from Queens, New York, observing that "people he worked with, people from his mosque and from his apartment building . . . began shunning one another, afraid that their own immigration violations would be discovered and reported to the authorities" (2005, 120). Profiling and surveillance irrevocably alter the lives of those who are forced to leave or who flee the country, but it also changes the lives of those left behind, altering the nature of social relationships and dissolving bonds of trust and dependence.

Many Muslim, Arab, and South Asian immigrant families ended up leaving the United States after indefinite separations and loss of the means of family support, creating new, global immigrant and refugee flows. At the same time, there were many cases of Muslim and Arab immigrant women who stepped into the breach and took over their husbands' businesses or tried to support their families, if only temporarily, as well as going to court and even campaigning against the detentions and deportations (for example, Sheikh 2003).[1] But as communities were shaken and inevitably transformed, some were also shrinking. In cities with large Muslim and Arab communities, some neighborhoods saw an emptying out of immigrants who were either deported or seeking to avoid detention, such as Brooklyn's "Little Pakistan" enclave on Coney Island Avenue in New York City (Ryan 2003). At least 500 Pakistanis were deported and many thousands more left the New York area, according to local estimates; 40 percent of businesses closed down on Coney Island Avenue, leaving the neighborhood a ghostly vestige of its former bustling self (Nguyen 2005,

17). By March 12, 2003, the Canadian immigration service reported 2,111 refugee claims by Pakistanis since January 1 of that year (Ryan 2003, 16), and refugee assistance centers along the border with Canada began overflowing with asylum applicants. More than 15,000 undocumented Pakistanis had reportedly left the country for Canada, Europe, and Pakistan by June 2003, according to the Pakistani embassy in Washington (Swarns 2003). The Canadian government began directing refugees back to the United States to await their immigration appointments as Canada's asylum policy came under attack for being too lenient and undermining border security (Nguyen 2005, 124–26). The ironic situation of Pakistanis leaving the United States to try to get political asylum elsewhere has generally received little attention in the American mass media, for it brings to light the uncomfortable fact that there are people who feel persecuted because of their national or religious identity in the United States—the self-professed champion of democracy and freedom.

For Muslim South Asian Americans, the War on Terror continued to be experienced most directly as racial assaults, suspicion, and discrimination in public sites, such as the workplace, that persisted well beyond 9/11. Among Indian Americans, the post-9/11 backlash was most violently directed against those identified as Muslim or mistaken for Arab. Sikh American men who were turbaned paid with their lives, in some cases, for this Orientalist distortion of what Arabs presumably looked like, based on massive public ignorance about the Arab world and fueled by images of a bearded Osama bin Laden wearing a white turban. The first attack on a Sikh American took place just minutes after the attack on the World Trade Center when a Sikh man who was fleeing from the collapsing towers was accosted by a group of men who said, "Take that f——ing turban off, you terrorist" (Singh 2003). The first man murdered in a hate crime linked to 9/11 was Balbir Singh Sodhi, who was killed at a gas station he owned in Mesa, Arizona, on September 15, 2001, by Frank Roque, a white man who later told the police, "I stand for America all the way" (Prashad 2003, 66). While photos of Sodhi were largely absent from the mainstream media, images of a turbaned, bearded Sikh man who was arrested and taken off an Amtrak train in Rhode Island a few days earlier, in September 2001, for carrying a ceremonial knife (the *kirpan*) were widely circulated, confirming the association of turbaned men with suspected terrorists (Grewal 2005, 210–11). Some Sikh men tried to protect themselves by removing their turbans and cutting their hair short, against their own religious proscriptions. Other immigrants and people of color also became targets of Islamophobia and anti-Arab racism after 9/11 when mistaken for Muslim or Arab, and African American Muslims who wore hijab were also viewed with suspicion in some instances. Post-9/11 profiling did not do not away with earlier fault lines of racial exclusion but perpetuated them, in many cases. For example, one of the early casualties after 9/11 was Kimberly Crowe, a Creek Indian who was murdered by young white men in Oklahoma; her killers yelled, "Go back to your country," without any trace of irony that their victim was actually the American native (Saito 2005, 53).

The War on Terror continued to affect Muslim, Arab, and South Asian communities in the United States well beyond 2001 though in ways that were less often publicly visible, more dispersed, and as painful. Using official reports of profiling—which are just the tip of the iceberg of actual incidents and also broader social experiences—hate crimes and incidents of discrimination against Muslims reportedly reached 1,717 by February 2002 (Nguyen 2005, 6). The backlash seemed to take a less dramatic and violent form over time but continued to affect Muslim and Arab Americans on a daily basis and in incidents that often went unreported. The Council on American Islamic Relations (CAIR) reported that after 2001, hate crimes began declining and incidents of airport profiling and workplace discrimination increased; despite underreporting, the U.S. Equal Employment Opportunity Commission (EEOC) received so many complaints of discrimination that it had to create a special category (Code Z).[2] "Employer discrimination against immigrants more than doubled" after 9/11, notes Nguyen (2005, xx), who records that by 2003 the EEOC had received over 800 complaints by individuals who had been dismissed from their jobs or harassed at work for being identified as "Muslim, Arab, Afghani, Middle Eastern, South Asian, or Sikh." Post-9/11 racial profiling, detentions, and deportations increasingly received less coverage in the mainstream media because, as one South Asian journalist working with an Indian American publication told me, sympathy and interest in these issues had faded and the media and general public simply did not want to hear these stories anymore. In addition to the ongoing problem of the mass media's short attention span for any issue, it seems to me that the collateral damage of the War on Terror had to be suppressed so that the nation could restore its image as a strong democracy and rally behind the ongoing war for "freedom."

Two Nations under Ashcroft:
Nationalisms after 9/11

I realized that after 9/11 there were, in effect, two nations under Ashcroft (and later, under Tom Ridge, who became the first secretary of the Department of Homeland Security, in 2003). The United States was divided into those who were, or believed they could be, targets of the War on Terror, and those who were not. The fault lines between the two nations were only exacerbated with time, for increasingly the general public heard less and less about the domestic War on Terror and its impact on Muslim and Arab Americans and most Americans began to go back to business as usual. These Americans belong to a nation shared with many in South Asian immigrant communities who were not Muslim, nor Sikh (as turbaned males continued to be attacked), and who were increasingly less aware of how profiling was affecting other South Asians and immigrants at large. The "other" nation continues to deal with ongoing issues of surveillance, detention, and deportations and, increasingly, less publicized or covert monitoring of individuals and FBI interviews, part of a private world not visible to the general public. An immigration lawyer in the Bay Area who has worked on many cases involving Muslim and Middle Eastern immigrants observed that this shift in state strategy, from mass detentions and deportations to individual targeting, also helped defuse public outrage and stifle potential dissent.

Yet the boundaries between these two nations within the United States are porous, as there are instances where those who thought they belonged to one nation realized that they actually belonged to another. Some who thought they were immune to racial profiling, because of their class status or professional privilege, found this illusion rudely shattered, often in a single moment. For example, South Asian American businessmen who were asked to get off airplanes or undergo repeated searches at airports, or whose bank accounts were investigated or closed down, were forced to acknowledge—after years of believing they were the model minority—that they belonged to the "other" nation after all. Vivek Wadhwa, a technology executive from India who had lived in the United States for twenty years, said, "I couldn't have cared less about race before Sept. 11," but he was forced to think about racism after the events of 2001 and began "speaking out" about his newly crystallized "sense of racial identity."[3] These epiphanies led to some shifts in racial thinking among South Asian Americans who were not Muslim, but only to a limited extent, in my view, because of the preexisting class, religious, and national cleavages within the community and the view that this was mainly a "Muslim" problem due to "Islamic terrorists," the brunt of which was born by Pakistanis, Bangladeshis, and Indian Muslims after 9/11. Profiling and responses to it highlighted divisions of class, religion, and nation and in some cases deepened them; some South Asian Muslims I spoke to observed that Muslim Americans increasingly turned to Muslim civil rights organizations, such as CAIR, for support and legal resources and that this further strengthened religious affiliations.

Some South Asian and Arab American professionals became part of larger efforts to challenge the assaults on civil liberties, but generally only on issues that affected them directly. For example, Bob Rajcoomar, an Indian American with U.S. citizenship, was part of a federal lawsuit by the ACLU charging the Transportation Security Administration (TSA) with racial profiling after he was detained illegally for four hours by federal air marshals who did not "like the way he looked." A settlement was reached with the Department of Homeland Security in 2003, requiring the TSA to change their "internal policies and training" (Nguyen 2005, 167). The galvanized civil rights campaigns of these South Asian Americans are important, not just for them or their communities but for challenging the broader War on Terror. However, most cases initiated by these professionals were driven more by outrage over inconvenience and mistreatment they felt they did not deserve, rather than disagreement with the fundamental premise of the War on Terror.

Service workers, taxi drivers, and small business owners bore the brunt of racial violence because their jobs leave them exposed to public ire and easy targeting; there were hundreds of incidents of taxicab drivers or store clerks being harassed and attacked after 9/11. For example, hours after Balbir Singh Sodhi's murder at a gas station, Waqar Hasan, a Pakistani man, was shot dead while working at a grocery store in Dallas, Texas (Prashad 2003, 66). Many South Asian and Muslim Americans, especially those working on the lonely front lines of public spaces rather than in offices, tried to plaster their gas stations, stores, or taxicabs with U.S. flags as a shield against racist violence. After 9/11, the sight of a lonely gas station on the highway covered in red, white, and blue or a taxi with flags fluttering over it often indicated that the person working inside was someone not accepted as fully American or, worse, considered a potential

enemy of the nation. There is a history of racial backlash and scapegoating of South Asians visible in the public sphere in times of social
crisis and economic anxiety, as illustrated by the attacks on South Asian
immigrants and their stores in Jersey City by the "Dotbusters" gang in
1987 (Misir 1996). Working-class immigrants are often hypervisible, as
was the case in Wellford for most of the South Asian immigrant youth
and their parents who worked in service jobs, not just those who were
Muslim. An Indian Sikh student at the high school told me that most
Punjabi immigrant men she knew in Wellford worked as taxi drivers, and
many of the Punjabi women, including her mother, worked at Dunkin'
Donuts. Race, class, religion, and gender intersect in the uneasy matrix of
so-called racial profiling after 9/11.

Many undocumented immigrants and less affluent South Asian and
Arab Americans who were detained (for much longer than four hours)
were not able to challenge their treatment by the government, because
they did not have the legal and economic resources and because their detention was considered a necessary if regrettable aspect of maintaining
"national security."[4] This lack of recourse persisted despite the revelations
of horrific abuse, including physical and psychological torture, of post-
9/11 detainees that was confirmed in an official report of the Department
of Justice's Office of Inspector General (OIG) that investigated conditions
at the Metropolitan Detention Center in Brooklyn and Passaic County
Jail in Paterson, New Jersey.[5] Released in 2003, the OIG's report found
300 videotapes documenting numerous incidents of cruel, inhumane, and
degrading punishment, including prison guards slamming detainees into
the wall, smashing their faces into a T-shirt with an American flag, beating them and dragging them over floors and stairs, conducting unneces-
sary strip searches and leaving detainees naked, and subjecting them to
verbal abuse, racist comments, and threats.

This report became public before the torture of Iraqi detainees by the
U.S. military in Abu Ghraib prison came to light, but it disappeared from
the media without any of the public outrage provoked by the Abu Ghraib
scandal. This discrepancy in public response shows that the war on Muslim, Arab, and South Asian Americans was, for many, still more justifiable than the increasingly unpopular war in Iraq, which was racking up
American casualties. Partly, this is because the American public was still
willing to believe that "something" needed to be done to prevent another
9/11 on U.S. soil, while the torture in Iraq, and the inhumane condi-

Protest in Coney Island, New York, 2003. Photograph by Irum Sheikh.

tions of detainees held in Guantánamo Bay prison, raised fears that U.S. prisoners of war might be similarly treated overseas or that these abuses would fuel greater anti-American blowback. Partly, too, this domestic prison abuse failed to be considered a "torture scandal," unlike Abu Ghraib, because it involved a vulnerable group of people, immigrants who were generally working class to lower middle class and whose lives did not have the added value of being equivalent to those of U.S. prisoners of war overseas.

The racialized rhetoric about Muslim men—and about Iraqis and Arabs in particular—as irrational terrorists from an alien, barbaric culture implicitly sanctioned the violence against post-9/11 detainees. But it must be noted that their experiences are part of a larger pattern of abuse in immigrant detention and U.S. prisons, many of them run by private contractors, which existed long before 9/11 (Dow 2004; Welch 2000). In fact, Angela Davis (2005, 69) points out that Charles Graner, who was convicted for his role in torture at Abu Ghraib, had been the object of at least two lawsuits for abuses while working as a prison guard in Pennsylvania; she observes that it is the "everyday tortures" and taken-for-granted warehousing of citizens presumed to be dispensable that underlies the link between prisons and warfare, for the military-prison-industrial complex rests on the assumption that "prisons are necessary to democracy." Dylan

Rodríguez argues that "the prison regime has become an indispensable element of American statecraft, simultaneously a cornerstone of its militarized (local and global) ascendancy and spectacle of its extracted (or coerced) authority over targeted publics" (2006, 44). This violence is the dark side of the modern imperial state that the general public chooses to ignore or, if confronted by accidental exposés, rationalizes as simply excesses of a system of discipline and security necessary for maintaining order and the American way of life. As Ruth Gilmore observes, the state uses "the prison industrial complex" as a "modus operandi for solving crises [through] the relentless identification, coercive control, and violent elimination of foreign and domestic enemies" (cited in Rodríguez 2006, 16). Paradoxically, "freedom" requires prison.

The Politics of Fear and Terror

The relationship between fear and nationalism is important to consider because the fear of terrorist attacks has been used to justify the state's repressive domestic policies, such as the PATRIOT Act, and military aggressions overseas. Fear has been used as a tool by nation-states for justifying repression at various historical moments. Both the fear and dissent of South Asian Muslim immigrant youth thus have to be placed in the context of this link between nationalism, fear, and repression. The politics of fear and terror shape the political climate and cultural environment for South Muslim immigrant youth and their understandings of citizenship and national belonging. The resurgence of U.S. nationalism after 9/11 and the definition of cultural citizenship as hyperpatriotism need to be examined as more than simply spontaneous responses of the national public to the events of 9/11. The "national public" is constructed in specific ways by the use of state symbols and rhetoric, and by public fear.

I think it is important to distinguish carefully between the kinds of fear experienced after 9/11 by various groups, for they perform different kinds of work in relation to citizenship and dissent. Much talked about after 9/11 was the fear of "terrorism," the fear of racist backlash, the fear of the "other," the fear of the erosion of civil liberties. But there are other, more complicated kinds of fear that were not as discussed, and that I think are key to understanding the nature of U.S. empire at this moment and to shedding light on the failures and problems in liberal, even progressive, responses to the War on Terror. Corey Robin's philosophical and historical analysis of the politics of fear is useful here: it demonstrates that fear is a political and economic strategy used by governments and elites to exacerbate and draw on "pervasive social inequities" (2004, 3). Governments have historically used fear as a political weapon for uniting national publics behind repressive or militaristic political agendas, as was clear in the strong support of the American public for Bush's overseas military interventions after 9/11. Robin astutely observes that political fear— "people's felt apprehension of some harm to their collective well-being," and the "intimidation wielded over men and women by governments and groups" (2004, 2)—obscures the political roots and functions of fear, and the "grievances and controversies that underlie it." So fear works as a political strategy precisely by the obscuring of its true political nature.

"Fear, American Style" is linked not just to the state but also to the workplace; Robin points out that repression is carried out by both "public and private sectors: what government officials cannot do well or with efficient ease, private elites do instead and vice versa" (2004, 199). Some have argued that the state's use of fear after 9/11 created a class of immigrant workers even more vulnerable than before and even more afraid of deportation, increasing the pool of cheap, compliant labor. This climate certainly allowed for a hyperexploitation of low-income workers after 9/11 from communities targeted in the War on Terror, and also other undocumented immigrants and members of refugee communities who were swept up in the wake of the PATRIOT Act (Vimalassery 2002; see Ong 1996 for a fuller discussion). The ongoing war on immigrants that had long targeted Latino and Latina, Asian, and other immigrants also drew new groups of immigrants and workers into its dragnet: Filipino and other immigrant airport workers were fired after 9/11 under the pretext of security threats, and Cambodian Americans were deported to Cambodia under a new treaty in 2002 between the United States and Cambodia that historically reversed the protection afforded to refugee communities (Hing 2005). Through these programs, it became clear that the state was effectively using fear of the threat to national security as a strategy not just for intimidation and repression of dissent, but also to benefit U.S. business and control immigration (Tirman 2004).

Robin argues that fear is generative and unifying for Americans because it is experienced as moral and spiritual—mainly for those who are included in the unifying discourse of belonging and have access to cultural citizenship—but it is also true that "the object of fear must belong to the realm of politics and yet somehow, in the minds of the fearful, stand apart from it" (2004, 4). Like fear, "terror" and terrorism are often relegated to the realm of culture, religion, or atavistic identities rather than to the arena of geopolitics. Political explanations for the 9/11 attacks that drew connections between al-Qaeda and the role of U.S. foreign policy were suppressed in mainstream discourse and viewed as treacherous justifications for the tragedy. The narrative proffered by state and mainstream media that was generally accepted as a frame through which to view 9/11 was a cultural argument dwelling on a clash of civilizational aspirations— a battle between (American) modernity and (Islamic) fundamentalism, a crusade dividing the "West" from the Middle East and South Asia, alternatively named "the Muslim world." Those who tried to offer political analyses for the roots of "terror" or historically contextualize the attacks were labeled traitors to the nation. The problem is that terror, and terrorism, too, are not just political but deeply ideological notions. While Robin's analysis of political fear is very astute, he does not fully acknowledge the ways in which the state is implicated in *generating*, not just using, terror. Robin cites various examples of state terrorism, from the Vietnam War to U.S.-supported terror in Argentina, Chile, and Guatemala, but he shies away from naming it as such. Robin (2004, 134) exposes the "liberalism of terror" to which progressives and others on the Left fall prey, but the complicity of liberalism with imperial nationalism has not received adequate attention in the debates about the War on Terror.

Liberalism, Complicity, Solidarity

Liberalism, as a tradition of political thought associated with eighteenth- and nineteenth-century Europe, rested on notions of individual autonomy, "freedom," rights, and property that have shaped modern conceptions of ethics, governance, and capitalism. Understanding the "liberalism of terror" is useful in shedding light on the larger question about the relationship of the imperial state to liberal nationalism, a key question in understanding the work of empire and the nature of imperial feelings at this time. At different moments of political repression in the United States, such as the McCarthy era and the post-9/11 period, liberals have been complicit with the government's use of fear to locate the origins of terror overseas and scapegoat an external threat. In doing so, liberals become complicit with or even actively support the economic, military, and political campaigns of the imperial project, as Robin acknowledges (2004, 155). This complicity is not just unique to American liberalism or to U.S. empire. Uday Mehta (1999, 2) shows how nineteenth-century British imperial thought and writings about India used a "liberal justification" to "endorse the empire as a legitimate form of political and commercial governance," to "justify and accept its largely undemocratic and nonrepresentative structure." While Mehta focuses on the liberal justification for British colonization of India, his work speaks on many levels to the rationalizations made by American liberals for the invasion of Afghanistan or the occupation of Iraq. Barry Hindess (2005, 242, 248) shows how liberal political philosophy links citizenship to empire, pointing out that liberal citizenship is key to the "civilizing mission" of Western colonial regimes, as "liberal political reason" viewed certain populations as incapable of being free, autonomous individuals capable of self-governance. Today, the imperial order uses notions of "democracy and basic human rights" to impose the indirect rule of international markets, development agencies, and financial institutions (Hindess 2005, 255–56), in addition to military and private security regimes.

Liberal complicity with empire often rests on a belief that liberal ideals must be exported and that assaults on sovereignty are justified by the emancipation of, or material benefit to, colonized peoples. The cruel paradox of liberal imperialism is, of course, that it justifies the undermining of sovereignty and the use of military force for the sake of presumably bringing freedom or modernity to the colonized through the doctrine of "humanitarian war" (Lutz 2006, 300). Tom Barry argues that after the Cold War, "progressives and liberals were among the main proponents of a more assertive U.S. military, especially in the cases of purported humanitarian intervention" (2003, 33). These analyses clearly show that nationalism and race serve as the link between liberalism and empire, but this deeper historical analysis of U.S. imperial history is generally overlooked in appraisals of the War on Terror by liberal intellectuals in America who were quick to rest their analysis on the Bush regime as the source of all political and cultural malaise.

Liberal nationalism in the United States is expressed through a much subtler nationalist discourse than that of right-wing jingoistic nationalism or the moral imperialism of neoconservatives and evangelical Christians (see Hernández-Truyol 2002). Liberal discourse is tangled with moral anxiety about imperialism that ends up, nonetheless, defending the moral supremacy and interests of the U.S. state using the pretext of "humanitarian intervention." In this vision, "terrorism" is a threat that necessitates the securitization of migration, the "liberation" of Afghan women justifies military intervention in Afghanistan, the occupation of Iraq is necessary for "reconstruction" after invasion, and the lives and choices of U.S. military personnel are always much more nuanced and complex than those resisting colonization and occupation. This is not to deny that there are real human rights issues around the world—not just in the Middle East or South Asia—and that strategies for fighting misogyny, religious fundamentalism, repression, or poverty are not simple, in the United States as well as in other places. The issue is which nation-states are permitted to violate the sovereignty of other states and the human rights of other populations, in the guise of humanitarian intervention or just war, and which state-sponsored invasions, occupations, and atrocities are exempt from international censure or action. The U.S. regime selectively uses human rights violations in other countries to justify interventions or sanctions while evading accountability for human rights issues within its own borders, from the death penalty and ongoing prison abuse to military trials and illegal detentions, brushing off condemnations from Amnesty International and Human Rights Watch of its own violations of international human rights and the Geneva Convention (Fernandes 2007; Hernández-Truyol 2002, 6). The absence of a genuine anti-imperialist critique, even after 9/11, is why liberal nationalism often bleeds into imperialist liberalism.

What needs to be pointed out is that American liberals sometimes fell prey to a political fear after 9/11 not just, or not always, because they were truly afraid of terrorism, but because they were afraid of something else: a social order in which their racial, national, or imperial privileges would be threatened or overthrown. It is not just that U.S. elites want to preserve their domestic rule over "women and workers" (Robin 2004, 3) but their dominance of the global order as well. White American liberals have an often unspoken identification with the imperial project of their nation, and with U.S. nationalism itself, as do liberals from minority or immigrant communities who wish to assert their cultural citizenship or who (want to) believe in the notion of liberal citizenship and individual freedom in the United States. Furthermore, the liberal belief in the inherently democratic governance of the state becomes the premise on which repression is enacted against those who are not worthy of cultural citizenship or inclusion in the democratic project. In moments of overtly state-sanctioned surveillance, such as the Red Scare during the Cold War or the PATRIOT Act era, ordinary, "law-abiding" citizens, of diverse racial and class backgrounds and with varying political orientations, inform on one another and participate in censorship and demonization themselves. The rule of law can maintain the illusion of justice and due process when these do not exist in the courts for those excluded from citizen or human rights, leading some critical legal theorists to be skeptical about using the law to fight for civil rights when the law itself is the weapon of repression. This predicament was very apparent in the precedent set by the U.S. Supreme Court in its upholding of the detention of more than 100,000 Japanese Americans, most of them U.S. citizens, in internment camps during the Second World War (Chan 1991). After 9/11, legal challenges to the secret, indefinite mass detentions of Muslim, Arab, and South Asian immigrant men were slow to appear in the courts, though cases were eventually filed against the government on behalf of the detainees abused and held indefinitely in the Metropolitan Detention Center in Brooklyn and in Guantánamo, including a class action suit by the Center for the Constitutional Rights in 2006 in which the court upheld the government's indefinite detention of noncitizens.[6]

It is also important to acknowledge that complicity was a part of the response to the War on Terror by the targeted communities themselves, and that this generated its own kind of internal fear and distrust. After 9/11, many Muslim and Arab Americans in particular, who were most directly dragged into the intelligence investigations of the CIA and FBI, were not sure who was informing on them to the government or where they were being surveilled, particularly given sensationalized cases of FBI informants in cases from Brooklyn, New York, to Lodi, California (Maira 2007; Rashbaum 2006).[7] Since 2001, the FBI made public that it was surveilling mosques and Muslim religious leaders and recruiting Muslim and Arab informants, as mosques were viewed as "breeding grounds" for terrorism (Cole 2003, 50). Previously considered a safe, if not sacred, space, the mosque was no longer a private space free from state surveillance. The public outcry over the alleged failure of U.S. intelligence and timely government anticipation of the 9/11 attacks prompted public announcements of FBI interviews of Arab immigrants to gather data, from interviews of Iraqi Americans before the invasion of Iraq and the Special Registration program to the less publicized "October plan" of FBI interviews and "extraordinary methods" of "aggressive" surveillance of Muslim Americans before the national election in 2004.[8]

The fear permeating the targeted communities kept many compliant, if not complicit, with the state's War on Terror. After 9/11, it became apparent that there were some Arab, Muslim, and South Asian American community organizations and leaders that were willing to cooperate with the government crackdown on their communities, and some maintained or established relationships with high-ranking officials in the Department of Homeland Security or other government offices. To assist them in obtaining information about the community, the FBI and INS recruited "community liaisons," who were often trusted figures in immigrant communities. Some of these liaisons became quasi-informants for the state, as in a story Nguyen (2005, 50) documents of Noorani, a Pakistani immigrant in Chicago who was visited by the FBI and "dutifully" gave them information about "divisions among Muslim political organizations in Chicago"; he also urged immigrants to participate in Special Registration, translated federal forms and instructions, and defended the government's policies. However, after several of the people Noorani encouraged to register were detained and deported and he heard about hundreds of others in similar situations, he acknowledged, "I was promoting Registration even more than Immigration [the INS] did. Knowing this is what was going to happen, I would not have promoted it" (Nguyen 2005, 67). Before 9/11, Noorani had displayed a large American flag outside his home because he admired the "meaning of the flag" and felt he had "made" himself in the United States; after the reality of racial profiling sunk in for Noorani, he said, "Why is this thing happening in this country?" Even those who had believed in the American Dream and in the government's fight against terrorism often found themselves disillusioned. But along the way, relations of trust and dependence were dissolved and people began to be wary of community or religious leaders they had previously looked to for guidance. In the case of an alleged terrorist sleeper cell in Lodi, which had been under FBI surveillance since 2001, it became apparent that a Pakistani informant for the FBI who was active in the mosque had befriended Hamid Hayat, a young Pakistani American man, and recorded implicating statements, though no evidence was found of a terrorist plot (Maira 2007). The fractures and tensions within South Asian, Arab, and Muslim American communities were not only exploited, but also deepened, by the seeds of mistrust and anxiety sowed by the state's programs of surveillance and infiltration.

I grappled myself with the implications of these feelings of fear and terror for Muslim and Arab American communities in Wellford and for the notion of community itself. "Community" is ideally believed to be represented and constituted in public spaces, but this notion changed for Muslim, Arab, and South Asian Americans after 9/11, as it had for some within these communities even before 9/11. For example, in spring 2003, SACH organized a public forum on civil and immigrant rights for Muslim, Arab, and South Asian immigrants in Wellford, and invited South Asian and Arab American lawyers to speak to members of the community at a university campus close to Prospect Square. We handed out fliers at the mosque and at local South Asian businesses and restaurants, and also spoke personally to individuals in the community who we knew were concerned about legal and immigration issues. On the day of the forum, however, not one person from these communities showed up who was not a civil or immigrant rights activist. Talking later to people in the South Asian Muslim community about why they were missing from the event, the explanation was simple: fear. The government's strategy was effective; not only did it produce self-censorship and repression, but it kept many from receiving help in defending themselves from the intrusions of the state or mobilizing collectively. The notion that people who were "missing" from public space after 9/11 were "the disappeared" is not simply a melodramatic phrase, but a condition produced in response to state strategies of disciplining and surveillance. These strategies were designed not just to "disappear" people, but also public dissent or resistance.

Fear, complicity, and self-censorship among those targeted by the War on Terror were some of the responses to state strategies of repression and intimidation—and were actively strategic or opportunistic responses for some—but there were other strategies that people used as well. Among these were expressions of courage, dissent, and solidarity. Many Muslim, Arab, and South Asian American activists challenged the state's assault on their communities by organizing in various ways and through different movements—based on civil and immigrant rights, prison reform or abolition, antiwar and human rights issues—and in alliance with others who had long experience in these movements in the United States. They did this despite government reprisals targeting Arab activists in the United

States, and dissidents more generally, both before and after 9/11. Most discussions of racial profiling, including liberal critiques, have tended to emphasize the suspicion held toward Arab and Muslim Americans after 9/11, or during the Iran hostage crisis, but few acknowledge the historical extent or political nature of this profiling or discuss the motivations for government intimidation of dissent in Arab American communities well before 9/11. Arab Americans have experienced heightened surveillance and harassment at various moments, including the 1967 Israeli-Arab war, the FBI's monitoring of the General Union of Palestinian Students in the 1980s, the attempted deportation of the pro-Palestinian activists known as the "L.A. 8," and the nationwide monitoring and interviews of Arab American individuals and organizations before and during the first Gulf War (Cainkar 2002; Cole and Dempsey 2002). In all these instances, state surveillance was tied to U.S. policies in the Middle East and designed to suppress movements or individuals critiquing U.S. support for Israel or resisting U.S. military interventions.

There may be a historical amnesia about the many acts of U.S. empire in the American public at large, but in many immigrant and minority communities and for many involved in civil rights, antiwar, and anticolonialist movements, regardless of ethnicity, there is a collective memory—however contained or dispersed—about imperial strategies and tactics. For example, Japanese American groups joined in protests of post-9/11 racial profiling, making links to the government's internment policies during the Second World War, and supported efforts to expose ongoing FBI surveillance and civil rights infringements of Arab and Muslim Americans. Arab Americans and South Asian Americans have worked with Latino and Latina immigrant rights activists around the country, for example, in the NEIDRN campaigns in New England and the "Deport the INS" (Deporten a La Migra) coalition formed to fight deportations in San Francisco (see also Naber 2002).

These alliances have given rise to new or strengthened relationships between various communities and have reconfigured the political landscape on some college campuses as well. These alignments have also fostered a certain kind of polycultural citizenship, or polycultural mappings of resistance that draw connections between areas of the world and national, ethnic, or racial groups, as well as forms of hegemony, presumed to be disconnected or distinct. The War on Terror has sparked new interconnections between movements and generated new kinds of political education, inadvertently producing new polycultural remappings of boundaries between movements and identifications. One instance on my own campus is a multiethnic group of students at the University of California, Davis, who created a South Asian / Middle Eastern Coalition after 9/11 and became engaged in making connections between the detentions of Muslim Americans and the warehousing of African Americans and Latinos and Latinas in the prison-industrial complex. Asian American and Latino and Latina students at UC Davis also became aware of the struggles of Arab American students to bring to light the Palestine question in the face of repression and censorship in the U.S. academy. In spring 2005, the Third World Forum (a multiethnic student group), along with South Asian, Palestinian, and Latino and Latina organizations, cosponsored a talk, "Palestine and Philippines: National Liberation Struggles and International Solidarity," which charted a history of U.S. imperial policies and overseas occupation, client states, and repression. Latino and Latina and Arab American students collaborated on a forum drawing attention to the militarization of the U.S.-Mexico border and the parallels between the building of a "security fence" to keep "terrorists" and unwanted aliens from crossing it and the Israeli wall that has encroached on Palestinian land and divided towns and villages in the West Bank. This event has echoes of the Third World solidarity of the Non-Aligned Movement and the era of the Bandung Conference (see Prashad 2007), re-created in the context of alliances forged among different immigrant communities in Northern California, where Latinos and Latinas, Asian Americans, and Arab Americans come together in coalitions focusing on immigrant and civil rights and in antiwar organizing, though clearly not in any kind of idealized way. These alliances, of course, are part of a much longer history of shifting "axes of affinity and identification" produced by global migrations that has, ironically, brought those who have knowledge of resistance to U.S. imperial power and global capital in their home countries to converge in "new social movements" within the United States, as noted by George Lipsitz (2001, 214).

After 9/11, as in other moments, there were innumerable and mostly untold acts of courage that were not identified as "political resistance," by individuals who were "ordinary" people—people who spoke, wrote, asked, stopped, initiated, persisted, protested, and refused to hesitate in the face of clear and present danger. The responses of many of the South Asian Muslim immigrant youth in this book exemplify some of these

Cross-ethnic solidarity in post-9/11 protest at Middlesex County Jail.
Photograph by Irum Sheikh.

dissenting actions: their speeches against racial profiling in the school, their analyses of Islamophobia, their opposition to the war, their insistence on international human rights, and their engagement with the histories of oppression of other groups. Solidarity was part of individual and collective responses to the War on Terror but is not easily or consistently produced, especially in a repressive climate of intimidation, fear, and distrust. Solidarity, Vijay Prashad (2000, 197) reminds us, is a desire that is actualized through a "tremendous act of production," for "unity is not waiting to happen." It is created through struggle—a struggle for understanding what differences and commonalities between groups are important, strategic, contradictory, or challenging for defining shared goals and interests. In the process of building a deeper solidarity, beyond short-term coalitions based on shared self-interests, the meaning of commonality sometimes shifts as members of groups come to a new definition of their shared identities, histories, or destinies. Coalitions are important and necessary to deal with immediate crises, such as Special Registration or violent attacks, but long-term, polycultural affinities are built on the awareness that groups such as South Asian Americans and Arab Americans share a history that is about more than the impact of 9/11: a history of shared experiences of European colonialism, partition, displacement, exile, occupation, migration, racialization, and Orientalism. There are gaps in awareness of these polycultural histories, for they are often suppressed in the United States. But even South Asian and Arab American youth who have grown up with the divide-and-rule tactics of race politics in the United States find their way to these common understandings, in some form, despite considerable barriers to making these alliances. The historical links and political connections forged by these youth in their everyday relationships are part of a daily process of polycultural affiliation that underlies solidarity. While the stories of South Asian Muslim immigrant youth are often missing from public discussion and academic research, their experiences teach us about the contradictions of citizenship in this moment of empire, through their reflections on displacement, belonging, work, aspiration, fear, difference, and dissent.

Conclusion

The post-9/11 moment underscores that notions of citizenship developed by South Asian Muslim youth, some of which I have explored here, are constructed in a dynamic relationship with various institutions and policies of the state, and that manifestations of the state are themselves mutable and multifaceted. Focusing on cultural citizenship allows for an analysis of how immigrant youth understand their relationship to the state and to imperial power in various realms in their everyday lives. Clearly, these South Asian Muslim immigrant youth understand the experience of "being Muslim," and being Indian, Pakistani, or Bangladeshi, after 9/11 in relation to a range of contexts that extend beyond religious practices and identifications and that include family, work, education, popular culture, and social relationships. This research is a small step in showing that the construction of "Muslimness" is produced by state policies and cultural discourses that tend to frame these youth as "Muslim" actors—ignoring that they may also be working-class, male or female, urban, Indian or Pakistani, Gujarati or Pathan—and give primacy to religion as the key explanatory rubric for the War on Terror, thus evading larger historical and political processes embedded in U.S. empire.

Immigrant youth express cultural citizenship through transnational ties to South Asia, evident in popular culture and family networks; through interethnic friendships and multicultural or polycultural affiliations in the context of work, urban space, and youth subcultures; and through critiques of war, nationalism, and human rights that speak implicitly, if not explicitly, to the workings of U.S. empire. The forms of citizenship identified here—flexible, multicultural or polycultural, and dissenting— exceed traditional notions of formal citizenship and provide new layers to notions of cultural citizenship by showing how young people grapple with the impact of the state in different realms of their everyday lives in subtle, and also tangible, ways. Situating this discussion in the ethnographic context of everyday life after 9/11 allows for an understanding of the impact of historical and political forces, such as that of empire, on the micropolitics of daily life for young people. Imperial power may not be explicitly mentioned by these young immigrants, but it has deeply shaped their experiences after, and even before, 9/11—it is the larger frame of empire that is often occluded or missing in discussions of South Asian Muslim immigrants after 9/11. In linking youth to citizenship and empire, this book aims to provide a deep and honest analysis of the questions of affiliation and exclusion, fear and dissent, empire and belonging, which face not just South Asian and Muslim immigrant youth but that confront us all today.

Amin and Sara

I left Wellford in fall 2003, to move to California. Amin called me several times on the phone to talk about the uphill battle that his romance with Sara was becoming, for her father had explicitly forbidden them to meet each other. He seemed alternately anxious and angry but was busy working at the family dry-cleaning store and simultaneously studying for the MCAS (state examinations). Amin's grades were beginning to suffer—even in biology, his favorite subject, which worried me. Understandably, Amin was upset about the roadblock that Sara's father's constantly posed to their relationship, and frustrated that Sara didn't seem to be standing up more to her father. He asked me once, "What do you think I should do?" Just be patient, I told him. Tell Sara how you feel but don't pressure her. Try to stay focused on your schoolwork and don't get too stressed. I told him that it was probably hard for Sara, particularly as a daughter, to oppose her father's wishes, and that I understood this well from my own experience. But Amin said to me one day, "If she loves me, she should be willing to fight for this. I would die for her, but she can't even talk to her father?" My attempts to soften his frustration by resorting to a gendered explanation fell away in the face of this simple statement. Although

I felt sometimes like I fulfilled the role of an older sister for Amin, yet someone outside his family and circle in whom he could confide, I don't know if Amin ever realized how much I respected his integrity and maturity.

In December 2003, Amin called me to say that Sara's sister Rukshana had divulged to their father that he and Sara were still in touch in defiance of his wishes. Sara's father was furious and decided to take her out of Wellford High and send her to the high school in the neighboring town of Granville. I happened to be visiting Wellford soon after his phone call, and when I arrived at the school I heard that Ellery had arranged a meeting with Sara's father and an interpreter to discuss the issue. The compromise Sara's father offered was that his daughter could choose between going to Granville High School or staying in Wellford and never talking to Amin again. Sara apparently rejected this choice as a false one, saying that it would not be possible for her to be in the same school as Amin and never talk to him or look at him again, so she would rather leave Wellford High. Wasn't this an expression of love? And of defiance? Although Amin might have recognized her stance as courageous, when I talked to him one rainy afternoon in the school hallways, he was unhappy that Sara had agreed to transfer to Granville because he believed that Wellford was a better high school—which was probably true. Amin knew that going to a new school in the middle of the year would be hard for her, especially since she didn't know anyone in Granville; he obviously cared deeply about her education and well-being. He told me, "I promised that if Sara stayed here, I wouldn't talk to her and I would keep to the agreement." We walked out into the rain together. I couldn't think of anything more to say.

A few months later, Amin called me once more, with some big news. Sara's father had arranged for her to marry her cousin in Gujarat, and she had finally relented. Amin was crushed. I was worried about him, but by the end of the year, he was reenergized and focused on applying to college. In the spring, he took the lead role in organizing the first South Asian culture show with other students at the high school which was to become an annual tradition. Perhaps he had come to terms in his own way with what was missing and what was yet to come in his life.

Anwar

I and others in SACH realized that organizing forums on immigrant rights after 9/11 was going to be difficult and unproductive if people in the South Asian Muslim community were simply too afraid to come to them. Over time, we talked to people in the area who were doing work on issues of detention and deportation and trying to connect the War on Terror to the larger questions of criminalization of immigrants and people of color, incarceration and prison abuse, and war and militarism. A woman from Rhode Island had started visiting prisons in New England after 9/11 and had managed to speak to many of the Muslim and Arab male detainees and document their situation, relaying information to their families and contacting the NEIDRN coalition for help with legal and medical resources as necessary. The work was arduous and very time-consuming, but she had been able by dint of sheer persistence to find out approximately how many Muslim and Arab men were in prisons across New England. Detainees had come to trust her and contact her for prison visits, and we in SACH were inspired by her committed work.

A Pakistani woman, Shirin, who was a criminal detention lawyer in Boston, suggested that if we were interested in trying to support South Asian detainees, we could start by working with her on a detention case which would link post-9/11 issues to the larger problem of immigrant detention and help us understand these issues. Shirin had been trying for a long time, with little result, to obtain travel documents for a Bangladeshi immigrant man, Anwar, who had been detained for over four months on immigration violations and who simply wanted to return home. He had been picked up on the docks in Boston after 9/11 and had no family in the United States. Anwar had had no visitors in the four months he had been locked up. Shirin tried, but was not able, to contact his sister in Bangladesh to find out if she could send Anwar his documents. Compounding the difficulty of the situation, the Bangladeshi consulate seemed to be reluctant to process his documents and give him a passport, even though Shirin had managed to get the Department of Homeland Security (DHS) to agree to release him if he could produce a Bangladeshi passport. It was an absurd situation, for here was a man who *wanted* to be deported and who was stuck in a Kafkaesque limbo between two states because his proof of citizenship was missing.

The first step Shirin suggested to us was to write to Anwar and see if we could visit him in prison to ask if we could work on his case and follow up with the consulate and the DHS. I wrote him a letter and Aparna, an Indian American woman in SACH, tried to contact the officer at the detention facility in Cranston, Rhode Island, where Anwar was held. Officer Hendricks was polite and responsive—particularly on e-mail with Aparna—and agreed to our visit, but it took us a couple of weeks to figure out the labyrinthine system of visiting schedules. By the time we had figured out that Anwar was in detainee group "E," and Anwar had officially requested that Aparna and I should be placed on his list of visitors, I had already moved to California. A few people in SACH had left, and the group had been whittled down to only three or four people. Since I had been the one to write to Anwar, we waited till I returned to Wellford in the fall to try to visit him. Group "E" detainees had visiting hours in the evenings on Thursdays. So one Thursday evening, I drove to Cranston with Aparna and Pawan, a young Indian American man who had recently joined SACH.

It took us almost two hours to get to Cranston, so by the time we arrived at the prison it was completely dark. The parking lot of the prison, which was set back from the highway atop a small hill, was almost empty. This was the first time any of us had visited a prison. We left our jewelry, wallets, and house keys in the car as instructed, and took some change and identification in a plastic bag. We had been warned by the visiting guidelines to dress appropriately and, in instructions specifically for women, not to wear revealing clothes. Officer Hendricks was alone at the desk behind the locked gate, and seemed to be delighted to see Aparna, with whom he had been almost flirtatious on e-mail. I could tell Aparna was wincing inside while outwardly laughing and chatting with Hendricks to make sure things went smoothly. There was one other visitor waiting in the reception area, a Latina woman in her early thirties, who was there to visit a detainee with her little daughter. Hendricks was brusque with her, and seemed to have seen her before at the prison. Another woman appeared at the entrance, apparently to visit the same detainee, and Hendricks buzzed her in. The woman at the desk turned away for a few seconds to look for her driver's license, and in that short interval, her daughter ran through the closing door. Pawan leapt and caught her just before she got caught in the sliding electric gate. It was a small moment of drama, but Hendricks was furious and rebuked the Latina woman for not taking care of her child. We stood there, embarrassed and angry. We were clearly not the "regular" visitors.

But the drama was to become bigger, and stranger. When we asked to see Anwar, Hendricks punched some information into his computer and then looked up and said, "He's gone."

DONALD PRICE FACILITY
VISITING SCHEDULE
DECEMBER 2003

RECEPTION DESK 462-1343   PO BOX 20983 CRANSTON, RI 02920

TIME	SUNDAY	MONDAY	TUESDAY	WEDNESDAY	THURSDAY	FRIDAY	SATURDAY
		1	**2**	**3**	**4**	**5**	**6**
5:30-7:15		A-DORM	C-DORM	E-DORM	B-DORM	D-DORM	A-DORM
8:00-9:45		B-DORM	D-DORM	A-DORM	C-DORM	E-DORM	B-DORM
	7	**8**	**9**	**10**	**11**	**12**	**13**
5:30-7:15	C-DORM	E-DORM	B-DORM	D-DORM	A-DORM	C-DORM	E-DORM
8:00-9:45	D-DORM	A-DORM	C-DORM	E-DORM	B-DORM	D-DORM	A-DORM
	14	**15**	**16**	**17**	**18**	**19**	**20**
5:30-7:15	B-DORM	D-DORM	A-DORM	C-DORM	E-DORM	B-DORM	D-DORM
8:00-9:45	C-DORM	E-DORM	B-DORM	D-DORM	A-DORM	C-DORM	E-DORM
	21	**22**	**23**	**24**	**25**	**26**	**27**
5:30-7:15	A-DORM	C-DORM	E-DORM	B-DORM	D-DORM	A-DORM	C-DORM
8:00-9:45	B-DORM	D-DORM	A-DORM	C-DORM	E-DORM	B-DORM	D-DORM
	28	**29**	**30**	**31**			
5:30-7:15	E-DORM	B-DORM	D-DORM	A-DORM			
8:00-9:45	A-DORM	C-DORM	E-DORM	B-DORM			

Attention Visitors: **(1) Anyone caught conveying contraband into this Facility maybe subject to loss of visiting privileges and/or criminal prosecution. (It is a *Felony* if you get caught bringing in illegal controlled substances.)**

(2) You must bring a valid picture I.D. (Drivers license, Passport or Military I.D.) Anyone attempting to use False Identification to gain entrance to this Facility will be turned over to the State Police for prosecution. Parents of minor children must bring the child's Birth Certificate. You must have written notarized permission to bring a minor that you are not the parent or legal guardian of. (See Reception Officer for permission slip.)

(3) You are not allowed to have *Anything* in your pockets or on your person other than One key (can be your car key), change for the vending machines and your I.D. *You can not ware any jewelry except wedding bands.*

(4) You must dress *appropriately.* NO REVEALING OUTFITS! See separate sheet for dress code.

Schedule and rules for visiting detainees in Cranston, Rhode Island, prison, 2003.

"What do you mean he's gone? We just e-mailed you, and you said yesterday we could visit him!" Aparna was shocked and confused.

"I know, hon', but he's not in my system. I think they came and took him out."

"Who did? Where did they take him?" I was anxious, and suspicious. How could he have disappeared, just as we were coming to visit him; was this purely coincidental?

"Like I told you, hon'; he just isn't here. They've moved him to Boston, it looks like. Maybe they're gonna send him home. Or maybe they re-leased him."

It was painfully anticlimactic. We had been waiting just to visit Anwar for almost two months, and now he was simply gone. Missing.

We drove back, frustrated, worried, and silent. On the way, we stopped for dinner at a Taco Bell on the highway and wondered where Anwar was. Later, we found out from Shirin that he had been transferred briefly to a Boston prison, which was notorious for being a difficult place for detainees, and then released on probation until his deportation hearing. We could have tried to find him, but we had no idea where he might have been and didn't want to put him in jeopardy. Maybe he had contacted his sister in Bangladesh, or maybe he was working on the docks again and had decided to stay here; we simply didn't know.

Two days after our visit, I got a letter from Anwar that had been wait-ing for me at an old address in Wellford. It seemed to have been written a month earlier by another detainee, since Anwar did not speak or write English. The letter said that he was very happy to have heard that we wanted to visit him, and he was grateful for any help we could offer. Anwar had been waiting to meet us. We had just missed him, in the maze of prisons, highways, docks, doors. He had slipped between the cracks of night and morning, letters and e-mails, home and away. Maybe he was in Bangladesh, maybe he was in the United States. Maybe he had found his own route through empire. We would never know.

Appendix

A Note on Methods

For this study, I did a total of sixty-seven interviews as well as participant-observation in various sites in Wellford in 2002–3. I interviewed thirty-eight high school students, of whom twenty-five were South Asian Muslim immigrant youth (twelve were Indian, eight Pakistani, and five Bangladeshi, roughly in proportion to their representation in the high school). I also interviewed seven second-generation South Asian Muslim youth, who were either born in the United States or came here before the age of seven or eight, and six non-Muslim South Asian or non–South Asian Muslim immigrant students (including Nepali, Tibetan, and African youth). Of the total group of high school youth, I ended up speaking to twenty-five students who were female and thirteen who were male. While I had ideally hoped for a gender balance among interviewees, I realized that some of the boys were a bit uncomfortable talking to girls and women outside their family circle, which is generally true of adolescent males, as I know from my previous research, and was particularly true for these immigrant youth.

The interviews were open-ended, informal conversations that took place in a range of settings, from prearranged meetings to conversations over lunch or while driving in my car or hanging out with them in the International Student Center at the high school. I made sure to meet with each of the students at least once for an intensive interview, but I also met them frequently and talked to them informally in many kinds of contexts, in and out of the school, and talked to them on the phone. In addition, with the help of my two primary research assistants, Palav Babaria and Sarah Khan, I interviewed a total of twenty-nine adults, including teachers and staff in the high school; parents of South Asian as well as non–South Asian students in the school; individuals active in the Indian community, Pakistani community, and Muslim organizations in the Wellford and Boston area; and local government employees working in youth programs. We interviewed leaders of the major South Asian (Indian and Pakistani) community organizations in the area as well as regional organizations representing the sizeable Gujarati community—Gurjar, Gujarati Samaj, and Patidar Samaj (a Hindu caste organization)—since most of the Indian Muslim students in the high school were from Gujarat, in western India.

My research also included fieldwork over a period of one year both in and outside the school, in the places that these young people traverse in their everyday lives: school, home, workplace, and community and cultural events. I visited the high school twice a week, on average, from September through mid-December 2002, while I was on leave from teaching, and continued to spend time at the school regularly after that so I came to know several of the teachers and staff quite well. With the help of the director of the International Student and Family Center at the school, I was able to "shadow" three South Asian Muslim students and sit in on their classes on three different days. This was an opportunity to see firsthand the daily interactions among students, teachers, and staff in the school and to get to know students whom I found difficult to meet because of their busy schedules after school. During the course of my fieldwork, I met with youth at the places where they worked, such as convenience stores, restaurants, movie theaters, and security guard posts. I was invited by some students to visit their homes and got to know their families and friends, and sometimes saw them around in the city, since I was living in Wellford at the time, not far from the high school. So I was very much a part of some of the worlds that they inhabited, but not others, and they helped me understand the politics of belonging and exclusion in the city more deeply than I ever had before.

Notes

Introduction   South Asian Muslim Youth in the United States

1 High school youth commonly referred to Latinos and Latinas and Latin American students as "Spanish."

2 See appendix A for detailed information on the study's research methods, including the interviews.

3 For example, the national population of Indian Americans was 1,678,765 in 2000, according to the U.S. Census (U.S. Census Bureau, 2000 Census).

4 The economic struggles of these often invisible Indian Americans challenge the model minority caricature: the 1990 U.S. Census found that 7.4 percent of Indian American families fall below the poverty line, slightly more than white American families (7 percent) (Hing 1993).

5 Wellford's population is 68.1 percent white American, 11.9 percent African American, 11.9 percent Asian American, and 7.4 percent Latino and Latina. Median household income in 1999 was $47,979, which is above the national median, but there were also 12.9 percent individuals living below poverty level, slightly above the national level, possibly due to the significant presence of students.

6 In 2000–2002, 33 percent of students had a first language other than English and 14 percent were in the bilingual program, which suggests that the immigrant student population in the school is somewhere between these figures.

7 See Suzanne Shanahan 1999 on the power of scripts of citizenship.

8 Jeff Coen, "Hate Crimes Reports Reach Record Level," *Chicago Tribune*, October 9, 2001.

9 Jane Lampan, "Under Attack, Sikhs Defend Their Religious Liberties," *Christian Science Monitor*, October 31, 2001.

10 Associated Press, San Jose, Calif., "Hate Crime Reports Down, Civil Rights Complaints Up," October 25, 2001; "Hate Crimes on Muslims Show Rise," *Boston Globe*, November 26, 2002, A11.

11 Also relevant, personal communication, Nancy Hormachea, immigration attorney and member of National Lawyers Guild and Arab Resource and Organizing Collective, Berkeley, Calif., July 8, 2007.

12 Developmental approaches to youth, particularly in the field of psychology but also in anthropology, assume a stage-based model of youth, as in the classic identity development theory of Erik Erikson 1994 (1968) that posits adolescence as a liminal period for testing of political attitudes and the formation of the relationship between the young person and society.

13 There is a growing body of work focusing on the transnational lives of Asian American, and particularly Latino and Latina, youth and "border" identities (for a recent example, see Cynthia L. Bejarano 2005). Studies of Asian American youth also increasingly focus on issues such as "parachute kids" from East Asia (Chiang-Hom 2004; Ong 1999; Orellana et al. 2001) and transnational Filipino American youth cultures (e.g., Bonus 2000). Less research has looked at the transnational experiences of South Asian youth in the United States, but there are emerging studies that focus on popular culture; for example, see Jigna Desai 2004.

14 This post-9/11 music of dissent was, of course, not free of controversy; in the hyperpatriotic climate of the aftermath of 9/11, several songs were censored. For example, the controversial song about the American Taliban soldier, "John Walker's Blues," by Steve Earle (Artemis Records), actually received less public attention than others, such as that by the Dixie Chicks, because it was banned from radio stations. "Last Year's Terror Attacks Have Changed America's Tune," *New York Times*, August 11, 2002, and "The World," 14; for a longer discussion, see Garofalo 2007.

15 See an early analysis by Perlo 1951.

16 For example, see Marjoie Agosin and Betty Jean Craige 2002; Kathleen Benson and Philip M. Kayal 2002; Brown 2003; Roger Burbach and Ben Clarke 2002; Joseph and Sharma 2003; Jee Kim et al., eds. 2002; Richard Leone and Greg Anrig Jr 2003; Bruce Lincoln 2003; Mahajan 2002; Norman Mailer 2003; Stephen J. Schulhofer 2002; Sandra Silberstein 2002; and Michael Sorkin and Sharon Zukin, eds. 2002

One   U.S. Empire and the War on Terror

1 See Andrew Bacevich 2002.

2 For example, Bacevich 2002; Ivan Eland 2004; Niall Ferguson 2004; Chalmers Johnson 2004; Robert W. Merry 2005; William Odom and Robert Dujarric 2004; Arundhati Roy 2004; Michael Scheur 2004; Neil Smith 2003.

3 Hardt and Negri (2000, 166) claim that the American notion of "frontier" was expansive, rather than expansionist unlike the Roman empire, and that the new "imperial sovereignty" does not "annex or destroy the other powers it faces," but absorbs and reforms them. They insist on an idealized vision

of the democratic principles enshrined in the U.S. Constitution, and of the radical possibilities of the New World republic in contrast to European imperial states that were monarchical and aristocratic.

4 See also Neil Smith 2005.

5 Mamdani (2004, 69–84) points out that proxy wars continued to be fought after American failures in Vietnam and Angola, despite countermeasures by critics of U.S. military policy to limit overseas military interventions and covert assistance, such as the War Powers Act (1973) and the Clark Amendment (1976), respectively.

6 Josh Meyer, "Human Rights Watch Lists 39 Secret CIA Detainees," *Los Angeles Times*, February 28, 2001, www.latimes.com.

7 See Kenneth Church 2002.

8 Historically, there was a shift in the United States from settler colonialism and direct acquisition of overseas colonies, as in the 1898 Spanish-American War, which resulted in U.S. control of the Philippines, Cuba, and Puerto Rico, to later phases of "neocolonialism" or indirect control through economic and political influence (Young 2001, 42).

9 George H. W. Bush said after the first Gulf War, "The specter of Vietnam has been buried forever in the desert sands of the Arabian peninsula.... By God, we've kicked the Vietnam syndrome once and for all" (cited in Gardner and Young 2007, 9).

10 As early as 1992, Paul Wolfowitz and Lewis Libby authored a report on Defense Policy Guidance, which called for a policy of preemptive military action and U.S. dominance in Eurasia to consolidate U.S. global power (Barry and Lobe 2003, 39). Building on this vision, the PNAC issued a report in September 2000, "Rebuilding America's Defenses: Strategy, Forces and Resources for a New Century"; it unabashedly proclaimed that America's "grand strategy" for global preeminence should rest on increased military spending, a stronger military presence in East Asia, a network of military deployment bases, global missile defenses, and space control technology (see Barry and Lobe 2003, and Feffer 2003, appendix B).

11 The PNAC was founded by neocons William Kristol and Robert Kagan in 1997, and initially operated out of media mogul Rupert Murdoch's right-wing newspaper, *The Weekly Standard* (Burbach and Tarbell 2004, 86). For a list of signatories of the PNAC's 1997 Statement of Principles, see Feffer 2003, appendix B.

12 Ernest R. May, *Imperial Democracy: The Emergence of America as a Great Power* (New York: Harcourt, Brace and World, 1961), 270. Cited in Bacevich 2002, 7.

13 See Caren Kaplan 2006.

14 This was a tenet espoused by previous revisionist historians of U.S. empire, such as Charles A. Beard, *A Foreign Policy for America* (New York: A. A. Knopf, 1940), 11. See the somewhat skeptical discussion in Bacevich 2002, 7–31.

15 The 1790 Naturalization Law denied naturalization rights to nonwhites and was repealed only in 1952. The civil rights struggles of the 1960s and '70s introduced the notion of "internal colonialism" to link the "disenfranchisement of racial minorities" within the United States to decolonization in the Third World; though this analogy was politically strategic, it had its limitations (Sharpe 1995, 183–84).

16 "Security" is an ideological and also politically strategic term for U.S. empire; Bacevich (2002, 121) points out that at the beginning of the Cold War, U.S. policymakers switched from using the term "national defense" to the more euphemistic term "national security" that could support interventions such as those in South Vietnam that had little to do with "defending" the United States. But "security" has clearly been a potent and persuasive idea for the Americans public to justify a range of actions.

17 Bernd Debusmann, "Fear and Distrust of Muslims Run Deep in U.S.," Reuters, December 1, 2006, www.asiamedia.ucla.edu (accessed December 7, 2006).

18 The 1996 Anti-Terrorism Act "reintroduced to federal law the principle of 'guilt by association' that had defined the McCarthy era" and applied this to groups defined by the state as terrorist, thus reviving the ideological exclusion of the Cold War–era McCarran-Walter Act. It also gave the state authority to deport noncitizens on the basis of secret evidence (see Cole and Dempsey 2002, 117–26). From 1996 to 2000, the government sought to use secret evidence to detain and deport two dozen immigrants, almost all of them Muslims, but ultimately the government evidence was thrown out and the accused were released (see Cole and Dempsey 2002, 127).

19 See Michael Welch 2000 and Mark Dow 2004 on the connections between immigration and incarceration in the United States.

20 The reregistration component of the program was officially ended by the Department of Homeland Security in December, 2003, after protests by immigrant and civil rights and grassroots community organizations, while other aspects of the program, including detentions and deportations, remained in place (see Cainkar 2004).

21 Adam Liptak, "In War of Vague Borders, Detainee Longs for Court," *New York Times*, January 5, 2007, www.nytimes.com.

Two   Cultural Citizenship

1 See Karen Leonard 1992 for a history of the Punjabi-Mexican marriages in California.

2 For more, see Nabeel Abraham 1994; and Akram and Johnson 2004, 12–13. This needs also to be placed in the context of the growing alliances between Hindu nationalist organizations and Zionist lobby groups in the United

States, who see common cause in their attack on "Islamic terrorism," in India as well as in Israel. See Sridevi Menon 2006; and Vijay Prashad 2003.

3   There have been numerous cases of surveillance and infiltration of antiwar groups and protests around the country. One famous incident was that of Aaron Kilner, a member of the Sheriff Department's Antiterrorism Unit in Fresno, California, who attended meetings and events of Peace Fresno for six months; his cover was blown when he was killed in an accident in 2003 that was reported in the media with a photograph of the man known to activists only as the person who "took a lot of notes" at antiwar meetings (see Rothschild 2007, 57, for this and other cases).

Three   Citizenship: Flexibility and Control

1   For a discussion of transnationalism, see Linda Basch, Nina Glick Schiller, and Cristina Szanton Blanc 1994.

2   Sam Rao, "Special 'Messengers' to Apprise Elders of City Services," *Indian Express/North American Edition*, August 10, 2007, 2.

3   See "Overseas Citizenship of India (OCI) Scheme," Embassy of India, Washington, D.C., www.indianembassy.org (accessed July 30, 2008).

4   Ibid.

5   "PM Promises NRIS 'Dual Citizenship,'" *Times of India*, January 10, 2003, 1.

6   "Dual Rhetoric," editorial, *Times of India*, January 11, 2003, 12.

7   "Advani Asks States to Deport Illegal Settlers," *Times of India*, January 8, 2003, 1; "Illegal Immigrants Cause Alarm in South Mumbai," *Times of India*, Downtown Plus, January 10, 2003, 1.

8   Neil MacFarquhar, "Fears of Inquiry Dampen Giving by U.S. Muslims," *New York Times*, October 30, 2006, www.nytimes.com.

9   John Mintz and Douglas Farah, "US Terror Probe Reportedly Targeting Muslim, Arab Stores," *Boston Globe*, August 12, 2002, A8.

10   Irina Slutsky, "Indian Couple Seeks Release: Jewelry Store Investigation," *Bradenton Herald*, Wednesday, July 17, 2002.

11   This is a reference to a production of *The Children of Herakles*, staged by Peter Sellars in January 2003. The cast included immigrant and refugee high school students, including a few South Asian students from the bilingual program.

12   Hamdi and Padilla were charged with links to al-Qaeda and detained indefinitely as "enemy combatants," without any rights to present evidence, or, in Padilla's case, to speak with his lawyer (Cole 2003, 43–45). After three years of being held in solitary confinement without trial on a navy brig, Padilla was finally indicted by a federal grand jury in November 2005, the original charge of an alleged plot to use a "dirty bomb" having been dropped by the government. Richard Schmitt, "Terror Suspect Indicted After 3 Years in Jail," *Los Angeles Times*, 1, A30.

Four   Work, Play, and Polyculturalism

1 In the high school at large, 64.8 percent of the graduating class of 2001 were admitted into four-year colleges, and only 15.7 percent attended two-year colleges (Wellford school document), so the difficulties of getting admission into a four-year college for immigrant students was clearly tied to the obstacles of English fluency and late entry into the American high school system, as well as ineligibility for financial aid due to immigrant status.

2 One of the exceptions is Nabeel Abraham and Andrew Shryock 2000, an edited collection of essays focusing on issues of work, politics, religion, and multicultural inclusion, but generally not in the context of the contemporary generation of Arab American and Muslim American youth.

3 It is often difficult to translate class categories across cultural or national contexts; immigrant populations may have varying understandings of the meanings of class, and may continue to identify with the class status they occupied in their home countries. Questions of defining class based on family income, occupation, or self-identification always arise with the complexity of class analysis, as class is a process, not just a "place in a social ranking," embedded in social and economic relations of "interpersonal domination and property ownership" (Gibson-Graham, Resnick, and Wolff 2000, 3; Kumar 2000, ix).

4 See Vimalassery (2002) for the broader implications of this policy.

5 Anand Vaishnav and Benjamin Gedan, "Debate Heats up over the Fate of Bilingual Classes," Boston Globe, October 2, 2002, A1, B6.

6 Anand Vaishnav, "Tamayo Targets Bilingual Changes," Boston Globe, June 12, 2003, B5. Ironically, but reflecting the divided cultural politics in immigrant communities, the chairman of the English for the Children campaign was a Latino educator, Lincoln Tamayo. Two-way immersion programs are those in which the instruction time is divided equally between two languages, taught by native speakers of each language, and the class is typically divided between students who are native speakers of each language.

7 Immigrant students in the bilingual program also struggled with new state-mandated testing requirements for graduation—those in the graduating class of 2003 were the first in the state who had to pass the tenth-grade test in math and English, required of all high school students in order to be eligible for admission into public four-year colleges. Many of the South Asian students had no problem with the math portion but had difficulty passing in English and so had to retake the test.

8 Park's (2005) study focuses on second-generation Korean American and Chinese American young adults, and raises issues of the roles of cultural translator and problem-solver played by youth in these businesses, as well as the resentment they felt due to the blurring of conventional boundaries of childhood and adulthood. This was not a critique expressed by the recently

arrived immigrant youth in my study, whose childhood had been dramatically transformed by migration, not to mention by the post-9/11 climate in the United States, so that work was just one of many, significant changes in their experiences of "childhood" or "adolescence."

9 See Maira (2000, 2002a) for a fuller discussion of the racial and class meanings of adoption of hip-hop by South Asian American youth, males and females.

10 An extreme form of this suspicion was manifested in the government targeting of Muslim American youth in cases that did not produce any evidence of terrorist activity or even plots: for example, the sensationalized allegations of attending a terrorist training camp that led to the detention of Hamid Hayat, a twenty-two-year old Pakistani American from Lodi, California, in 2005 (Maira 2007), and the less publicized case the same year of the deportation of Tashnuba Hyder, a sixteen-year-old Bangladeshi girl, for writing a school essay about religious views of suicide bombing and entering an Internet chat room discussing the views of a radical Muslim cleric (Bernstein 2005).

11 Michael Muhammad Knight (2006), a white Muslim convert, has drawn attention to a nascent Muslim punk movement in the United States and to an eclectic synthesis of anarchism, Sufism, black nationalism, and radical politics. For a discussion of urban African American youth fusing hip-hop with Islam via the Nation of Islam or subcultures such as the Five Percenters, see Hisham Aidi (2007).

12 In 2006, the former British foreign secretary Jack Straw called for the regulation of headscarves worn by British Muslim women and a comment by the former prime minister Tony Blair that veils were a "mark of separation" sparked national debate about the "integration" of Muslims; see "Muslim Face Veil Draws Criticism in Britain," *Los Angeles Times*, November 24, 2006, www.latimes.com; Alan Cowell, "Blair Criticizes Full Islamic Veils as 'Mark of Separation,'" *New York Times*, October 18, 2006, www.nytimes.com.

13 For more on the ambivalent portrayals of working women and commentaries on traditional gender roles and the "New Indian Woman" in Indian television serials, see Purnima Mankekar 1999.

Five   Dissenting Citizenship

1 For more on this issue as affecting second-generation South Asian youth, see Maira 2002a.

2 For example, Ignatieff "The Burden"(2003), the pro-empire historian Ferguson's "The Empire Slinks Back" (2003), and the cover story of *Harper's Magazine*, titled "The Economics of Empire," by William Finnegan (May 2003): 41–54.

3 I am currently doing new research on South Asian, Arab, and Afghan American youth in Silicon Valley, California, where there are large Muslim

American communities. These include a new generation of Muslim American youth who are actively engaged in local and campus politics, often in the context of Muslim Student Association groups but also in broader coalitions, including civil and immigrant rights, antiwar, Palestinian rights, and social justice organizing.

4 These "moderate" Muslim feminists and authors have been funded and promoted by various right-wing think tanks, particularly Irshad Manji (2003), who calls herself a "Muslim refusenik." Asra Nomani (2005) was catapulted into fame by the death of her friend the journalist Daniel Pearl, and launched a "Muslim Women's Freedom Tour." More shrill spokespersons include Brigitte Gabriel, the Lebanese Christian founder of American Congress for Truth, and Wafa Sultan, a Syrian American psychiatrist who became famous for declaring on Al Jazeera television (February 21, 2006), "There is no clash of civilizations but a clash between . . . civilization and backwardness, between the civilized and the primitive, between barbarity and rationality."

5 Comments such as these are perhaps why the New York Museum of Film and Radio withdrew its support for the film just as the United States was about to invade Iraq.

6 Khan's comment was echoed by other Muslim American leaders, who noted that a year after George W. Bush's meeting with Muslim activists at the White House, there had been a "reversal" of outreach by the White House and a failure by the president to condemn comments by Christian conservatives, such as evangelist Franklin Graham, who called Islam "a very evil and wicked religion." They pointed out that Bush actually courted Southern Baptists at a conference where Muhammad was called a "demon-possessed pedophile," and that the celebration of Muslim holidays at the White House had not been accompanied by a shift in policy on issues concerning Muslim Americans—an incipient critique of U.S. multicultural rhetoric. Rachel Zoll, "U.S. Muslims Say Bush Ignores Them," Associated Press, August 17, 2002, www.A P.org.

7 Hussein Ibish, "The War on Terrorism: Arab Americans, South Asian Americans, and Civil Liberties," talk given in the Asian American Studies Speaker Series, University of Massachusetts, Amherst, April 25, 2002.

8 In a southern case, the appellate court ruled in Dow v. The United States (1915) that "Syrians" were of the Semitic branch of the Caucasian race and thus eligible for U.S. citizenship. In Detroit, John Mohammed Ali argued before a U.S. District Court (1925) in a case that sought to revoke his naturalization (based on the Thind decision) that although he was born in India, he was "Arabian," since his ancestors had originated in Arabia. The judge replied that regardless of Ali's ancestry, he had dark skin and fit all the other criteria that defined the "common understanding" of being nonwhite. Judges in Detroit and Buffalo during the first few decades of the twentieth century consistently denied Arabs naturalization rights, without issuing written opinions that could be appealed (Cainkar and Maira 2006, 19).

9   Sami Al-Arian was acquitted of the key charges against him in December 2005 but remained behind bars, at the time of writing this book, for refusing to testify before a federal grand jury. In spring 2007, he went on a hunger strike to protest the violation of his plea agreement with the Department of Justice after he had already been convicted and was due to be released from prison and deported. Jeff Markon, "Support for Hunger Strike Growing," *Washington Post*, February 26, 2007, www.washingtonpost.com.

10 For example, the No Child Left Behind Act ties federal aid to local schools' protection of students' right to pray in schools, outside classes, a right the school district had to certify at the time that I was doing the research. Megan Tench, "US Aid Tied to School Prayer," *Boston Globe*, City/Region, March 23, 2003, B5.

11 Zachary Coile, "Bay Area Lawmakers Say They Back Troops Involved in Strikes," *San Francisco Chronicle*, October 8, 2001; Edward Epstein, "Bush Gets Power to Strike Iraq," *San Francisco Chronicle*, October 11, 2002.

12 For example, in November 2002, two Latinos and one Cambodian American were arrested in Easton, Massachusetts, for beating a Pakistani man in a 7–11 store, while shouting "You are from Afghanistan, you are Osama bin Laden's brother, you are a —— terrorist." Marcella Bombardieri, "3 Minorities Accused of Hate Crime in Attack on Store Clerk," *Boston Globe*, November 20, 2002, B6.

13 Robert Burns "Army: Recruiting Young Blacks Tougher Now," Associated Press, March 8, 2005, 8:19 a.m. ET, www.AP.org.

14 Matthew LaPlante, "U.S. Territories: A Recruiter's Paradise," *Salt Lake Tribune*, August 5, 2007, www.sltrib.com.

15 Melissa Scott Sinclair, "Peace Center Fights Back with 'Counter-Recruiting,'" *Style Weekly* (Richmond, Va.), January 11 2006; Jim Warren, "Tactics Questioned," *Kentucky Herald-Leader*, December 27, 2005.

16. For example, the AWOL hip-hop magazine for youth (see www.objector .org/awol, accessed December 25, 2005; printouts of Web pages in author's files).

17 See "Dream Act"/"Student Adjustment Act" Overview (Publications), National Council of La Raza, www.nclr.org (accessed September 3, 2007).

18 See the National Immigration Law Center's briefs, "Dream Act Summary," www.nilc.org (accessed September 3, 2007).

19 AWOL magazine points out, "The military is not a 'way out' for low-income youth. The DOD [Department of Defense] advertises financial aid for college. However, between 1986 and 1993, the military actually took $720 million more from GIs in non-refundable deposits than they paid out in college benefits, according to a report in Army Times. Military job training is also a myth. Only 12% of male veterans and 6% of female veterans report using skills learned in the military in their current jobs. In fact, according to the Veterans Administration, veterans overall earn less than non-veterans, 1/3 of homeless men are veterans, and at least 20% of federal and state prisoners are

veterans. Even former Secretary of Defense Cheney admitted, 'The reason to have a military is to be prepared to fight and win wars. . . . The military is not a social welfare agency, it's not a jobs program.'" Www.objector.org/awol, accessed December 25, 2005; printouts of Web pages in author's files. See also "Project on Youth and Non-military Opportunities," Committee Opposed to Militarism and the Draft (COMD), www.comdsd.org, and "Youth and Militarism," American Friends Service Committee, www.afsc.org.

20 "Military Recruiting in Schools," WHO-TV, Des Moines, January 10, 2006, www.whotv.com (accessed January 16, 2006). A new defense authorization bill increased funding for military recruiters, as enlistment dropped with increasing casualties in the war in Iraq, providing enhanced incentives such as down payments on houses for those enlisting in the army. Megan Scully, "Defense Bill Allows Military Recruiters to Offer New Incentives," December 20, 2005, www.govexec.com (accessed January 16, 2006).

21 See articles and debates in *Resistance Studies Magazine* (www.rsmag.org), the journal of the Resistance Studies Network (www.resistancestudies.org).

22 See Toufic El Rassi's graphic novel/autobiography, *Arab in America* (San Francisco: Last Gasp, 2007), for a thoughtful and also poignant reflection on these issues.

23 For example, the FBI's Community Relations Executive Seminar Training (CREST), a euphemistically named program for encouraging Muslim and Arab Americans to report on suspicions of terrorist plots, organized meetings with Pakistani and Sikh Americans as well as town meetings cosponsored by the Muslim Public Affairs Council, as noted in the Indian press. Arun Kumar, "FBI Reaches out to Muslim, Sikh Communities to Fight Global Terror," *Hindustan Times*, June 14, 2006, www.hindustantimes.com.

24 James Risen, "Bush Signs Law to Widen Reach for Wiretapping," *New York Times*, August 6, 2007, www.nytimes.com; Richard Schmitt, "FBI Abuses May Lead to Patriot Act Limits," *Los Angeles Times*, March 10, 2007, www.latimes.com; Doug Thompson, "White House Keeps Dossiers on More than 10,000 'Political Enemies,'" *Capitol Hill Blue*, November 8, 2005, www.capitolhillblue.com.

25 For example, see the essay about Shazia Mirza by Marshall Sella, "Did You Hear the One about the Suicide Bomber?" *New York Times Magazine*, June 15, 2003, 44–46.

26 See the press release for the show www.bapd.org; see also the flier at www.koshercomedy.com.

27 For example, among many other works, some that deserve mention are films such as *Lest We Forget* (directed by Jason DaSilva, 2003) and *Brothers and Others* (directed by Nicolas Rossier, 2002); plays such as *Jihad Jones and the Kalashnikov Babes* (by Yussef El Guindi, 2008) and *The Domestic Crusaders* (by Wajahat Ali, 2005); music by hip-hop artists such as Arab Summit, Iron Sheik, N.O.M.A.D.S., and The Philistines; spoken word poetry by artists such as Suheir Hammad and Shailja Patel; and novels such as *Arab in Amer-*

ica, by Toufic El Rassi (2007), *Ask Me No Questions*, by Marina Budhos (New York: Atheneum Books, 2006), and *Once in a Promised Land*, by Laila Halaby (Boston: Beacon Press, 2007).

Six   Missing: Fear, Complicity, and Solidarity

1 See also documentary films such as *Brothers and Others* (directed by Nicolas Rossier, 2002), and *Whose Children are These?* (directed by Theresa Thanjan, 2004).

2 Mary Beth Sheridan, "Backlash Changes Form, Not Function," *Washington Post*, March 4, 2002, www.washingtonpost.com.

3 Deepti Hajela, "After 9/11, Issues of Race Crystallize," *Boston Globe*, September 22, 2002, A26.

4 For example, the Supreme Court refused to hear a Freedom of Information Act suit challenging the government's secret detentions after 9/11 and asking it to release the names of the hundreds of Muslim, Arab, and South Asian immigrant detainees. U.S. attorney general John Ashcroft praised the court for seeing the "dangers of giving terrorists a virtual road map to our investigation," although not a single one of the men had been charged with terrorism. David Savage, "High Court Refuses to Take up Case of Sept. 11 Detainees," *Los Angeles Times*, January 13, 2004, A1, A14.

5 *The September 11 Detainees: A Review of the Treatment of Aliens Held on Immigration Charges in Connection with the Investigation of the September 11 Attacks*, report by Office of the Inspector General, Department of Justice, April, 2003, www.fas.org (accessed February 20, 2007). See also Camille T. Taiara, "American Payback," *San Francisco Bay Guardian*, May 26, 2004, 19.

6 Nina Bernstein, "Judge Rules That U.S. Has Broad Powers to Detain Non-Citizens Indefinitely," *New York Times*, June 15, 2006, www.nytimes.com; Richard Serrano, "9/11 Prisoner Abuse Suit Could Be Landmark," *Los Angeles Times*, November 20, 2006, www.latimes.com.

7 Demian Bulwa, "Muslims in Lodi Believe Mystery Man Who Spoke of Jihad Was a Federal Mole in Investigation," *San Francisco Chronicle*, August 27, 2005. Andrea Elliott, "As Police Watch for Terrorists, Brooklyn Muslims Feel the Eyes," *New York Times*, May 27, 2006, A1.

8 Chrisanne Beckner, "A Kinder, Gentler Surveillance," *Sacramento News and Review*, October 14, 2004.

Bibliography

Abbas, Tahir. 2005. "British South Asian Muslims: State and Multicultural Society." In *Muslim Britain: Communities under Pressure*, edited by Tahir Abbas, 3–17. London: Zed Books.

Abraham, Nabeel. 1994. "Anti-Arab Racism and Violence in the United States." In *The Development of Arab-American Identity*, edited by Ernest McCarus, 155–214. Ann Arbor: University of Michigan Press.

Abraham, Nabeel, and Andrew Shryock, eds. 2000. *Arab Detroit: From Margin to Mainstream*. Detroit: Wayne State University Press.

Abraham, Sameer. 1983. "Detroit's Arab-American Community." In *Arabs in the New World: Studies on Arab American Communities*, edited by Sameer Abraham and Nabeel Abraham, 85–108. Detroit: Wayne State University Center for Urban Studies.

AbuKhalil, As'ad. 2002. *Bin Laden, Islam, and America's New "War on Terrorism."* New York: Seven Stories Press.

Abu-Laban, Sharon M., and Baha Abu-Laban. 1999. "Teens Between: The Public and Private Spheres of Arab-Canadian Adolescents." In *Arabs in America: Building a New Future*, edited by Michael Suleiman, 113–28. Philadelphia: Temple University Press.

Abusharaf, Rogaia. 1998. "Structural Adaptations in an Immigrant Muslim Congregation in New York." In *Gatherings in the Diaspora: Religious Communities and the New Immigration*, edited by R. Stephen Warner and Judith G. Wittner, 235–61. Philadelphia: Temple University Press.

Agamben, Giorgio. 2005. *State of Exception*, translated by Kevin Attell. Chicago: University of Chicago Press.

Agarwal, Priya. 1991. *Passage From India: Post-1965 Indian Immigrants and Their Children: Conflicts, Concerns, and Solutions*. Palos Verdes, Calif.: Yuvati.

Agosin, Marjorie, and Betty J. Craige. 2002. *To Mend the World: Women Reflect on 9/11.* Buffalo: White Pine Press.

Ahmad, Aijaz. 2000. *Lineages of the Present: Ideology and Politics in Contemporary South Asia.* London: Verso.

———. 2004. *Iraq, Afghanistan, and the Imperialism of Our Time.* New Delhi: LeftWord Books.

Ahmad, Muneer. 2002. "Homeland Insecurities: Racial Violence the Day after September 11." *Social Text* 72:101–15.

Ahmed, Akbar. 2003. *Islam under Siege.* Cambridge: Polity Press.

Ahmed, Leila. 1992. *Women and Gender in Islam: Historical Roots of a Modern Debate.* New Haven: Yale University Press.

Ahmed, Nilufer, Gladis Kaufman, and Shamim Naim. 1996. "South Asian Families in the United States." In *Family and Gender among American Muslims: Issues Facing Middle Eastern Immigrants and Their Descendants*, edited by Barbara Bilgé and Barbara Aswad, 155–72. Philadelphia: Temple University Press.

Aidi, Hisham. 2007. "Jihadis in the Hood: Race, Urban Islam and the War on Terror." *Middle East Report* 224. Website of the Middle East Research and Information Project, www.merip.org (accessed January 4, 2007), printout in author's files.

Ajrouch, Kristine. 1999. "Family and Ethnic Identity in an Arab-American Community." In *Arabs in America: Building a New Future*, edited by Michael Suleiman, 129–39. Philadelphia: Temple University Press.

Ajrouch, Kristine J. 2004. "Gender, Race, and Symbolic Boundaries: Contested Spaces of Identity Among Arab American Adolescents." *Sociological Perspectives* 47(4): 371–91.

Akhtar, Parveen. "(Re)turn to Religion and Radical Islam." 2005. In *Muslim Britain: Communities under Pressure*, edited by Tahir Abbas, 164–76. London: Zed Books.

Akram, Susan. 2002. "Orientalism Revisited in Asylum and Refugee Claims." In *Moral Imperialism: A Critical Anthology*, edited by Berta Esperanza and Hernandez-Truyol, 61–77. New York: New York University Press.

Ali, Tariq. 2003. *Bush in Babylon: The Recolonisation of Iraq.* London: Verso.

Ali, Wajahat. 2005. *The Domestic Crusaders* (play).

Allison, Aimee, and David Solnit. 2007. *Army of None: Strategies to Counter Military Recruitment, End War, and Build a Better World.* New York: Seven Stories Press.

Alsultany, Evelyn. 2007. "Selling American Diversity and Muslim American Identity through Nonprofit Advertising Post-9/11." *American Quarterly* 59(3): 593–622.

Andreas, Peter. 2003. "A Tale of Two Borders: The U.S.-Canada and U.S.-Mexico Lines after 9–11." In *The Rebordering of North America: Integration and Exclusion in a New Security Context*, edited by Peter Andreas and Thomas J. Biersteker, 1–23. New York: Routledge.

Appadurai, Arjun. 1996. *Modernity at Large: Cultural Dimensions of Globalization*. Minneapolis: University of Minnesota Press.

Aronowitz, Stanley. 2003. "The New World Order." In *Debating Empire*, edited by Gopal Balakrishnan, 19–25. London: Verso.

Aronowitz, Stanley, and Heather Gautney. 2003. "The Debate about Globalization: An Introduction." In *Implicating Empire: Globalization and Resistance in the 21st Century World Order*, edited by Stanley Aronowitz and Heather Gautney, xi–xxx. New York: Basic Books.

Arrighi, Giovanni. 2003. "Lineages of Empire." In *Debating Empire*, edited by Gopal Balakrishnan, 29–42. London: Verso.

Asad, Talal. 2003. *Formations of the Secular: Christianity, Islam, and Modernity*. Stanford, Calif.: Stanford University Press.

Bacevich, Andrew. 2002. *American Empire: The Realities and Consequences of U.S. Diplomacy*. Cambridge, Mass.: Harvard University Press.

Bacon, Jean. 1996. *Lifelines: Community, Family, and Assimilation among Asian Indian Immigrants*. New York: Oxford University Press.

Balakrishnan, Gopal, ed. 2003. *Debating Empire*. London: Verso.

Barazangi, N. H. 1991. "Parents and Youth: Perceiving and Practicing Islam in North America." In *Muslim Families in North America*, edited by Earle Waugh, Sharon M. Abu-Laban, and Regula Qureshi, 132–47. Edmonton: University of Alberta Press.

Barkey, Karen, and Mark von Hagen, eds. 1997. *After Empire: Multiethnic Societies and Nation-Building—The Soviet Union and the Russian, Ottoman, and Habsburg Empires*. Boulder: Westview Press.

Barry, Tom. 2003. "How Things Have Changed." In *Power Trip: U.S. Unilateralism and Global Strategy After September 11*, edited by John Feffer, 28–38. New York: Seven Stories Press.

Barry, Tom, and Jim Lobe. 2003. "The People." In *Power Trip: U.S. Unilateralism and Global Strategy After September 11*, edited by John Feffer, 39–49. New York: Seven Stories Press.

Bascara, Victor. 2006. *Model-Minority Imperialism*. Minneapolis: University of Minnesota Press.

Basch, Linda, Nina Glick Schiller, and Cristina Szanton Blanc, eds. 1994. *Nations Unbound: Transnational Projects, Postcolonial Predicaments, and Deterritorialized Nation-States*. Amsterdam: Gordon and Breach.

Bayoumi, Moustafa. 2001/2002. "How Does It Feel to Be a Problem?" *Amerasia Journal* 27(3)/28(1): 69–77.

Beard, Charles A. 1940. *A Foreign Policy for America*. New York: A. A. Knopf.

Beinin, Joel. 2006. "The New McCarthyism: Policing Thought about the Middle East." In *Academic Freedom after September 11*, edited by Beshara Doumani, 237–66. New York: Zone Books.

Beit-Hallahmi, Benjamin. 1993. *Original Sins: Reflection on the History of Zionism and Israel*. New York: Olive Branch Press.

Bejarano, Cynthia L. 2005. ¿Qué Onda? Urban Youth Culture and Border Identity. Tucson: University of Arizona Press.

Benmayor, Rina, Rosa Torruellas, and Ana Juarbe. 1992. Responses to Poverty among Puerto Rican Women: Identity, Community, and Cultural Citizenship. New York: Centro de Estudios Puertorriqueños, Hunter College.

Benson, Kathleen, and Philip M. Kayal. 2002. A Community of Many Worlds: Arab Americans in New York City. New York: Museum of the City of New York.

Berlant, Lauren. 1997. The Queen of America Goes to Washington City: Essays on Sex and Citizenship. Durham, N.C.: Duke University Press.

Bernstein, Nina. 2005. "Questions, Bitterness and Exile for Queens Girl in Terror Case." New York Times, New York/Region, June 17.

Best, James. 2003. "Black like Me: John Walker Lindh's Hip-Hop Daze." East Bay Express, September 23, 13–23.

Bhavnani, Kum-Kum. 1991. Talking Politics: A Psychological Framing for Views from Youth in Britain Cambridge: Cambridge University Press.

Birt, Jonathan. 2005. "Lobbying and Marching: British Muslims and the State." In Muslim Britain: Communities under Pressure, edited by Tahir Abbas, 92–106. London: Zed Books.

Bobbio, Norberto. 1996. The Age of Rights. Cambridge: Polity Press.

Boggs, Carl. 2003. "Introduction: Empire and Globalization." In Masters of War: Militarism and Blowback in the Era of American Empire, edited by Carl Boggs, 1–16. New York: Routledge.

Bonus, Rick. 2000. "Of Palengkes and Beauty pageants: Filipino American-Style Politics in Southern California." In Cultural Compass: Ethnographic Explorations of Asian America, edited by Martin Manalansan IV, 67–84. Philadelphia: Temple University Press.

Bourdieu, Pierre. 1977. Outline of a Theory of Practice. Cambridge: Cambridge University Press.

Bowen, John. 2006. Why the French Don't Like Headscarves: Islam, the State, and Public Space. Princeton: Princeton University Press.

Brinkley, Alan. 2003. "A Familiar Story: Lessons from Past Assaults on Freedoms." In The War on Our Freedoms: Civil Liberties in an Age of Terrorism, 23–46. New York: Century Foundation, Public Affairs Reports.

Brothers and Others (documentary film). 2002. Directed by Nicolas Rossier. Baraka Productions (Arab Film Distribution).

Brown, Wendy. 2006. Regulating Aversion: Tolerance in the Age of Identity and Empire. Princeton: Princeton University Press.

Buckingham, David. 2000. The Making of Citizens: Young People, News, and Politics. London: Routledge.

Buck-Morss, Susan. 2003. Thinking Past Terror: Islamism and Critical Theory on the Left. London: Verso.

Budhos, Marina. 2006. Ask Me No Questions. New York: Atheneum Books.

Burbach, Roger, and Ben Clarke, eds. 2002. September 11 and the U.S. War: Beyond the Curtain of Smoke. San Francisco: City Lights.

Burbach, Roger, and Jim Tarbell. 2004. *Imperial Overstretch: George W. Bush and the Hubris of Empire*. London: Zed.

Cainkar, Louise. 2002. "No Longer Invisible: Arab and Muslim Exclusion after September 11." *Middle East Report* 224 (fall). Middle East Report Online—Web site of the Middle East Research and Information Project, www.merip .org (accessed January 19, 2004; printout in author's files).

———. 2004. "Post 9/11 Domestic Policies Affecting U.S. Arabs and Muslims: A Brief Review." *Comparative Studies of South Asia, Africa, and the Middle East* 24(1): 245–48.

Cainkar, Louise, and Sunaina Maira. 2006. "Crossing the Boundaries of Asian And Arab American Studies: Criminalization and Cultural Citizenship of Arab / Muslim / South Asian Americans." *Amerasia Journal* 31(3): 1–27.

Canclini, Néstor García. 2001. *Consumers and Citizens: Globalization and Multicultural Conflicts* Minneapolis: University of Minnesota Press.

Caplan, Pat. 2003. "Introduction: Anthropology and ethics." In *The Ethics of Anthropology: Debates and Dilemmas*, edited by Pat Caplan, 1–33. London: Routledge.

Chan, Sucheng. 1991. *Asian Americans: An Interpretive History*. New York: Twayne.

Chang, Nancy. 2002. *Silencing Political Dissent: How Post–September 11 Anti-Terrorism Measures Threaten Our Civil Liberties*. New York: Seven Stories.

Chari, Sharad. 2006. "Son of Bush or Son of God: Politics and the Religious Subaltern in the United States, from Elsewhere." *South Atlantic Quarterly* 105(1): 37–54.

Chiang-Hom, Christy. 2004. "Transnational Cultural Practices of Chinese Immigrant Youth and Parachute Kids." In *Asian American Youth: Culture, Identity, and Ethnicity*, edited by Jennifer Lee and Min Zhou, 143–58. New York: Routledge.

Church, Kenneth. 2002. "Jihad." In *Collateral Language: A User's Guide to America's New War*, ed. John Collins and Ross Glover, 109–24. New York: New York University Press.

Churchill, Ward. 1998. *Pacifism as Pathology*. Winnipeg: Arbeiter Ring.

———. 2003. *On the Justice of Roosting Chickens*. Oakland, Calif.: AK Press.

Clarke, John, et al., eds. 1976. Subcultures, Cultures, and Class. In *Resistance through Rituals: Youth Subcultures in Post-war Britain*, edited by Stuart Hall and Tony Jefferson, 9–79. London: Hutchinson.

Clifford, James. 1997. "Diasporas." In *The Ethnicity Reader: Nationalism, Multiculturalism, and Migration*, edited by Montserrat Guibernau and John Rex, 283–90. Cambridge: Polity Press.

———. 1998. "Mixed Feelings." In *Cosmopolitics: Thinking and Feeling beyond the Nation*, edited by Pheng Cheah and Bruce Robbins, 362–70. Minneapolis: University of Minnesota.

Clifford, James, and George Marcus. 1986. *Writing Culture: The Poetics and Politics of Ethnography*. Berkeley: University of California Press.

Cohen, Lizabeth. 2003. *A Consumer's Republic: The Politics of Mass Consumption in Postwar America*. New York: Knopf.

Cohen, Stanley. 1997. "Symbols of Trouble." In *The Subcultures Reader*, edited by Ken Gelder and Sarah Thornton, 149–62. London: Routledge.

Cole, Alyson M. 2007. *The Cult of True Victimhood: From the War on Welfare to the War on Terror*. Stanford, Calif.: Stanford University Press.

Cole, David. 2003. *Enemy Aliens: Double Standards and Constitutional Freedoms in the War on Terrorism*. New York: New Press.

Cole, David, and James Dempsey. 2002. *Terrorism and the Constitution: Sacrificing Civil Liberties in the Name of National Security*. New York: New Press.

Cole, Jennifer, and Deborah Durham. 2007. "Introduction: Age, Regeneration, and the Intimate Politics of Globalization." In *Generations and Globalization: Youth, Age, and Family in the New World Economy*, edited by Jennifer Cole and Deborah Durham, 1–28. Bloomington: Indiana University Press.

Coll, Kathleen. 2002. "Problemas y necesidades: Latina Vernaculars of Citizenship and Coalition-Building in Chinatown, San Francisco." Paper presented at the conference "Racial (Trans)Formations: Latinos and Asians Remaking the United States," Center for the Study of Ethnicity and Race, Columbia University, March.

Comaroff, Jean, and John Comaroff. 2001. "Millennial Capitalism: First Thoughts on a Second Coming." In *Millennial Capitalism and the Culture of Neoliberalism*, edited by Jean and John L. Comaroff, 1–56. Durham, N.C.: Duke University Press.

Comaroff, Joshua. 2007. "Terror and Territory: Guantánamo and the Space of Contradiction." *Public Culture* 19(2): 381–405.

Cooper, Christine M. 2007. "Worrying about Vaginas: Feminism and Eve Ensler's The Vagina Monologues." *Signs: Journal of Women in Culture and Society* 32(31): 727–58.

Cooper, Fred. 2004. "Empire Multiplied: A Review Essay." *Comparative Study of Society and History* 46(2): 247–72.

Dabashi, Hamid. 2006. "Native Informers and the Making of the American Empire." Website of Al-Ahram Weekly, www.weekly.ahram.org.eg (accessed November 16, 2006).

Daniels, Roger. 1989. *History of Indian Immigration to the United States: An Interpretive Essay*. New York: The Asia Society.

Dasgupta, Shamita, and Sayantani Das Dasgupta. 1996. "Women in Exile: Gender Relations in the Asian Indian community." In *Contours of the Heart: South Asians Map North America*, edited by Sunaina Maira and Rajini Srikanth, 381–400. New York: Asian American Writers' Workshop.

Davidson, Lawrence. 1999. "Debating Palestine: Arab-American Challenges to Zionism, 1917–1932." In *Arabs in America: Building a New Future*, edited by Michael W. Suleiman, 227–40. Philadelphia: Temple University Press.

Davis, Angela Y. 2005. *Abolition Democracy: Beyond Empire, Prisons, and Torture.* New York: Seven Stories Press.

De Genova, Nicholas P. 2002. "Migrant 'Illegality' and Deportability in Everyday Life." *Annual Review of Anthropology* 31:419–47.

Delgado, Richard. 2003. *Justice at War: Civil Liberties and Civil Rights during Times of Crisis.* New York: New York University Press.

Desai, Jigna. 2004. *Beyond Bollywood: The Cultural Politics of South Asian Diasporic Film.* New York: Routledge.

DeYoung, Karen. 2007. "Distrust Hinders FBI in Outreach to Muslims." *Washington Post*, February 8, A01.

Diouf, Mamadou. 1999. "Urban Youth and Senegalese Politics: Dakar 1988–1994." In *Cities and Citizenship*, edited by James Holston, 42–66. Durham, N.C.: Duke University Press.

Doolittle, Douglas. 2002. *American Orientalism: The United States and the Middle East since 1945.* Chapel Hill: University of North Carolina Press.

Doumani, Beshara. 2006. "Between Coercion and Privatization: Academic Freedom in the Twenty-First Century." In Academic Freedom after September 11, edited by Beshara Doumani, 11–57. New York: Zone Books.

Dow, Mark. 2004. *American Gulag: Inside U.S. Immigration Prisons.* Berkeley: University of California Press.

Dubal, Veena, and Sunaina Maira. 2005. "The FBI 'Witch-Hunt' in Lodi." *India Currents*, August 2. Website of *India Currents*, www.indiacurrents.com (accessed March 30, 2006).

Dunbar-Ortiz, Roxanne. 2004. "The Grid of History: Cowboys and Indians." In *Pox Americana: Exposing the American Empire*, edited by John B. Foster and Robert W. McChesney, 31–40. New York: Monthly Review Press.

Eisenlohr, Charlene J. 1996. "Adolescent Arab Girls in an American High School." In *Family and Gender among American Muslims*, edited by Barbara Bilgé and Barbara Aswad, 250–70. Philadelphia: Temple University Press.

Eland, Ivan. 2004. *The Empire Has No Clothes: U.S. Foreign Policy Exposed.* Oakland, Calif.: Independent Institute.

El Guindi, Yussef. 2008. *Jihad Jones and the Kalashnikov Babes* (play).

Elliott, David. 2007. "Parallel Wars? Can 'Lessons of Vietnam' be Applied to Iraq?" In *Iraq and the Lessons of Vietnam: Or, How Not to Learn from the Past*, edited by Lloyd C. Gardner and Marilyn B. Young, 17–44. New York: New Press.

El Rassi, Toufic. *Arab in America.* San Francisco: Last Gasp.

Erikson, Erik H. 1994 [1968]. *Identity: Youth and Crisis.* New York: W. W. Norton.

Faith, Karlene. 2000. "Reflections on Inside/Out Organizing." In *Critical Resistance to the Prison-Industrial Complex*, special issue of *Social Justice* 27(3): 158–67.

Falk, Richard. 2004. "Citizenship and Globalism: Markets, Empire, and Terror." In *People Out of Place: Globalization, Human Rights, and the Citizenship Gap*, edited by Alison Brysk and Gershon Shafir, 177–89. New York: Routledge.

Feffer, John, ed. 2003. *Power Trip: U.S. Unilateralism and Global Strategy after September 11*. New York: Seven Stories.

Fenton, John Y. 1988. *Transplanting Religious Traditions: Asian Indians in America*. New York: Praeger.

Ferguson, Niall. 2002. *Empire: The Rise and Demise of the British World Order and the Lessons for Global Power*. London: New England.

——— 2003. "The Empire Slinks Back: Why Americans Don't Really Have What It Takes to Rule the World," *New York Times Magazine*, April 27, 2003, 52–57.

——— 2004. *Colossus: The Rise and Fall of the American Empire*. New York: Penguin.

Fernandes, Deepa. 2007. *Targeted: Homeland Security and the Business of Immigration*. New York: Seven Stories Press.

Fields, Alison. n.d. "The Youth Challenge: Participating in Democracy." Carnegie Corporation of New York website, www.carnegie.org (accessed September 2005).

Finnegan, William. 2003. "The Economics of Empire." *Harper's Magazine* (May), 41–54.

Flores, William V., and Rina Benmayor, eds. 1997. *Latino Cultural Citizenship: Claiming Identity, Space, and Rights*. Boston: Beacon Press.

Foley, Douglas E. 1994. *Learning Capitalist Culture: Deep in the Heart of Tejas*. Philadelphia: University of Pennsylvania Press.

France, Alan. 1998. "'Why Should We Care?': Young People, Citizenship and Questions of Social Responsibility." *Journal of Youth Studies* 1(1): 97–111.

Fraser, Nancy. 1997. *Justice Interruptus: Critical Reflections on the Postsocialist Condition*. New York: Routledge.

Freedman, Jane, and Carrie Tarr. "Introduction." In *Women, Immigration, and Identities in France*, edited by Jane Freedman and Carrie Tarr, 1–12. Oxford: Berg, 2000.

Frith, Simon. 1997. "Formalism, Realism, and Leisure: The Case of Punk." In *The Subcultures Reader*, edited by Ken Gelder and Sarah Thornton, 163–74. London: Routledge.

Ganguly, Keya. 2001. *States of Exception: Everyday Life and Postcolonial Identity*. Minneapolis: University of Minnesota Press.

Gardner, Lloyd C., and Marilyn B. Young, eds. 2007. *Iraq and the Lessons of Vietnam: Or, How Not to Learn from the Past*. New York: New Press.

Garofalo, Reebee. 2007. "Pop Goes to War: U.S. Popular Music After 9/11." In *Music in the Post-9/11 World*, edited by Jonathan Ritter and J. Martin Daughtry, 3–26. New York: Routledge.

Gelder, Ken, and Sarah Thornton, eds. 1997. *The Subcultures Reader*. New York: Routledge.

Ghayur, A. 1981. Pakistani Immigrants in the United States: A Socio-demographic Study. *Pakistan Studies* 1(1): 3–23.

Gibson-Graham, J. K., Stephen A. Resnick, and Richard D. Wolff. 2000. "Class in a Poststructuralist Frame." In *Class and Its Others*, edited by J. K. Gibson-Graham, Stephen A. Resnick, and Richard D. Wolff, 1–22. Minneapolis: University of Minnesota Press.

Gilroy, Paul. 2005. *Postcolonial Melancholia*. New York: Columbia University Press.

Glick Schiller, Nina, and Georges Fouron. 2001. *Georges Woke up Laughing: Long-Distance Nationalism and the Search for Home*. Durham, N.C.: Duke University Press.

Goldberg, David Theo. 2002. *The Racial State*. Malden, Mass.: Blackwell.

Grandin, Greg. 2004. "The Narcissism of Violent Differences." In *Anti-Americanism*, edited by Andrew Ross and Kristin Ross, 17–31. New York: New York University Press.

Green, Jordan. 2003. "Silencing Dissent." *ColorLines* 6(2): 17–20.

Grewal, Inderpal. 2005. *Transnational America: Feminisms, Diasporas, Neoliberalisms*. Durham, N.C.: Duke University Press.

Gupta, Sangeeta, ed. 1999. *Emerging Voices: South Asian American Women Redefine Self, Family, and Community*. New Delhi: Sage.

Haddad, Yvonne Y. 1994. "Maintaining the Faith of the Fathers: Dilemmas of Religious Identities in the Christian and Muslim Arab-American Communities." In *The Development of Arab-American Identity*, edited by Ernest McCarus, 61–84. Ann Arbor: University of Michigan Press.

———. "Make Room for the Muslims?" In *Religious Diversity and American Religious History*, edited by W. H. Conser Jr. and S. B. Twiss. Athens: University of Georgia Press.

Haddad, Yvonne Y., and Jane I. Smith. 1993. "The Ahmadiyya Community of North America." In *Mission to America: Five Islamic Sectarian Communities in North America*, 49–78. Gainesville: University Press of Florida.

———. 1996. "Islamic Values among American Muslims." In *Family and Gender among American Muslims: Issues Facing Middle Eastern Immigrants and Their Descendants*, edited by Barbara Bilgé and Barbara Aswad, 19–40. Philadelphia: Temple University Press.

Halaby, Laila. 2007. *Once in a Promised Land*. Boston: Beacon Press.

Hall, Stuart. 1997. "The Local and the Global: Globalization and Ethnicity." In *Dangerous Liaisons: Gender, Nation, and Postcolonial Perspectives*, edited by Anne McClintock, Aamir Mufti, and Ella Shohat, 173–87. Minneapolis: University of Minnesota Press.

Hall, Stuart, and Tony Jefferson, eds. 1976. *Resistance through Rituals: Youth Subcultures in Post-war Britain*. London: Hutchinson.

Hammer, Rhonda. 2003. "Militarism and Family Terrorism." In *Masters of War: Militarism and Blowback in the Era of American Empire*, edited by Carl Boggs, 293–309. New York: Routledge.

Hanassah, Shideh. 1993. "Caught between Two Cultures: Young Iranian Women in Los Angeles." In *Irangeles: Iranians in Los Angeles*, edited by Ron Kelley, 223–29. Berkeley: University of California Press.

Hansen, Thomas B., and Finn Steputat. 2001. "Introduction: States of Imagination." In *States of Imagination: Ethnographic Explorations of the Postcolonial State*, edited by Thomas B. Hansen and Finn Steputat, 1–38. Durham, N.C.: Duke University Press.

———. 2005. "Introduction." In *Sovereign Bodies: Citizens, Migrants, and States in the Postcolonial World*, edited by Thomas B. Hansen and Finn Steputat, 1–36. Princeton: Princeton University Press.

Hardt, Michael, and Antonio Negri. 2000. *Empire*. Cambridge, Mass.: Harvard University Press.

———. 2004. *Multitude: War and Democracy in the Age of Empire*. New York: Penguin.

Harvey, David. 2003. *The New Imperialism*. Oxford: Oxford University Press.

———. 2005. *A Brief History of Neoliberalism*. Oxford: Oxford University Press.

Hasan, Asma G. 2000. *American Muslims: The New Generation*. New York: Continuum.

Helweg, Arthur, and Usha Helweg. 1990. *An Immigrant Success Story: East Indians in America*. Philadelphia: University of Pennsylvania Press.

Hernández-Truyol, Berta E., ed. 2002. *Moral Imperialism: A Critical Anthology*. New York: New York University Press.

Hess, Gary. 1976. "The Forgotten Asian American: The East Indian Community in the United States," in *The Asian American: The Historical Experience*, edited by Norman Hundley Jr. Santa Barbara, Calif.: Clio Books.

Hindess, Barry. 2005. "Citizenship and Empire." In *Sovereign Bodies: Citizens, Migrants, and States in the Postcolonial World*, edited by Thomas B. Hansen and Finn Steputat, 241–56. Princeton: Princeton University Press.

Hing, Bill O. 1993. *Making and Remaking Asian America through Immigration Policy, 1850–1990*. Stanford, Calif.: Stanford University Press.

———. 2000. "No Place for Angels: In Reaction to Kevin Johnson." *University of Illinois Law Review* 2:559–601.

———. 2001. "The Dark Side of Operation Gatekeeper." uc *Davis Journal of International Law and Policy* 7(2): 123–67

———. 2002. "Vigilante Racism: The De-Americanization of Immigrant America." *Michigan Journal of Race and Law* 7(2): 441–56.

———. 2004. *Defining America Through Immigration Policy*. Philadelphia: Temple University Press.

———. 2005. "Detention to Deportation: Rethinking the Removal of Cambodian Refugees." *U.C. Davis Law Review* 38(3): 891–971.

Hitchens, Christopher. 2004 [1990]. *Blood, Class, and Empire: The Enduring Anglo-American Relationship*. New York: Nation Books.

Ho, Enseng. 2004. "Empire through Diasporic Eyes: A View from the Other Boat." *Comparative Studies of Society and History* 46(2): 210–46.

Hobson, Barbara. 2000. "Introduction." In *Gender and Citizenship in Transition*, edited by Barbara Hobson, 293–309. New York: Routledge.

Holston, James, and Arjun Appadurai. 1999. "Introduction: Cities and Citizenship." In *Cities and Citizenship*, edited by James Holston, 1–18. Durham, N.C.: Duke University Press.

Hossain, Mohammed. 1982. South Asians in Southern California: A Sociological Study of Immigrants from India, Pakistan, and Bangladesh. *South Asia Bulletin* 2(1): 74–83.

Howell, Sally, and Andrew Shryock. 2003. "Cracking Down on Diaspora: Arab Detroit and America's 'War on Terror.'" *Anthropological Quarterly* 76(3): 443–62.

Huntington, Samuel P. 1996. *The Clash of Civilizations and the Remaking of World Order*. New York: Simon and Schuster.

Hutnyk, John. 2000. In *The Right to Difference is a Fundamental Human Right*. Stephen Corry and Iris Jean-Klein vs. Richard Wilson and John Hutnyk, edited by Peter Wade, 40–52. GDAT debate no. 10. Manchester: Group for Debates in Anthropological Theory, University of Manchester.

Ibish, Hussein. 2002. "The War on Terrorism: Arab Americans, South Asian Americans, and Civil Liberties." Public lecture sponsored by Asian American Studies Speaker Series, University of Massachusetts, Amherst, April 25.

Ignatieff, Michael. 2003. "The Burden." *New York Times Magazine*, January 5, 2003.

Ileto, Reynaldo. 2005. "Philippine Wars and the Politics of Memory." *positions* 13(1): 215–34.

Isin, Engin. 2000. "Introduction: Democracy, Citizenship and the City." In *Democracy, Citizenship and the Global City*, edited by Engin Isin, 1–21. London: Routledge.

Jacobson, Jessica. 1998. *Islam in Transition: Religion and Identity among British Pakistani Youth*. London: Routledge.

Jain, Usha. R. 1989. *The Gujaratis of San Francisco*. New York: AMS.

Jensen, Joan. 1988. *Passage from India: Asian Indian Immigrants in North America*. New Haven: Yale University Press.

Johnson, Chalmers. 2004. *The Sorrows of Empire: Militarism, Secrecy, and the End of the Republic*. New York: Metropolitan Books (Henry Holt).

Jones, Gill, and Claire Wallace. 1992. *Youth, Family, and Citizenship*. Buckingham: Open University Press.

Joseph, Ammu, and Kalpana Sharma. 2003. *Terror, Counter-Terror: Women Speak Out*. New Delhi: Kali for Women.

Joseph, Suad. 1999. "Against the Grain of the Nation: The Arab." In *Arabs in America: Building a New Future*, edited by Michael Suleiman, 257–71. Philadelphia: Temple University Press.

Joxe, Alain. 2002. *Empire of Disorder*. Los Angeles: Semiotext(e).

Kaplan, Amy. 1993. "Left Alone with America": The Absence of Empire in the Study of American Culture." In *Cultures of United States Imperialism*, edited by Amy Kaplan and Donald Pease, 3–21. Durham, N.C.: Duke University Press.

———. 2002. *The Anarchy of Empire in the Making*. Cambridge, Mass.: Harvard University Press.

———. 2005. "Where Is Guantánamo?" *Legal Borderlands: Law and the Construction of American Borders*, edited by Mary Dudziak and Leti Volpp, special issue of *American Quarterly* 57(3): 831–58.

Kaplan, Amy, and Donald Pease, eds. 1993. *Cultures of United States Imperialism*. Durham, N.C.: Duke University Press.

Kaplan, Caren. 2006. "Precision Targets: GPS and the Militarization of U.S. Consumer Identity." *American Quarterly* 58(3): 693–713.

Kaufman, Gladis, and Shamim Naim. 1996. "An International Family: A Case Study from South Asia." In *Family and Gender among American Muslims: Issues Facing Middle Eastern Immigrants and Their Descendants*, edited by Barbara Bilgé and Barbara Aswad, 173–78. Philadelphia: Temple University Press.

Kelley, Robin D. 1999. "People in Me." *ColorLines* 1(3): 5–7.

Kim, Jee, et al., eds. 2002. *Another World is Possible: Conversations in a Time of Terror*, 2nd ed. New Orleans: Subway and Elevated Press.

Knight, Michael Muhammad. 2006. *Blue-Eyed Devil: A Road Odyssey through Islamic America*. Brooklyn: Autonomedia.

Koshy, Ninan. 2003. *The War on Terror: Reordering the World*. New Delhi: LeftWord Books.

Kumar, Amitava. 2000. "Foreword: In Class." In *Class and Its Others*, edited by J. K. Gibson-Graham, Stephen A. Resnick, and Richard D. Wolff, vii–xii. Minneapolis: University of Minnesota Press.

Kurien, Prema. 2003. "To Be or Not to Be South Asian: Contemporary Indian American Politics." *Journal of Asian American Studies* 6(3): 261–88.

Kymlicka, Will. 1995. *Multicultural Citizenship: A Liberal Theory of Minority Rights*. Oxford: Oxford University Press.

Laffey, Mark, and Jutta Weldes. 2004. "Representing the International: Sovereignty after Modernity?" In *Empire's New Clothes: Reading Hardt and Negri*, edited by Paul Passavant and Jodi Dean. New York: Routledge.

Lamb, Sarah. 2007. "Aging across Worlds: Modern Seniors in an Indian Diaspora." In *Generations and Globalization: Youth, Age, and Family in the New World Economy*, edited by Jennifer Cole and Deborah Durham, 133–63. Bloomington: Indiana University Press.

Lazreg, Marnia. 2008. *Torture and the Twilight of Empire: From Algiers to Baghdad*. Princeton: Princeton University Press.

Leonard, Karen I. 1992. *Making Ethnic Choices: California's Punjabi Mexican Americans*. Philadelphia: Temple University Press.

———. 1997. *The South Asian Americans*. Westport, Conn.: Greenwood Press.

———. 2003. *Muslims in the United States: The State of Research*. New York: Russell Sage Foundation.

Leone, Richard, and Greg Anrig Jr., eds. 2003. *The War on our Freedoms: Civil Liberties in an Age of Terrorism*. New York: Century Foundation.

Lessinger, Joan. 1995. *From the Ganges to the Hudson: Indian Immigrants in New York City*. Boston: Allyn and Bacon.

Lest We Forget (documentary film). 2003. Directed by Jason DaSilva. In Face Films.

Lewis, Theodore, et al. 1998. The Transition from School to Work: An Examination of the Literature. *Youth and Society* 29(3): 259–92.

Lincoln, Bruce. 2003. *Holy Terrors: Thinking about Religion after September 11*. Chicago: University of Chicago Press.

Lipsitz, George. 2001. *American Studies in a Moment of Danger*. Minneapolis: University of Minnesota Press.

Little, Douglas. 2002. *American Orientalism: The United States and the Middle East since 1945*. Chapel Hill: University of North Carolina Press.

Lopiano-Misdom, Janine, and Joanne De Luca. 1997. *Street Trends: How Today's Alternative Youth Cultures Are Creating Tomorrow's Markets*. New York: Harper-Business (HarperCollins).

Lovato, Roberto. 2006. "Cruising on Military Drive: 'Good' Latinos and 'Bad' Latinos in the Age of Homeland Security and Global War." *Public Eye Magazine* 20(3) (fall). Website of *Public Eye Magazine*, www.publiceye.org (accessed September 9, 2007; printout in author's files).

Lutz, Catherine. 2006. "Making War at Home in the United States: Militarization and the Current Crisis." In *The Anthropology of the State: A Reader*, edited by Aradhana Sharma and Akhil Gupta, 291–307. Malden, Mass.: Blackwell.

MacCabe, Colin, et al. 2006. "Multiculturalism after 7/7": A CQ Seminar." Roundtable convened by Colin MacCabe, with Monica Ali et al. *Critical Quarterly* 48(2): 1–44.

MacMaster, Neil. 2003. "Islamophobia in France and the 'Algerian Problem.'" In *The New Crusades: Constructing the Muslim Enemy*, edited by Emran Qureishi and Michael A. Sells, 288–313. New York: Columbia University Press.

Magdoff, Harry. 2003. *Imperialism without Colonies*. New York: Monthly Review Press.

Mahajan, Rahul. 2002. *The New Crusade: America's War on Terrorism*. New York: Monthly Review Press.

———. 2003. *Full Spectrum Dominance: U.S. Power in Iraq and Beyond*. New York: Seven Stories Press.

Mailer, Norman. 2003. *Why Are We at War?* New York: Random House.

Maira, Sunaina. 2000. "Henna and Hip Hop: The Politics of Cultural Production and the Work of Cultural Studies." *Journal of Asian American Studies* 3(3): 329–69.

———. 2002a. *Desis in the House: Indian American Youth Culture in New York City*. Philadelphia: Temple University Press.

————. 2002b. "Temporary Tattoos: Indo-Chic Fantasies and Late Capitalist Orientalism." *Meridians: Feminism, Race, Transnationalism* 3(1): 134–60.

————. 2004. "Imperial Feelings: Youth Culture, Citizenship, and Globalization." In *Globalization: Culture and Education in the New Millennium*, edited by Marcelo Suárez-Orozco and Desirée B. Qin-Hilliard, 203–34. Berkeley: University of California Press.

————. 2007. "Deporting Radicals, Deporting La Migra: The Hayat Case in Lodi." *Cultural Dynamics* 19(1): 39–66.

Maira, Sunaina, and Peggy Levitt. 1997. "Variations on Transnationalism: Preliminary Lessons from Gujarati Immigrant Experiences in Massachusetts." Paper presented at the symposium "Globalization and South Asia," 26th Annual Conference on South Asia, University of Wisconsin, Madison, November.

Maira, Sunaina, and Magid Shihade. 2006. "Meeting Asian/Arab American Studies." *Journal of Asian American Studies* 9(2): ix–xiii, 117–40.

Maira, Sunaina, and Elisabeth Soep, eds. 2005. "Introduction." In *Youthscapes: The Popular, the National, the Global*, 15–35. Philadelphia: Temple University Press.

Mamdani, Mahmood. 2004. *Good Muslim, Bad Muslim: America, the Cold War, and the Roots of Terror*. New York: Pantheon.

Manji, Irshad. 2003. *The Trouble with Islam Today: A Muslim's Call for Reform in Her Faith*. New York: St. Martin's Griffin.

Mankekar, Purnima. 1999. *Screening Culture, Viewing Politics: An Ethnography of Television, Womanhood, and Nation in Postcolonial India*. Durham, N.C.: Duke University Press.

Mariscal, Jorge. 2005. "Homeland Security, Militarism, and the Future of Latinos and Latinas in the United State." *Radical History Review* 93:39–52.

Marshall, T. H. 1950. *Citizenship and Social Class*. Cambridge: Cambridge University Press.

Marshy, Mona. 1994. "'Offensive' Art by Palestinian Children." In *Food for Our Grandmothers: Writings by Arab-American and Arab-Canadian Feminists*, edited by Joanne Kadi, 120–24. Boston: South End Press.

Martin, Randy, and Toby Miller. 1999. "Fielding Sport: A Preface to Politics." In *SportCult*, edited by Randy Martin and Toby Miller, 1–13. Minneapolis: University of Minnesota Press.

Marvasti, Amir, and Karyn McKinney. 2004. *Middle Eastern Lives in America*. Lanham, Md.: Rowman and Littlefield.

Mattson, Ingrid. 2003. "How Muslims Use Islamic Paradigms to Define America." In *Religion and Immigration: Christian, Jewish, and Muslim Experiences in the United States*, edited by Yvonne Haddad, Jane Smith, and John Esposito. 19–215. Walnut Creek, Calif.: AltaMira.

McAllister, Melani. 2001. *Epic Encounters: Culture, Media, and U.S. Interests in the Middle East, 1945–2000*. Berkeley: University of California Press.

McCarthy, Timothy P., and John McMillian, eds. 2003. *The Radical Reader: A Documentary History of the American Radical Tradition*. New York: New Press.

McKechnie, Jim, and Sandy Hobbs. 2002. "Work by the Young: The Economic Activity of School-Aged Children." In *Youth in Cities: A Cross-National Perspective*, edited by Marta Tienda and William J. Wilson, 217–45. New York: Cambridge University Press.

McRobbie, Angela. 1994. "New Times in Cultural Studies." In *Postmodernism and Popular Culture*, 24–43. London: Routledge.

Mehta, Uday S. 1999. *Liberalism and Empire: A Study in Nineteenth-Century British Liberal Thought*. Chicago: University of Chicago Press.

Menon, Sridevi. 2006. "Where Is West Asia in Asian America? 'Asia' and the Politics of Space in Asian America." *Social Text* 24: 55–79.

Mernissi, Fatima. 1991. *The Veil and the Male Elite: A Feminist Interpretation of Women's Rights in Islam*. Reading, Mass.: Addison-Wesley.

Merry, Robert W. 2005. *Sands of Empire: Missionary Zeal, American Foreign Policy, and the Hazards of Global Ambition*. New York: Simon & Schuster.

Miller, Toby. 1993. *The Well-Tempered Subject: Citizenship, Culture, and the Postmodern Subject*. Baltimore: Johns Hopkins University Press.

———. 1999. "Competing Allegories." In *SportCult*, edited by Randy Martin and Toby Miller, 14–38. Minneapolis: University of Minnesota Press.

Misir, Deborah. 1996. "The Murder of Navroze Mody: Race, Violence, and the Search for Order." *Amerasia* 22(2): 55–75.

Missing (feature film). 1982. Directed by Constantin Costa-Gravas. Universal Studios.

Mitchell, Timothy. 2006. "Society, Economy, and the State Effect." In *The Anthropology of the State: A Reader*, edited by Aradhana Sharma and Akhil Gupta, 169–86. Malden, Mass.: Blackwell.

Mizen, Philip. 2002. "Putting the Politics Back into Youth Studies: Keynesianism, Monetarism, and the Changing State of Youth." *Journal of Youth Studies* 5(1): 5–20.

Moallem, Minoo. 1999. "Transnationalism, Feminism, and Fundamentalism." In *Between Woman and Nation: Nationalisms, Transnational Feminisms, and the State*, edited by Caren Kaplan, Norma Alarcón, and Minoo Moallem, 320–48. Durham, N.C.: Duke University Press.

———. 2005. "Am I a Muslim Woman? Nationalist Reactions and Postcolonial Transgressions." In *Shattering the Stereotypes: Muslim Women Speak Out*, edited by Fawzia Afzal-Khan, 51–55. Northampton, Mass.: Olive Branch Press (Interlink Publishing).

Modood, Tariq. 2002. "The Place of Muslims in British Secular Multiculturalism." In *Muslim Europe or Euro-Islam: Politics, Culture, and Citizenship in the Age of Globalization*, edited by Nezar AlSayyad and Manuel Castells, 113–30. Lanham, Md.: Lexington Books.

―――. 2006. "British Muslims and the Politics of Multiculturalism." In *Multiculturalism, Muslims and Citizenship*, edited by Tariq Modood, Anna Triandafyllidou, and Richard Zapata-Barrero, 37–56. London: Routledge.

Moore, Kathleen. 1999. "A Closer Look at Anti-terrorism Law: American Arab Anti-Discrimination Committee v. Reno and the Construction of Aliens' Rights." In *Arabs in America: Building a New Future*, edited by Michael Suleiman, 84–99. Philadelphia: Temple University Press.

Murray, Nancy. 2004. "Profiled: Arabs, Muslims, and the Post-9/11 Hunt for the 'Enemy Within.'" In *Civil Rights in Peril: The Targeting of Arabs and Muslims*, edited by Elaine C. Hagopian, 27–68. Chicago: Haymarket Books.

Naber, Nadine. 2002. "So Our History Doesn't Become Your Future: The Local and Global Politics of Coalition Building Post September 11th." *Journal of Asian American Studies* 5(3): 217–42.

Nader, Laura. 1989. "Orientalism, Occidentalism and the Control of Women." *Cultural Dynamics* 11(3): 323–35.

Newman, Katherine S. 1999. *No Shame in My Game: The Working Poor in the Inner City*. New York: Alfred A. Knopf.

Nguyen, Tram. 2005. *We Are All Suspects Now: Untold Stories from Immigrant Communities After 9/11*. Boston: Beacon Press.

Nomani, Asra. 2005. *Standing Alone: An American Woman's Struggle for the Soul of Islam*. New York: HarperSanFrancisco (HarperCollins).

Nussbaum, Martha C. 2002. "Patriotism and Cosmopolitanism." In *For Love of Country*, edited by Martha Nussbaum and Joshua Cohen, 3–17. Boston: Beacon Press.

Nussbaum, Martha C., and Joshua Cohen, eds. 2002. *For Love of Country*. Boston: Beacon Press.

Odom, William, and Robert Dujarric. 2004. *America's Inadvertent Empire*. New Haven: Yale University Press.

Okihiro, Gary Y. 1994. *Margins and Mainstreams: Asians in American History and Culture*. Seattle: University of Washington Press.

Ong, Aihwa. 1996. "Cultural Citizenship as Subject-Making: Immigrants Negotiate Racial and Cultural Boundaries in the United States." *Current Anthropology* 37(5): 737–62.

―――. 1999. *Flexible Citizenship: The Cultural Logics of Transnationality*. Durham, N.C.: Duke University Press.

―――. 2003. *Buddha is Hiding: Refugees, Citizenship, the New America*. Berkeley: University of California Press.

―――. 2005. "Splintering Cosmopolitanism: Asian Immigrants and Zones of Autonomy in the American West." In *Sovereign Bodies: Citizens, Migrants, and States in the Postcolonial World*, edited by Thomas B. Hansen and Finn Stepputat, 257–75. Princeton: Princeton University Press.

―――. 2006. *Neoliberalism as Exception: Mutations in Citizenship and Sovereignty*. Durham, N.C.: Duke University Press.

Orellana, Marjorie F., Lucila Ek, and Arcelia Hernández. 2000. "Bilingual Education in an Immigrant Community: Proposition 227 in California." In *Immigrant Voices: In Search of Educational Equity*, edited by Enrique T. Trueba and Lilia I. Bartolomé, 75–92. Lanham, Md.: Rowman and Littlefield.

Orellana, Marjorie, et al. 2001. "Transnational Childhoods: The Participation of Children in Processes of Family Migration." *Social Problems* 48(4): 572–91.

Pakulski, Jan. 1997. "Cultural Citizenship." *Citizenship Studies* 1(1): 73–86.

Panitch, Leo, and Sam Gindin. 2003. "Global Capitalism and American Empire." In *The New Imperial Challenge*, edited by Leo Panitch and Colin Leys, 1–42. London: Merlin Press.

Parenti, Christian. 2003. *The Soft Cage: Surveillance in America. From Slave Passes to the War on Terror*. Cambridge, Mass.: Basic Books (Perseus).

Park, Lisa S. 2005. *Consuming Citizenship: Children of Asian Immigrant Entrepreneurs*. Stanford, Calif.: Stanford University Press.

Passavant, Paul. 2004. "Introduction: Postmodern Republicanism." In *Empire's New Clothes: Reading Hardt and Negri*, edited by Paul Passavant and Jodi Dean, 1–20. New York: Routledge.

Pease, Donald. 1993. "New Perspectives on U.S. Culture and Imperialism." In *Cultures of United States Imperialism*, edited by Amy Kaplan and Donald Pease, 22–37. Durham, N.C.: Duke University Press.

Perlo, Victor. 1951. *American Imperialism*. New York: International Publishers.

Peutz, Nathalie. 2006. "Embarking on an Anthropology of Removal." *Current Anthropology* 47(2): 217–41.

Poitevin, René F. 2000. "Political Surveillance, State Repression, and Class Resistance: The Puerto Rican Experience." In *Critical Resistance to the Prison-Industrial Complex*, special issue of *Social Justice* 27(3): 89–100.

Pozzano, Claudia, and Alessandro Russo. 2005. "After the Invasion of Iraq." *positions* 13(1): 205–14.

Prashad, Vijay. 2000. *The Karma of Brown Folk*. Minneapolis: University of Minnesota.

———. 2001. *Everybody Was Kung Fu Fighting: Afro-Asian Connections and the Myth of Cultural Purity*. Boston: Beacon Press.

———. 2003a. "The Green Menace: McCarthyism After 9/11." *The Subcontinental: A Journal of South Asian American Political Identity* 1(1): 65–75.

———. 2003b. *Namaste Sharon: Hindutava and Sharonism under U.S. Hegemony*. New Delhi: LeftWord Books.

———. 2007. *The Darker Nations: A People's History of the Third World*. New York: New Press.

Prashad, Vijay, and Mathew, Biju, eds. 2000. *Satyagraha in America: The Political Culture of South Asian Americans*, special issue of *Amerasia Journal* 25(3): 139–49.

Qureshi, Regula. B. 1991. "Marriage Strategies among Muslims from South Asia." In *Muslim Families in North America*, edited by Earle Waugh, Sharon

M. Abu-Laban, and Regula B. Qureshi, 185–212. Edmonton: University of Alberta Press.

Rafael, Vicente. 1993. "White Love: Surveillance and Nationalist Resistance in the U.S. Colonization of the Philippines." In *Cultures of United States Imperialism*, edited by Amy Kaplan and Donald Pease, 185–218. Durham, N.C.: Duke University Press.

Rajagopal, Arvind. 1998. Being Hindu in the Diaspora. *SAMAR (South Asian Magazine for Action and Reflection)* 9:15–21.

Rangaswamy, Padma. 2000. *Namaste America: Indian Immigrants in an American Metropolis*. University Park.: Pennsylvania State University Press.

Rashbaum, William. 2006. "Terror Case May Offer Clues into Police Use of Informants." *New York Times*. April 24, B1.

Rayaprol, Aparna. 1997. *Negotiating Identities: Women in the Indian Diaspora*. New Delhi: Oxford University Press.

Razack, Sherene H. 2004. *Dark Threats and White Knights: The Somalia Affair, Peacekeeping, and the New Imperialism*. Toronto: University of Toronto Press.
———. *Casting Out: Race and the Eviction of Muslims from Western Law and Politics*. Toronto: University of Toronto Press.

Robbins, Bruce. 1998. "Introduction, Part I: Actually Existing Cosmopolitanism." In *Cosmopolitics: Thinking and Feeling beyond the Nation*, edited by Pheng Cheah and Bruce Robbins, 1–19. Minneapolis: University of Minnesota.
———. 1999. *Feeling Global: Internationalism in Distress*. New York: New York University Press.

Robin, Corey. 2003. "Fear, American Style: Civil Liberty After 9/11." In *Implicating Empire: Globalization and Resistance in the 21st Century World Order*, edited by Stanley Aronowitz and Heather Gautney, 47–64. New York: Basic Books.
———. 2004. *Fear: The History of a Political Idea*. New York : Oxford University Press.

Roche, Jeremy. 1997. "Children's Rights: Participation and Dialogue." In *Youth in Society: Contemporary Theory, Policy, and Practice*, edited by Jeremy Roche and Stanley Tucker, 49–58. London: Sage.

Rodríguez, Dylan. 2006. *Forced Passages: Imprisoned Radical Intellectuals and the U.S. Prison Regime*. Minneapolis: University of Minnesota Press.

Rogers, Wendy, et al. 1997. "Worlds Apart: Young People's Aspirations in a Changing Europe." In *Youth in Society: Contemporary Theory, Policy, and Practice*, edited by Jeremy Roche and Stanley Tucker, 27–33. London: Sage.

Rogin, Michael. 1993. "'Make My Day!' Spectacle as Amnesia in Imperial Politics (and the Sequel)." In *Cultures of United States Imperialism*, edited by Amy Kaplan and Donald Pease, 499–554. Durham, N.C.: Duke University Press.

Román, Ediberto. 2002. "Membership Denied: An Outsider's Story of Subordination and Subjugation under U.S. Colonialism." In *Moral Imperialism: A Critical Anthology*, edited by Berta E. Hernández-Truyol, 269–84. New York: New York University Press, 269–84.

Rosaldo, Renato. 1997. "Cultural Citizenship, Inequality, and Multiculturalism." In *Latino Cultural Citizenship: Claiming Identity, Space, and Rights*, edited by William F. Flores and Rina Benmayo, 27–38. Boston: Beacon Press.

Rosenberg, Emily. 2006. "Ordering Others: U.S. Financial Advisers in the Early Twentieth Century." In *Haunted by Empire: Geographies of Intimacy in North American History*, edited by Ann L. Stoler, 405–24. Durham, N.C.: Duke University Press.

Ross-Sheriff, Fariyal, and Azim Nanji. 1991. "Islamic Identity, Family and Community: The Case of the Nizari Ismaili Muslims." In *Muslim Families in North America*, edited by Earle Waugh, Sharon M. Abu-Laban, and Regula B. Qureshi, 101–17. Edmonton: University of Alberta Press.

Rothschild, Matthew. 2007. *You Have No Rights; Stories of America in an Age of Repression*. New York: New Press.

Roy, Arundhati. 2004. *An Ordinary Person's Guide to Empire*. Cambridge, Mass.: South End Press.

Rudrappa, Sharmila. 2004. *Ethnic Routes to Becoming American: Indian Immigrants and the Cultures of Citizenship*. New Brunswick, N.J.: Rutgers University Press.

Russell, Stephen T. 2002. "Queer in America: Citizenship for Sexual Minority Youth." *Applied Developmental Science* 6(4): 258–63.

Ryan, Oliver. 2003. "Empty Shops, Empty Promises for Coney Island Pakistanis." *ColorLines* 6(2): 14–16.

Said, Edward. 1981 [1978]. *Orientalism*. New York: Vintage.

———. 1992 [1979]. *The Question of Palestine*. New York: Vintage.

———. 1981. *Covering Islam: How the Media and the Experts Determine How We See the Rest of the World*. New York: Vintage.

———. 1993. *Culture and Imperialism*. New York: Vintage.

Saito, Natsu T. 2005. "The Costs of Homeland Security." *Radical History Review* 93:53–76.

Salaita, Steven. 2006a. *Anti-Arab Racism in the U.S.A.: Where It Comes from and What It Means for Politics Today*. London: Pluto Press.

———. 2006b. *The Holy Land in Transit: Colonialism and the Quest for Canaan*. Syracuse, N.Y.: Syracuse University Press.

Saliba, Therese. 1994. "Military Presences and Absences." In *Food for Our Grandmothers: Writings by Arab-American and Arab-Canadian Feminists*, edited by Joanne Kadi, 125–32. Boston: South End Press.

Sarroub, Loukia. 2001. "The Sojourner Experience of Yemeni American High School Students: An Ethnographic Portrait." *Harvard Educational Review* 71(3): 390–415.

Sassen, Saskia. 1991. *The Global City: New York, London, Tokyo*. Princeton: Princeton University Press.

———. 1999. "Whose City Is It? Globalization and the Formation of New Claims." In *Cities and Citizenship*, edited by James Holston, 177–94. Durham, N.C.: Duke University Press.

———. 2004. "The Repositioning of Citizenship: Emergent Subjects and Spaces for Politics." In *Empire's New Clothes: Reading Hardt and Negri*, edited by Paul A. Passavant and Jodi Dean, 175–98. New York: Routledge.

Scheur, Michael. 2004. *Imperial Hubris: Why the West is Losing the War on Terror*. Dulles, Va.: Brassey's.

Schlosser, Eric. 2001. *Fast Food Nation: The Dark Side of the All-American Meal*. New York: Perennial.

Schrecker, Ellen. 1998. *Many are the Crimes: McCarthyism in America*. Princeton: Princeton University Press.

———. 2005. "History in Red—and White and Blue." *Radical History Review* 93:159–69.

Schudson, Michael. 1998. *The Good Citizen: A History of American Civic Life*. Cambridge, Mass.: Harvard University Press.

Schulhofer, Stephen J. 2002. *The Enemy Within: Intelligence Gathering, Law Enforcement, and Civil Liberties in the Wake of September 11*. New York: Century Foundation Press.

Schultz, Bud, and Ruth Schultz. 2001. *The Price of Dissent: Testimonies to Political Repression in America*. Berkeley: University of California Press.

Scott, James C. 1990. *Domination and the Arts of Resistance: Hidden Transcripts*. New Haven: Yale University Press

The September 11 Detainees: A Review of the Treatment of Aliens Held on Immigration Charges in Connection with the Investigation of the September 11 Attacks. 2003. Report by the Office of the Inspector General, Department of Justice. April. www.fas.org/ (accessed February 20, 2007).

Shafir, Gershon. 2004. "Citizenship and Human Rights in an Era of Globalization." In *People Out of Place: Globalization, Human Rights, and the Citizenship Gap*, edited by Alison Brysk and Gershon Shafir, 11–25. New York: Routledge.

Shaheen, Jack G. 1999. "Hollywood's Reel Arabs and Muslims." In *Muslims and Islamization in North America: Problems and Prospects*, edited by Ambreen Haque, 179–202. Beltsville, Md.: Amana Publications.

Shanahan, Suzanne. 1999. "Scripted Debates: Twentieth-Century Immigration and Citizenship Policy in Great Britain, Ireland, and the United States." In *Extending Citizenship, Reconfiguring States*, edited by Michael Hanagan and Charles Tilly, 67–96. Lanham, Md.: Rowman and Littlefield.

Sharma, Aradhana, and Akhil Gupta. 2006. "Rethinking Theories of the State in an Age of Globalization." In *The Anthropology of the State: A Reader*, edited by Aradhana Sharma and Akhil Gupta, 1–41. Malden, Mass.: Blackwell.

Sharpe, Jenny. 1995. "Is the United States Postcolonial? Transnationalism, Immigration, and Race." *Diaspora* 4(2): 181–99.

Sheikh, Irum. 2003. "The Female Detainee: Reading, Tracing, and Locating Gender in 9/11 Detentions." *The Subcontinental: A Journal of South Asian American Political Identity* 1(3): 71–78.

Shepard, Benjamin, and Ronald Hayduk, eds. 2002. *From ACT UP to the WTO: Urban Protest and Community Building in the Era of Globalization*. London: Verso.

Shryock, Andrew. 2000. "Family Resemblances: Kinship and Community in Arab Detroit." In Arab Detroit: From Margin to Mainstream, ed. Nabeel Abraham and Andrew Shryock, 573–610. Detroit: Wayne State University Press.

Shukla, Sandhya. 2003. *India Abroad: Diasporic Cultures of Postwar America and England*. Princeton: Princeton University Press.

Sigel, Roberta, and Marilyn Hoskin. 1981. *The Political Involvement of Adolescents*. New Brunswick, N.J.: Rutgers University Press.

Silberstein, Sandra. 2002. *War of Words: Language, Politics, and 9/11*. New York: Routledge.

Singh, Amritjit. 1996. "African Americans and the New Immigrants." In *Between the Lines: South Asians and Postcoloniality*, edited by Deepika Bahri and Mary Vasudeva, 93–110. Philadelphia: Temple University Press.

Singh, Jaideep. 2003. "Interpreting Media Representation at the Intersections of White and Christian Supremacy." In *Race/Gender/Media: Considering Diversity across Audiences, Content, and Procedures*, edited by Rebecca Lind, 117–24. New York: Allyn and Bacon.

Sinnar, Shirin. 2007. "Returning Home: Watch Lists and Profiling at the Border." Talk given at Asian Law Caucus, San Francisco, August 1.

Siu, Lok. 2001. "Diasporic Cultural Citizenship: Chineseness and Belonging in Central America and Panama." *Social Text* 19: 7–28.

Smith, Jane I. 1999. *Islam in America*. New York: Columbia University Press.

Smith, Neil. 2003. *American Empire: Roosevelt's Geographer and the Prelude to Globalization*. Berkeley: University of California Press.

———. 2005. *The Endgame of Globalization*. New York: Routledge.

Sorkin, Michael, and Sharon Zukin, eds. 2002. *After the World Trade Center: Rethinking New York City*. New York: Routledge.

Soysal, Yasemin N. 1996. "Changing Citizenship in Europe: Remarks on Postnational Membership and the National State." In *Citizenship, Nationality, and Migration in Europe*, edited by David Cesarani and Mary Fulbrook, 17–29. London: Routledge.

Spivak, Gayatri C. 1988. "Can the Subaltern Speak?" In *Marxism and the Interpretation of Culture*, edited by Cary Nelson and Lawrence Grossberg, 271–313. Urbana: University of Illinois Press.

Stephens, Sharon. 2005. "Introduction: Children and the Politics of Culture in 'Late Capitalism.'" In *Children and the Politics of Culture*, edited by Sharon Stephen, 3–48. Princeton: Princeton University Press.

Stoler, Ann L. 2006a. "Intimidations of Empire: Predicaments of the Tactile and Unseen." In *Haunted by Empire: Geographies of Intimacy in North American History*, edited by Ann L. Stoler, 1–22. Durham, N.C.: Duke University Press.

————. 2006b. "Tense and Tender Ties: The Politics of Comparison in North American History and (Post) Colonial Studies." In *Haunted by Empire: Geographies of Intimacy in North American History*, edited by Ann L. Stoler, 23–67. Durham, N.C.: Duke University Press.

Storrie, Tom. 1997. "Citizens or What?" In *Youth in Society: Contemporary Theory, Policy, and Practice*, edited by Jeremy Roche and Stanley Tucker, 59–67. London: Sage.

Swanson, Jon. 1996. "Ethnicity, Marriage, and Role Conflict: The Dilemma of a Second-Generation Arab American." In *Family and Gender among American Muslims*, edited by Barbara Bilgé and Barbara Aswad, 241–49. Philadelphia: Temple University Press.

Swarns, Rachel L. 2003. "More than 13,000 May Face Deportation," *New York Times*, June 7, A1.

Tannock, Stuart. 2001. *Youth at Work: The Unionized Fast-Food and Grocery Workplace*. Philadelphia: Temple University Press.

Thornton, Sarah. 1996. *Club Cultures*. Cambridge: Polity Press.

Thrupkaew, Noy. 2003. "The Policies: Culture." In *Power Trip: U.S. Unilateralism and Global Strategy after September 11*, edited by John Feffer, 106–16. New York: Seven Stories Press.

Tilly, Charles. 2003. "A Nebulous Empire." In *Debating Empire*, edited by Gopal Balakrishnan, 26–28. London: Verso.

Tirman, John. 2004. "The Movement of People and the Security of States." In *The Maze of Fear: Security and Migration After 9/11*, edited by John Tirman, 1–16. New York: New Press.

Tuan, Mia. 1998. *Forever Foreigners or Honorary Whites? The Asian Ethnic Experience Today*. New Brunswick, N.J.: Rutgers University Press.

Turner, Bryan S. 2001. "Outline of a General Theory of Citizenship." In *Culture and Citizenship*, edited by Nick Stevenson, 11–32. London: Sage.

Twain, Mark. 2002 [1923]. *The War Prayer*. New York: Perennial.

U.S. Census Bureau. 2000. "American Fact Finder—Census 2000 Summary File." Accessed at http://factfinder.census.gov/.

Vimalassery, Manu. 2002. "Passports and Pink Slips," *SAMAR (South Asian Magazine for Action and Reflection)* 15:7–8, 20.

Volpp, Leti. 2002. "The Citizen and the Terrorist." *UCLA Law Review* 49:1575–1600.

Welch, Michael. 2000. "The Role of the Immigration and Naturalization Service in the Prison-Industrial Complex." *Critical Resistance to the Prison-Industrial Complex*, special issue of *Social Justice* 27(3): 73–88.

Werbner, Pnina, and Nira Yuval-Davis. 1999. "Women and the New Discourse of Citizenship." In *Women, Citizenship, and Difference*, edited by Nira Yuval-Davis and Pnina Werbner, 1–38. London: Zed Books.

Whose Children Are These? (documentary film). 2004. Theresa Thanjan.

Williams, Patrick, and Laura Chrisman. 1994. "Colonial Discourse and Post-Colonial Theory: An Introduction." In *Colonial Discourse and Post-Colonial*

Theory, edited by Patrick Williams and Laura Chrisman, 1–20. New York: Columbia University Press.

Williams, Raymond. 1977. *Marxism and Literature*. Oxford: Oxford University Press.

Williams, William A. 1980. *Empire as a Way of Life: An Essay on the Causes and Character of America's Present Predicament*. New York: Oxford University Press.

Willis, Paul. 1990. *Common Culture: Symbolic Work at Play in the Everyday Cultures of the Young*. Milton Keynes, England: Open University Press.

Yegenoglu, Meyda. 1998. *Colonial Fantasies: Towards a Feminist Reading of Orientalism*. Cambridge: Cambridge University Press.

Young, Iris M. 1990. *Justice and the Politics of Difference*. Princeton: Princeton University Press.

Young, Marilyn. 2005. "Against Preemptive War." *Permanent War*, special issue of *positions: East Asia cultures critique* 13(1): 177–93.

Young, Robert. 2001. *Postcolonialism: An Historical Introduction*. Malden, Mass.: Blackwell.

Visweswaran, Kamala, and Ali Mir. 1999/2000. "On the Politics of Community in South Asian American Studies." *Amerasia Journal* 25(3): 97–108.

Zine, Jasmin. 2006. "Between Orientalism and Fundamentalism: The Politics of Muslim Women's Feminist Engagement." *Muslim World Journal of Human Rights* 3(1): 1–24.

Zwick, Jim. 2002. "Mark Twain's Anti-imperialist Writings in the 'American Century.'" In *Vestiges of War: The Philippine-American War and the Aftermath of an Imperial Dream 1899–1999*, edited by Angel V. Shaw and Luis I I. Francia, 38–56. New York: New York University Press.

Index

Absconder Apprehension
   Initiative, 70
Abu Ghraib, 270; Graner
   and, 271
Afghanistan, 55, 62–63,
   115, 124, 177, 217, 275;
   economic liberalization
   of, 137; "liberation" of,
   225, 276; occupation of,
   64, 73, 76, 205; Operation Enduring Freedom
   and, 58, 70; Vagina
   Monologues and, 237;
   war on, 11, 32, 35, 53,
   59, 70, 77, 103, 190,
   198
Al-Arian, Sami, 238
al-Qaeda, 13, 67, 73, 78, 114,
   211, 244, 274
American-Arab Anti-
   Discrimination Com-
   mittee, 92, 228
American Council of
   Trustees and Alumni, 31
"American Dream," 18, 81,
   102, 105, 136, 140, 142,
   157, 278
AmeriCorps, Teach for
   America and, 137
Amnesia, 23, 36, 57, 58, 280
Anti-Defamation League,
   90
Anti-imperialism, rewrit-
   ing of movements based
   on, 54

Anti-Imperialist League,
   43
Anti-Terrorism and Ef-
   fective Death Penalty
   Act, 68
Antiwar movement,
   249; Act Now to Stop
   War and End Racism
   (ANSWER) and, 237;
   Military Out of Our
   Schools, 21; Prison
   Moratorium Project
   and, 20–21
Ashcroft, John, 61, 66, 268;
   Bush-Ashcroft era and,
   68
Asian Americans, 9, 82, 87,
   93, 102, 105, 158, 176–77,
   180–81, 260, 281
Asylum, 266

Bharatiya Janata Party
   (BJ), 109, 185
Bill of Rights Defense
   Campaign, 255
Bollywood: films, 110;
   music, 165, 198, 210

Campus Watch, 31
Capital: human, 140;
   social, 141
Capitalism, 148; American
   capitalist culture and,
   142, 146; entrepreneurial,
   146; flexible, 102, 117;
   free-market, 50; global, 7,

Capitalism (*cont.*)
19, 47–49, 102, 105, 117, 136, 177, 200; labor and, 139, 149; liberalism and, 274; "millennial," 156; multiculturalism and, 171; neoliberal, 17–18, 87, 102, 136–37, 142–43, 146, 149, 161

Citizen Corps Council, 137

Citizenship, 5–6; active, 17–18, 233; aspirational, 111; consensual, 17; consumer, 155–59, 161, 171; cultural, 10–13, 82–85, 135, 221, 243–47, 264, 272–73, 276; democratic, 13, 17; denationalized, 101; dialectics of, 168; dissenting, 11, 89–90, 138, 145, 167, 197–202, 205, 211, 216–22, 226, 234, 241, 247–50, 255–56, 263; dual, 101, 108; economic, 143, 145–55; flexible, 11, 89–90, 101–112, 115–17, 145, 157, 166–67; global, 101; "good" vs. "bad," 15–17, 21, 69, 82, 86, 143, 234–40, 244; latitudinal, 102; liberal, 275–76; multicultural, 84, 89–90, 155, 168, 170–74, 180, 249–50; neoliberal, 136–45; participatory, 21; patriotic, 17, 247; polycultural, 11, 88–90, 135, 155, 179–82, 206, 280; postnational, 101; private vs. public spheres of, 158; privatization of, 137; racial exclusion and, 61; subcultural, 87, 155, 159–65, 264; theories of, 81–82, 86; urban, 90, 135, 165–70; youth, 16, 18

Civilizations: alien, 11; Bush's discourse of, 211; "clash of," 13, 27, 30, 230, 235, 275; conflict and, 178; democracy and, 57; imperialism and, 54; media and, 200; settler-colonialism and, 173; War on Terror discourse and, 245

Civil rights: alliances, 280–83; Japanese American protests and, 280; law and, 277; Muslim activists for, 232, 239–40; secularism and, 239–41; South Asian and Arab American professionals and, 269

Class, 34; American foreign policy and, 60; citizenship and, 5, 81–83, 86–87; consumption and, 156–59; differences of, amongst South Asians, 8–9, 269–70, 188–89; flexible citizenship and, 104, 108, 111; in high school, 145–55, 175, 217; imperial feelings and, 242–47; model minority myth and, 176; multiculturalism and, 176; Muslim and South Asian activism and, 232–33, 254; national anxieties and, 13; Pakistani working, 188; racial profiling and, 268–73, 277; South Asian immigration and, 7, 106; South Asian Muslim working, 214; sports and, 159; the state and, 122; women and, 106, 225; work and, 135–45; working, culture of, 144; working, youth of, 17–18, 89, 111, 118, 164, 168, 199

Colonialism, 23, 282; British, 173; multiculturalism and, 172; settler, 51–56, 173. *See also* Empire; Imperialism

Consumer nationalism, 156

Consumption, 22, 26, 99, 153, 155, 156, 168–69; armored, 206–7; citizenship and, 154, 171; cultural, 81, 101, 110, 135, 160–61, 165, 176; cultural difference and, 183; popular culture and, 111. *See also* Dissent

Cosmopolitanism, 116, 205, 206

Crowe, Kimberly, 267

Decolonization movements, 44. *See also* Youth activism

Democracy, 17, 111, 266; Bush's discourse of, 53; capitalist, 157; liberal rhetoric of, 49, 51; neoconservatism and, 4; political discourse of, 210, 223, 230; prisons and, 283; U.S. imperial power and, 34, 45, 57, 64,

69, 169, 177, 275; War on Terror for, 36, 52–54, 205, 223, 267; Western liberal, 12, 96, 212, 238, 250, 254

Department of Homeland Security, 71, 269; community liaisons with, 278

Department of Justice, Office of the Inspector General, 270

Deportation, deportations, 70, 265; activism against, 93, 223, 226, 238, 265, 280, 286; "disappeared" and, 27, 70; as disciplining technology, 138, 145, 209, 273; effects of, 93, 264–65, 268; "L.A. Eight" and, 231, 280; mass, 70, 72, 73; media coverage of, 267; men as targets of, 223; Muslims and, 203; neoliberalism and, 136; Special Registration and, 252; systemic racism through, 228; U.S. imperial policies and, 65; War on Terror cases of, 12, 24, 31, 34, 69, 73. See also Detention

Detention, 34, 43, 65, 70–72, 83, 281; "disappeared," 70, 82; fear and, 105, 145; human rights and, 276; intelligence gathering and, 42; Japanese Americans and, 116; media coverage of, 267; multiculturalism and, 228, 240; Muslim men and, 71, 85, 215, 223, 226, 236, 271, 277; numbers of persons in, 71, 73, 84, 223; PATRIOT Act and, 78, 80, 136; racial profiling and, 222; Special Registration and, 84, 252; War on Terror and, 12, 24, 85–86, 94, 136, 138, 221, 238, 264–65, 268, 270, 286

"Disappeared," 24, 70

Discrimination, in workplace, 144, 267. See also Profiling

Dissent, 62, 282; affective responses and, 207; ambiguous, 213; communities of, 232; complicity and, 247–51; feelings of, 214; gender and, 218; repressive tolerance and, 249;

resistance and, 281; views of, 208; vocabulary of, 28

Dotbusters, 270

DREAM Act, 246

Education: bilingual, 152–53; citizenship and, 5, 25, 86, 135, 137–40, 233; consumption and, 157; higher, 31, 154; migration and, 102, 104, 140–41; military and, 245–46; multiculturalism and, 170, 172, 174; vocational, 146–50; work (labor) and, 87, 101, 111, 143–45, 152, 157; youth and, 15, 17–18, 22, 151

Empire, 6; definition of, 23; discourse of, 43–44; domestic and foreign aspects of, 60–61; "imperial feeling" and, 24–26, 32, 62–64, 207–8, 242–44, 274; imperialism and, 45–46; informal vs. formal, 49; intimacy of, 26; invisibility of U.S., 56; "New," 45, 48; rationalization of U.S., 58; significance of term, 36; spectacle of, 60; theories of, 44–64; United States as, 47; vocabulary of, 28; as way of life, 24. See also Colonialism; Imperialism

Ethnography: ethics of, 30–31; ethnographic methodology, 5, 31–35; of Empire, 25

Fair Labor Standards Act, 147

FBI (Federal Bureau of Investigation), 12; COINTELPRO and, 66, 124, 254; intelligence investigations and, 277; National Security Higher Education Advisory Board and, 31; October plan and, 277; Special Registration and, 30; "voluntary" interviews and, 30, 268

Fear, 272–74, 278–80

Federal Bureau of Investigation. See FBI

Feminism: imperialist, 224–26; liberal, 219, 222–23, 226; Orientalist, 225

General Union of Palestine Students, 231, 280

Globalization, 18, 26, 28, 101, 107–8, 166; capitalist, 47; conditions of, 101; economics and, 48, 53, 140; labor migration and, 145; migration and, 159; neoliberal, 106; political crises of, 19; popular discourse of, 116; War on Terror and, 55. *See also* Empire; Transnationalism

Guantánamo Bay, 50–51, 57, 271, 277

Gujarat, 7–8; diaspora from, 105; immigrants from, 7–8; massacre in, 202–4; riots in, 171, 185

Gulf War, First, 58, 115, 231, 280

Hamdi, Yasser, 74, 124

Hammad, Suheir, 20

Hardt, Michael, 23, 46–48, 69, 101, 230

Harvey, David, 49

Hassan, Waqar, 269

Hayat, Hamid, 13, 278

Hip hop, 20; culture of, 214; marketing through, 237; youth culture styles and, 160–61, 233

H.R. 3077 (bill to regulate TITLE VI funding for area studies), 30–31

H.R. 3477 ("immigration reform bill"), 83, 102

Huntington, Samuel P., 230–31, 235. *See also* Civilizations

Illegal Immigration Reform and Immigrant Responsibility Act, 68

Immigrant rights, 10, 23, 43, 69–70, 83, 85, 92, 103, 187, 222, 226, 279–80; movements for, 241, 253–54

Immigrants, 7; "good" vs. "bad," 81, 102, 135, 142, 244; green card marriages and, 88; War on Terror and, 67–68

"immigrant time," 118, 121–27

Immigration and Customs Enforcement, Bureau of. *See* Immigration and Naturalization Services

Immigration and Naturalization Services (INS), 71, 145

Imperialism, 45–51; amnesia and, 280; benevolent, 51–54, 225; contradictions of culture of, 241; cultures of U.S., 58, 63; for "democracy," 52; discourse of U.S., 63–64; evangelical, 53; feminism and, 224–26; informal empire and, 48–50; Monroe Doctrine and, 51; nostalgia or melancholy for, 63; paradox of liberal, 275; of United States, 47, 49–60. *See also* Colonialism; Empire

International Emergency Economic Powers Act, 113

International Monetary Fund, 47, 49, 106

Iraq, 177; occupation of, 76–77, 275; Operation Iraqi Freedom and, 70; Vietnam syndrome and, 54

Islam: American, 112; discourse of, 24; "Islamic terrorism" and, 109; jihadism and, 27; politicization of, 232; "radical," 13. *See also* Muslim organizations; Muslims

Israel, 53–55

Israeli-Arab War, 231, 280

Kaplan, Amy, 50, 57, 64; cultures of U.S. imperialism and, 58

Labor: bilingual education and, 152–53; consumption and, 156–58; flexible, 136, 142; immigration status and, 152; law and, 154; leisure and, 155; merit and, 153–54; service sector, 7–8, 87, 102, 136, 142, 146; South Asian students and, 150; undocumented, 138, 145; unpaid, 142; vocational education, 148–51; youth, 136, 144, 147–48, 151. *See also* Work

L.A. Eight, case of, 231, 280

Liberalism, liberals, 45, 48, 64, 90, 274–83; consumer nationalism and, 158; imperial feelings and, 243;

liberal citizenship and, 156, 209, 229, 233, 247, 249; liberal democracy and, 13, 84, 86, 137, 238, 242, 248; liberal dissent and, 222; liberal feminism and, 219, 223, 225; "liberalism of terror," 274; liberalization, 137; liberal multiculturalism and, 20, 28, 85, 171, 173, 176–78, 218, 228, 250, 255; liberal Orientalism and, 224, 226; liberal rhetoric and, 49, 223; liberal theorists and, 206; "liberal world order" and, 80; pluralism and, 171; responses of, to War on Terror, 272. *See also* Neoliberalism

Lindh, John Walker, 13, 74

Mamdani, Mahmood, 50, 53–54, 235, 240

Marri, Ali al-, 74

Militarism, 19–20, 47, 58, 61, 86, 149, 216, 237, 243, 286; culture of, 245–47; Junior ROTC and, 245; recruitment programs and, 247; ROTC and, 246; Troops to Teachers program, 245

Military recruitment, 245–47; counter-recruitment programs and, 20, 246

"Missing": "disappeared" and, 24, 70; as idea, 35

Missing (film), 36

Model minority, 7, 82, 87, 105, 109, 141, 150, 176–77, 181, 232, 268; imperialism and, 177; pre-9/11 stereotypes of, 176; War on Terror and, 176

Multiculturalism, 135; armored, 247–51; British, 173; Canadian, 172; French, 172; liberal, 20, 28, 228; multiculture and, 175; pluralist, 174; polyculturalism and, 135, 179, 181–82; problems with liberal, 171; school and, 170; state-sponsored, 250

Muslim organizations: American Muslim Alliance, 233; Council on American-Islamic Relations (CAIR), 11, 267, 269; Islamic Circle of North America, 237; Muslim American Society, 237; Muslim American Society's Freedom Foundation, 91

Muslims, 88; as comedians, 255; construction of, 283; "good" vs. "bad," 21, 176, 232–41; as men, 271; *Muslim Girl Magazine* and, 234; politicization of identity of, 209, 239; representations of, 218–19; as women, 53, 60, 221–26, 233, 250. *See also* Islam; Muslim organizations

National Security Entry-Exit Registration System, 72. *See also* Special Registration

National Security Higher Education Board, 31

Negri, Antonio, 23, 46–48, 69, 101, 230

Neoliberalism, 19; ideology of, 141; millennial capitalism and, 156; multiculturalism and, 173; neoliberal capitalism and, 87, 136–37; neoliberal exception and, 102; "Washington consensus" and, 136

New England Immigrant and Detainee Response Network, 222

9/11 attacks, 4, 16, 56, 224, 289; African American reaction to, 178, 242–43; backlash after, 23; climate of fear and, 67, 209, 215, 244; mainstream discourse of, 286; media portrayals of, 71, 218; minorities after, 115, 244; South Asian responses to, 219; white trauma and, 194

No Child Left Behind Act of 2002, 245

Non-Resident Indians (NRIS), 108, 204; Overseas Citizenship of India and, 108, 109

Ong, Aihwa, 84, 101, 106
Operation Enduring Freedom, 58, 70.
  See also Afghanistan
Operation Iraqi Freedom, 70
Operation Tarmac, 72
Operation TIPS (Terrorist Informa-
  tion and Prevention System), 74
Orientalism, 11, 64, 218, 283; discourses
  of, 106, 230; liberal, 226–28; liberal
  feminism and, 219, 222–23; Muslim
  masculinity and, 223; Muslim youth
  and, 163; neo-, 200, 224
Overseas Citizenship of India, 108;
  Non-Resident Indians, 108, 109

Padilla, Jose, 74, 124
Pakistani Americans, 204–5; deporta-
  tion of, 265; refugee claims by, 266
Palestine, occupation of, 53, 55, 115,
  214–15, 231, 238
PATRIOT Act, 22, 65–70, 113
PATRIOT Act II (Domestic Security
  Enhancement Act), 75
Patriotism, 255; coercive, 69; hyper-,
  242, 272; "statist American," 47
Pentagon, Joint Vision 2010 and, 54
Personal Responsibility and Work
  Opportunity Act (1996), 141
Persons of Indian Origin (PIO), 108
Philippines, 55, 249; colonization of,
  23, 281; war (1898), 43, 48–49, 57,
  126; War on Terror and, 231
Polyculturalism, 179, 181–82; citi-
  zenship and, 135. *See also* Multi-
  culturalism
Popular culture, 110, 135, 144, 154–55;
  consumer citizenship and, 156–59;
  consumption of, 87, 110–11; national
  belonging and, 165; sports and masculinity, 159–60; transnational, 110,
  158
"Post-9/11 moment," 23–24; definition
  of, 6; media interest in, 29
Post-9/11 studies, 29–32

Profiling, 11–12, 27, 30, 43, 80, 82, 124,
  209, 251, 265–67, 269; discrimination and, 144, 267; of Muslims, 103,
  110, 177, 182, 219, 228, 231, 238–42,
  255, 264; political, 180; racial, 9, 11,
  28, 43, 67–68, 181–82, 198, 206, 210,
  222, 227–32, 242, 267–70, 278–82;
  religious, 68; youth response to, 232.
  See also Racism
Project for the New American Century, 4, 55, 57

Racial Profiling Act of 2001, 242
Racism: anti-Arab and anti-Muslim,
  10, 178, 267; antiblack, 180; construction of Islamic threat, 240;
  cultural, 172; discourse of intolerance and, 178; discrimination and,
  144, 267; Green McCarthyism and,
  228; hate crimes, 11–13; imperial,
  230; Sikhs and turbans and, 266;
  War on Terror and, 177, 232. *See also*
  Profiling: racial
Resistance, 281. *See also* Antiwar
  movement; Dissent
Ridge, Tom, 268

Said, Edward, 31, 63–64, 224
September 11th. *See* 9/11 attacks
Sikh Americans: attacks on, 4, 11, 109;
  employer discrimination against,
  267; hate crimes against, 11; as turbaned males, 59, 266, 268
Sodhi, Balbir Singh, 11, 266
Space: city as, 166–68; subaltern
  counterpublics and, 168; urban,
  plural public and, 167
Special Registration, 12, 252–53,
  277–78, 282; activism against, 222,
  252–53, 282; arrests and, 72; Muslim men and, 30, 223, 252; Pakistanis and, 73; public criticism
  and, 75
State, the, 25–26

"State of exception," theory of, 23–24, 205

Stoler, Ann, 26, 44

Teach for America, AmeriCorps and, 137

Temporality, 122–23; "immigrant time" and, 118, 121–27

Terror: liberalism and, 274; terrorism and, 276. *See also* 9/11 attacks; War on Terror

Thind, Bhagat Singh, 229, 300

Total Information Awareness, 74

Transnationalism, 87; diaspora and, 114; flows of funds and, 113–14; migration and, 7; resistance and, 115; return migration and, 74; transmigrants and, 201. *See also* Citizenship; Globalization; Undocumented immigrants

Transportation Security Administration, 269

Undocumented immigrants, 9, 68–69, 72, 84, 95, 102, 114–15, 128, 136, 138, 145, 150, 157, 162, 164–65, 255, 270, 273

United Nations Convention on the Rights of the Child, 83

U.S. Equal Employment Opportunity Commission, 267

U.S. House of Representatives, bills of, 30–31, 83, 102

Vishwa Hindu Parishad (VHP), VHPA and, 109, 204

War on Terror, 5, 22, 64–75, 109, 145; anxiety about, 13; civil liberties, security, and, 61; detentions under, 12, 270; discourse of, 13; effect of, on Muslim communities, 265, 267; framing of, 45; immigrants and, 67, 69, 114; in media, 58–60, 207, 267; multicultural citizenship and, 180; normalization of, 251–56; PATRIOT Acts and, 22, 65–70, 75, 113; politics of, 114; roots of, 231; Special Registration programs and, 12, 30; state surveillance under, 11–12; U.S. foreign policy and, 55; youth critique of, 198–99. *See also* FBI

Willis, Paul, 21, 155

Women: Afghan, 225, 276; Arab, Muslim, and South Asian American, 218–23, 233, 250, 265; citizenship and, 61, 111; as feminists, 225; as immigrants, 226; Iraqi, 93; Mexican, 88; middle-class, 106; Orientalism and, 200, 224; political fear and, 273; popular culture and, 163; Puerto Rican, 83; Punjabi, 270; rights of, 224–25; work and, 144, 149, 276. *See also* Muslims: as women

Work, 135; family obligations and, 158; post-Fordist hourglass economy and, 136; symbolic, 155. *See also* Labor

World Bank, 47, 49, 106

Youth, youths: as active consumers, 17; of color, solidarity of, 181–82; cultural displacement, 161; desi identity, 196; dissenting views of, 208–14, 210; employment programs and, 147; gender and, 163–65, 196; as Muslim immigrants, 15–16, 27–28, 162–64; neoliberalism and, 17, 143; studies of, 151; subcultures of, 161, 164; theories of, 13–15, 17, 18, 161

Youth activism: Active Arts Youth Council, 20; civil rights and, 232; political music and, 20. *See also* Hip hop

SUNAINA MARR MAIRA is an associate professor of Asian American Studies at the University of California, Davis. She is the author of *Desis in the House: Indian American Youth Culture in New York City* and the co-editor of *Youthscapes: The Popular, the National, the Global* and *Contours of the Heart: South Asians Map North America.*

Library of Congress Cataloging-in-Publication Data

Maira, Sunaina, 1969–
Missing : youth, citizenship, and empire after 9/11 / Sunaina Marr Maira.
p. cm.
Includes bibliographical references and index.
ISBN 978-0-8223-4391-2 (cloth : alk. paper)
ISBN 978-0-8223-4409-4 (pbk. : alk. paper)
1. South Asian Americans—Civil rights.
2. South Asian Americans—Attitudes.
3. South Asian Americans—Social conditions.
4. Muslim youth—Civil rights—United States.
5. Muslim youth—United States—Attitudes.
6. Muslim youth—United States—Social conditions.
7. September 11 Terrorist Attacks, 2001—Influence.
8. Citizenship—United States.
I. Title.
E184.S69M35 2009
973.931—dc22
2008053651